C000301121

YES
Perpetual Change

David Watkinson

Foreword by Rick Wakeman

Plexus, London

Dedicated to my son

Charles David Watkinson

Dream it, think it, believe it and

YES it can happen

All rights reserved including the right
of reproduction in whole or in part in any form
Text copyright © 2001 by David Watkinson
Copyright © 2001 by Plexus Publishing Limited
Published by Plexus Publishing Limited
55a Clapham Common Southside
London, SW4 9BX
www.plexusbooks.com

Watkinson, David
Yes : perpetual change: thirty years of Yes
I.Yes (Group) 2.Rock musicians – Great Britain – Biography
3.Progressive rock music
I.Title
782.4'2166'0922

ISBN 0-85965-297-1

Printed and bound in Spain by Bookprint S.L., Barcelona

Cover image by Roger Dean
Cover design by Bradley Davis at White Light
Book design by Bradley Davis at White Light

This book is sold subject to the condition that it shall not, by way of trade or otherwise, be lent, re-sold, hired out, or otherwise circulated without the publisher's prior consent in any form of binding or cover other than that in which it is published and without a similar condition including this condition being imposed on the subsequent purchaser.

CONTENTS

ACKNOWLEDGEMENTS

A huge thank you must go to Roger Dean for his support and for providing artwork, paintings, photographs and logos; Rick Wakeman for writing the Foreword; Jeff Varner and Annecke at Left Bank Management; Simon Arnold for the website and support; Ian Hartley for bootleg listings; Clifford Loeslin for the Yes discography; Pam Bay, Henry Potts, Chris Jones, Martin Standen and the Old Hippie store for assistance; Jo Munns at Eagle Rock; Tanya Coad and Sue Smith from *Relayer* magazine for general information; Mike Tiano and Jeff Hunnicut at *Yesworld* & *Notes From The Edge* for the Chris Squire interview; MGT pictures and various news clippings; Steve Wehner for tapes listings; *Record Collector* magazine for the Jon Anderson interview; *Melody Maker* and *Sounds* music magazines for information plus the *Accrington Observer*; Brockum and Winterland for tour merchandise; Jim Halley for contacts; Jeremy Weissenburger; Steve and Kim (Fragile); Cams and Vick; John Watkinson for general help; Yes tour dates were compiled with help from Bill Bruford, Peter Banks and Julie Warren. Asia tour dates provided by Dave Gallant.

Other invaluable research material for this book came from the following sources: Yesworld, NFTE, Dan Hedges' *Yes: The Authorised Biography*, Yesyears' booklet *Yes* by Shilow Kuloda, Chris Welch's *Yes: Close to the Edge*. Thanks also to Pete Whipple and Steve Sullivan for cross-referencing material and Bob Hagger for the Marquee Club dates. Thanks to Eileen Niland for the Warriors diary. Thanks to everyone who was interviewed: Jon Anderson; Chris Squire; Steve Howe; Bill Bruford; Rick Wakeman; Geoff Downes; Trevor Horn; Patrick Moraz; Roy Clair; David Foster; Rod Hill; Bob Hagger; Dave Potts; Bill Turner; Michael Tait and Mr. Booth.

For the use of photographs and memorabilia thanks as follows: Yes artwork and photographs used courtesy of Electra Entertainment Group Inc; Roxi Cook; Gottlieb Brothers; Bob Hagger; Rob Packard; David Watkinson Collection; Chris Zinn; East Mersea Youth Camp; Don Rogers; Julie Warren; Paul Punter; Mike Leander at MCA Records; Dave King; A. Braun; Olias Of Bolton; EMI Records archives; Atlantic Records archives; Urban Archives; Temple University (Philadelphia, Pennsylvania); Decca Records; Digimode Entertainment Ltd; Shoji Yamada; Dave Gallant for Asia dates; Jon Dee; Barry Plummer; Purple Pyramid and Victory Records; Eagle Records; New Millennium Communications Ltd; Victory Records and Island Records.

I send a huge thank you to my dear wife Laura for putting up with my Yes interests for so long and for being supportive throughout the completion of this book. I couldn't have done it without you. Thank you Mum and Dad for always being there for me, backing whatever I do.

And finally a big thank you to all of the members of Yes for the great shows and albums over the years, and for having such a positive impact on so many people's lives.

FOREWORD
Rick Wakeman

There seem to have been so many books about Yes over the years that I have lost count! Most of them, starting with the appalling Dan Hedges effort back in the seventies, should , in my opinion, have each page perforated and then suitably installed in the smallest room in the house.

The problem is basically two fold. Either the text becomes the opinionated view of the author, or it is a collection of one sided views based on a mixture of fact and fiction from various band members both past and present. The members from the past are nearly always cynical for obvious reasons: that they either missed out or didn't last very long, whereas those in the present line up tend to hold those no longer present responsible for anything they would rather not take the blame for.

The fact of the matter is that Yes are unique, and this is what has made Yes music unique, and it has always taken a strange blend of musicianship and alter-egos in order to make it work at its very best, which is why some line ups worked better than others.

In this respect this book is probably one of the most accurate to date .

Whilst it takes care to draw heavily on statements made publicly by various members of Yes throughout the years, it must be remembered that a lot of what we all said was heavily influenced by such outside sources as frustration, success, failure, elation, bitterness, love, hatred, alcohol and one or two other substances that I understand have yet to attain the status of legality.

In most of these areas I am as guilty as the next man. In retrospect whilst a lot of what I said is true, an equal amount is fuelled by either exaggeration or emotion. Many of the quotes from everybody else suffer from some of the same ailments, but this is what made Yes what it was and what it is today . . . a band of total excess and total commitment. We listened to no-one as regards to what we should do musically. We did listen to well-meaning advice, but then we ignored it. The band has always been pretty much unmanageable and, thankfully, because of all this, has created some music that is totally uninfluenced or tarnished by the people who have surrounded the band over the years in various managerial capacities, most of whom could not tell the difference between a hatchet and a crotchet, and in many cases managed to bleed the band dry.

Here I go again, blaming third parties!

The fact is, Yes was a major part of my life, and still is. I have much genuine love and respect for all the guys I worked with in the band during my various membership periods and the legacy that has been built will hopefully last long after I've collected my free bus pass.

A true untarnished account of the life of Yes can never really be written, but to be honest, if it could be done without the exaggerated emotions that fuelled us as members of Yes, it would be pretty boring. Reading what we all said throughout the last thirty years, whilst under the influence of everything from vast amounts of alcohol to large breasted women, is much more fun.

It was at the time too!

INTRODUCTION

YES ARE, UNQUESTIONABLY, one of the most progressive rock bands in the world, a position that they have retained for over thirty years. In the 1960s, they produced a unique fusion between pop rock and traditional orchestral sounds, whilst in the 1970s, they became, for a time, the biggest band in the world through sheer musical virtuosity coupled with stage presentations of the highest quality. In the 1980s, Yes re-invented themselves once again, and conquered the world with a number one album and single. The 1990s saw Yes attract a whole new generation of fans around the world with their *Union* line-up tour, the music constantly evolving while new band members introduced new concepts. Into the millennium, the Yes phenomenon remains in perpetual motion, with sell-out world tours and a refreshing sense of innovation in their albums and shows.

With the Yes discography spanning 33 years, we can now look back at those classic Yesshows and key moments from their illustrious career in this visual documentary book. *Yes: Perpetual Change* brings together unpublished material including memorabilia, photographs, every Yes show date, the largest discography and bootlegography ever published and exclusive interviews with key members of the group, both past and present.

Many words have been written on Yes' meteoric rise from the Marquee Club to rock stadiums around the world, but this book is different in that it aims to show what has been created alongside their music, and how the artwork and stage designs have become an integral part of the Yes image.

The memorabilia illustrating this book is predominantly from the author's personal collection. The assembled tour dates represent a complete Yesshows guide and, for the first time, the old tour diaries of Bill Bruford and Peter Banks have been cross-referenced to produce an accurate guide to Yes' live dates in the early days.

A Yesshow is about the unique sound that evolves almost organically, in a heady atmosphere that draws the band and audience together. Say the words 'Yes show' to a fan and you suggest a merging of rich pageantry and colour, with tremendous musicianship, incredible sounds, light shows, costumes, stage sets, the introduction music as a prelude that sets the tone for the whole of the night. Yes fans attend their shows time and again to experience the camaraderie of an event that brings together like-minded people to create that special Yes atmosphere.

The Yes story is certainly an interesting one, with many twists and turns in their history, many of which could have put an end to the band over the past 30 years. However, Yes have battled on, with total belief in their music, and their fans have stuck with them worldwide. What makes the Yes story unique is the impact that they have had on the music world, as both a group and with their solo performances.

When I listened to my first ever piece of Yes music, 'The Revealing Science of God' back in 1975, it had an immediate and profound impact on me. Those unique sounds reverberating around my head, the cover artwork and the whole package, at just sixteen, I was spellbound. Yes is not just about music, but also the images, the style and the underlying positive messages of the lyrics.

YES FAMILY TREE

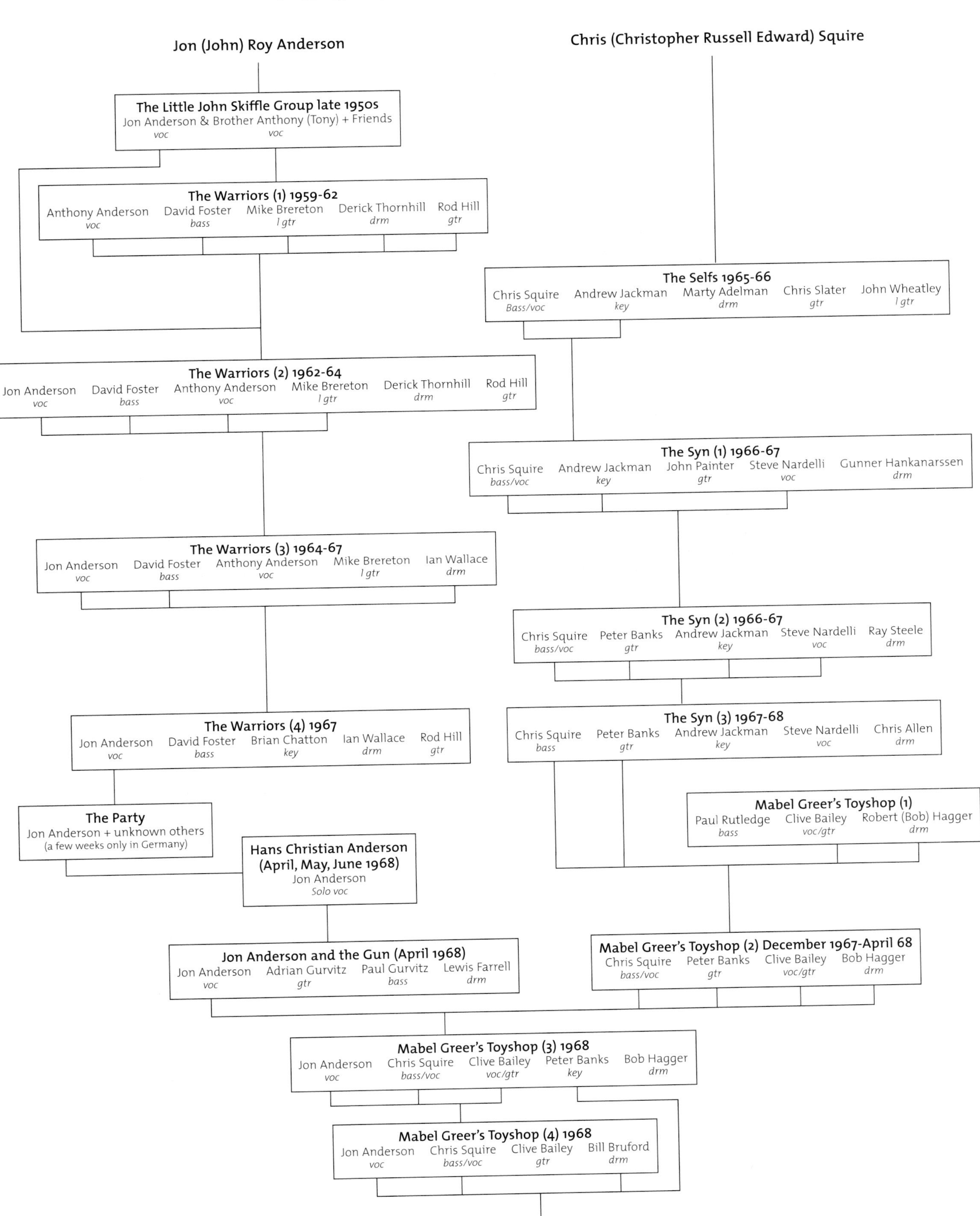

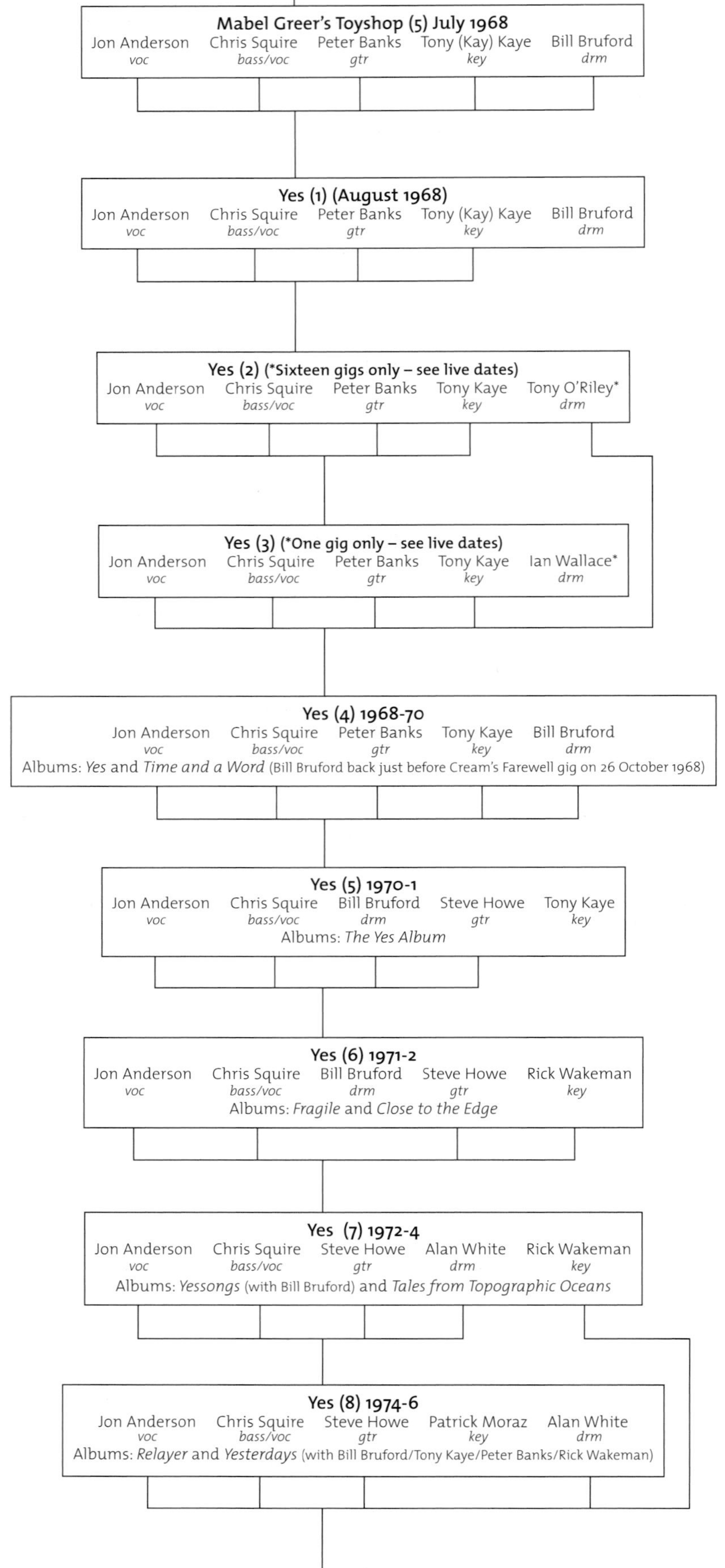

Mabel Greer's Toyshop (5) July 1968
Jon Anderson voc
Chris Squire bass/voc
Peter Banks gtr
Tony (Kay) Kaye key
Bill Bruford drm
Yes (1) (August 1968)
Jon Anderson voc
Chris Squire bass/voc
Peter Banks gtr
Tony (Kay) Kaye key
Bill Bruford drm
Yes (2) (*Sixteen gigs only – see live dates)
Jon Anderson voc
Chris Squire bass/voc
Peter Banks gtr
Tony Kaye key
Tony O'Riley* drm
Yes (3) (*One gig only – see live dates)
Jon Anderson voc
Chris Squire bass/voc
Peter Banks gtr
Tony Kaye key
Ian Wallace* drm
Yes (4) 1968-70
Jon Anderson voc
Chris Squire bass/voc
Peter Banks gtr
Tony Kaye key
Bill Bruford drm
Albums: Yes and Time and a Word (Bill Bruford back just before Cream's Farewell gig on 26 October 1968)
Yes (5) 1970-1
Jon Anderson voc
Chris Squire bass/voc
Bill Bruford drm
Steve Howe gtr
Tony Kaye key
Albums: The Yes Album
Yes (6) 1971-2
Jon Anderson voc
Chris Squire bass/voc
Bill Bruford drm
Steve Howe gtr
Rick Wakeman key
Albums: Fragile and Close to the Edge
Yes (7) 1972-4
Jon Anderson voc
Chris Squire bass/voc
Steve Howe gtr
Alan White drm
Rick Wakeman key
Albums: Yessongs (with Bill Bruford) and Tales from Topographic Oceans
Yes (8) 1974-6
Jon Anderson voc
Chris Squire bass/voc
Steve Howe gtr
Patrick Moraz key
Alan White drm
Albums: Relayer and Yesterdays (with Bill Bruford/Tony Kaye/Peter Banks/Rick Wakeman)

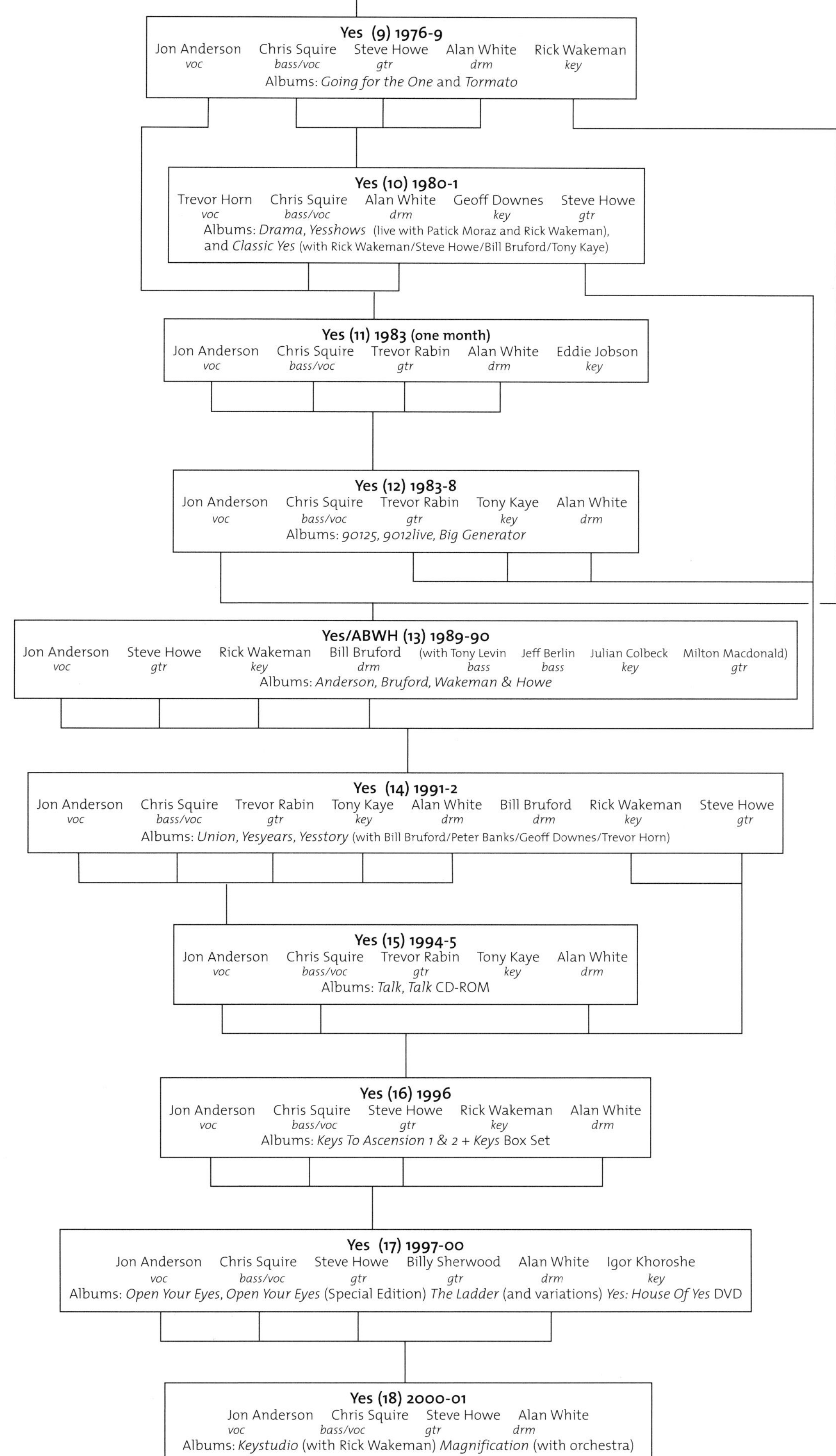

Yes (9) 1976-9
Jon Anderson voc
Chris Squire bass/voc
Steve Howe gtr
Alan White drm
Rick Wakeman key
Albums: Going for the One and Tormato
Yes (10) 1980-1
Trevor Horn voc
Chris Squire bass/voc
Alan White drm
Geoff Downes key
Steve Howe gtr
Albums: Drama, Yesshows (live with Patick Moraz and Rick Wakeman),
and Classic Yes (with Rick Wakeman/Steve Howe/Bill Bruford/Tony Kaye)
Yes (11) 1983 (one month)
Jon Anderson voc
Chris Squire bass/voc
Trevor Rabin gtr
Alan White drm
Eddie Jobson key
Yes (12) 1983-8
Jon Anderson voc
Chris Squire bass/voc
Trevor Rabin gtr
Tony Kaye key
Alan White drm
Albums: 90125, 9012live, Big Generator
Yes/ABWH (13) 1989-90
Jon Anderson voc
Steve Howe gtr
Rick Wakeman key
Bill Bruford drm
(with Tony Levin bass
Jeff Berlin bass
Julian Colbeck key
Milton Macdonald) gtr
Albums: Anderson, Bruford, Wakeman & Howe
Yes (14) 1991-2
Jon Anderson voc
Chris Squire bass/voc
Trevor Rabin gtr
Tony Kaye key
Alan White drm
Bill Bruford drm
Rick Wakeman key
Steve Howe gtr
Albums: Union, Yesyears, Yesstory (with Bill Bruford/Peter Banks/Geoff Downes/Trevor Horn)
Yes (15) 1994-5
Jon Anderson voc
Chris Squire bass/voc
Trevor Rabin gtr
Tony Kaye key
Alan White drm
Albums: Talk, Talk CD-ROM
Yes (16) 1996
Jon Anderson voc
Chris Squire bass/voc
Steve Howe gtr
Rick Wakeman key
Alan White drm
Albums: Keys To Ascension 1 & 2 + Keys Box Set
Yes (17) 1997-00
Jon Anderson voc
Chris Squire bass/voc
Steve Howe gtr
Billy Sherwood gtr
Alan White drm
Igor Khoroshe key
Albums: Open Your Eyes, Open Your Eyes (Special Edition) The Ladder (and variations) Yes: House Of Yes DVD
Yes (18) 2000-01
Jon Anderson voc
Chris Squire bass/voc
Steve Howe gtr
Alan White drm
Albums: Keystudio (with Rick Wakeman) Magnification (with orchestra)

LOOKING AROUND

1950s–1968

JON ROY ANDERSON was born October 25 1944 in the town of Accrington, Lancashire in the north of England. Life was extremely difficult for Jon in his early years: his family had little money and everyone was forced into manual work. Jon himself worked as a farm labourer from the age of fifteen with his brother Tony, and it was during these harsh years that he developed a desire to get away. He later said, 'Being in a working-class area of Accrington, you work for a living. You don't become an artist. You don't paint. For me it was a fight to get away from that kind of situation. I didn't want to end up all my life driving long distance lorries or delivering milk.'

Although times were tough, Jon still has happy memories of watching his parents perform. 'My mother and father were ballroom dancing champions of East Lancashire,' Jon explains. 'They had cups on display and photographs of my mother in her beautiful ballroom gown and my father in his bow tie. Basically they were a couple of show offs!'

Jon and his brother Tony began performing music at the same time – forming the Little John Skiffle Group, a simple family musical get-together. 'Me and my brother Tony did a milk round for a local farmer, only we had to go to the field, catch the cows and milk them first. That's when we started singing together, Everlys, Buddy Holly. When I was ten, I played washboard in the Little John Skiffle Group and a bit later Tony dragged me into the Warriors.'

The English beat scene at the time was booming and the Warriors wanted to be a part of it. The line up consisted of David Foster on bass, Rodney Hill on guitar, Michael Brereton on lead guitar, Derick Thornhill on drums and Jon Anderson on vocals. David Foster explains how Jon got involved with the Warriors, 'We knew his brother Tony, he was a rocker, and he had a Norton bike and all the leathers. We knew Tony could sing well and then he told us that his brother Jon was a singer too, so I waited for Jon to deliver the milk one day to my house and asked him to join.' They played in working men's clubs and small halls in and around Lancashire. They teamed up with Methodist minister Fletcher Richardson at Antley Church and started a Rock Gospel movement called Rock Goes to Church.

Although the Warriors' early gigs were not lucrative, they provided an excellent training ground. They built a good reputation in local towns such as Blackburn, Bury and Bolton where they would play gigs most nights for the sum of £25. Asked about whether they had got into the Mersey sound too late, Anderson replied 'I don't think so, in fact I think we may have got in on time. In any case, we have not stuck to one brand of music and are not typecast like a lot of other groups, and now that the trend is turning more in favour of ballads, we are quite happy about it. Of course the vast majority of our fans are teenagers, but we also go out and try and please the older set.'

The Warriors' popularity started to rise, as the manager of the Bolton Palais later explained. 'The Warriors were the only group to ever get the offer to play there every Monday night because they were so popular. They would play a set of about

THE WARRIORS
Decca Records

COPYRIGHT

two half-hour slots, we had one of the few round revolving stages at the Palais, and it was just like the London Palladium. One side of the stage would have the local DJ on it and when it was time for the group's turn then we would turn it round and they would be ready waiting behind the dividing wall, it worked really well.' Rodney Hill remembers, 'We used to call Jon "Johnny Electric Boy" because just when you would have set up all the equipment for the gig, he would come along and blow the fuses for the whole place.'

In 1963, they came fourth in a music competition called The Big Chance, run by the local paper. This was followed by a national competition sponsored by the *New Musical Express* where they reached the finals in London. Midway through 1964, the band was invited to participate in a film called *Just for You* at Shepperton Studios in London. The film showcased popular bands of the time, a kind of *Top of the Pops* of the 1960s, and was showed at cinemas nationwide. Other bands featured included the Merseybeats and Peter and Gordon. The Warriors performed their single track 'Don't Make Me Blue,' which, along with its predecessor, 'You Came Along', would later feature on a series of compilation albums by Decca Records.

More work came their way with a TV appearance on *Thank Your Lucky Stars*, swiftly followed by the release of their first single 'You Came Along' by Decca. It did very well locally but didn't reach the charts. The band then toured Germany, playing similar-sized gigs to those they had performed in the UK. Jon felt he had taken the Warriors as far as he could and it was no longer rewarding for him; they had spent a great deal of time together, and were still good friends, but they all agreed it was time to call it a day. They returned to the UK without Jon, who decided to stay on in Munich. Back home the Warriors spent the summer of 1964 making regular appearances at the Bolton Palais and Leigh Beachcomber Clubs.

Jon remained in Munich for a few weeks. Although he was a little homesick, he was still eager to find another band. While in Germany, he received a telegram forwarded by his mum, stating that a local Bolton band called Party was in the same town and looking for a singer. This group, unknown to all but their closest friends, thought Jon was a great singer. 'I felt I had a lot to say, and they listened and followed instructions,' he remembers. 'That's when I realised I had a talent for getting people together and formulating a direction. We were playing the worst clubs in Germany, but were getting a great reaction just re-arranging the hits – doing our own soul versions.' Unfortunately, they suffered management problems which caused their downfall, so Jon returned to the UK where he moved to London to begin the search for a job and a new musical vehicle with which to involve himself.

The vibrancy of the music scene in May 1968 (and the reason for Jon coming to London) was located in a few key music clubs in Soho, central London. To help set the scene of the years immediately preceding the formation of Yes, it is worth looking at the Marquee Club, 90 Wardour Street, London. Here, many legendary performers played during their formative years, including the Rolling Stones, the Who, the Yardbirds, David Bowie, Cream, the Moody Blues, Eric Clapton, the Move, John Mayall, Pink Floyd, Led Zeppelin and Fleetwood Mac.

The Marquee Club opened its doors to thousands of music-loving youngsters on Saturday 12 April 1958. Situated then in the basement of the Academy Cinema in Oxford Street, it was originally called the Marquee Jazz Club and its programmes were controlled by the National Jazz Federation Organisation, but it moved to its well-known and loved spot at 90 Wardour Street on 13 March 1964. During its first ten years from 1958 to 1968, the Marquee Club gradually moved away from jazz to

marquee club
GERRARD 8923 | 90, WARDOUR STREET, LONDON W.1.

provide a home for the new pop and rock acts. Any musician playing there had an almost direct line to the record companies who frequented the place on a weekly basis. Through the sheer quality of the bands that played there, the Marquee forged its reputation and represented a real cross section of musical styles, from jazz to pop and rock to folk. Consequently, the Marquee became the place to be, mirroring the status that the Cavern Club had in Liverpool. Moreover, for the future members of Yes, who attended regular gigs there, the Marquee proved to be a valuable education. There were many bands in the 1960s that influenced Yes, including the Who (Chris Squire's favourite band), the Spencer Davis Group (Bill Bruford's favourite r'n'b band), John Mayall's Blues Breakers, Simon and Garfunkel, Cream, the Action, the Graham Bond Organisation, Moody Blues, the Crazy World of Arthur Brown and the Nice. Most of these bands would have played at the Marquee at some stage in their early careers, the future members of Yes rubbing shoulders with them.

On his arrival in London, Jon was befriended by Jack Barrie, part owner of the Marquee Club and owner of the La Chasse Club, situated at 100 Wardour Street, where he offered Jon a job cleaning glasses. Meanwhile, a regular at the club, Paul Korda (who happened to be a record producer) was looking for a singer to do some demos for EMI, so Jon recorded some tracks and his demo subsequently turned into his first single.

The single 'Never My Love', was recorded under the pseudonym of Hans Christian. Secrecy was essential whilst the record company prepared a coordinated marketing campaign, and they wanted to keep their young talent under wraps until the release of the record. In the meantime, Jon had decided to join another band called Les Cruches, to keep himself busy, and flew out to meet them in Holland. He was soon called back when EMI announced the release of 'Never My Love', in March 1968. It was not a hit, but EMI were still keen to release the second Hans Christian single in May, 'Autobiography of a Mississippi Hobo', but alas this one was as unsuccessful as the first. From then on Hans Christian gave up and Jack Barrie endeavoured to find a new band for his young protégé, Jon Anderson.

It was Paul Korda who alerted Jack and Jon's attention to psychedelic trio the Gun. Run by the Gurvitz (Curtis) brothers, Adrian and Paul, offspring of the Kinks' exuberant road manager Sam Curtis, and accompanied by drummer Louie (Brian) Farrell, they played mostly cover versions of the major bands at the time. Jon had already seen them perform and was so impressed that he decided to join them, performing two gigs at the Marquee Club in London. Much to the irritation of the Gurvitz brothers, the record company promoted the two gigs as Jon Anderson with the Gun, since Jon's name was now relatively famous. The gigs were well received, but the line-up didn't last: Jon was fired after a falling out between himself and the brothers, leaving Adrian, Paul and Louie on their own again.

The Gun went on to have a major hit single in 1968 with the riff-laden 'Race with the Devil', illustrating that they could flourish without Anderson. However, they seemed unsure of

Hans Christian.

their appeal in the popular music market and disbanded in the early seventies. (Interestingly the Gun later enlisted the artistic talents of Roger Dean to design their album cover.)

Chris Squire, born 4 March 1948 in Kingsbury, North West London, spent his childhood singing in church choirs. As he moved into his teens, his choral commitment dwindled. Chris left school and, without a job, quickly picked up a guitar to while away the hours of boredom. 'I became totally absorbed in the idea of bands, electric guitars and stuff,' remembers Chris. 'But as soon as I started formulating bands with friends, obviously my knowledge of church music and harmonies entered into it. Prior to that, despite having all that musical knowledge, I never played any instrument at all. Although I used to sneak into the church or cathedral when it was closed and start up the organ – just blow everything away for a couple of hours.' Chris took up the guitar and worked at a London music store for a year during which time he discovered the Rickenbacker. He persuaded his boss to import Rickenbacker guitars into the shop, thus ensuring that he was able to buy one at cost price to replace his Futurama.

Chris and his old choral buddy, Andrew Jackman, recruited three young musicians and became the five-piece teenage band the Selfs. Andrew played the keyboard, while the size of Chris's hands dictated he play bass guitar. The band played weekly in local clubs and school halls, and according to an article in the *Wembley News* on Friday 8 January 1965, the Selfs' first major appearance was at the New Years Eve Ball at Kingsbury Town Hall. The headline in the paper read 'Beat Group's Big Break'. The Selfs played a twenty-minute set to an audience of 930.

However, the Selfs had numerous line-up changes, and, with little stability, they soon split. Chris decided to form a new band with Andrew Jackman and another local north London lad, Steve Nardelli. Bouncing back into the limelight, they renamed and regrouped to become the Syn, joined by Martin Adelman on drums and John Painter on guitar, who was replaced soon after by Peter Banks.

Born 15 June 1947 in Barnet, North London, Peter Banks' early influences were a combination of blues, r'n'b, skiffle artist Lonnie Donnegan, folk singer Woody Guthrie, Motown group Martha and the Vandellas and emerging bands such as the Beatles and the Who. His parents would buy him records inspiring him to play the guitar, which he mastered in his early teens. Peter left school at sixteen and went to art college briefly, joining his first band Devils Disciples, who were based in Borehamwood, and played the local youth clubs and halls. 'A guy that influenced me was the guy who used to play with the Nice, Davey O'List,' recalls Peter. 'He was an extremely chaotic, anarchic guitar player, who would play either very, very well or very, very badly. I liked his approach, but whatever happened to him, I have no idea.' He was soon thrown out of art college and went to Germany to play in Hamburg with the band. Their set list, however, consisted mainly of Rolling Stones covers, and, not surprisingly, didn't set the world on fire. Peter moved back to London to look for another band. At this time, the music scene was fairly incestuous – everyone seemed to know everyone else, and it wasn't long before Peter joined the Syn after being introduced by Martin Adelman.

Finally, a line-up had come together that looked promising and had real potential. The Syn were a five-piece band playing Motown hits in their own unique style, until 1967, when they moved headlong into the flower power era and became more psychedelic. They also wrote themed songs in the vein of the popular rock-operas being staged by other bands at the time, primarily basing their stories around gangsters. They were fairly well known around London, building up a strong fan base and managing to gain a weekly spot at the prestigious Marquee Club. They were swiftly spotted at the Marquee by Deram, who signed them up, and they were managed by Kenny Bell. Kenny would book gigs all over the country and the band would travel around in their Ford transit van from one town to another.

It was during the Syn days that Chris Squire acquired a reputation for lateness, 'In the Syn, we went to pick Chris up,' Peter Banks remembers. 'We were going to a gig in Stoke-on-

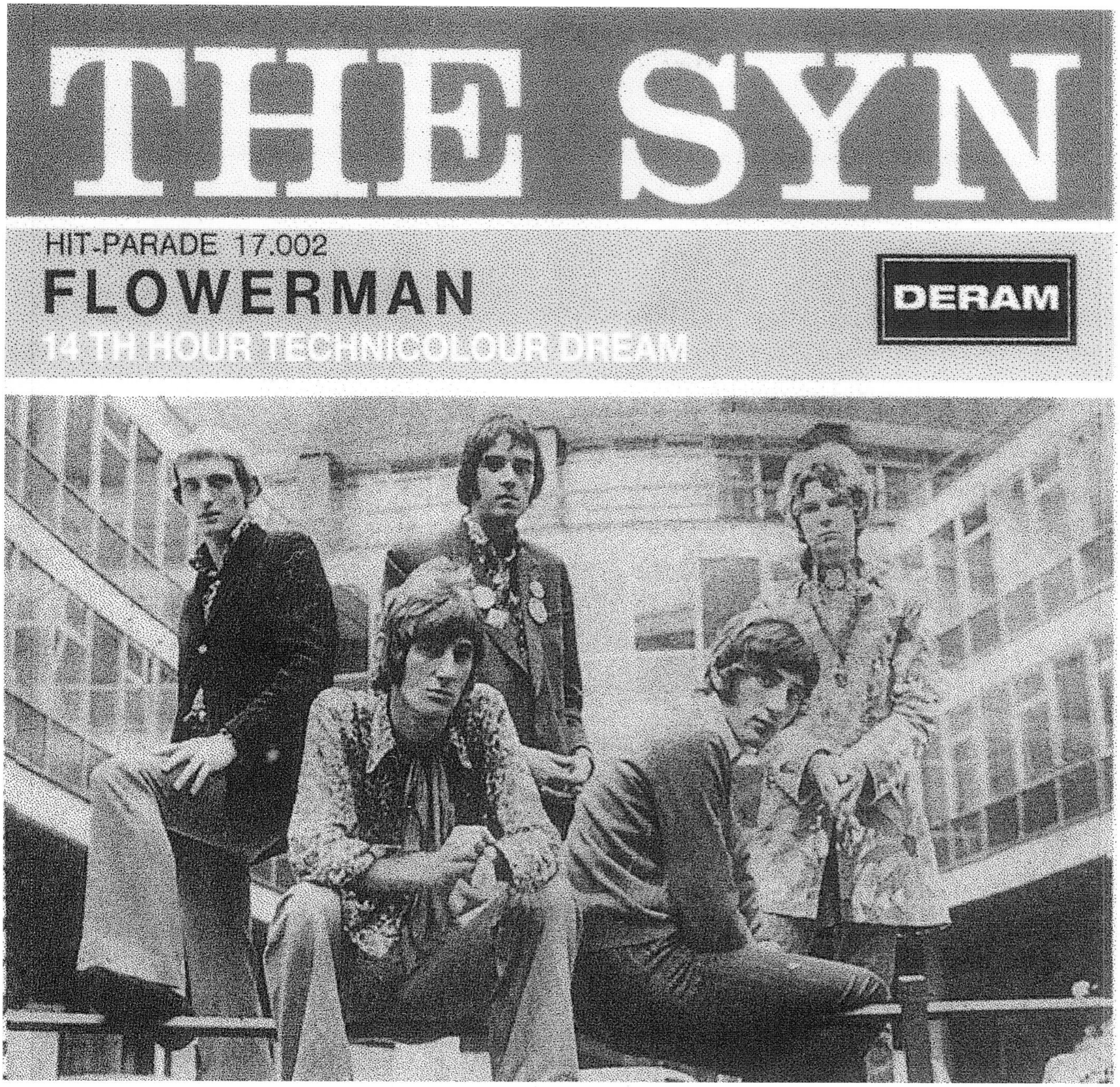

THE SYN

HIT-PARADE 17.002

FLOWERMAN

14 TH HOUR TECHNICOLOUR DREAM

Trent which was about one hundred miles away. He was traditionally always late and he had this girlfriend whose name was Sheila who would make excuses for him. And we'd wait for about half an hour while he got out of the bath or finished his breakfast or whatever. This could be happening midday, one o'clock in the afternoon, or something like that. But this one time, we had been waiting outside because we weren't invited in, something snapped and someone just said, "Let's go without him." And we did. We went to this place in the Midlands and we did the gig without a bass player to teach him a lesson. It didn't work, it didn't make any difference whatsoever. I think he was a little hurt about it. He said, "Why did you go without me?" He wasn't angry, but he said, "I was nearly ready." That was always his line.'

The Syn produced all their own original compositions, releasing a single in June, 'Created By Clive'/'Grounded', and another in September, 'Flowerman'/'14-Hour Technicolour Dream' both of which did better in France than they did in the UK. However, the band could not last, the consistent lack of success saw a creeping deterioration in the band's morale. They split in 1968.

In March 1998 Chris Squire was interviewed by Mike Tiano for the Yes internet information service Notes from the Edge. In an extremely candid interview, Chris spoke about the Syn days and how he met guitar legend Jimi Hendrix at a UK show. (This was prior to the first Hendrix UK tour, which started in March 1967, and before the album *Are You Experienced?* was released in May 1967.) 'We had been touring around England and it was kind of a miserable time of the year; it was wet and cold and a lot of the shows we'd been doing were in the north of England where it was particularly bad weather, it hadn't been very well attended and we didn't get our percentages and we were kind of looking forward to coming down to playing at the Marquee Club. Because that was in London, usually that was well attended because we had the regular Tuesday night support band spot, and that usually meant there'd be a major band playing on the Tuesday night and we'd be the support band but we also got a cut of the profits, and so we were looking forward to that.

'When we got down there we unloaded our equipment out of the van and there was this band rehearsing on the stage, and the bass player was trying to learn the riff to what we later knew would be 'Purple Haze'. And being an English rock musician this was one of my very early encounters of actually … apart from Muddy Waters and things like that, I'd never really met any black players in rock 'n' roll so it was quite a novelty watching this band rehearsing, and also it was kind of frustrating because the bass player didn't seem to be able to learn to play the riff very well, and I kept thinking I'd go and grab the bass and show him exactly what the notes were that the black guy was telling him, how he could do it. That was Noel Redding, of course, not the greatest bass player of all time.

'However, what happened then was that I wandered around to the front because I got bored with listening to this sort of rehearsal and I was wondering how long they'd been renting the place out in the afternoons for people to just go in and rehearse! And the assistant manager came in and I said to him, "Wow, is this band going to stop rehearsing soon? Because you've got to get Cliff Bennett in," who was going to be the main band that week; they had covered the Beatles' 'Got to Get You into My Life' and had a hit with it in England. So we were expecting a lot of people to come and they were pretty high in the charts with that song. The assistant manager said to me, "Yeah, I just got a phone call from the office and they told me the band that's rehearsing, they're the main band tonight," and I kind of said [laughs], "You're kidding, aren't you! They can't even learn to play five notes! I listened to them painfully rehearse for half an hour." He said "Well, that's what I've been told." So of course we were all kind of pretty upset about that, so they finished rehearsing and we set our equipment up in front of theirs, as we would do being the first band on, and we kind of counted out our last spare change, and we decided to go down and grab the cheapest possible something or other to eat at this café that was pretty local to the Marquee, just down the street.

'So as was customary to me I went off the stage after we did our little sound check and I was changing strings on my Rickenbacker in this small dressing room at the Marquee Club, and Jimi came in and started talking to me, which I found was quite surprising because guitarists didn't usually talk to bass players much in those days, let alone this black guitar player, so I ended up kind of having about a 30 minute conversation with him about bass guitars, and how his friend in Seattle used to have a Rickenbacker, and various stuff. And so I left the dressing room after this rap thinking, "Well, he's a real nice guy, it's a shame that the band can't play and no-one's going to come and see us tonight," because we'd been away and we weren't really aware of what had been going on in town.

'So I went down to the café to eat and we all had the cheapest thing on the menu, and as we were sitting there the line for the Marquee Club started to pass the window of the café and we thought, wow, that's amazing, there's actually a line for the show tonight. We thought that's good, for some reason people are just coming out. We all ordered dessert because we figured we'd be able to afford the gas money to get home, then we went back to the Marquee Club and we could hardly get through the doors; and there was the same assistant manager just taking money hand over fist

APRIL, 1967 **PROGRAMME** **APRIL, 1967**

Sat. 1st
SYN
The Footprints

Sun. 2nd
Closed

Mon. 3rd
THE HERD
Tony Knight's Chessmen

Tues. 4th
THE ACTION
The Stalkers
(Members' Tickets 7/- in advance from March 28th)

Wed. 5th
Folk Night :
WESTON GAVIN
plus Stephen Delft and guests

Thurs. 6th
MARMALADE
Fancy Bred

Fri. 7th
1-2-3
The Time Box

Sat. 8th
SYN
The Love Affair

Sun. 9th
Closed

Mon. 10th
THE HERD
Fleur de Lys

Tues. 11th
West End Premiere :
THE JEFF BECK GROUP
Wynder K. Frog
(Members' Tickets 7/6 in advance from April 4th)

Wed. 12th
Folk Night :
THE FRUGAL SOUND and Guests

Thurs. 13th
MARMALADE
The Nite People

Fri. 14th
TONY RIVERS
and the CASTAWAYS
Time and Motion

Sat. 15th
SYN
C Jam Blues

Sun. 16th
Closed

Mon. 17th
THE HERD
Warren-Davis Monday Band

Tues. 18th
CHRIS FARLOWE
and the Thunderbirds
Wynder K. Frog
(Members' Tickets 7/- in advance from April 11th)

Wed. 19th
Folk Night :
DEREK BRIMSTONE and Surprise Guests

Thurs. 20th
THE SAVOY BROWN BLUES BAND
Cock-a-Hoop

Fri. 21st
THE LONG JOHN BALDRY SHOW with
Stuart Brown, Alan Walker, and Bluesology
The Time Box

Sat. 22nd
SYN
The Stalkers

Sun. 23rd
THE LONDON YOUTH JAZZ
ORCHESTRA and Guests (Admission 3/-)

Mon. 24th
THE HERD
The Summerset

Tues. 25th
JIMMY JAMES and the VAGABONDS
Wynder K. Frog
(Members' Tickets 7/- in advance from April 18th)

Wed. 26th
Folk Night :
AL STEWART and Special Guests

Thurs. 27th
JOHN MAYALL'S BLUES BREAKERS
featuring PETE GREEN
Blues City Shakedown
(Members 6/-, Non-members 8/6)

Fri. 28th
1-2-3
The Time Box

Sat. 29th
SYN
Skip Bifferty with Graham Bell

Sun. 30th (2.30 – 5.30)
Theatrescope presents
JESSE FULLER
Weston Gavin
Peter Baughen
Paul Layton
(Members 6/- Non members 8/6)

Evening Session (8—10.30)
Weston Gavin
Jo Ann Kelly
Peter Baughen
Paul Layton
(Members 5/- Non-Members 7/6. Special double session tickets: Members 8/6 Non-Members 12/6).

(All Programmes are subject to alteration and the Management cannot be held responsible for non-appearance of artistes.)

Printed by Hepworth and Co., (Tunbridge Wells) Ltd., Tunbridge Wells, Kent

One of the regular programme flyers for the Marquee Club, featuring a listing for the Syn on Satuday 8th April 1967.

from people and it was just crazy, and of course I had no idea that during the week we'd been away that Hendrix had played a couple of late night clubs and jammed with Mick Jagger or somebody at this late night club, and there was this whole buzz around town, and this was his first ever gig to the public.

'We went to the dressing room and we got changed and we went on stage and the place was really packed. And then they had a few chairs in the front there, about the first, I don't know, four rows, and there's about sixteen chairs in each row and the rest was standing room, and then as we were beginning to start our first song I looked down at the front rows and realised that all my rock heroes of all time, like the Beatles, the Stones, the Who, everyone was sitting in the chairs in the front row! We went through our set and we got really good applause after each song, and later on I asked Pete Townshend, who was one of the guys sitting there, I said, "God, did anyone like us or were they just applauding us so that we'd get off?" then politely "Thank you very much," because they were obviously all waiting to see Hendrix, and there was Eric Clapton, and all these people sitting there. And Townshend said, "Oh no, no, I've always liked the band, I thought you were really good that night," because we'd supported the Who a couple of times.

'We finished our set, Hendrix came on, and that was his first ever show in England. Of course, he completely brought the place down and it was amazing. So that's my little story of meeting Jimi Hendrix and actually it was so packed in the place I couldn't even leave the dressing room, so I just decided to hang on the stage while he played his set. There was this piano at the back of the stage, this grand piano, I just wanted to kind of lay on top of it and watch the Hendrix set from behind the drums, so I obviously got a real close-up view of the whole thing. The amazing thing was that after that show every chick who'd never, ever really wanted to talk to me before, down at the clubs and late nightclubs [laughing] all suddenly became my best friend. They wanted to know how Jimi was, and of course I played that one up and said, "When Jimi and I were rapping before the show ..." That was the funny twist to it, that all of a sudden all these chicks who hadn't been interested in talking to me before became real friendly.'

Chris went on to explain, 'And that's the only time I was ever with him. It's amazing that I just didn't know who he was or what the band were capable of or anything during that half-hour conversation, so it was a completely untainted conversation I suppose, in terms of me being in awe or anything like that, it's just a natural thing. So I'll always remember that.'

Initially Chris and Peter had gone their separate ways since Chris was still a little disillusioned after the split of the Syn. He decided to take some time out and concentrate on his bass work and soon met up with Clive Bailey and Robert (Bob) Hagger (alias Alexander Belmont) who were playing under the name of Mabel Greer's Toyshop. Their line-up was clearly unsettled, and after a series of gigs, their bass player Paul Rutledge quit the band. In January 1968 Chris was ready to play with another band and accepted Bob Hagger's invitation to join the Toyshop. Once on board Chris then invited Peter Banks and they became a four-piece. John Peel liked the band, and invited them to play live on his radio show *Night Ride*.

It was at this time that Jack Barrie thought it would be a good idea to introduce Chris to Jon – having become acquainted with Chris on the club circuit, he thought that they would probably hit it off. Jack was also keen for Jon to become involved with other aspiring young musicians, in the hope that they might join forces and create a group of their own. Their first encounter at the La Chasse Club proved to be fruitful. Chris remembers, 'We had a lot of similar tastes, mainly vocal stuff and that's when we decided to form a band. The very next day Jon came round to my flat and we sat down and attempted to write a song together and we actually came up with "Sweetness" which is on the first Yes album.' Naturally Chris was inclined to invite Jon to play with the Toyshop occasionally, but the rest of the band did not respond well to the irregular sessions with Jon, especially Peter Banks, who – tired of having no money and resenting the way different musicians were invited to come along and join in – decided to leave and join Neat Change, who had steady Marquee dates. Then drummer Bob Hagger left, disillusioned with the way the band was heading, and joined another band called Heather. 'I had a great time in the band,' Bob recalled, 'they were really good years. I was pleased that Bill Bruford joined the band; he is a fine drummer, one of the best. I was a crap drummer.' Chris was keen to get Peter back and within a month he had managed to persuade him that they would make a fresh start. The Toyshop were now looking for another drummer.

Originating from Sevenoaks in Kent, born 17 May 1950, Bill Bruford's introduction to drumming came via his sister's boyfriend. 'He gave her some brushes and said "If you play them on the back of an album sleeve" – which used to be made of thick white card – "it sounds just like a drum." So she passed them on to me and said "play these". So I learned to play the brushes first, then got a pair of sticks, then I got a practice pad, then I got a drum, then I got two drums ... now

Bill on his drum set.

Mabel Greer's Toyshop. Peter Banks second from left and Chris Squire far right.

I understand kids buy seventeen drums at once.' Bill grew up with a passion for jazz, and was inspired by the likes of Max Roach, Art Blakey, Dizzy Gillespie and listening to and playing jazz rather than rock 'n' roll, unlike most teenagers at the time.

With his middle-class upbringing, the pre-destined route of school, university and then a steady profession lay ahead of Bill, but during his gap year in 1967 he decided to join a band to fill in time waiting for the start of university. He was keen to play with a band and started to follow up the ads in the music press for auditions and managed to get his first gig with Savoy Brown. He talked his way into the band but within three nights, it was clear that he was not at all suitable and he was asked to leave. He now had a background in music as an 'ex-Savoy Brown' and, after a few months spent with a group called Paper Blitz and a residency in Rome at the Piper Club, he was looking for a new challenge. It was at this time that Chris and Jon saw Bill's ad in *Melody Maker*, 'Named Drummer Seeks Work', and offered him the job on the strength that he said he used a Ludwig kit.

Chris had been thinking of changing the band's name for some time, as Mabel Greer's Toyshop was far too long. It was Peter who came up with the name Yes. 'I was a big fan of the Who and I liked very short names. In fact, instead of the Who, I always thought it should be just Who. Because you don't say the Yes. And when you had posters and people would put up flyers of who was playing, the less letters you had in your name, the bigger the name could be printed. If it was three letters, it could be printed very big!'

Now that they had Bill, the group needed to broaden their sound with a keyboard player: Chris got in touch with a guy called Tony Kaye, whom he had met originally in Leicester four years earlier and again at the La Chasse Club during the days of Syn.

Born 11 January 1946 in Leicester, Tony Kaye's early years were spent surrounded by music. His grandmother had been a concert pianist, who left him a grand piano when she died, and his grandfather had been a jazz saxophonist. He started piano lessons before the tender age of five and, by the age of eight, knew many classical pieces, by twelve, he was playing solo and duet concerts. However, things would soon change. 'Until I was seventeen, I wanted to be a classical pianist,' Tony explains. 'But I started getting interested in other forms of music at school. A buddy was a traditional jazz fan, and another had a collection of modern jazz records. We formed a sort of Temperance Seven band at grammar school. I was carrying on with classical music, but listening to other forms. Modern jazz seemed very exciting and I liked the big bands – Basie and Ellington. In fact, I joined a big band in Leicester when I was fifteen – the Danny Rogers Orchestra.'

At eighteen, he was offered a place at the Royal College of Music: 'There was quite heavy competition in classical piano playing and I didn't think I was good enough. The alternative was a teaching career and I didn't want that.' So instead Tony decided to go to Leicester Art College. He was still passionate about music and involved himself in session work, but the late nights led to skipped classes and he was soon kicked out.

'After I left art college,' Tony recalls, 'I saw an ad in *Melody Maker* and went for an audition with a group called the Federals. They were backing Roy Orbison on tour and in two hours, I learned the entire Roy Orbison chart and went on the road. They were a good band, but into the comic showband thing. At this time, I used to go to the Marquee and watch Graham Bond, Ginger Baker and Jack Bruce. Bond was mind-shattering. I liked the sound he got from the organ. I had been playing my vox like a piano. Actually, it wasn't until six months after joining Yes that I got a Hammond.'

Tony had been connected to three bands following the Federals: Yellow Passion Loaf, Jimmy Winston and his Reflections (also known as Winston's Fumbs) and Bittersweet, all of which bought him experience and the opportunity to travel, but were not forthcoming financially. Back in the UK, Tony met up with Chris Squire in the famous La Chasse Club where he wowed Chris with his credentials and was subsequently offered the role of keyboardist with Yes. Now the Yes line up was officially complete: Anderson, Squire, Bruford, Kaye and Banks.

THE SURVIVAL YEARS

1968–71

LIFE WAS HARD for the band at the beginning. Despite having a complete belief in their music, they barely had enough money to live on. The true driving forces that kept Yes going were Jon and Chris. With their combined experience – Jon's solo work in various bars and clubs and Chris's gigs with both the Toyshop and the Syn – they began to nurture assiduously their entire list of club contacts in order to forge the band's progress. Jack Barrie still helped out but it was a chance meeting with John Roberts, a wealthy Warriors fan who frequented the La Chasse Club, that really boosted their resources. He liked what the band were doing, and gave them £500 to help them on their way. This enabled the purchase of some new equipment and paid the rent on the basement beneath the Lucky Horseshoe Café on Shaftesbury Avenue where the band spent hours rehearsing.

Their ideas at this time were influenced by bands such as Cream, the Nice and Deep Purple, all of whom were bringing in orchestras and spending time on arrangements, reflecting the mood of the 1960s as it moved away from psychedelia towards progressive rock. It was an experimental time in London, with musicians such as Led Zeppelin and King Crimson all creating new sounds and new forms of music. Bill Bruford admitted that the unique style he brought to Yes at the time was 'A clanging snare drum sound, some off-kilter, odd-metre rhythms and rhythmic drama.'

East Mersea Youth Camp, where Yes played their first gig.

The first official Yes gig was on 3 August 1968 at the East Mersea Youth Camp in Essex and within days they performed the first of many gigs at the Marquee Club. 'At the beginning, we did covers of other people's songs like the Beatles thing, the Buffalo Springfield thing, a couple of others like "America", that kind of stuff,' Tony explains. 'And we just put it into a different musical ball park and embellished it and made it more symphonic and more instrumental. Although the first two albums didn't really reflect what was coming, it was the start of the way we were thinking.' Although Yes played well-known covers, they were barely recognisable from the originals, and it took audiences a while to understand and warm to the extraordinary way in which the band changed them.

Jon became noted for his disciplinarian charge over the band. He was always at the forefront of their plans, determined to keep the band focused and committed to their goals. Peter remembers, 'Jon Anderson was always the ring master of the Yes circus. I once unkindly compared him to Napoleon. If anybody did have a grand vision of Yes it would be him.' The band all shared a house in Drayton Gardens, Fulham and Bill recalls, 'It was a very exciting time. Time was just going, very, very fast. We just lived for the band. We all lived in the same house, or most of us did. And as far as I can make out, we were confined to the property, because at 24 hours notice we'd have to do a gig somewhere. So you couldn't leave the building for more than twelve hours in case a gig came through … We used to be like firemen … with a greasy pole and when the bell rang, we did a concert.'

Many years later, Bill would comment on the band's early days and their legendary drinking habits. 'We used to drink an awful lot of alcohol. There was a club here in London called the Speakeasy that the band's manager [Roy Flynn] was managing as well. The Speakeasy stayed open late, until two or three in the morning. So you could pretty much play a gig in England within a hundred-and-fifty-mile radius and still make it back to the Speakeasy at about two o'clock.'

Yes performing at the Red Car Jazz Club.

They began to obtain regular gig bookings, thanks to Jon's perseverance, securing a couple of gigs at the Marquee club in London, making £20 a night. Then on 15 September came their lucky break. Blaise's Club was a hip new joint which had been opened by the manager of the Speakeasy, Roy Flynn. He had seen Yes play at the Marquee and Jack Barrie was always promoting them to him, so when Sly and The Family Stone let him down half an hour before a show he called Yes. Peter remembers, 'Jon phoned me up and said, "Come on, we've got a gig tonight." This was about 11pm. So we all rushed down to play at Blaise's. There were lots of famous people there all waiting for Sly and the Family Stone. Instead they got Yes. And we went down very well. Keith Emerson was there and so was Peter Townshend and Eric Clapton … a lot of faces!' Roy Flynn was highly impressed by the band and on the strength of their performance, offered to be their manager.

Jack Barrie had to take a back seat, but he knew that Yes now had a financial backer with huge contacts in the business who was able to promote them and take them further than he was able to. So strong was his belief in Yes that Flynn bought them a van, an organ, a drum kit and found them better accommodation. He also provided their first big break by obtaining the key residency slot at the Marquee, which was a major achievement. They enjoyed several months of regular gigs until their first setback.

Following a decision to get an education, and perhaps earn some money, Bill Bruford enrolled at Leeds University to study economics. He was still unsure about his future and felt that there was more to life than playing in a band. So Yes were forced to employ stand-in musicians over the course of the next few months. For a while, Tony O'Riley stood in for Bruford, who had previously been with a band called the Koobas, managed by Beatles boss Brian Epstein. (The Koobas appeared in a number of films, including *Ferry Cross the Mersey* and *Money Go Round*, and released two singles with Columbia, in 1967, and an album in 1968.) He only played a few gigs with Yes, since his unreliability and musical unsuitability was clear from the outset, and it wasn't long before he moved on to another band.

Yes then turned to Dave Potts whose first band, Crying Shame, was formed in 1966 and was also managed by Brian Epstein. Crying Shame did not last very long and Potts joined Skip Bifferty, an underground band that had influenced the future members of Yes, playing many times at the Marquee Club in the spring of 1968. Potts spent a brief period of time rehearsing with Yes but never actually had the opportunity to play live with them. He went on to play with rock acts such as Ozzy Osbourne and Praying Mantis.

Ian Wallace was the next drummer to grace the Yes platform. Friends with Jon from the Warriors days, Ian now lived in the same block of flats as Chris, Tony and Jon and agreed to stand in as an emergency drummer. Despite various attempts at persuading Ian to join, he refused, due to commitments to another band, Sleepy, and thus holds the record for the shortest stay in Yes; one gig lasting an hour or so!

Everyone agreed that Bill was the best man for the job – no-one came close to him in terms of reliability or performance. So it was fortunate that when Yes played at Leeds University, Bill went to watch. He could see that they were struggling with their current drummer, 'I'd said to all my new-found mates, "Come and have a look at this band, they're really good. I used to play with them." But they were dismal. The rest of the group were all right, but the drummer was at least a beat behind everybody else. I was absolutely crippled with embarrassment.' Realising just how much he had missed the band, he decided that quality of work was more important to him than making money and elected to go back to London and re-join the band.

As with most bands in their early years, it was a constant struggle to obtain a gig, transport the equipment and then earn money from it. Yes would travel to and from gigs in their Ford Transit van, everyone's equipment vying for the best spot in the back. Micky (Michael) Tait, the long-serving Yes sound and light man was with the band from the beginning, starting as their driver and then helping out with equipment development. 'They were amazing days,' recalls Micky. 'When I look back and compare them to today's tours with eighteen trucks and nine buses, I don't know why anyone would want to do it now, because it's just a job. Then it was an adventure. I did that consistently with Yes on the road for fifteen years and they were incredible days, something I would never trade.'

The band would check out the bar first and then in no particular order, the size of the stage, electric points and quick exit routes (just in case). It would be all hands on deck for a quick set up, carrying in six or eight speaker cabinets and about four amplifiers. If they were lucky, they may have had time for a tune up, a sound check, a quick practice, and maybe even a beer or two, but pulling the whole operation together would have been a last-minute job. For the fans themselves,

Main photo from left: Chris Squire, Tony Kaye, Peter Banks, Jon Anderson and Bill Bruford at the front.

attending a Yesshow way back in the beginning was a pretty basic event. The lighting was of a very simple nature and the only special effects used on stage were the oil projectors, the simple but effective device popular in the seventies that projected fluid images onto white sheets hung from amplifiers.

Roy Flynn's next breakthrough was engineering Yes' appearance of the year, playing Cream's farewell concert at the Royal Albert Hall in London on 26 November 1968. Cream were the first real supergroup at the time and they would be playing in front of 5,000 people that night, so it was easy to think that, finally, Yes had hit the big time. It was a significant event for Yes – from then on they were perceived as pioneers of progressive rock music, as if Cream were passing down the mantel to the band of the next decade. The press were right behind Yes and, following the Albert Hall gig, maintained that they were the band to watch out for. Within a few months, in January 1969, Yes had an offer to record sessions at the BBC for John Peel's show *Top Gear*, which was aired on 23 February. Among the four numbers they performed was the one which became the first Yes single, entitled 'Sweetness'/'Something's Coming', released on 4 July 1969.

The early Yes years between 1968-71 were documented by handbills for gigs where the band played as support. From 1973 onwards, Yes had their own programmes and tour merchandise, pioneering the use of mass-produced rock-tour memorabilia. The earliest piece of Yes live memorabilia is a flyer for their appearance, accompanied by the Nite People, at the Marquee on 5 August 1968. A Yes gig in 1968-69 would be listed on the monthly club handbills or flyers, most likely to be

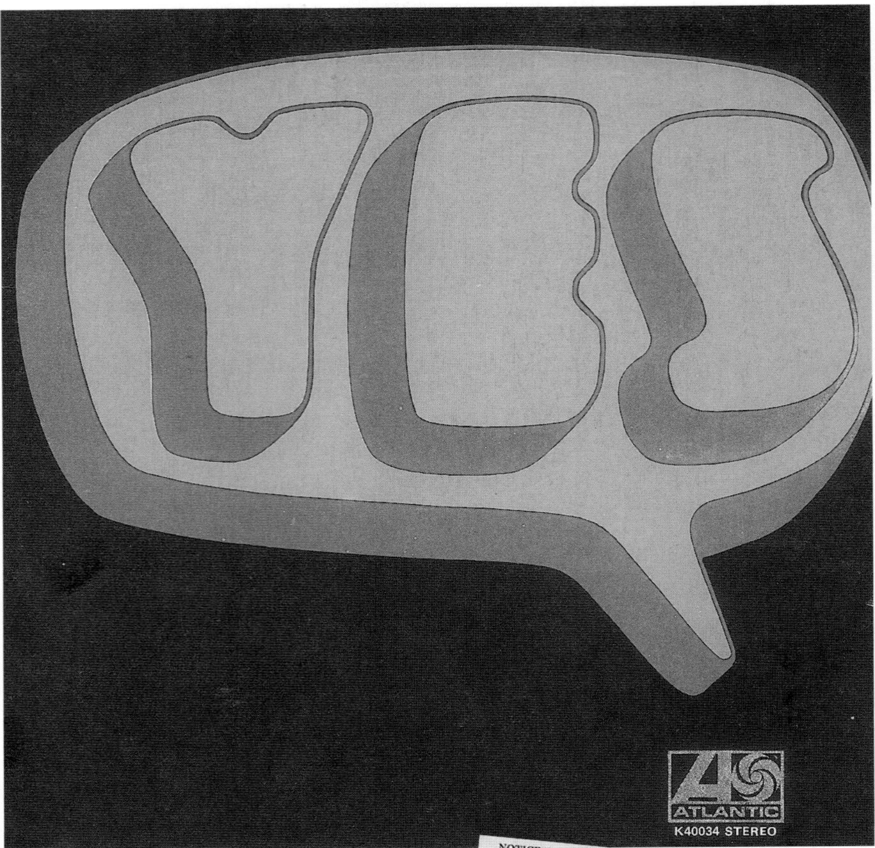

NOTICE TO CLUB MEMBERS

YES

are having their first Solo Concert at the
QUEEN ELIZABETH HALL,
Royal Festival Hall, London.

on Saturday 21st March, 1970

Seat Prices: 21/- 15/- 10/- & 7/6

Available at:-

Th~ Queen Elizabeth Hall Telephone 01-928 3191

or Harold Davison Ltd., Telephone 01-734 7961
235 Regent Street,
London, W.1.

New single and Album both called "TIME AND A WORD"
available on Atlantic Records in March.

A5 in size and cheaply produced. The Marquee flyers were double sided, black and white, and vaguely resembled the design layout of a newspaper. The front usually carried details of who was appearing in the coming month, admission prices, a review of last month's gigs, any special events, membership details and a stop press section – very comprehensive for such a small flyer. The back stated the date and a complete monthly programme of all acts and support bands.

For the first six months of 1969, Yes spent their time in residency at the Marquee Club, only venturing outside the UK on a couple of occasions. As the attention on the band increased, Roy negotiated and secured a record deal with Atlantic records. 'The band was doing really well in London, getting a real good name for itself,' explains Jon. 'It toured England twice. We were ready to do some recording. We didn't know very much at that time about getting the right engineer/ producer so we went and just recorded for about three or four weeks... At that time, there was an internal decision that we wouldn't specifically try for singles. There were enough people doing that. We wanted to formulate some style of music and package it as an album. That gives you a better chance of staying around.'

Yes' first venture into the studios for Atlantic wasn't hugely successful, however. The band were a little taken back with Advision's studio equipment and felt that, although the music they had was definitely worth recording, they desperately needed a producer to help them pull it together. The one they secured, Paul Clay, had produced film soundtracks but never produced a band before, so it was a learning experience for all concerned. The band recorded their set list from the previous months' gigs and added some new compositions. It consisted of a good mixture of cover versions like Lennon and McCartney's 'Every Little Thing' and Roger McGuinn and David Crosby's 'I See You' complementing new tracks by Anderson, Squire, Bailey and Bruford. A couple of songs from the album – 'Survival' and 'Looking Around' – would become Yes standards.

The self-titled first album *Yes* came packaged in a gatefold sleeve with the original Yes logo emblazoned upon the front. Inside the liner notes, a leading journalist for *Melody Maker*, Tony Wilson, predicted that Yes would become one of the most significant bands of 1969.

The album *Yes* and first single 'Sweetness'/'Something's Coming', were released in July and received good reviews but sales were sluggish, the single sold poorly, and the album didn't even enter the charts due to lack of airtime exposure. Nevertheless, the band themselves were just happy to get their first album out to the public and to work hard to improve their playing, arrangements and writing. Although *Yes* was a tentative start, it cemented a real home for all the members of the band. Bill Bruford described the band as a warm and cosy place: 'I was an eighteen year old virgin, she was my first girlfriend.'

The band supported the album with more concert dates in the UK and then went to Switzerland and Germany later in the year to play clubs and festivals. For the most part, 1969 saw Yes touring, establishing a following in London, recording another session for the BBC and gaining encouraging reviews in the press.

Early praise for the band was featured on the front page of the March 1969 Marquee flyer, which commented: 'Finally, a reminder that the original sound of Yes can be heard on Wednesday evenings in March and should be meeting with bigger audiences than they have been getting of late.'

Whilst on the tour, Yes pieced together their next album, entitled *Time and a Word*, released soon after *Yes*. Most of the band had been influenced by classical music, which became increasingly apparent in their music as they searched for a bigger overall sound. Jon wanted to include a brass section or an orchestra like the Nice and Deep Purple had been doing. Having now gained confidence within a traditional studio setting, they used the orchestral backing of the London Sinfonia, who had approached the band after hearing of their desire to experiment with other musical styles.

Atlantic allocated Yes an excellent producer, Tony Colton, and arranger Tony Cox. Featuring six new band compositions and two covers, *Time And a Word* opened with a grand cover version of Richie Havens 'No Opportunity Necessary, No Experience Needed'. Yes were going for the big sound that they so desperately wanted here, aided by the exceptional skills of sound engineer Eddie Offord.

Time and a Word was clearly an improvement on the first album in terms of style and arrangements. Bill commented, 'The difference between the first and second LP's is immense. Consequently, I envisage a huge improvement between the second and third.' The album would give the world a few classic tracks that Yes would perform for many years such as 'Time and a Word' and 'Sweet Dreams' and Yes' own space odyssey 'Astral Traveller', clearly influenced by Jon's love of science fiction. This highlighted the emerging interest in all things spiritual and cosmic that would soon become a trademark of the band. In the remaining tracks 'Then', 'Clear Days' and 'Prophet', we hear Yes in various moods, pooling influences from the Beatles, Holtz and jazz.

Jon Anderson later remarked of the classical influences on this album: 'I had speakers at the bottom of my bed, blasting out classical music all the time. I was interested in opening up the sound of the band, developing a string sound, and we talked about trying a Mellotron, but we thought it only had a certain sound, and that it relates to only a certain type of music. We did try it out a couple of times, then we decided to use real musicians, string and brass and things like that. So, in some ways, it was kind of an adventure really. For the most part it worked but sometimes the musicians weren't really up to it. They were session men, but they didn't sound like they were really *up*. They were just doing their job.'

Time and a Word, released on 25 July, entered the charts on 1 August where it spent three weeks, hitting no. 45 at its peak. The band were not pleased with the album. 'It was the same problem all over again,' Chris explains, 'I'd imagined it sounding much grander somehow, but we didn't quite get there.' Two singles were released, the title track plus 'The Prophet', but both only sold in very small quantities and Yes decided after this that they weren't a singles band.

Page 4—MELODY MAKER, May

BANKS
new forms

Yes guitarist Banks has quit

ANOTHER SPLIT has hit a top British group—guitar star Peter Banks has quit Yes. And the group have cancelled all their appearances until they can find a replacement.

They played their last date together at Luton recently. Peter says he is leaving to "explore new forms of music and to work with other musicians."

Manager Roy Flynn told the MM: "The group and Peter felt that their music had begun to stagnate and the Yes have cancelled all their engagements and are not accepting any bookings until they find a suitable guitarist to replace Peter."

The group recently gave a successful solo concert at London's Queen Elizabeth Hall, and have been widely tipped for stardom by critics.

The line-up includes singer/writer John Anderson, organist Tony Kaye, drummer Bill Brufford and bassist Chris Squire. They have an LP ready for release, but have cancelled plans to release a single.

Still only two years old as a band, Yes began to play in larger venues and focused on playing festivals. The band were still very much a support band despite all their hard work and constant touring. Although Yes were beginning to share the stage with bigger acts and were benefiting from better sound systems and superior lighting, visually it was still a basic show. The standard set up would be twelve to fifteen 500-watt lights and that was it. *Time and a Word* offered the opportunity for more touring and live performances, but the inclusion of a twenty-piece orchestra created absolute chaos.

Then, on 2 May, Roy Flynn made an official announcement: 'The group and Peter felt their music had begun to stagnate and Yes have cancelled all their engagements and are not taking any more bookings until they find a suitable guitarist replacement.' Peter had become increasingly distant from the rest of the band, and he was the only member who had been opposed to using an orchestral sound on the album. He had, reputedly, found recording *Time and a Word* very difficult and, as time passed, discovered that his style of playing and the direction Yes were moving in were diametrically opposed.

Time and a Word was selling only slightly better than the first album, and by the time it was released in the US Roy Flynn had quit as manager. Roy had worked really hard and loved the band, but had reached the point where he could no longer subsidise their existence. Sad to see him leave, the band appreciated how much of his life he had given to their pursuit of success and have remained eternally grateful – but were keen for a new manager to step in and push them into the big time.

At this point, the band's members were thoroughly depressed, not knowing for sure whether they could or should continue. Questions were raised about whether they ought to find a replacement guitarist or even stop playing altogether. Without a manager, money, guitarist or a record company who had faith in them, times were tough for the band and Yes needed some time away to rethink. Decamping to Devon in order to contemplate the future and work on new material, the only hope the band retained came from a singular belief in their music.

'It was a very bleak period after the second album where nothing had really happened at all,' Bill recalled. 'And we were still stunningly unfamous! Bands don't get that long now, three years into our career and we were still in staggeringly bad shape. I think the feeling was in those days, you give the band three albums, pretty much. Now you'd have about three seconds, so there's no chance to develop anything at all. So I was grateful to be a young musician at the time I was a young musician.'

Fortunately, there was a glimmer of hope on the horizon when Jon and Chris found a new guitarist. Before leaving for Devon, they recalled seeing Steve Howe play in a number of London clubs. Impressing them with his style, performance and overall technique, the band called him to a meeting in the hope he would consider joining Yes.

Born 8 April 1947, Steven James Howe hailed from London. Through his family, he soon grew to love music. His brother played the clarinet and Steve became fascinated with jazz – a style he was later to incorporate into his own playing. He picked up his first guitar aged twelve and began the long process of teaching himself. 'Not being a very studious child, I had to work at it even harder – there were no rock guitar teachers around who I could communicate with.'

His early inspiration came from Bill Haley and the Comets, featuring guitarist Fran Beecher, whilst Les Paul and Chet Atkins were also favourites. And then, as Rock 'n' Roll hit the airwaves, Steve would copy the likes of the Shadows, Chuck Berry and Buddy Holly. Added to his interest in classical music, jazz, rock and rhythm and blues, it was inevitable that his burgeoning style would embrace all these influences. His first teenage band, the r'n'b-based Syndicats, had a lucky start in the music business when they were signed by EMI.

The Syndicats were a promising band that had quickly become well known and developed a strong and loyal following. EMI backed them to the hilt, releasing three singles in quick succession, but none of them became hits and the group realised they were not destined to make it. Steve left soon after this, deciding success was a long way off, and in early 1967 joined another band, the In Crowd, which turned out to be a short-lived affair. As the line-up changed over a period of time, they changed their name to Tomorrow.

'I'd always wanted to have my own guitar style, but other people said I had one before I was aware of it…' remembers Steve. 'In 1968 I was in a band called Tomorrow when I realised there were things I did that other guitarists didn't do. I've always enjoyed not using ordinary guitar licks, for instance. For a long time, people played blues guitar. Although I like playing blues guitar, you don't hear me playing many blue phrases. In some ways, it's a question of finding the most obvious things I play and then digging in around them to be more unusual and more original. I'm not limited to just one instrument. I've played a bit of mandolin, the koto and some steel guitar because the guitar isn't enough for me.'

Tomorrow were a psychedelic band and had considerable success for a time, releasing an album and two singles with EMI. They briefly rivalled the success of Pink Floyd, gaining a good following around London, and their singer, Keith West, had a Top 30 solo hit called 'Excerpt from a Teenage Opera (Grocer Jack)'. However, West's solo success resulted in internal difficulties within the band. So Steve left and joined an outfit called Canto, who changed their name to Bodast in May 1968, released an album but never reached the same heights as Tomorrow.

His time with Bodast was not all wasted: they toured as support for bands such as the Nice, and also found time to play at Blaise's in London with Keith West, Twink and Freddie (from the Pink Fairies) under the name of the Joint. In 1969, Steve also played some gigs at the Roundhouse in London with Tomorrow (who had reformed without Keith West), as the lead vocalist, which he enjoyed immensely. But although this was a varied and productive time for Steve, it became clear that Bodast were going nowhere fast and, by 1970, the record company decided to let them go. Steve moved on once more, almost joining the Nice at one stage, before auditioning for Jethro Tull. Both these ventures came to nothing.

Whilst searching for the right band, Steve played on sessions for his friend Keith West and also performed on the Delaney & Bonnie European Tour, which featured stars such as Eric Clapton and George Harrison. Soon after, when Chris Squire rang him and asked if he wanted to join Yes, Steve agreed almost immediately.

Jon recalled his meeting with Steve. 'I actually saw Steve a month before we got together, when I went to the Speakeasy and he was playing. I remember walking right past him, underneath the stage, just looking at this guy with this beautiful guitar playing.' When they auditioned him, Jon remembered, 'He sat down, played some music to us, and it was spontaneous and unanimous. We wanted him to join Yes.'

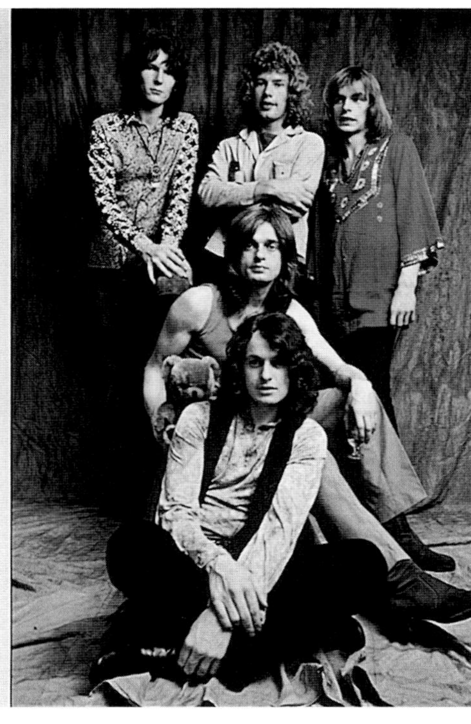

SWEET DREAMS, CLASSIC YEARS

1971 – 79

THE BAND SET out to write all the material for the next album without relying on any covers, deciding that a strong musical identity had to be forged this time. In late Spring 1970, the band weaved their way down to Devon where they started work, their confidence returning over the next six months as they composed and recorded with a renewed enthusiasm. 'We were in Devon rehearsing *The Yes Album*,' remembered Jon. 'Staying in a beautiful valley. Nature was all around us and it was amazing,' adding, 'We worked so hard while we were away on the farm we were exhausted. It was like four years on the road!'

Co-producer Eddie Offord (who had worked as engineer on the previous album) and new manager Brian Lane would be instrumental in ensuring the future success of the band – Offord helping them achieve a clearer defined sound, Lane managing their business affairs, record deals and tours. Chris had stumbled upon Brian Lane whilst having his hair cut, his hairdresser suggesting he consider Brian for the job of manager. Brian had previously managed singer Anita Harris, and, although he had not been heavily involved in the music industry for a long time, 'Brian was a very energetic manager and was a big boost to the whole thing,' as Chris explained. 'He was one of those people who always had a phone glued to his ear. He was very impressive because in those days that was the beginning of the age when people were constantly on the phone. It was a new trendy thing.'

The Yes Album was released in January 1971 and the result was stunning. Heralding new sounds, arrangements and styles that simply had never been done before, it was light years ahead of their previous material and produced what is now commonly known as the Yes sound. This very English sound (which, doubtless, helped its UK success), also provided a huge jump forward for the band in the US. In the UK the album went to Number 7 and in the US, the track 'Your Move', released as a single, managed to reach number 40 in the Billboard charts.

The band did not use session musicians, as they had done with *Time and a Word* and concentrated on their own material. The album featured six very long tracks that heralded the beginning of an interest in more complex arrangements, expansive ideas, and creating a form of music with greater feel, depth, mood and emotion which still retained the band's all-important accessibility. With hindsight, it is clear that Yes had produced a classic record. Virtually the whole album became a 'Best of' selection, all-

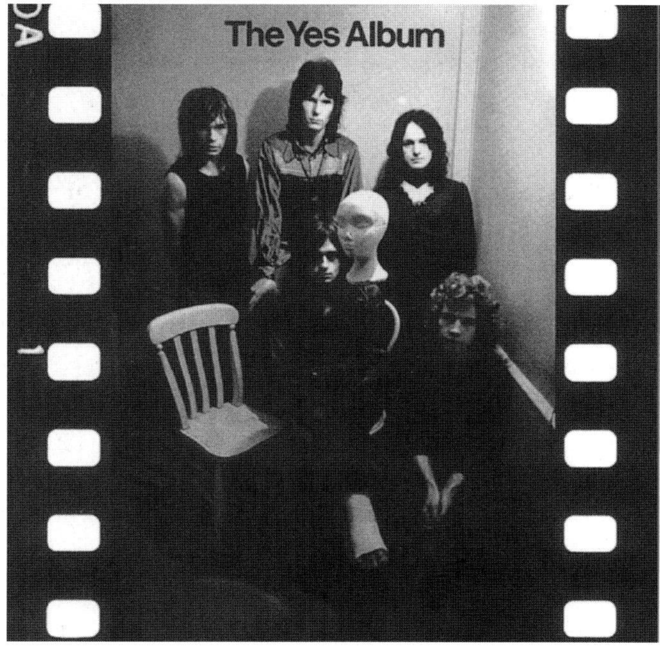

time greats such as 'I've Seen All Good People', 'Clap', 'Starship Trooper', 'Perpetual Change' and 'Yours Is No Disgrace' all becoming regular features at Yesshows over the past 28 years.

In November 1970, Yes started a UK and European tour also featuring progressive bands such as Iron Butterfly and Focus, playing to large audiences at home and on the continent. But it was to be their success in the US that was the turning point for Yes. Through giving up some publishing rights, Yes pulled enough money together to buy a sound system that their sound engineer, Michael Tait, claimed 'made Yes sound better than anyone else in Europe'. In the early months of 1971 Yes made an appearance on *Top of the Pops* which precipitated their rise to the top of the UK album charts.

YES: "The Yes Album" (Atlantic). Undoubtedly their best release, the third Yes album, is a milestone in the history of the group, and one of the finest from a British band. The quality of production equals the quality of performance at last and bite, showcased by superb instrumental ability. There is teamwork and the individual talent of Steve Howe (guitar), Bill Bruford (drums), and Tony Kaye (organ). Chris Squire's meaningful bass, combined with Bill's drums make them a formidable rhythm section. The songs and arrangements are rich in melody, surprises and excitement. There is a quality and depth to their work that is earning them new friends daily.

The Yes Album was released in the US in March 1971. The US radio stations' play lists have always had a profound impact on how well a record performs in the charts, but it took a good deal of time for American DJs to get used to Yes and to start playing their music on a regular basis. At this time, the US was flooded with English musical imports, but, eventually, the band did break through on the East Coast.

One of the biggest British acts at the time was Jethro Tull, who would play to audiences of between 15-20,000 people every night. In the summer of 1971 Yes made their north American debut in Edmonton, Canada, before Brian Lane secured a six-week tour as support to Jethro Tull. When the band arrived for their first US tour, they genuinely believed that no-one would know who they were. Surprisingly, the reaction that they received was excellent, especially in New York and Philadelphia where they were greeted on stage like old friends and benefited from a great deal of radio DJ support. 'We were an immediate success,' recalls Bill. 'And we wiped the floor with the other bands and everybody loved us.'

One of Yes' biggest fans in the US was a sound engineer called Roy Clair: 'The first time I heard them I was most impressed, because the music was so different. They were so talented and they worked really well together.' Roy ran his own audio engineering company where he'd worked with Elton John and Cat Stevens, and offered to build Yes a new sound system. 'Their music is very dynamic and they needed a lot of power. So we used big amplifiers. This enabled the speakers to cope with the dynamics of the band, quiet sometimes and then remarkably loud. Yes were famous for that.' With Eddie Offord still working as the band's official sound engineer, between the two of them Eddie and Roy created a very effective sound.

Following the US tour, which was a huge success, the band flew back to the UK in August to finish the dates booked at home. They supported Elton John at the Crystal Palace Bowl in south London before going back to the studio to start work on their next album. While Yes were naturally feeling pleased with themselves over the success of the US tour, external forces were having an impact.

The emergence of new technology had seen keyboard players such as Keith Emerson of ELP and Mike Pinder of the Moody Blues expanding the musical horizons of their bands by introducing, respectively, the Moog synthesiser and the Mellotron. Although Yes were on a wave, they still needed a more vibrant variety of sounds. Differences had arisen on the last tour between the rest of the band and keyboardist Tony Kaye, whose playing style had now become out of sync with Yes' mood and tone. Soon after, Tony left the band and Yes appointed a younger man as keyboardist.

Born May 18 1949 in west London, at the age of five Rick Wakeman followed in the footsteps of his father and took up the piano. 'My earliest memory of the piano was probably from when I was about four years old. I saw my dad playing and of course I wanted to play piano like daddy.' By the age of ten, Rick had won around 30 child prodigy competitions. At fourteen, he joined his school friends in a group called Atlantic Blues who were fortunate enough to get steady weekly gigs in a local club. His next band, the Concords, went nowhere, but Rick spent a great deal of energy on his music, resulting in his school grades deteriorating. Though he achieved his dream of attending the Royal College of Music, he didn't last long since he continued to play gigs with rock bands and was dismissed for neglecting his studies.

Between the ages of eighteen and 21 Rick played on over 2,000 studio sessions for artists including Cat Stevens and David Bowie. Then he was offered the chance to join the Strawbs, where he was paid £50 per week and gained a passion for performing in front of live audiences.

After eighteen months with the Strawbs, it was becoming clear to everyone that Rick needed a new challenge. He was the rising star of the day, still only 21, a stylish and charismatic keyboard player, whom the music press had hailed as 'The Star of Tomorrow'. 'I had been doing a lot of sessions and was lying in bed after having done a three-day stint with about six hours sleep. And that was typical. I had just arrived home having had no sleep again, and fell into bed. It was one of those things where the minute my head hit the pillow, I fell asleep. It felt so good, and then the phone rang. I couldn't believe it, and Ros picked up the phone. I could hear the conversation, "He's only just come in. He hasn't been back for three days... you know he's really tired." I was awake by then and let me tell you I was furious. "Gimme that phone... who's that?" I said. And this voice said, "Oh, hello. It's Chris Squire from Yes." It's three in the morning and he said, "How are you?" I said, "You phone me up at three in the morning to ask how I am?" I told him I was very tired and asked him if he would phone back. "Well," he said, "We've just come back from an American tour and we're thinking of having a change in personnel. I saw you doing some sessions down at Advision Studios and all I wanted to know was if you'd be interested in joining the band." And I, like a prick, said "NO!" and slammed the phone down. I was furious!'

Rick later conceded to rehearse with Yes, which became his initiation into the band. Within his first week with the band they had written 'Heart of the Sunrise' and 'Roundabout' and Rick was now a firm member of the band.

'We did an American tour that really energised us incredibly,' recalled Jon. 'We wanted to get back in the studio and make another album quickly because we knew that we were on sort of a roll on many levels. And all of a sudden there was this definite feeling of "we've got Steve and he's very multi-talented and maybe we should look for a more multi-talented keyboard player." That's when Rick Wakeman joined the group. He was the darling of the universities and colleges, he was the man to go see. Rick was very talented and individual in his style ... he joined the group and again we were injected with that energy.'

Rick's style and ideas fitted perfectly with the others, and the early composition sessions were extremely productive. Rick and Steve provided Yes with a complete sound overhaul: Steve's different guitar styles and instruments moving the Yes soundscape into areas of jazz, blues, rock and classical music, epitomised by his contribution to 'Starship Trooper'. Rick's classical training on keyboards and his introduction of grand piano, Mellotron, Moog and electric piano were exactly what Yes needed to create a bigger orchestral classical sound without actually using an orchestra.

'I remember thinking how different the band were as musicians,' recalls Rick. 'Everything almost seemed wrong. Jon had an alto voice unlike other rock singers, who were raunchy tenors. Steve had a true style of his own with his individual Fender amp, unlike every other guitarist who was using Marshall stacks, and Chris played bass with the treble turned full on through his Sunn amps. Bill was even more different, if that's possible, with a totally focused precise way of playing the drums. I remember thinking that I'd fit in quite well here!' Rick continues, 'In reality, I had a couple of important roles. Firstly, that of adding new colours to the music through the keyboards and as new keyboards became available so I was able to add more sounds. I think my classical background helped a lot as well, as I could work out exactly what everybody was doing and help shape the arrangements. I also enjoyed doing harmony solos and "orchestrations" with guitar and keyboards.'

Melody Maker

NEW YES MAN

RICK WAKEMAN: "I'd reached my peak within the Strawbs"

Yes had written much of the next album on the last tour, so Rick was coming late to the project. The band based themselves in the Advision Studios in London for five weeks where they worked with an intensity that was exhausting. They spent four to five weeks recording *Fragile*, working sixteen hour days with hardly any time off, an intense and inspiring time for the band.

Rick himself was shocked by the attention to detail. 'I couldn't believe it. I mean, we would spend three or four hours just musically discussing three bars – whether the link was right or not. And trying it all sorts of ways and then coming back to the way we started. I thought, "This is totally over the top! This is totally unnecessary." But at the end of the day after all those hours were put into the little bits... when you listened back to the tracks, you realised that it was those little attentions to detail that make the pieces what they are.'

The album features some of the most memorable Yes compositions, split between four band collaborations and five solo efforts. Classic tracks on the album include 'Heart of the Sunrise', the longest track Yes attempted up to that time; 'Long Distance Runaround' and the mighty solos from Chris – 'The Fish' and Steve – 'Mood for the Day'. Jon's multi-tracked vocals feature in 'We Have Heaven', Bill's first solo-written percussive piece 'Five Percent for Nothing'. They all showed off their individual talents without threatening the collective entity that was Yes, the album linking together their carefully crafted arrangements, atmospheric vocals, impressively complex playing, rich textures and moving, emotional lyrics. The band's partnership with producer Eddie Offord was crucial. 'He knew a lot about studio techniques,' explained Chris, 'and I personally learned more from him about studios and the ideas behind them than I ever will from anyone again. There were a lot of unspoken things that worked because he grasped what we were trying to do.'

Earlier on in the year, the band's path had crossed for the first time with the artist Roger Dean. Roger had originally been approached by the record company to design the cover of *The Yes Album*, but this never actually happened. Once taken on board by Yes, his cover designs introduced the spacey fantasy landscapes of Yesworld and fostered a love affair with Roger Dean's artwork for many Yes fans. *Fragile*'s album cover was a seminal moment, bearing the revised Yes logo by Roger and containing a booklet, designed by him, including photographs of every member of the band. The lengthier tracks, with their cosmic lyrics, and the grandiose artistic covers, attracted journalistic labels like 'symphonic rock', 'progressive rock' or 'art rock'. As non-musician, artist, visionary and designer of the classic Yes logo, Roger Dean has developed the image of the band over nearly thirty years. Roger's contribution to the success of Yes is huge; his unique, dreamy artwork lending itself perfectly to their mysterious lyrics and sound.

It seemed that at this point in their career Yes could do no wrong: they had their strongest musical line-up, a hit album and single, a string of tours under their belts, all combining to give them an enormous amount of confidence. The live shows had also changed greatly, with the band investing £6,000 in new instruments, lighting and sound equipment. Following the album's release, they continued to tour the US and Europe to increasingly large audiences, better reviews and bigger sales. In November 1971 they hit the US for their second tour, supporting Ten Years After and the J. Geils Band. 'That second tour was gruelling – like an endurance test,' recalls Steve. But

Yes' audience had grown with the band since the start, and they appreciated the longer, more complex musical arrangements.

Fragile was released both in the States and the UK on 4 January 1972 and reached number four in the US charts and number seven in the UK charts, where it remained for seventeen weeks. At the same time, the record company released 'Roundabout' as an edited single in January for the American market, managing to get a large amount of airplay and charting reasonably well as a result. It seemed that Yes had finally made their mark on the North American market.

The band were both bemused and startled by this change in their status, as Bill recalls: 'The first idea I got of any success was sitting in a limo, in New York perhaps. And somebody was showing me *Billboard* and I think *Fragile* was number four on the American charts and above us was Frank Sinatra and a couple of other people. It said *Fragile* by Yes and all I can remember is what a pathetically short word the word Yes seemed and a vague feeling that somehow we had done it. I think the minute the band became popular, my overriding memory was that somehow we'd pulled off a band heist. It felt like somehow we had gotten away with it and really it was much more exciting doing the bank heist than running away with the riches. Somehow getting there is much more interesting than arriving.'

Massive Yes tour

YES will headline a 30 - day concert tour of Britain in November — but there won't be any UK dates for the group before then.

The British itinerary will be part of a massive European tour, organised by manager Brian Lane in conjunction with the Chrysalis Agency and Kinney Records. A top American act — also from the Kinney group — will join Yes.

Italy (October 1-7), Switzerland (8-10), Scandinavia (18-25), Britain (November 1-30), Holland and Belgium (December 1-7) and France (7-10) will all be visited.

Plans are under way for Yes to be recorded "live" on both the British and European dates for a 1972 album.

The group's first US tour is now set to open in New York on June 9 and will last four-and-a-half weeks. A projected visit to Mexico in early June has been cancelled because of recording commitments. Their next album is due for August release.

Manager Brian Lane told the MM this week: "The group are away in the country preparing new material and they want to get it all down on record before playing any more British dates. They're getting a brand new act together and in this way they'll avoid getting stale.

"They need a break and they want to get away from

JON A… of Britai…

Jon Anderson spent a great deal of time reading for inspiration, one of his favourite books being *Siddhartha* by Hermann Hesse, and listening to classical music by Sibelius amongst others. These influences started to merge into the Yes ethos and it seemed that the next project would carry an underlying classical tone.

Early meetings to discuss the album's potential direction and form were held in the West End of London, where they decided once again to record at Advision Recording Studios. Once ensconced in the studio, the band recorded lots of material and the inspiration was flowing. Jon and Steve then dissected the recordings and continuously edited the myriad pieces together, often working late into the night, while Chris worked closely with Eddie Offord as he made countless tiny adjustments to the recordings.

Bill recalls, '*Close to the Edge* had a sense of discovery for us – and presumably for the people who bought it. I'm sure it sounds trite now, but in those days, it was quite a big deal. Rock musicians hadn't been capable of an arrangement of any kind of complexity at all. But now I find it's fundamentally good music, its form, its shape are timeless.'

The process was anything but scientific, however. Yes failed to assemble the recordings in the normal manner, leaving bits of tape on the floor, in the bin, under the desk, all vying for that place in the final mix. With the desire to create a large orchestral sound, they moved towards the type of themed work that only the Beatles, with *Sgt. Pepper,* and the Who, with *Tommy* had realised with any success.

'The idea with *Close To The Edge* was to start with the river – something very natural – and then the river to become electronic and develop into some music and go through a few dreams that I've had... It's very difficult to explain,' Jon tried to articulate to *Melody Maker*.

But whilst Jon Anderson viewed the recording process positively, Bill Bruford recalls things differently. 'If we'd known how horrible it was going to be, we would never have done it. But it's like five guys trying to write a novel at the same time. One guy has a good beginning, and the second guy had quite a good middle and the third guy thinks he knows what the ending is, but the fourth guy doesn't like the way the middle goes towards the ending, and the second guy who used to like the third section has changed his mind and now likes the first section. It was torture. None of these arrangements were written and they weren't really composed. We all sat in the rehearsal room and said, "Let's have the G after the G#." And every instrument was up for democratic election, you know, and everyone had to run an election campaign on every issue. And it was horrible, I mean it was incredibly unpleasant and unbelievably hard work. And Squire was always late for every rehearsal. And after about two months of this unbelievable punishment, people still say to me, "Bill, why didn't you do another one?"'

This would be Yes' fifth album with Atlantic, with the record company giving the band a free hand in recording and production. *Close to the Edge* was released on 13 September 1972 to excellent reviews and wide acclaim from the fans. The album only featured three tracks, the whole of the first side dedicated to a title track, which lasted nearly twenty minutes and contained all the ingredients that had made Yes' music

ATLANTIC
YES
ROUNDABOUT
TUBS

Clockwise from top: Rick Wakeman, Jon Anderson, Steve Howe, Chris Squire and Bill Bruford.

COLORA

unique: as it was termed, merging a 'sound painting', soaring vocals, shifting moods, grand themes, virtuosity and tangible emotion. The other two tracks on the album were 'And You And I' and 'Siberian Khatru', both of which were around ten minutes in length.

After *Close to the Edge* was released, a journalist suggested that Yes would probably put *The Bible* to music next! Although it was only said in a jocular manner, Jon replied, 'Yes why not, we can do it, we can do anything we like.'

As before, the overall presentation was important to the success of the album, Roger Dean was again enlisted to design the cover, which perfectly complemented the feel of the album. How many of us have let the fluidity of *Close to the Edge* fill our heads while imagining the endless flow of the island waterfalls on the inner sleeve? Who hasn't listened to 'Gates of Delirium' without seeing those riders passing through the canyons of stark, grey rock with the ever-present omen of the snake threatening their safety? And, when Jon sings the introduction to 'The Revealing Science of God', what better embodiment of the line 'Chased amid fusions of wonder' than the school of fish flying through the crazy topographic landscape? There could be no greater visual complement to the music of Yes than Roger Dean's amazing work. He was also responsible for the newly created Yes logo, a curvy, bubble-like design which would become the band's trademark for the next 27 years, instantly recognisable the world over.

In the UK, the album spent thirteen weeks in the charts, reaching its highest point at number four, whilst in the US it reached number three in the *Billboard* chart. Yes' stature at this point in the US can be gauged by their number one spots on both the *Cashbox* and *Billboard* charts. They also came away with the 1972 *Billboard* mid-year award for the Top Group on Album. Yes were suddenly big news – with good transatlantic album sales, their singles receiving airtime, and converts in the press suddenly advocating the Yes sound. Everything seemed to be just right, except for one member of the band.

The making of the album had been a great strain on Bill Bruford and, although he was delighted with the end result, he didn't see how a follow up album could possibly be any better. The constant high standards required by the band had put immense pressure on Bill, and unbeknownst to the other guys, he decided that his days were numbered. Bill had long had an inkling to join King Crimson, whose dark jazz element he felt an empathy with, and decided on the eve of the next US tour that it was better to jump than to be pushed. He would later explain, 'I did get irritated, but then I was like all twenty year olds, I thought I knew everything. But it was all so slow! We had to work all night and knew it would take at least three months to make this record because Simon and Garfunkel had taken two and a half months to make theirs.' But it came as a huge surprise to the rest of the band and the shock hit them very hard. Rick recalls, 'When Bill suddenly left I couldn't believe it. I thought the band would crumble. For the first time I had started to feel part of the band and then it seemed it was about to end.' Yes, always resilient in times of adversity, had a week to overcome the task of finding a replacement drummer. Although a number of names were drawn up for the vacant position, the most obvious one had been known to the band for a while. A friend of Eddie Offord's, Alan White was fully aware of Yes and their rapidly burgeoning success.

Born 14 June 1949 in Pelton, County Durham, Alan White's introduction to music was via the piano rather than the drums. But when his drum playing uncle spotted the way he hammered the keys on the piano, he suggested that his nephew learn the drums instead.

'I was on the stage within three months of getting my first kit. At that time, I joined a band called the Downbeats. Basically, we did a lot of Beatles, copy stuff with some original material. I think that the best place to learn is on stage. It makes demands of you and you really start creating. I was in that band two years and they changed their name to the Blue Chips and we won a bunch of competitions nationwide in England.'

However, he left the band to go to college for a while – although it wasn't long before he was lured back to his drum kit to play for Billy Fury's backing band, the Gamblers, and spent a few depressing months slogging around Germany. On his return to the UK, Alan put a band together with Alan Price, called Happy Magazine, who soon changed their name to Griffin and continued to scrape a living from playing live, but Alan was also playing sessions and had, in the past two years, contributed to approximately 50 albums.

His big break was to come shortly. 'I got a telephone call and someone said, "John's on the phone for you," and I said, "I don't know any Johns." And it was a telephone call from John Lennon. I thought that it was a hoax initially, but he'd seen me somewhere and he said, "I'd like you to do a gig with myself the day after tomorrow." I said, "I think we have a gig, but I'll see what I can do!" I turned up at the VIP lounge in Heathrow airport and there was Eric Clapton, John, Yoko and Klaus Voormann. We literally rehearsed on the airplane, John and Eric playing acoustic guitars and me with a pair of drumsticks on the back of an airplane seat. All of a sudden, we were being picked up in Toronto and taken straight to the gig and on stage. Me being young and naïve to that big star kind of thing… I didn't realise what I'd just been through. Playing on stage, with Eric Clapton and John Lennon in front of all those people was the biggest break of my career.'

An album of the event was later recorded, entitled *Live Peace in Toronto* by the Plastic Ono Band, and then the offers came flooding in. He initially remained with Griffin, involved with Denny Laine's band Balls, recording

White joins Yes

ALAN WHITE has joined Yes, replacing founder member Bill Bruford, who quit the group last week to work with the new King Crimson line-up, as reported exclusively in the MM.

Yes have postponed their American tour which was to have started this week and instead they are rehearsing day and night with White. They leave for America on Saturday, thus missing four gigs of the three week schedule.

White will make his British debut with the band at the Crystal Palace Garden Party concert on September 2.

On their return from America, the Yes British tour will now include Belle Vue, Manchester, on September 10 and two shows at Glasgow's Kelvin Hall on October 4 and 5.

■ SEE FEATURE on P.9.

Following founder-member Bill Bruford's decision to quit Yes -- revealed exclusively in last week's MM -- comes news that his replacement is ex-Lennon, ex-Cocker drummer ALAN WHITE. Chris Charlesworth talked to White and to Yes leader JON ANDERSON...

YES -now with added Whiteness

IT seems to happen once a year—a split within Yes But it comes as something of a shock, especially as the group are riding on crest of a wave in terms of popularity. Never has the band's following or earning potential been so great as it is now, but despite it all Bill Bruford quits.

It was around 12 months ago that Rick Wakeman took over from Tony Kaye, and a year before that Steve Howe took over from Pete Banks. Only Jon Anderson and Chris Squire now remain as original members of the group.

Balls

Taking over from Bruford is Alan White, the nomadic drummer of rock whose prowess as a session man took him into Lennon's Plastic Ono Band, Balls (which never got off the ground) and his most recent stint as a member of Chris Stainton's All Stars, backing Joe Cocker on their European tour which ended last week.

Yes's manager Brian Laine planned a gradual introduction to the group with White travelling with them while Bruford played drums.

Eventually is was planned that two drummers would play with the group — and Bruford would be gradually phased out. Now he will take over immediately.

ALAN WHITE: decided to settle down with Yes

This week White is taking part in intensive rehearsals with Alan about the possi- their American tour. His British debut will be at Crystal Palace in September, following the American tour which, he hopes, will enable him to slot right into the band.

Anderson, the undisputed leader of Yes, views the future with confidence. He doesn't consider the change of drummer will effect the band adversely and, although Bruford's abrupt decision to quit came as a shock, he had secretly admired White's drumming and considered the possibility of working with White long before the opportunity arose.

"It was a shock to see it in the paper this week, but Bill had told me that if there was anybody he would like to work with in the future it would be Bob Fripp. I think the change would definitely have developed in the next couple of years but this came sooner than anticipated," Anderson told me this week.

"I had been in touch with Alan about the possibility of working together and making some tapes within the framework of Yes. When Bill said he wanted to leave it was an obvious move to ask Alan to join and he is as interested as us.

JON: confident about the future

"It probably came as a shock to Bill that we found a replacement so easily. We are happy with the outcome and we hope Bill will be happy."

Coincidentally, Yes seem to lose a man as they record a new album, and Anderson considers the intensity of their work a contributing factor to each split.

"All artists have a lost period after doing intense work. The ideas are drained out of you and frustration creeps in.

"It was the same thing when Tony left, and we though that Rick could do a better job and bring in new ideas. The next album we do will be a live album, and as this is to be recorded on our next American tours, Aan will be featured on it.

Boost

"I don't think it is as hard fitting in a drummer as it would be a new instrumentalist. The instrumentalists are soloists in Yes, and the drummer is the root. Chris and Alan can work together and I think they will learn things from each other. Alan writes music and it will be interesting to see what he can contribute to the band in this way.

"Yes have a style for arranging things, but no permanent style of music. There are no boundaries as to what we can do. I think the addition of a new musician will help to boost morale in the band because that's what happened when Rick joined."

The group plan to develop the percussion ideas within the band by introducing fringe percussion instruments like timpani and gongs. At present Wakeman uses nine different keyboards, Steve Howe has six guitars and Chris Squire three basses.

"The possibilities for de velopment are endless," says Jon.

"The only way in which I can see our music changing is that Alan might make things a bit heavier and funkier. Bill was a technical drummer, and Alan is more of a rock drummer. The next six months are going to be really interesting."

White, who heard about the vacancy while touring Europe with Cocker, maintains he can adopt to the Yes style quite easily.

Blows

Last week he spent hours playing Yes' records over and over again, and listening to Yes tapes with their engineer Eddie Offord. Offord, who now travels with Yes as their sound engineer as well as working with them in the studio, has worked with White before.

He worked on an album by Terry Reid with Offord, and one with P. P. Arnold. His most recent album with Offord was a Johnny Harris Orchestra collection — and the same album featured Steve Howe on guitar and Jon Anderson singing.

"I've had a few blows with Yes at various places and it always felt good. It was just a matter of someone getting rid of Bill Bruford," Alan joked.

"I've got about a week to learn several million drum breaks but this is a better way of doing things than travelling around watching Bill playing. I couldn't be a spectator for 20 concerts.

"For the present it's down to playing what Bill was playing as opposed to my version of it, but in the future I'll be putting in my own ideas. Yes are a co-operative group and I'll have a co-operative role in the band.

"I've been looking for a band to settle down in and I think this is it.

an album and a single and going on a promotional tour of Germany.

Alan then spent two months with Ginger Baker's Airforce (ex Cream), followed by a lengthy period with Terry Reid and Bell and Arc before coming to Yes in 1972. 'At the time, I had just completed a tour with Joe Cocker. I was in Rome when Tony Dimitriades called me and said, "Yes wants you to join the band." As it happened, I was finishing the tour that night, so I flew back to England and we had a meeting in Eddie Offord's apartment. I was sharing an apartment with Eddie then. We had met numerous times through Eddie. Chris had seen me play with Joe Cocker at the Rainbow Theatre in London. Chris and Jon came up to Eddie's apartment and said "Listen. You're joining the band or we'll throw you out this third-storey window!"'

An intense four days work for Alan followed, as he had to learn the new set before his first Yes concert in Dallas, Texas on 30 June 1972. Over the next five months Yes toured the US and UK to promote *Close to the Edge*, garnering good reviews and growing audiences. Alan settled into the line-up quickly, after passing a three-month trial period with flying colours.

RICK WAKEMAN: solo album in January

Rick's Six Wives

RICK WAKEMAN, keyboardsman with Yes, has completed work on his first solo album "The Six Wives Of Henry The Eighth," which is scheduled for release by A & M in early January.

The album features six lengthy instrumental tracks, one of which will be released as a single in the States, but Wakeman stresses that no British single will be issued.

On the album, Rick plays organ, Mellotron, Moog, harpsichord, piano, electric piano, ARP Synthesiser and the church organ of St. Giles, Cripplegate.

Yes colleagues Steve Howe, Chris Squire and Alan White assist him on the album, and others in on the sessions include guitarists Mike Egan and Dave Lambert, bassists Dave Wintour, Chas Cronk and Les Hurdle, and drummers Bill Bruford and Barry De

The 1972 shows can be viewed in all their glory as immortalised in the concert film, *Yessongs*. Whilst this is classic Yes music, played with power, commitment and feeling, it's performed on a basic stage setting with minimal effects and lighting. The highlight on stage was a mirror ball effect during the beginning and end sections of 'Close to the Edge': a flat disc covered in reflective glass hung down from the rig, centrestage, with spotlights hitting it directly to create a starlight effect as it spun.

Again, the classic track 'Close to the Edge' benefited from the use of dry ice in the middle section, which drifted over the stage to provide an eerie atmosphere for the quieter section. Rick Wakeman's solo spot was magnificent, incorporating dry ice, flashing lights and amazing sound effects to end the show.

Merchandise for this tour was on a larger scale than before: in many ways, Yes pioneered this kind of concert memorabilia: T-shirts, iron-on Yes logos, programmes, stickers and badges – some of it was official, most of it pirated.

Before he started work on *Close to the Edge*, Rick Wakeman had spent some time recording a solo album. A purely instrumental album, *The Six Wives of Henry VIII* was approached in a modern rather than a medieval style, utilising grand piano, hammond organ, and the talents of Steve Howe, Chris Squire and Bill Bruford. The album was a successful solo debut for Rick, selling millions of copies worldwide over the years.

Yes were becoming known for their precise and polished albums and yet, despite touring for years, had no real recorded representation of their live shows. Nevertheless, they had carved out a niche for themselves as *the* band to see live, surpassing their recordings on albums and creating a tremendous atmosphere at the gigs.

The 1972 UK and US tours had been recorded at various points including London, New York and South America, in an attempt to capture the excitement and raw energy that had made them a top live act. Intended as a double album, *Yessongs* was released as a triple live set on 4 May 1972 and provides a permanent record of how finely tuned those Yessongs actually were. It became Yes' biggest selling work up to that time, featuring an imaginative gatefold Roger Dean cover and a booklet of live band photographs.

Yessongs represented a whole live Yesshow, from the opening bars of Stravinsky's *Firebird Suite* through 'Heart Of The Sunrise', 'And You And I', 'Perpetual Change', 'Roundabout' and 'Close To The Edge' – featuring solo high

Yes deliver with style

THERE WAS an atmosphere of slightly more than usual expectancey at the Rainbow Theatre for Yes' concert last weekend. The Yes audience perhaps sees itself as slightly more discriminating than your average rock audience — not as highbrow as King Crimson's followers, but they know good music when they hear it and come expecding to hear it played.

Yes were aware they had to is no small part due to the help of their regular engineer Eddie Offord, who they thanked at the end of the set.

"Close To The Edge", as Jon Anderson told the audience, "relates very closely to the way I've been thinking lyrically and we've been thinking lyrically and we've been thinking musically for the last year". It exemplified the formal beauty of Yes' music with the airy voice of Jon An-

fall. Wakesman's harpiscord punctuating the mood of the piece as it swells towards the climactic Gothic chords of the organ.

It's clearly Yes' finest accomplishment yet, but it seems to me to fall into a compromise between an overtly structured, chemetic and a collection of impressionistic musical episodes loosely joined together.

spots from Rick, Steve and Chris and a rip-roaring finale of 'Yours Is No Disgrace' and 'Starship Trooper'. 'The energy on a live album is generated because of the audience,' explained Chris, 'and unless you can get an audience in the studio you're never going to get that on an studio album. A combination of the audience *and* the live band makes the show, not one or the other alone.'

At the time Jon told *Rolling Stone*, '*Yessongs* signifies an end of an era for us. For the past few years, we've been on a continuous cycle of hard work where we tour, record a new album, tour to promote it, then record another album . . . it can go on and on if you let it. Yes has outgrown that now.'

The album made number twelve in the US and number 7 in the UK, eventually selling enough to reach gold status. Featuring tracks from *The Yes Album*, *Fragile* and *Close to the Edge*, it represented the Bill Bruford years whilst serving also as an introduction to Alan White.

Chris Welch, the veteran rock journalist and Yes supporter, said of *Yessongs*, 'There probably isn't another group in the world that could sustain such a high standard of variety and brilliance over six sides of one release, and yet leave [one] the feeling they have a lot more music to come.'

Yes' successful tour of Australia, New Zealand, Japan, UK and the US came to an end in April 1973. For the band, it was not before time. Jon and Chris had gone through a period of heated disagreements over their music which had caused a serious rift in their relationship. However, it never became serious enough to cause a major split and the band survived. Jon remembers, 'To make points with music, you have to be helpful to one another and definitely not set up barriers. To work towards a very harmonious sort of sound is the law of the land with this band, and I think it was broken on a few occasions . . . A time finally came when I decided that my weight *should* be heard. It was a time when I felt the music was suffering because of this . . . inner conflict.'

The world tour had ensured that the band had long periods of time in which to write new material and exchange ideas for the next album. Everyone agreed that they would concentrate on longer pieces of music, carrying strong themes, or stories, and covering entire sides of the album.

Ideas were sought from the entire band, but it was Jon who came up with the final idea. He had been reading books on the inner self, specifically *The Finding of the Third Eye* by Vera Stanley-Adler, and Paramhansa Yogananda's *The Autobiography of a Yogi* (given to Jon by King Crimson member Jamie Muir) which immediately captured his imagination. Jon admitted that he learnt a lot from Jamie Muir. 'We

Atlantic promotional photo. From left: Alan White, Chris Squire, Rick Wakeman, Jon Anderson and Steve Howe.

and it was a big risk, although one that Jon and Steve had total belief in.

Steve added, 'We had so much space on that album that we were able to explore things, which I think was tremendously good for us. Side one was the most commercial or easy-listening side of *Topographic Oceans*, side two was a much lighter, folky side of Yes, side three was electronic mayhem turning into acoustic simplicity, and side four was us trying to drive the whole thing home on a biggie. So we saw them much smaller than they are in reality.'

While touring, Jon and Steve underwent intensive writing sessions, often leading into the early hours of the morning. The first two sections of the album had been organised mid-way through the US tour and, by late April 1973, the third and fourth sections had also been sketched out. The pair presented the concept to the band back in the UK – with a decidedly mixed reaction. At first, they were taken back by the sheer scale of the project and the key concepts, and not convinced that this was a positive step forward from *Close to the Edge*.

started talking about meditation in music – not the guru-type but some really heavy stuff, and he gave me these books of Shastric scriptures. As I read them, I became engrossed with the idea of making music around the concepts they spoke of, making a four-part epic built around the four-part themes of which I was reading.'

Spirituality had become a big part of Jon's life and was increasingly reflected in Yes' music. Many years later, he acknowledged this in an interview where he talked about his daily schedule: 'I wake up, I meditate, I'm very in tune with keeping fit. I like to go for a walk. And I write some music on a piano. Review the work I'm going to do that day. Have a light breakfast. Then go back to bed for an hour, maybe. Just rest. Get ready for the day. The day can consist of a zillion things at once. It's a question of balancing everything out. I tend to want to do two or three things a day. When I'm not working, I'm travelling. And when I'm travelling, I tend to read. I enjoy reading books and I love listening to Sibelius, I listen to Sibelius whenever I can. I love Frederick Delius. I love to read Henry Miller and Carlos Castaneda... dreaming is really where I get into the mysteries of life. I love my dreams very much. I've been practising dreaming now for about ten years. There's an art to dreaming. You can find books about it. You can wake up in your dreams. You can have focused discussions with people in your dreams. Life is a dream, really. But it's a physical one. But when you are in your sleeping dream, it is a highly spiritual one.'

The concept for *Tales from Topographic Oceans* had already been chosen, covering subjects such as religion, medicine, music, art, society and architecture, and it would be a mammoth project that would engulf the band over the next five months. No other band had tried anything like it before

The band suffered differences of opinion over suitable recording studios. Jon, Steve and Alan wanted to record away from the hustle and bustle of city life – to actually record in a forest or field, taking the album's concept to the extreme, embracing nature, all its lifeforms, and the whole planet. Following many heated discussions as to how they could achieve the same effect in a studio setting, a compromise was made. During the first few months the band held rehearsals at Manticore Studios in London, followed by a move to Morgan Studios. The compromise was that Studio Three at Morgan Studios would be made into a miniature countryside, with straw bales to stand keyboards on, a white picket fence to keep Alan in, farm implements to add authenticity and, of course, a full-sized cow! Jon also had a bathroom built, copying his own from home with the exact tiles so he could recreate the same echo sounds he'd discovered while singing in the bath.

The album, which had originally been called *Tales From Tobographic Oceans* but changed to *Topographic Oceans*, was meant to consist of four tracks over one album. However, as time went by, the concept developed into a double album because the tracks began to get longer and longer, some running over 25 minutes, producing a total of only four tracks. This was a decision that would affect the band in a big way, guiding the style of music that would take Yes forward over the next few years.

Chris Squire commented that, 'It wasn't a particularly happy album. It was a busy time then; we were going all the time. It was a major project and there wasn't enough time to do something that difficult and still capture people's interests as a commercial thing. So, it fell a little short.' Rick added,

Opposite page: Jon Anderson.
Clockwise: Jon Anderson with his daughter Deborah, Steve Howe, Rick Wakeman and Chris Squire with his daughter Carmen.

'*Tales from Topographic Oceans* is like a woman's padded bra. The cover looks good, the outside looks good; it's got all the right ingredients, but when you peel off the padding, there's not a lot there. I think it's a dreadfully padded album. . . there are some nice parts but it's like wading through a cesspool to get to a water lily.'

The album, naturally, took Atlantic Records by surprise as they had no idea of the content and their feelings were kept decidedly mute. Seeing Yes as a band who could exploit their previous success and make further inroads into the US market, Atlantic decided that their next album could and should be even bigger than *Close to the Edge*. However, when Atlantic first listened to it, the mood was one of sheer incredulity – only four tracks on a double album was unheard of at that time. Luckily for Yes, Atlantic ignored their own doubts and backed the release.

The promotional tour for *Topographic Oceans* opened to mixed reviews at the famous Rainbow Theatre in north London. The critics had a field day panning the new album, which affected Yes for quite some time, while the fans embraced the work. The album should have been aired on Radio One in the UK, prior to the tour and official release date but, due to a mix up, the wrong tapes were sent to the station. Because of this, Yes lost their only chance of giving their fans a preview of *Topographic Oceans* before the tour started. Despite the public's initial shock, *Tales From Topographic Oceans* hit the UK charts (two months later than expected) on 22 December 1973 and stayed there for fifteen weeks, reaching Number 1 in the UK in January 1974, whilst also making the Top Ten in the US Billboard chart. It went gold on pre-sales alone and was nominated for Grammy awards in the US.

There is little doubt that, had the public and press been given the chance to hear the album first, then the reaction that was to come might have been moderated. Quite unlike anything before it, *Tales From Topographic Oceans* did receive some good press, but, for the first time, Yes were also attracting negative reviews. With no time to acclimatise themselves to the work, the press could not comprehend the scale of what Yes had done. The band's gamble in playing all 80 minutes of the album, plus *Close to the Edge*, in the same set was just too much for them. Headlines such as 'Over The Edge', 'Wishy Washy Tales from the Deep' and 'Adrift on the Oceans' ran in the same music papers that had recently hailed them as the best band in the world. This was a new experience for Yes, whose relationship with the press had been extremely amicable up to this point. Ironically, back in September, Yes had been voted Band of the Year in the *Melody Maker* 1973 Pop Poll Awards, defeating the likes of Led Zeppelin to the coveted position.

The four tracks that made up *Tales From Topographic Oceans* were 'The Revealing Science of God', 'The Remembering', 'The Ancient' and 'Ritual'. A stunning album, light years ahead of its time, it is full of contrasts and a huge diversity of arrangements and styles: from simple acoustic sounds to the all-out, fast and furious guitar and keyboard runs, from ancient rhythms to eerie, esoteric lyrics and noises, all engineered to form a unique musical adventure.

Yes started the *Tales from Topographic Oceans* Tour at

YES

Winter Gardens, Bournemouth in November 1973 and covered the entire country before ending in December. Following the fantastically successful collaboration between Roger Dean and his brother Martyn on the *Tales From Topographic Oceans* album cover, the Deans copied a number of stylistic features for the stage design. Yes wanted to present their show as an extension of listening to the album, incorporating other elements to provide a complete sensory experience.

The stage set-up for the shows saw the band situated in their standard positions, with Alan on a centre drum riser. To his right, Rick played stylised organ pipes, which looked extremely dramatic alongside Alan's fibreglass canopy drum rostrum – lit from the inside creating the appearance of changing shapes, representing anything from animals and flowers to machines. The split canopy would slowly move during the finale of 'Ritual' and an array of coloured lights would flood out from within. 'When you think we worked on minuscule budgets, compared to what other people were getting, we achieved quite dramatic effects,' recalls Roger. 'Some designers were working with budgets literally a hundred times greater than we were spending.'

By this stage Steve had become a vegetarian, like most of the band. 'Travelling and performing caused me to think more about what I was eating,' explained Steve. 'For a long time, something bothered me about eating meat, although I couldn't quite place it. Then, while travelling in America, having dinner one night, and having this chicken placed in front of me – it was typically overcooked, greasy, you know, probably microwaved – I just right there made this decision not to eat it and I felt good about the decision. It stuck with

Yes at the Rainbow Theatre, 20 - 24th November, 1973.

me. My wife and I became interested in classes offered at the East West Centre like reflexology and psychosynthesis. I began going for treatments. We were really getting going. And we gave up the idea of "take-away" instant solutions to health.'

Rick was the only member of the band not drawn into vegetarianism, following instead, a more orthodox, rock 'n' roll star lifestyle. Besides his legendary drinking habits, he was also seriously into cars. 'I have a Rolls Royce, which is about fifteen years old. Also a Cadillac and a Jaguar XK 150s, which is in immaculate condition – well, they all are! I don't believe in sticking my money in the building society so I invested in cars instead. As time goes by, they'll be worth a bomb!' Years later, Rick admitted that he believed the two main reasons Yes stayed together were; 'One... it owes too many people too much money! Two... it spends any income before it's earned it!'

Bill Turner, a roadie for Yes between the years 1972-74 remembers, 'I started to work with Yes through Hemdale films. I basically humped stuff around on various Yes tours. I did the famous five nights at the Rainbow Theatre for the *Tales From Topographic Oceans* tour.

I did the dry ice for 'Close To The Edge' and I used to winch the wings up and down on top of Alan's drum staging for 'Ritual'. Rick was so cheesed-off in those days that he would just walk off stage, he either had crates of beer behind his keyboards or he'd resort to a glove puppet that would wave to the audience when he was bored. That was great, ha! When it got too much, he would bring out the green plastic dinosaur toy and wind it up and let it walk across the stage. Very funny that one.'

Bill continued, 'Yes were into football in a big way. We played in the music industry league. It was funny. We played teams like EMI and the Wormwood Scrubs Prison. They would turn up in a van and the rest of Yes would come along in about five different Bentleys, crazy times.'

Whilst waiting for the US tour to start, Rick Wakeman began work on his next solo project based on Jules Verne's science-fiction classic *Journey to the Centre of the Earth*, a huge financial undertaking that carried more than a few risks. Rick planned to record the album from an evening's live performance at the Royal Albert Hall, where he would be accompanied by a five-piece electric band, the 60-strong English Chamber Choir and the 100-piece London Symphony Orchestra. Despite various setbacks, on 18 January 1974, Rick pulled it off. It was an enormous feat and subsequently the album was a huge success. Then, in February, Yes began their Spring North American tour.

As the tour progressed, it became clear that Yes had taken a huge risk in a set list comprised only of *Edge* and the four sides of *Topographic*. Consequently the old favourites were reintroduced and two sides of *Topographic* dropped, increasing the divide that had already arisen between Rick Wakeman and the rest of the band.

Rick began to express his unhappiness with the album in various interviews. 'Despite all our different lifestyles, we had survived because when we got together musically, it all worked. We had five totally different people in the band. Usually the music brought us together. Then we did *Tales From Topographic Oceans* which, to put it bluntly, was not my favourite album. I'll own up. Jon and I have had some conversations about this since. We both agree that if CDs had been available then there was enough good material on that album to make a 50-minute CD. We had a bit too much to go on an album of 36 minutes but not enough for a double album. So it was padded mercilessly. And that really upset me.'

Yes had a massive fan base and were achieving big sales at this point, something that they did not want put at risk by Rick's unease. Press indifference to the album had resulted in heated discussions within the band. After speaking openly amongst themselves, it became obvious that it wasn't just Rick who had not enjoyed performing *Topographic Oceans* on tour, but also Chris. Set against them were Jon and Steve, threatening a schism within the band. At the end of the tour, Rick decided to leave the band and, on 18 May 1974, his birthday, he quit Yes and took refuge at his farmhouse in Devon, whilst his second solo album went to the number one spot in the UK charts.

Rick commented, 'I had some great times and some lousy

Jon and Eddie Offord waiting to board a plane during the Topographic Oceans *tour.*

times. It was a band that was bonded together by music. There was little love lost. It wasn't bad until things got to a stage where I didn't know what direction the music was going in. I didn't enjoy *Tales from Topographic Oceans*, so I finished out the European tour we were doing and left.'

With Rick now out of the picture, speculation was steadily mounting in the press regarding his replacement. The list was as follows: Keith Emerson (ELP), Nick Glennie (Wally), Patrick Moraz (Refugee), Vangelis (a solo artist by now) and Jean Roussel. All possibilities were tried, including friends and acquaintances. One main contender, Vangelis, was already known to the members of Yes, who were highly impressed with his musicianship. He spent a number of weeks rehearsing with the band and seemed at one point to be on the verge of replacing Rick.

NEW MUSICAL EXPRESS

WORLD'S MOST RELAXING ROCK WEEKLY

Wakeman quits Yes

ZEPPELIN CANCEL

VELVETS REFORM FOR TOUR
With Eno 'replacing' Lou Reed

ANOTHER CHARLTON SUPERGIG
With Stones or Faces on bill?

Black Oak, Sabbath
Slade
Purple
Lou Reed
Cassidy
Uriah Heep

Melody Maker and *New Musical Express* carefully followed the process until it became clear that Vangelis' immense talent was probably limited to solo work.

Time was starting to pass them by and, as hard as the band tried, a new keyboardist could not be found. They carried on rehearsing and writing material for a new album for around three months before Patrick Moraz, the Swiss keyboard player with Refugee, came to their attention.

Born on 24 June 1948, in Switzerland, Patrick had a modest upbringing in an artistic family. His father was a tap dancer who had danced with Fred Astaire and Maurice Chevalier, and was also the road manager for the violinist Paderewski. Patrick began to study the violin and piano at the age of five, influenced by Bach and Beethoven, but stopped at age nine to concentrate instead on keyboards, at a time when jazz and pop influences were spreading across Europe.

In 1964, aged sixteen, Patrick came to the UK to learn English. A few years later, he gained a degree at Geneva University whilst playing with a band. 'My first professional band was called Mainhorse. The other people in the band were Jean Ristori, a guitar player, and a very heavy English drummer, but the type of music we were doing at that point was just representative of the progressive music that was happening at the time. I guess you could call it orchestral rock – we had a pretty good following ourselves with Mainhorse . . . We were just doing local things [in Europe]. Different! We had two English guys as well, Peter Lockett and Bryson Graham. Those were fantastic times!

'After Mainhorse broke up in 1972, Jean and I did a tour of Japan with a Brazilian dance company that played heavily rhythm-orientated folk music. I had been interested in Brazilian music for some time, so I was familiar with the way that type of music had to be phrased and accented.'

On his return to the UK, Patrick settled down to writing film scores and completed fifteen in six months. He then played for Refugee, a three piece band in the style of ELP, with Brian Davison and Lee Jackson, Keith Emerson's former bandmates from the Nice. 'Refugee was somewhat different from the Nice, maybe a little less bombastic in a way,' explained Patrick. 'More classically and jazz orientated. With original music as opposed to recreating the classics. I never saw the Nice live but I loved their sound. One day, Lee Jackson called me; I was back from the Far East, in early 1973. I had met him in 1969 – he suddenly calls me out of the blue in Switzerland four years later. He said, "Get your arse over here, I want to form a trio." And I did! The name Refugee was found later. We started the trio with Brian Davison and Lee Jackson and we just rehearsed in Battersea somewhere. For three or four months we played, composed, rehearsed. Then we did that first [and only] Refugee album. It was very well received and critically acclaimed.'

Although they recorded one album, they had managerial problems and Patrick began having doubts. Soon, he would be in Yes, however. 'I was invited to have a little jam with the band. I knew what it was all about. They had been looking for a keyboard player for several weeks. They had even tried Vangelis for two weeks, but although Vangelis is a very

July 13, 1974

NEW MUSIC

News Desk

VANGELIS PAPATHANASSIOU:

Could he fill Yes vacancy?

THE LEADER OF the now-disbanded Greek group Aphrodite's Child, Vangelis Papathanassiou, is understood to be the principal contender for the keyboards vacancy in Yes — created by the recent departure of Rick Wakeman.

Aged 31, he has recently been fronting his own Paris-based band. He plays organ, piano, vibes, synthesiser, drums, flute and various Greek instruments. He had training in classical music and speaks English fluently.

Aphrodite's Child achieved the peak of their success in late 1968 and early 1969, when they became the first Greek group to appear in the British charts. At that time, their line-up included current European superstar Demis Roussos, who was featured on bass and vocals. Papathanassiou

original player, he couldn't bend to the musical and psychological discipline of being in the band. At that time, I felt it was time to leave Refugee anyway, so I said okay.'

Patrick remembers, 'Brian Lane picked me up and brought me to a Yes rehearsal, the first part of August 1974, on a Wednesday afternoon. Then the next evening, Brian called me and said; "You got the gig." I was so shocked! I didn't even have time to think about it, to ponder, and so on. I was not really sure I wanted the gig but Brian said, " I've organised everything, everything's taken care of." He also told me that, from then on, I was a member of Yes, and that I would get twenty per cent of everything, equally shared.'

During the next four months the band worked on the follow-up to *Tales from Topographic Oceans*. The *Relayer* album was recorded in Chris Squire's home studio in his garage (the Barn), as opposed to the usual central London location. With state-of-the-art equipment provided by Eddie Offord, and the rural setting, Yes found this change of environment creatively stimulating.

Steve recalls, 'I suppose it was one of the first records I ever made that felt like a location record, because all of the others had been made in London. I was looking out the window thinking, "This is a different way of recording!" There's nobody telling us the studio is about to close and it didn't cost anything, we could take our time and get things done. It was hard work, but we conjured up some good music.'

Patrick Moraz remembers the recording period: 'Never early mornings with the group, although I had to get up early to learn most of the material, not only for the new album, but for the six or seven other albums that we were going to be playing. Each guy in the band was very helpful. Jon, Chris, Steve, Alan, either separately or as a group, explaining all they could. All the notes I could imagine, I put in my memory. All the things I could write, I wrote down at the time. So that was very helpful. It was also, of course, in the interest of the group, so we could go on tour as soon as possible. I think the record company wanted a new album. Brian Lane wanted to get us on tour, and so on.'

Jon knew exactly what he wanted and at a meeting to discuss the album, presented his ideas for one of the epic pieces called The Gates of Delirium (GOD). Jon's ideas were gleaned from the book *War and Peace* by Tolstoy and his vision was to base the whole album on it. But considering the reaction to *Topographic Oceans*, it was agreed that Jon's epic should remain rooted to one side of an album only.

Pictured in Chris Squire's garden while working on the Relayer *album. From left: Steve Howe, Jon Anderson, Chris Squire, Alan White, Patrick Moraz*

Relayer was released in November 1974, making number four in the UK charts and number five in the US charts. The album cover features one of Roger Dean's best paintings: a castle built out of rock, rising majestically into the sky, with riders and snakes in the foreground.

Yes wanted this album to be a confirmation of their willingness to experiment with technology, and it certainly showed. The calming atmosphere of Chris Squire's recording studio seemed to have had the very opposite effect on the epic-length tracks that comprise the album. Both 'Sound Chaser' (nine and a half minutes) and 'The Gates of Delirium' (twenty-one minutes) were energetic pieces of jazz-rock synthesis. In fact, the only calming influence on the whole album came with the quietest of its three tracks, the splendidly atmospheric 'To Be Over' (nine minutes). The sound of Yes had been completely overhauled, Jon's vocals and lyrics considerably sharper, angrier and more aggressive than his established utopian style.

The accompanying tour, beginning in February 1975, was an updated version of 1973's show. Patrick remembers, 'We played some very big gigs in Philadelphia and Chicago, playing to 100,000 people at a time. We needed sixteen different PA systems from Clair Brothers just to cater for all the various concerts.' Roger Dean designed the stage

Yes captured live on the Relayer *tour stage set.*

backdrop, onto which different lights and images were projected – still a relatively simple design compared to future variations. When recalling the 100,000-strong gig at JFK Stadium in Philadephia, Roy Clair of Clair Brothers said, 'That's something that will never happen again. A lot of people gatecrashed that event. After it, the authorities clamped down and made it more secure. That's when Yes were at their biggest, playing outdoors in stadiums.' Before having been ousted out of the band Patrick stated, 'It was unbelievable! From behind the scenes, you could see the whole stadium, the whole audience from the top of the stadium, behind the stage, in the afternoon. The gig, I tell you! (laughing) was absolutely unbelievable! And not only just our concert but the whole event was amazing! That is probably the biggest concert Yes has EVER had. The opening acts were Peter Frampton and Gary Wright who had had both very big hits.'

A rock show doesn't get any more spectacular than the 1976 *Relayer* tour, which was a visually stunning event, enlisting once more the sensational designs of Roger and Martyn Dean, who built the marvellous Crab Nebular stage. The whole Yes tour was a massive logistical operation. With four enormous semi-trailers (trucks) and a total crew of about forty, the show had it all: an amazing Dean-designed backdrop suspended all around the stage to provide a scenic Yes painting of epic proportions. The show began with the gentle sounds of Japanese music drifting around the auditorium as fans poured in. When the curtain opened, the whole stage was elevated, uncovering a blaze of light, sound, and colour with the band in full flight. Along with the three-headed Crab Nebular, which was a cross between a machine, a dragon, a flower and an alien, which would gently light up, pulsate, move, flash, rise and fall, shine boldly, or glow dimly to appropriately reflect the mood of each track, clouds of dry ice floated around the stage, creating a magical atmosphere penetrated only by laser beams.

1975 saw the various members of Yes working on solo projects. Without an album to promote, Atlantic Records decided to release *Yesterdays*, a compilation culled from the first two albums, plus a previously unreleased extended

JFK Stadium, 12th June, 1976, Yes's largest gig up until that time.

version of the Simon and Garfunkel song 'America' and the single b-side 'Dear Father', in March.

Steve Howe's *Beginnings,* the first of the solo albums, was a varied collection of songs. Although Steve's voice was probably not strong enough to carry off lead vocals with total aplomb, the album highlights his versatility in different modes of guitar playing. Released in October 1975, it reached number 63 in the US and number 22 in the UK chart where it spent four weeks.

Chris Squire's album *Fish out of Water* was the most successful of the solo albums released that year. Released in the UK in November, it spent seven weeks in the charts and reached number 25. In the US, it was released on 30 December and reached number 69. Solo projects aside, Yes spent five months touring from April up to August 1975 in the Europe and the US, but cancelled a proposed Far Eastern tour due to the solo projects. The Yesshows changed once again, when Roger and Martyn Dean came up with what they called the barnacle stage design. The barnacle-shaped lighting rig was huge and spread all across and above the keyboards and drums, it was meant to look like marine wildlife, which changed colour, as if in seawater, depending on the light used. With Yes playing medium-sized venues in the UK, they were not always able to use the full stage set, but at larger events, such as festivals, and arena shows in the US, the full show would be in place. Consisting of a front-of-stage curtain, large lighting rig, spotlights, rear-projection screen, dry ice, lasers, and the Dean brothers' staging, these acclaimed stage spectacles began, as usual, with the *Firebird Suite* which, along with 'Roundabout', became synonymous with the opening of Yes' shows.

chris squire

The long awaited Yes movie, *Yessongs*, filmed back in 1972, was finally made ready for release featuring live footage of Yes playing material from the *Yes Album*, *Fragile* and *Close to the Edge* with Rick Wakeman at the Rainbow Theatre. It went on national release in cinemas, in some places even outselling the major film release of the time, *Jaws.*

'*Yessongs* was one of those films that was made very quickly and organised a day before we did a show in London at the Rainbow Theatre,' explained Chris Squire. 'And anyone who has seen it will have noted that it's quite dark – you don't see very much. But on the other hand, it's a kind of piece-of-history type of film at the time when Rick Wakeman was playing with us. And as a piece of footage, it is interesting. It's good history, but it's not a particularly good film.' The movie

Record company promotional flyer for Yessongs the Movie.

included film footage of Steve Howe and Chris Squire's solo track performances.

The solo albums had kept Yes in the public eye in 1975-76, while there was no new Yes project on release. Although they only achieved average sales, they did prove to Atlantic that Yes had built up a strong fan base during nearly a decade as a band.

The solo albums also highlighted all too clearly that, together as a five-piece band, Yes were a much stronger force than anything that they could produce as individuals. Chris added, 'Through making solo records, we'd all learned a lot and had much more to bring back and feed to each other. It also made us all appreciate that it was probably more enjoyable playing together than doing a solo thing, which is definitely much harder work because you're in charge of it all and there isn't anyone to share it with. Going through those vibes brings you back together and gives you a sense of release – relief as well – and also a lot of knowledge has been gained.'

At the start of 1976, the focus was still on solo projects. Chris Squire released the single 'Lucky Seven'/'Silently Falling' on 1 March in the US, taken from *Fish out of Water*. Alan White's solo album, which he produced himself, was released in the US on 15 April. Entitled *Ramshackled*, it was the furthest away from Yes in terms of style, staying closer to Alan's basic rhythm 'n' blues and rock roots. The single from the album 'Oooh Baby'/'One Way Rag' followed on 15 June. Patrick Moraz's album *I* had a complex, percussive ambience. Electronic, eclectic and extremely manic, it showed what Patrick might have come up with in the group context of Yes, given the time.

However, it came as no surprise to anyone that the most ambitious of the solo projects was Jon's. *Olias of Sunhillow* was a true solo album in every sense of the word, with Jon playing all the instruments. The album was based on ideas that had been formulating in his mind over the previous three years, and the recording kept him busy for six solid months.

Collectively, the band began the year rehearsing intensely for the forthcoming American tour, which ran from May to August. A film was started based around the tour, *Yessongs 2: The Movie*, financed by Atlantic Records, but the producers encountered difficulties and it is still unknown as to how much footage they shot and why filming was halted. Directed by Peter Neal and produced by David Speechley, the location of the footage remains a mystery even to the members of Yes.

At this time, the band were still keen to widen their audience appeal via greater radio airplay. The problem was that, although the FM radio stations were still interested in what the band were up to after the success of their first hit single 'Roundabout', releasing singles would not become a priority for Yes until much later in their career. Their immediate concern was the next album, which they began recording in September 1976 at Mountain Studios in Montreux, Switzerland, only yards away from Lake Geneva.

Patrick Moraz had a preliminary role in writing and planning the album but, as time progressed, it became clearer that he and Yes had reached the limits of their collaboration, and it was time for him to move on. Whilst not in the band anymore, Rick Wakeman had remained on the outskirts and kept in touch. Yes and manager Brian Lane, had always wanted him back. Musical differences also arose with the band over the new material, and so, after a few good years spent with Yes at their peak, Patrick left in November 1976.

The band claimed afterwards that they were aware Patrick was uneasy in his role, primarily due to language difficulties,

Official Ludwig advertising campaign, 1975, featuring Alan White.

or as Patrick explains, 'I was kind of gently eased out of Yes, I was too young in the business to know what was happening. The motivation, of course, was that Brian Lane wanted to have Rick Wakeman back in the band. He was managing Rick and Rick was not happening as one would have thought, although he had two number-one albums, I think. *Journey to the Centre of the Earth* and *The Six Wives of Henry VIII* had been very well received and we thought that he was going to be the biggest keyboard rock star since sliced bread and it was not really happening. I was not fired as such. But it clearly happened one afternoon in November 1976, we had written most of *Going for the One*'s parts and I was having increasing difficulty trying to express my own voice within the confines of the band and what I've called the festival of egos. Although maybe it might be argued by the other guys that I was not comprehending the depths of whatever.'

Atlantic also began to grow restless, noticing a fall in album sales with the release of *Relayer*. Although Yes could still fill giant stadiums, Atlantic executives also felt that the return of Rick Wakeman would be a huge boost to the band. Despite enjoying much success with his solo career at the time, he was in financial debt due to his large, extravagant stage shows. As Steve Howe recalls of his inevitable return, 'I was very excited when we got Rick Wakeman back into the band, because I felt that he was a more colourful and therefore more suitable keyboardist for Yes.'

With Yes enjoying continued success all over the world, *Relayer* winning accolades and stadium shows selling out, they maintained their position as one of the premier rock bands in the world.

Jerry Greenberg, the president of Atlantic Records at that time, wanted a new album ready for release in 1976, but grudgingly accepted that creativity could not be forced. With the solo albums now out of the band's system, and Rick Wakeman re-installed, a feeling of optimism had been restored within the band. A fresh approach was taken to the writing, rehearsing and recording of the next album, with a

RICK WAKEMAN JON ANDERSON ALAN WHITE STEVE HOWE CHRIS SQUIRE

Rick and Jon deep in creative thought.

greater degree of improvisation and an openness to new ideas. Since it would be over two and a half years between the releases of *Relayer* and its successor, it was critical that this album was a commercial success.

In a change of direction, Atlantic pressed Yes to try for a hit single this time – but within six months it became clear that the band only cared about the album, and Atlantic relented. When it eventually arrived, entitled *Going for the One*, the label's reaction was hugely positive, speculating that it would probably be the biggest album yet for the band. Striving to grant each track its own distinct personality, and to introduce as many new sounds as they could, Yes had taken a risk that paid off handsomely.

Having taken the narrative concept as far as it would go on their previous albums, Yes went in a different direction on the celebratory *Going for the One*. Chris emphasised this point: 'It is a spontaneous-sounding record with a lot of good feeling on it. Without being egotistical, I could foresee that feeling would make it through to the record and that people would listen to it and feel it as well. A clear emotion produces a successful record.' Steve merely commented, '*Going for the One* is a dynamic piece of music; unlike anything we ever did. It's very underrated, or very underrequested and underplayed.'

The only taint of controversy was when Patrick accused the band of not giving him due credit on *Going for the One*. This was an issue that would run and run – he believed he had contributed to and helped write all the tracks on the album, but without any acknowledgement. Steve retorted, 'He

Star Trek's William Shatner Goes Punk!
SHATNER
Live On Stage With Solo LP

NUGENT FEVER POSTER

CIRCUS

K48243

THE LEADING ROCK & ROLL BI-WEEKLY

ISSUE NUMBER 163 SEPTEMBER 8, 1977 UK 45p $1.00

YES
'Going For The One'—Wakeman And Squire Square Off On The New LP And Return Of Yes To The US

ELP/KEITH
The Keith Emerson Tapes: "I've Never Had A Vacation From Music"

DOOBIES
Disaster Rock Hits LA—Doobie Brothers Debut 'Livin' On The Fault'

GEILS
'Monkey Island'—Peter Wolf On The Brave New Sound From The Original Boston Badboys

LP GOLD
Collectors' Bonanza! Up To Hundreds Of Dollars For Your Old Records!

ALICE
New Tour! New Snake! New Tricks Unveiled In LA Sendoff Concert

AUDIO
How To Customize Your Stereo For Four-Speaker Sound

PINBALL
Death Race, Space Stinger, Battle Of The Raymen—The Electrifying World Of Super Pinball

MARTY FELDMAN
'The Last Remake of Beau Geste' Is Only The Beginning For Madcap Film Star Marty Feldman

RUNAWAY
Teenage Disappearances Are On The Rise—What Drives Them Away?

FRISBEE
How I Floated To Victory—The US Champ's Own Golden Saucer Story

ALAN PARSONS
Space Music For A New Generation From 'Abbey Road''s Brilliant Engineer

0 71896 48243 63

RICK WAKEMAN REJOINS YES

helped to get the album going. But you see, the problem is, what was our choice? He didn't make it in the end. We couldn't make the record without him. We prepared some of the material, and we did try to lose as much as would be offensive to him, or to us, of his style. We did take a lot out. But what he's sensing, of course, is the familiarity. He knows this. He hears this music and he says, "I was there when we were writing this." But of course, what we did was take out his idea and put in another idea. We had already heard his idea. So in some ways, it's a compliment to him that he still feels he's in there. There are a couple of references to Patrick's music in there. And we intended in all good faith to put on the album something about Patrick. But, it's too late now.'

The band also changed the packaging of the album as well as the musical content. Roger Dean had designed the last six album covers and established an artform that was universally loved by the fans. But by the time the band had recorded *Relayer*, Jon's influence and interest in art had grown considerably and his persistent suggestions about the artwork led to a falling out with Roger Dean. As a replacement, the established graphic studio of Hypgnosis were brought in – though with hindsight, it appears that Yes lost some of their

Chris (above) and Jon (right) playing open air on the Going for the One tour.

identity with the new cover designs.

Released in July 1977, *Going for the One* became an instant hit, reaching the number one position in the UK and the Top Ten in the US. The single 'Wondrous Stories' gave Yes their biggest hit single in the UK at number seven and, later on in the year, the title track 'Going for the One' reached the Top 30. The singles were a more accessible side of Yes. FM radio-friendly, shorter, more instantly recognisable songs. The result was that many fans who had grown tired of their drawn-out epics, regained their interest in the band. Jon Anderson commented at the time that Yes were taking a more relaxed approach, having spent enough time being serious. Not only did the music become simpler but the lyrics did too – with no big conceptual strands running throughout, each song relied on its own strengths.

They followed the release with a large tour from August through December 1977, playing mostly indoor arenas. Retaining their tradition of staging the most lavish show they could, the stage was divided by curtains into four layers. One resembled arches which were tensed at slight angles to give a distorted effect and acted as a projection screen for the many multicoloured lights. Rick and Alan were, once again, on higher platforms, Rick on two levels due to the massive amount of equipment he had. The centre section was also raised and used by Jon to perform 'Awaken' on a full-sized harp.

The success of the album and single in the UK was a pleasant surprise, as opposed to an angry new rock 'n' roll movement, punk. Punk rock was taking over the western world, and would even affect the future of an established band like Yes. The Sex Pistols had been the overnight heralds of the movement, and, though they would implode quickly, had created the ethos – young, energetic and raw, they were part of a new rock 'n' roll that had dire consequences for all big stadium bands. Within a matter of months Yes were downgraded in the press, from favourite band to forgotten heroes. To survive this new onslaught they would be forced back on their wits, to revitalise themselves with a fresh energy.

Following the ascendance of punk rock, Yes had an uphill battle in following the popular *Going for the One*. Before they even started working on the follow-up album, the decision to record in London had caused problems. Some of the band members wanted to go abroad again for tax reasons, preferably to Switzerland, where they had had such a good time making the last album – but, after heated debate, they all regrouped in London, to record at Advision and R.A.K. Studios in St. John's Wood.

Seven months of writing, rehearsing and recording led to *Tormato*, released in September 1978. It was a big disappointment after *Going for the One*, which had captivated and delighted so many people – even the band members agreed that it was a messy, strained effort. *Tormato* hit the UK charts on 8 October for a stay of eleven weeks, reaching number eight at its highest point. The first reaction to the album from fans was one of disbelief, particularly at the sight of the cover, which they were not impressesd by. Press reaction was mixed: 'Arriving UFO' and 'Circus of Heaven' were given a rough ride, whilst the Chris Squire-written 'Onward' accompanied by a string section, 'On the Silent Wings of Freedom' a longer more typical Yes composition with a strong bass opening by Chris, and the mellow, classical Wakeman piece 'Madrigal' were considered to be better tracks. US fans, more tolerant than their UK counterparts, were more appreciative of the album. But, for all its faults, *Tormato*'s best tracks stand up to a contemporary listen. Yes showed their affection for 'Onward' in 1996 by

From left: Chris, Rick, Jon, Steve and ALan recording Tormato in London.

recording a live version for the *Keys to Ascension* album.

Rick summed it up by saying, '*Tormato* could have been tremendous but suffered from appalling production. If I could be given one album to remix and to get the guys to add a couple of extra bits to, it would be that one. If ever an album had unfulfilled potential it was *Tormato*, but totally our fault as it had probably the worst final production mix of anything I have ever been involved with.'

What started as a change of direction with *Going For The One* continued with *Tormato*. It was a conscious effort to lighten the band's material and increase the number of tracks on an album. Following the hit single 'Wondrous Stories', which had been a pleasant surprise to everyone, Yes realised the potential of a wider audience for their music and the need for hit singles to make it happen. From this point, they would continue to record their albums with some tracks aimed at mass-market appeal.

If the album had been a disappointment to some, then the 1978 shows on the *Tormato* tour more than made up for it! Touring from August to October, Yes absolutely blew the audiences away with the spectacular, unforgettable In the Round stage show, which topped all previous tours, something that seemed impossible beforehand. Whilst discussing the future presentation of the Yesshow in 1978, Chris Squire had suggested to Michael Tait that the band should play in the middle of an auditorium. Once an auditorium was filled to capacity, the lights were dimmed and the overture music began (either a piece from Benjamin Britten's *Young Person's Guide To The Orchestra*, or the soundtrack from the film *Close Encounters of the Third Kind* by John Williams) as the band emerged from the side entrance of the arena.

Picked out by spotlights, Yes would walk towards the stage. Once set up, they would open with the classic 'Siberian Khatru'. The stage slowly moved round at about two to three miles per hour, giving the crowd an unrestricted view of the band from all angles, bringing the audience much closer to them than ever before.

At one point, however, the audience got *too* close, as Rick Wakeman recalls. 'I remember the second night in Chicago when we were on stage. . . when you're moving, you tend to look at the audience; you don't normally. There

Clockwise from left: Chris, Rick, Jon, Steve and Alan.

Jon and Chris in the round.

was a whole block in the front of about twenty seats that were empty and this was very strange because I knew the show was sold out. Now, with any show that is sold out with thousands of seats, there are going to be twenty to thirty no-shows, it's a fact of life. But I thought this is really weird that there's twenty to thirty no-shows, but they're all in the front row – this is crazy! We came to the part of the show where Steve Howe played Clap and while he played we all used to disappear. I would jump off stage and go to where my road crew were. When I went under there. . . I'd never seen so many people in my life! And I said to my guy, "What on earth is going on?" He said, "The motor that turns the stage burned out. So we've taken twenty people from the front two rows." And they were underneath pushing the stage around!'

The band also endured some strange incidents on the *Tormato* tour. On one night in Pittsburgh, someone ran onto the stage and tried to strangle Jon! He wasn't hurt, but police had to scramble up onto the stage to help him shake off his attacker.

By the time the 1978 world tour climaxed in October, back home in England, the show's contents were becoming widely disseminated – not only had BBC Radio One recorded some gigs, but they also made it onto a number of well-known bootleg tapes and albums.

Jon Anderson.

Steve and Jon in the round.

Yes began work on various projects in the New Year, taking them through to April 1979. Rick worked on his solo album *Rhapsodies* – a double album without a concept, featuring shorter songs, covers of a few classics, and a much lighter overall feel.

In February, Jon worked on a piece called 'Ursprung' for a Scottish Ballet production also featuring music by Jethro Tull's Ian Anderson. Entitled *Underground Rumour*, it opened on 7 March in Glasgow, then toured a limited number of venues in Scotland and the north of England, finally reaching London for its last performance. Around this time, Jon had also caught up with the keyboard maestro Vangelis, and they began meeting regularly, putting down demos for an album together whilst Steve worked on his second solo album, a more guitar-orientated project using outside vocalists.

Confidence was extremely high in the band. Not content to rest on their 1978 laurels, they regrouped and headed off to the US for another three-month tour. With no new product or album to promote, they took in different parts of the US and Canada not covered in the earlier tour, smaller venues in far-flung places, as an alternative to the usual arenas.

Although the attendances were down, due to the smaller halls and the fact that Yes hadn't played in America for some time, the intimate locations, coupled with the larger East Coast arenas, made the unusual tour a great success. On their 10th anniversary tour, with the classic Yes line-up of Jon, Chris, Steve, Alan and Rick, the band of 1969 had definitely made it to the top. The spectacular In the Round stage shows were a resounding triumph and, in a sense, saw the end of a special era for Yes. As Roy Claire remembers: 'We had the most amazing sound system then, but it was Rick, he was a real star you know. Such charisma, he had the lot. His solos were wonderful; he'd have the flashing lights, mirrors, smoke and the crashing sounds – A *real showman*.'

Returning home, tired, at the end of June, all of the band were looking forward to taking time out before rehearsals started for the next album. Although on 19 July, Jon, Rick and

Steve all performed at the Montreux Jazz Festival, Steve performing solo and Jon and Rick as a duo.

The Yesshows of 1978/9 had been recorded with the intention of releasing a follow up to the *Yessongs* live album. Anticipated as a double album, to be released by the end of the year, the intention of including material from the earlier *Topographic Oceans* tour, suggested it might need to expand to a triple set.

Chris Squire spent many hours going through live tapes but (soon) realised it was going to take longer than originally thought to pick a core selection. Moreover, the band couldn't reach an agreement on which mixes to use, and ultimately decided that *Yessongs 2* should be delayed until after the next studio release.

Because of the musical climate at the time, it had become a great deal more difficult to get airplay and publicity for Yes and their contemporaries. Rick remembers, 'After *Tormato* everything started to go horribly wrong because punk was hitting big time and Yes were out of fashion.' More than a year on from the release of *Tormato*, rehearsals for the next album took place in Paris during November and December 1979. The location was a compromise – everybody lived in London, apart from Rick, who resided in Switzerland.

The band were originally planning to produce the next album by themselves, but their management had other ideas – a speedily delivered product with a potential hit single. Aiming to capitalise on the successful tours, management enlisted producer Roy Thomas Baker. Known for his work with Queen, Baker brought in new ideas and challenged the way Yes worked. For a short while this worked but soon the band split into two separate writing outfits: Jon and Rick in one corner and Steve, Chris and Alan in the other. The latter trio envisaged Yes moving into a rockier area, slightly heavier than before, having spent a while writing and rehearsing together as a power trio. Rick and Jon's material was of an opposing style, with a lighter approach. It was surely going to be yet another difficult time for Yes.

At every meeting where they expected to move things forward, the two sides were driven further apart, never once agreeing on either music or lyrics. 'We were trying to record the new album in France and there was terrible animosity,' explains Rick. 'Jon and I teamed up tightly together and although we had written a lot of stuff, it wasn't liked by the other guys and they didn't even turn up to the studio. It all became a mess.' After only a few weeks Roy Thomas Baker left, deciding that the band were in too disharmonious a state to work together and in serious trouble. Worse was to come. Alan White broke his foot while ice skating, and there were personal and financial problems for other members of the band. Ten years on from their inception, the band were becoming tired with one another. Everyone returned home for Christmas to think about how they could save Yes.

Chris and Steve reviewing 'Money' and 'Don't Kill the Whale' after a mixing session at RAK studios.

DRAMATIC TIMES AHEAD

1980–82

YES HAD SPENT very little time apart over the last decade. Being on the road for that length of time, and in each other's space so intensely, had ensured that any split was in the process of becoming wider. The band returned to London in February to salvage the album and give some press interviews, claiming that Yes were looking to the future with optimism. According to the press reports, completion of the forthcoming album would be in March or April and a tour would follow soon after.

However, it was also reported that tax problems were prohibiting Rick Wakeman from entering the UK for rehearsals, forcing him to stay in Switerland. In reality, the upbeat nature of the press conferences was a front for a gigantic split within the band. Management remained optimistic, not realising the extent of the problems, and booking both US and UK tours for later in the year. Everyone had, originally, great enthusiasm for the next album, and as usual Jon presented many ideas to the band. Unusually for the band, though, things began to fall apart: having the wrong producer, being in the wrong place, personal and financial problems, a lack of respect for one another and a lack of direction musically.

The music that Jon had presented, in conjunction to some extent with Rick, was rejected by Steve, Alan and Chris as it was just too different from the direction that the latter three had in mind. This great divide seemed to be too wide for a compromise to be reached. Meanwhile, financial issues pertaining to the division of songwriting royalties were also creating a strain. Tensions were coming to a head, with no-one able to rise above it and lead from the front. Something had to give, and in March 1980 Jon and Rick parted company with Yes. The announcement of the Yes split was broadcast on BBC Radio One, *Friday Rock Show*. As host Tommy Vance played very early Yes sessions featuring material from the first two albums, Jon and Rick went on record expressing their sadness at leaving the band, emphasising that this was not what they had wished to happen. Steve later looked back with hindsight, 'It was no good anymore and it all collapsed. People got very suspicious, there were accusations and the whole thing escalated into a major problem. We were analysing, looking back into the past, dragging out skeletons from cupboards and absolutely nothing was achieved by this. It was all totally negative.'

The fan's shock and disbelief soon gave way to a central question: was Jon pushed or did he jump? It remains pure speculation, but with Jon gone, Rick soon followed suit when he decided that both personal differences and the musical gulf were too wide to bridge. For the first time in the band's history, Yes' star performers were out, leaving the remaining Yesmen – Chris, Alan and Steve – to compose and record the next album.

Contemporary commentary from Rick Wakeman shed some light on the situation: 'It all worked well up until about 1979. That's when it really started falling apart. The problems were both internal and musical. Jon and I formed a partnership of playing and writing and a way of working. We just felt we weren't getting any input at all from any other areas. Everything became a struggle. We ended up recording an album which we never finished, and what happened was we got halfway through . . . and it was like Jon and I met one day in Paris in a little café and just said, "We've both had enough" I mean, the band's just run out of . . . we were digging into a gold mine that just had a few nuggets left.'

Jon's music had become too folk-orientated for the rest of the band, management were making precarious financial decisions, and the band were spending their money faster than they were making it. The solo works began flooding out: Steve Howe released his second album, imaginatively titled *The Steve Howe Album*, in November, making it to number 68 in the UK charts. A Jon and Vangelis single, 'I Hear You Now', made the Top Ten in the UK and helped pave the way for a long and commercially successful partnership.

Jon became a reluctant but prolific solo artist. Over the coming year, he would release his first solo album since *Olias* of *Sunhillow* and tour the UK as a solo artist for the first time, playing medium to large venues from 21 November to 16 December. He began work with keyboard wizard Vangelis on *Short Stories* which made number four in the UK, followed by his second solo album *Song of Seven*. Raised in Greece by artistic parents and with a schooling in classical music, film and art at the Academy of Fine Arts in Athens, Vangelis formed a beat group in 1965 called Forminx. By 1967 the band had split up and over the following few years, 1967-72, Vangelis played many sessions and formed his own outfit, the Papathanassiou Set. They were signed by the Philips record label in 1968, and following a name change to Aphrodite's Child, released their debut album. After many years living and working in Paris on solo projects, Vangelis finally achieved his dream of moving to the UK in 1974, where he set up his own recording studios called Nemo behind London's Marble Arch.

Melody Maker

September 27, 1980 25p weekly USA $1.75

MADNESS

"'ABSOLUTELY' is evidence that Madness are, and always have been, a pure pop group at heart ... if Stiff release this album track by track, they'll have satellite hit after hit on their hands." The new Madness longplayer gets a civilised thumbs up on page 17.

SECRET AFFAIR

SECRET AFFAIR are still tagged as a Mod band, even though their music's become more diverse and individual – and they're suffering because of the label. Their current tour isn't selling out and they admit they're having problems. Behind Secret Affair's closed doors – Page 22.

LENNON

JOHN LENNON breaks a five-year silence with the admission that he'd rather be a housewife than a Beatle. "Going back to the Beatles would be like going back to school ... I was never one for reunions. It's all over!" See As It Happens ... – Page 9

REBIRTH OF JON ANDERSON

EXCLUSIVE INTERVIEW: PAGE 24

... but the end of an era for the Specials

THE SPECIALS' tour looks like being the last with the band's current format and intentions.

The end of the current Specials' era will be marked by a 2-Tone film, featuring live footage of all the bands associated with the label, that will be released as a cinema movie as soon as it is completed.

Speaking to MM last week on the road, Specials leader Jerry Dammers, recovering from the strains of producing the new "More Specials" album, spoke of the next phase of the band, a time when they are likely to stay off the road to plan and re-think their career, a period that will include solo work by members of the band.

The film, which includes the Specials, the Selecter, the Beat, the Bodysnatchers, Madness and Bad Manners, is currently being filmed and is financed by Chrysalis Records, 2-Tone's parent company.

Full details and the Jerry Dammers interview as the Specials hit Newcastle: Page 21.

Meanwhile, Rick released two singles, which garnered minimal sales and toured Europe to diminishing audiences. Standing firm on his musical integrity, Rick missed a prime opportunity by turning down an offer by manager Brian Lane to be part of a new supergroup. A deal with Geffen Records had been signed and sealed before executives heard so much as a note of music! Rick, perhaps justifiably, couldn't see the creative validity in a line-up planned to feature himself, John Wetton, Carl Palmer, and possibly a new guitarist called Trevor Rabin who had just arrived on the scene from South Africa.

What now for Yes? The momentous happenings throughout 1979 and into 1980 had seemed to rip the heart from the group. Clearly this was an important time; the band could quite easily have split for good over the next year, and finding replacements was not going to be an easy task. Steve Howe, Chris Squire and Alan White continued rehearsing their new material in London, with their thoughts on a fresh direction and the prospect of finding two new members. By fortuitous coincidence, pop sensations the Buggles were rehearsing in the same studios at the time – in May 1980, fans would be stunned by the press announcement that Trevor Horn and Geoff Downes, both leading Buggles, had joined forces with Yes.

Trevor Horn, born 15 July 1949 in Hertfordshire, was musically inclined from an early age. 'I used to play double bass in the youth orchestra. I was playing classical music with them for about four years in the north of England. Well, my father was a musician – a double bass player in a dance band. I sort of drifted into it, playing in the school orchestra, and then in a youth orchestra. And then I started to play the bass guitar in a group and I started doing it for a living. Then, I came down to London and got involved in session work.' He worked on some of the cheap UK '70s compilation albums featuring second-rate covers of well-known hits, impersonating stars such as Bryan Ferry.

Having built a production studio, with the aim of producing albums rather than simply playing sessions on them, he became involved with Euro-pop artist and *Top of the Pops* regular Tina Charles. Trevor dealt with everything, from booking Tina's gigs to playing the bass. Through her, he soon met Geoff Downes, who would later become the other permanent member of the Buggles.

Geoff Downes was born on 25 August 1952 in Manchester, northern England, and was introduced to music through the classics. 'I studied classical music early on, but I didn't really get interested in pursuing music as a career until I was thirteen or fourteen years old, when rock 'n' roll caught my ear. My hero at that point was Keith Emerson. He was the archetypal rock keyboard player. He was the first virtuoso keyboard player in rock. I was in a trio that played a lot of material that Emerson did with the Nice. We used to play around the north of England.'

On reaching eighteen, he enrolled at a music college in Leeds.

OH YES, OH NO!

RICK WAKEMAN

JON ANDERSON

BUGGLES

WHAT DO Steve Howe, Chris Squire and Alan White think they are playing at! How can those two turds out of Buggles believe they can replace such brilliant musicians as Jon (God) Anderson and Rick Wakeman.

Can you imagine that burk who looks like Brains out of "Thunderbirds" daring to go on stage and sing "Wonderous Stories" or "And You And I". It is indeed blasphemy. And if they don't intend to do the old Yes material then why retain the name? To cash in on the publicity and lull Joe Public into believing this new joke will be anything like the perfection that Jon Anderson instilled in the group. How can they expect us to "re-invent the Yes idea" when Jon Anderson was that idea and indeed was Yes. Good God! Next Johnny Logan will be replacing Robert Plant in Led Zeppelin!

Cathy, Birmingham

HOW DISAPPOINTED I am that Buggles are joining forces with Yes. It's such a shame because they were doing so well as a duo.

How can Trevor and Geoff do it? I mean, have they given any thought to their fans? Don't they realise that it just wouldn't be the same without them as a duo? Even the name 'Buggles' does something for them. To lose the novelty name comes as a shattering blow.

Well, it's Buggles' future that Trevor and Geoff predicted, not Yes'. If they can go and do that kind of thing, then I can't see a bright future for them. Has my following of Buggles since their first hit been a waste of time?

Disappointed Buggles Fan, Surrey

On finishing the course, he moved to London and started session work, which provided a good, steady source of income for over two years, before branching out into writing and producing jingles for TV and radio. He then auditioned for Tina Charles's backing band and, through her, met Trevor Horn. After the tour, the pair kept in touch and, around 1976, began to produce demos for no-hope performers. However, when this ultimately proved frustrating, they began writing, arranging and recording their own material together.

After two years struggling with no money, they figured that the quickest way to resolve the situation would be to create a hit single. Island Records liked what they heard, and promptly launched them as a plastic-techno pop band for the eighties using the silliest name that they could dream up.

Releasing the single 'Video Killed the Radio Star' under the worst joke name they could dream up, the Buggles, they would spawn the huge smash hit single which reached number one in many countries around the world. The subsequent album, *The Age of Plastic*, also stayed in the Top Thirty for six weeks.

The conceptual pop band had turned overnight into the real thing, which, despite their meticulous planning, left them in need of a proper manager. When Yes' manager Brian Lane came aboard, it wasn't long before a chance meeting at the rehearsal studios took place between Trevor Horn and Chris. Trevor and Geoff offered Yes a track called 'We Can Fly from Here' for their forthcoming album. Chris, ever the visionary, saw a thematic link between the song and Yes' current material and asked the duo to sit in on the album sessions. Following three weeks of rehearsals, it became clear to Chris Squire that this combination might work in the long-term. Not only were the Buggles successful, they had been fans for many years. Geoff played keyboards, Trevor sang at a similar pitch to Jon Anderson, they were in need of a manager and desired stardom. With a Yes tour already booked for the US, Chris saw the answer to all their problems.

'Chris said, "Why don't you join?",' recalls Trevor. 'Then, he asked us again. And we sat down and talked to him for about two hours. He said, "I really want you to join. I've got this feeling that it could be really good. And it's finished, it's over

The new Yes line-up for the eighties. From left: Steve Howe, Geoff Downes, Alan White, Chris Squire and Trevor Horn.

with Jon and Rick. It's just like the end of an era. It's not working anymore and whether you join or not, it won't stay together. But I really think it'll be good if you join." And of course, I went through all of the reasons against it. Because I knew that if I said yes, I was going to have to take a lot of shit. I didn't really know if I wanted to take it. I knew that I'd have to do Jon Anderson's songs. And I knew that however I did the Jon Anderson songs, whether I did them like Jon, unlike Jon... whatever I did, there would be no way I could win... in certain people's eyes. I just didn't know whether I wanted to go through all that shit.' However, after much agonising, Trevor and Geoff joined Yes.

The new Yes album, despite the fresh line-up, brought back many of the old familiar names and faces behind the scenes. Eddie Offord came back as producer; the album artwork and stage design were once again in the capable hands of Roger and Martyn Dean; the sound system was created by the Clair Brothers and Michael Tait. The focus for new Yessongs would include turning to *The Yes Album* for inspiration; it seemed that the old Yes was being updated for the 1980s.

'It was a very well titled album [*Drama*] under the circumstances, because it seemed to swing from week to week into another apocalyptic nightmare,' explained Geoff. 'From the Paris sessions to Alan breaking his leg so he couldn't do the drums, then Anderson and Wakeman left and Yes started recording in London. Then they got myself and Trevor working with them, then Eddie Offord was in and then out... he freaked out and left. Everybody was totally on the edge, you know? I think Chris wanted to re-establish more of the old sound, or what he considers to be the old sound of Yes. That's why he was so into the Hammond I wanted to play on the record and Mini-Moog and that sort of thing. He viewed it more as being the spirit of the early Yes... the revitalised Yes with the original concept. It was a good experiment from my

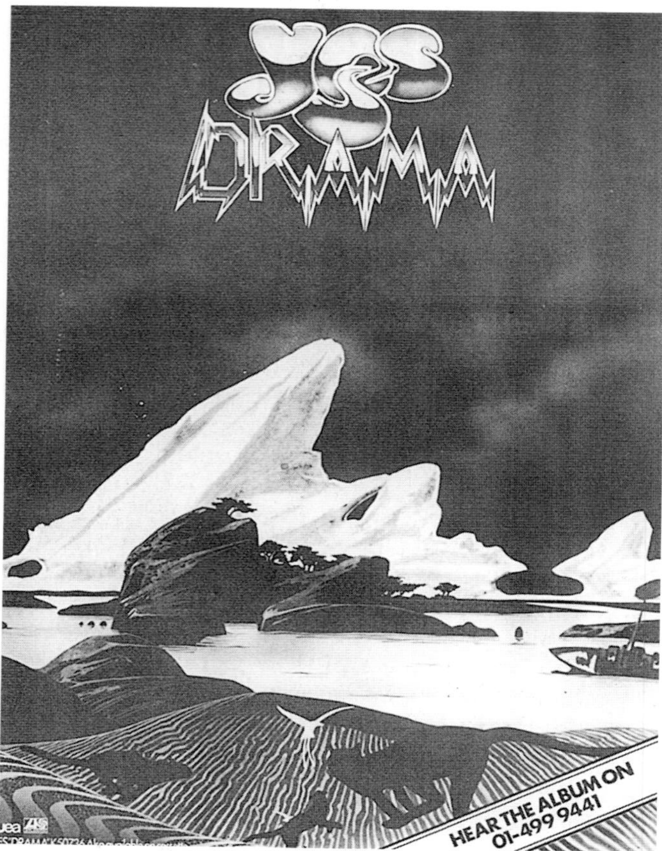

New Yes break through

YES
Hammersmith Odeon, London

I THINK I'm going to like this new Yes.

The young man sitting beside me plainly didn't agree. He kept shouting "rubbish" when either Geoff Downes or Trevor Horn contributed anything to the proceedings, demanded the presence of Jon Anderson at inappropriate moments of quiet, and generally indicated a lack of sympathy with the palace revolution which has taken place.

It's true, Trevor had something sounding suspiciously like laryngitis, and I wish he didn't dress up to look so much like Ronnie Corbett – even to the Billy Bunter glasses – but the concert worked, instrumentally at least on a level equal to anything Yes did in its great days.

One good thing that happened is that, just as the departure of Peter Gabriel brought Phil Collins out from under his drumkit, it has changed the focus of attention towards Steve Howe and Chris Squire, particularly the latter. I thought the Fish's long bass solo much more interesting, musically, than such things usually are, even including it's "Amazing Grace" opening and close.

Despite the plaudits of the audience for "The Clap", Howe still isn't a clean enough instrumentalist to really cut it acoustically, but his range of electric tone colours really is remarkable. One of the new, so far unrecorded songs was credited to him, which promises well for future creativity.

In fact, this on-stage premiering of new material was something of a break-through, and though it was fascinating to hear how much Trevor Horn could sound like Jon Anderson on songs like "Starship Trooper" and "Yours Is No Disgrace", it was the material from "Drama" which came over best.

I hadn't found the album very strong – indeed, what Yes album has been strong enough since "Topographic Oceans"? – but these performances caused instant re-evaluation.

Geoff Downes is no Rick Wakeman, true, but his solo excursion had wit, melody, and a lot of light and shade. He doesn't look very comfortable, but he has quickly established a stage persona for himself.

Which leaves us with Trevor Horn. It would be unfair to judge his obviously sick voice on this outing, and he is working well at getting over with an (at least partly) hostile audience. I'll pass on him, this time, and hope he'll have less of a sore throat next time round.

But, on this showing, I've got to stand up on the opposite side of the fence from the young lad so vocal in his disapproval next to me. This Yes is no disgrace. – KARL DALLAS

DOWNES in action.

standpoint, that I had the opportunity of blending a lot of things that I had grown up with, the classic sort of keyboard sound with also the technology that I had started to build up, synths and that kind of thing. It was a sort of cross-breed, which is quite different to do in a group situation, but particularly a group so ethnic-sounding as Yes.'

It was during the recording of this album that Trevor Horn got married. 'We were supposed to have two weeks holiday in Miami before the tour but because it all got delayed, we ended up with three days in Baltimore. There was hardly anytime to get married, but eventually we got married halfway through the album, at lunchtime on a Monday. I was back in the studio recording at three o'clock in the afternoon.'

Drama had been recorded in SARM East studios in Commercial Road, London and released in August 1980. Commercially, it did very well, reaching number two in the UK album charts, where it stayed for eight weeks whilst reaching the top twenty in the US. Yes had pulled off yet another hit album. Geoff Downes explains, 'As well as acknowledging the classic sound of the previous keyboardist, I tried to inject broader techno-sounds to the *Drama* album i.e. with the addition of the first use of samples on the Fairlight CMI. I think it stands up as a well-written and performed album. I am proud of my own contribution on this album. To be elevated from the pop field into Yes was an enormous step: I have great memories of my first USA tour, and being part of the rock 'n' roll circus. You've got to be mad to be in Yes – and if you weren't when you started, you certainly will be when you leave!

'I still maintain the *Drama* album was a good album, it was a good Yes album. I think a lot of the Yes fans do appreciate it. Obviously, there were the criticisms aimed at us, "It isn't really Yes, no-one can take over from Jon Anderson." It wasn't such a bad situation from my standpoint, because I was the fourth Yes keyboard player, but Yes had never replaced a vocalist before. Just from an image standpoint, Trevor's image was totally unsuitable to the sort of iconoclastic Yes image of what a vocalist should be in that group, which is sort of esoteric, cosmic if you like, which is its hallmark. Trevor's image didn't fit into that at all. Having said that, I do think the record is a good record. I've heard from various sources that Jon Anderson doesn't really even sort of recognise it as being a Yes record.'

Looking back on his days with Yes, Trevor Horn claims to have been feeling 'slightly ill'. He was aware that the band were at an all-time low, and has few happy memories. He suggests the main reasons for the band's endurance were: 'One, none of them could do anything else. Two, they had Chris Squire in the band. Three, Jon Anderson isn't particularly tall.' Asked what he brought to the band's unique sound, Trevor replied, 'Out-of-tune vocals.'

The tour to promote the album began in Canada in August 1980. Geoff remembers the first show: 'Opening night of the *Drama* tour in Toronto, the sound of the [18,000 strong] crowd was spine-tingling, and something I'd never heard from the stage before.' The North American part of the tour was a huge success, selling out stadiums including the massive Madison Square Gardens arena on three consecutive nights (which beat Led Zeppelin's record by a cumulative total of sixteen sell-out shows at the venue throughout Yes' career). When asked to recall the favourite moment of his brief career with Yes, Geoff said, 'Probably the last night of the three at the Madison Square Gardens. In the space of one year, I had moved from being an unknown back-room boy to a world-rated musician on a world-famous stage.'

On return to the UK, however, Geoff Downes pointed out that the UK fans simply could not accept Trevor as the lead singer. Although they had accepted different keyboard players, guitarists and drummers, it appeared that the band-name 'Yes' was totally synonymous with that of Jon Anderson.

Melody Maker

September 13, 1980 25p weekly USA $1.75

HE new-look Yes arrived in New York last week – and earned an ecstatic ception. Former Buggles men Geoff wnes (below) and Trevor Horn (bottom ght) joined with longstanding Yes usicians Chris Squire (above), Steve owe (top right) and Alan White (centre ght) in performing old favourites like Yours Is No Disgrace" and "Starship ooper" plus material from the new Drama" album – which rises to No 1 in e MM chart this week. Full report, and terviews, from Patrick Humphries at Ma son Square Gardens on pages 14 and 15. ictures by Lisa Tanner.

NEW YES CONQUER NEW YORK

Paul Simon dates

PAUL SIMON'S London concerts, exclusively revealed by MM a fortnight ago, have been confirmed with three dates at the Hammersmith Odeon on November 6, 7 and 8. Tickets go on sale during the week beginning September 22 with prices fixed at £8.50, £7, £6 and £4.50.

These will be his first UK concerts for five years. They follow the release of his new album "One-Trick Pony", the soundtrack from Simon's new movie of the same name co-starring Rip Torn.

No details of the line-up have yet been released, but it is widely expected that the touring band will include the nucleus of Simon's recording line-up: Eric Gale, Richard Tee, Steve Gadd, Joe Beck and Hugh McCracken.

Stonk and bravado

TAKING a year away from any job is a risky business. Yet that's exactly what Ian Dury has been doing. Now with new member Wilko Johnson a complete Blockhead and a new album due at the end of November, Ian plus bassist Norman Watt-Roy reveal the trouble and strife behind the making of "Do It Yourself" and the philosophy of their new single "I Want To Be Straight".

They also talk about anything and everything – from success, politics, theatre and the departure of Chas Jankel to the "stonk and bravado", as Dury calls it, of their new songs.

Paulo Hewitt donned his New Boots And Panties and grabbed a lift to the Top Of The Pops studio to hear all – pages 24 and 25.

Seizing the moment, Atlantic realised this was a perfect opportunity to release the long overdue live album *Yesshows*. Although most of the band were unable to agree on a final track listing, Atlantic knew *Yesshows* would appeal to different generations of fans, both old and new. When the label released *Yesshows* without consulting the band, Rick Wakeman was furious: 'I think it's disgraceful. We recorded some of the dates and there were enough tapes to produce a "live album. . ." We always thought the group was better live than on record. We're dreadfully clinical in the studio; we're well aware of it and the music suffers from it. Chris mixed some stuff, which was good, but nothing exciting. The next thing I knew was that somebody gave me a copy of *Yesshows*, and it turned out to be those horrible demo mixes. I can't do anything about it, but nobody told us it was coming out.'

During the *Drama* tour, rumours began circulating in the press of problems. *Sounds* reported on 13 December 1980 that Yes were about to split up because of major differences, which the band's office in London dismissed as 'absolute rubbish'.

'Come the begining of 1981, nobody was really sure of the

destiny of Yes,' remembers Steve Howe. 'We had a meeting and the egg sort of cracked on the floor and it ended up that really only Geoff and I were sitting there saying, "Well, I think I'm still in Yes. I haven't left. I haven't been fired or axed by anybody." So that's what happened. Geoff and I sort of felt, "Well, can we carry on Yes?" And I thought, "God, I've been doing this for a long time... trying to work out how the group continues."... I said, "No, Geoff, you do the Buggles and I'm going to take a short break." But within a couple of weeks, I'd realised that we couldn't resurrect this, we couldn't piece this back together. It's really cracked wide open. So we started on the next project.'

As planned, Atlantic released another attempt at an elusive hit single, 'Run through the Light'/'White Car' in January 1981. Unfortunately, this failed also. And then, a few months after the tour and after much soul searching, everyone agreed that they couldn't maintain Yes in its current form. Long-term manager Brian Lane was fired and it seemed that, technically, Yes were dead.

An official announcement came through that Yes had finally broken up and this time the split seemed irreparable. Chris and Alan tested their resolve however, to see whether they could rescue anything from their long partnership within Yes. A few months after the demise of the band, they began working on new material with Jimmy Page, until recently the guitarist of Led Zeppelin. They had spoken about the possibility of working together and arranged a meeting in Chris Squire's home studio in his house in Virginia Water. Over the next two months, the threesome created a sound that married a powerful rock backing to an eastern feel, similar to Zeppelin's 'Kashmir'. The former vocalist of Led Zeppelin, Robert Plant was going to contribute to the sessions but, since the 1980 death of Zeppelin's drummer John Bonham, he had been unable to put his heart into an outside musical project – this one carrying the provisional title of XYZ, ex Yes Zeppelin.

The press got hold of the story celebrating the formation of the new supergroup – but, with Plant out of the picture, Page's interest waned and the project came to an end before it had really started. Interestingly, the record company denied all knowledge of the XYZ sessions, presumably keeping it under wraps until something concrete came of it. But the end of XYZ heralded a new beginning for Chris and Alan.

Retaining their enthusiasm, the pair carried on writing and playing together. They collaborated with friends Pete Sinfield (lyricist), Greg Lake (singer) and Andrew Jackman (arranger) who had previously worked with Yes, as well as with the Cathedral choir at St. Paul's, on a single recorded at SARM Studios in October 1981. Released for the Christmas market, 'Run with the Fox' received only minimal radio play and subsequently sank without trace. The only Yes product released that year was the compilation album *Classic Yes*, in December. Featuring another Roger Dean cover, it contained an inspired selection of the best of Yes from the early 1970s.

Meanwhile, Jon Anderson was consolidating his post-Yes career with the second Jon and Vangelis album *The Friends of Mr Cairo.* Released on 11 July 1980, it reached number seventeen in the charts, where it stayed for eight weeks. Drawing its inspiration from the glamour years of Hollywood, it was an excellent follow up to *Short Stories*. Elsewhere, Rick Wakeman released his first solo album since he and Jon quit Yes in 1980. Entitled *1984*, inspired by George Orwell's novel, it reached number 24 in the UK charts, where it spent nine weeks.

With Yes now defunct as a band, and musicical trends shifting rapidly away from their progressive-rock style, Chris and Alan continued to write new material together. Continuing in

Asia at the end of a triumphant show at Wembley Arena. From left: Carl Palmer, Steve Howe, John Wetton and Geoff Downes.

the business without Yes, a band which had provided a backbone and a way of life for the past thirteen years, was extremely difficult. Jon, Rick and, to some extent, Steve Howe, were all safe in the knowledge that they could prosper outside of Yes but Chris and Alan, as a rhythm section, really needed a group.

Meanwhile, the early 1980s saw activity from the other ex-members of Yes. Jon Anderson released his second solo album without Vangelis, entitled *Animation*, a concept album based on the birth of his child, reaching number 43 in the album charts. The first single from the album 'Surrender' reached the Top 100 but a second single 'All in a Matter of Time' failed to do as well despite a US tour to promote the album.

Further rumours that a major supergroup was about to form hit the music press with a headline in *Melody Maker*: 'From the Ashes of Yes. . . Comes Asia'. With plenty of press interest laced with a dash of scepticism, Asia prepared to

conquer the world. A collaboration between Carl Palmer, John Wetton, Steve Howe and Geoff Downes, they were the brainchild of Brian Lane. Following the Yes split in 1981, Lane saw a huge gap in the market for a progressive rock supergroup. Their March 1982 debut album, imaginatively entitled *Asia*, exceeded all commercial expectations. Released on Geffen Records, the album contained vital ingredients culled from the members' previous bands, repackaged as an instantly recognisable sound. Their timing was impeccable: FM US radio audiences were starting to demand a change from the increasingly stale new-wave music.

The familiar faces from prog-rock bands ELP, King Crimson, UK and Yes released three singles in 1982: 'Heart of the Matter' reached number 4 in the US and number 46 in the UK, while the other two singles – 'Only Time Will Tell' and 'Sole Survivor' – failed to do anything. The album spent 38 weeks in the UK chart, reaching number eleven, going straight to number one and holding the spot for nine weeks in the US. Asia fever was everywhere: their tours were sell-outs and, by 1982, they were winning various music polls and selling millions of albums. Any worries that Steve Howe and Geoff Downes may have had about life outside of Yes were proven to be groundless.

Back in the world of Yes, Chris Squire and Alan White were trying to hold things together. After their brief time spent playing with Jimmy Page, ex-manager Brian Lane recommended they meet with a South African guitarist named Trevor Rabin. Trevor had played in the top stadium-rock band Rabbitt in his homeland and was in the US looking for a recording deal. Lane, intrigued by Rabin's multi-instrumentalist tag and consummate musicianship, called up Chris and suggested that he should listen to Rabin's tape.

Born 15 January 1955 in Johannesburg, South Africa, his introduction to music was via the piano: 'I come from a family of musicians. My mother is a piano teacher, my father was the lead violinist of the Johannesburg symphony for twelve years, my brother was winning every classic music competition in sight from the age of seven on violin and my sister is a classically trained ballet teacher and she's a great pianist. . . So I come from a kind of pretty talented family.'

At eleven years old, Trevor received his first guitar and, only six months later, having never taken a music lesson in his life, confidently formed his first band, Conglomeration. In his mid-teens, a local producer spotted Trevor and offered him work as a session player, which he managed to turn into a successful full-time career. Later, still in his teens and heavily influenced by jazz and fusion, Trevor was a member of a jazz quartet for a year before joining his first professional rock band, Freedom's Children. The political scene at the time affected everyone in the country and was of particular concern to Trevor's family, who had forged close links with the anti-Apartheid movement. These political sympathies led Rabin to write and perform original songs in defence and support of the movement.

Moving away from politics, Trevor founded a new band, Rabbitt, with some of his colleagues from Conglomeration. Signed up to the Capricorn label, they became incredibly

Future Yes guitarist, Trevor Rabin.

popular in South Africa, with platinum-selling records, sell-out concerts, and a huge teen fan base. They had to put the band on hold for two and a half years whilst carrying out their military service, but when they returned to the band they released two albums: *Boys Will Be Boys* and *A Croak and a Grunt*. Even with his massive success on home soil, Trevor was not entirely happy, since the political situation in South Africa was becoming increasingly intense. He made a brave decision in the summer of 1977 to leave the band at the height of their collective career, and Rabbitt broke up soon after in January 1978.

With his sights set on further success in Europe, Trevor left South Africa to work in Italy and Germany. On arriving in the UK, he headed to London where he was signed to Chrysalis Records and released two solo albums, *Trevor Rabin* in 1978 and *Face to Face* in 1979. Not only did he produce them himself, but he also played almost every instrument. As he carved out a reputation as both a producer and a multi-instrumentalist, he worked with many bands, including Manfred Mann, whose *Chance* album he produced.

Following the *Face to Face* album, Trevor went on to tour the UK as a support act to Steve Hillage. Whilst his albums were a great showcase for Trevor's many talents, none of them sold well enough for him to secure a deal for his third album, so he moved to Los Angeles in 1981 with a bunch of demos tucked safely under his arm. Whilst in LA, word got out that Trevor was looking for a deal or project and he was approached to join a band fronted by Keith Emerson and Jack Bruce. Although he decided against joining them, he was more responsive when he recieved a call from Chris Squire.

'I was suspicious of Trevor when I was first made aware of him,' recalls Chris. 'It was about '79 and the manager I had at the time, Brian Lane, gave me this tape and said, "Here, you know what you should do. . . ?" He was like this scheming-manager type guy who would secretly go to every guy in the band and just sound everyone out until he got some sort of reaction. So I was a little suspicious of Trevor for that reason. I heard this tape that Brian had given me and the guy played and sang everything on it and it sounded just like the last Foreigner album prior to that time, whatever it was. So I thought, "Who is this guy? What does he actually do?" But he did it all very well – he could sing like Lou Gramm and he could play like any guitarist I'd ever heard, more or less. And produce his records and play drums! So I thought, well, the guy is obviously a bit of a clever dick – but what is he really saying? But when I actually met him, we got on really well. In fact, the first time he came over to London to talk about forming this new band, we had this awful jam. We didn't really play very well at all, but we actually liked each other, so we didn't really care.'

Rabin, Squire and White began working on new material together. As they gelled into a band, they realise they needed a keyboard player to flesh out the sound. Chris' thoughts returned to Yes' original keyboard player, Tony Kaye, and his premature departure. Tony was still involved with music, called to a meeting with Chris, he came along with an open mind, excited and a little apprehensive at the thought of rejoining the old mates who previously made him redundant. All components were soon in place for creating a dynamic new rock band; with Chris Squire and Trevor Rabin sharing lead vocals, and Trevor Horn at the helm as producer, Cinema, as they would be known, promised to be more than a new incarnation of Yes.

Rick Wakeman had also been extremely busy, completing three soundtrack albums and a studio album. As well as appearing on various TV and radio programmes, which marked the beginning of a whole new career for him.

Tony Kaye playing at John Henry's rehearsal studios in London at the formation of Cinema.

CINEMATIC CHANGES

1983–89

CINEMA LABOURED HARD on their new material for nine months, at John Henry's rehearsal rooms in London. The music sounded incredibly tight and powerful. While the band's management fought off legal challenges from several US-based bands who shared the same name, they decided to track down Jon Anderson, to listen to their new music. The band arranged a meeting in a London pub where Jon expressed his interest in becoming involved. Jon remembers, 'Chris asked if I'd listen to his music. I said, "yes" and it was really good stuff. I said, "What's the band called?" Cinema! I said "if I'm going to sing on the thing it's going to sound like Yes. Is that the deal, do you want to do Yes again?" He said, "Yeah."'

After recording some demos, it soon became clear to everyone that Jon's unique vocal range was not only perfect but helped to create a sound directly evolved from the latterday period of Yes. 'What we did [on the *90125* album] based on the demos I had written was so different from *Close to the Edge* or *Fragile*,' Trevor Rabin recalled. 'If I knew that it was going to turn into a Yes album, I would have done things differently; more from my orchestral point of view.'

Soon after, the record company issued a press release stating that, for the first time since the break-up of Yes over two years ago, the band's members had been working together

New Yes line up. From left: Chris Squire, Trevor Rabin, Tony Kaye, Alan White and Jon Anderson.

Tony and Trevor rehearsing as Cinema in London.

again in the studio. With most of the material already written, the band went into the studio to lay down tracks. However, after a short period of time, Tony Kaye decided to leave to go back to LA and play with the band Badfinger. He had become unsure of whether he wanted to tour with the band, since they were pressurising him, once again, into using new-fangled keyboard technology he was not familiar with.

With Tony out of the picture, at least temporarily, Trevor Rabin added keyboard sections, working closely with producer Trevor Horn. Although they didn't always see eye to eye, their collaboration produced an excellent album. In order to shoot a promotional video and then, ultimately, to begin touring again as Yes, the band needed a keyboard player quickly. It was during this time, in 1983, that keyboard player and violinist Eddie Jobson, well known for his work with Roxy Music, became available.

Previously known for his work with Curved Air, Roxy Music and Frank Zappa's band – Mothers of Invention, Eddie joined forces with other young musical 'veterans', Bill Bruford, John Wetton and Allan Holdsworth in 1977, to form the progressive jazz-rock ensemble UK.

Their eponymously titled album, was released in April 1978, the band garnering good live reviews on extensive US and UK tours. Despite this, both Bruford and Holdsworth left to pursue other opportunities. Eddie carried on with John Wetton and introduced a new band member, ex-Frank Zappa drummer Terry Bozzio, the trio playing as a three-piece on the 1979 album *Danger Money*.

Although the albums were good, progressive rock had rapidly declined in popularity during the post-punk new wave era, and UK folded after the 1979 live album *Night After Night*. Eddie continued working in London with a number of musicians but had no definite plans, other than completing a solo album entitled *Zink*.

Jobson was offered Tony Kaye's place in the band just a week before Yes had to go on tour to promote the new album. He stayed for only a short period of time – long enough however to be photographed and interviewed by the press as a new member of Yes, although he never actually played live with them – making him one of the shortest-lived members ever. Tony Kaye was then persuaded to come back and continue his sporadic career history with Yes.

The new Yes album was to be called *80102* originally but was changed a while later to *90104,* and then *90125*, all dictated by the album's changing catalogue numbers! From the ashes of the old Yes rose a revitalised line-up with a cutting-edge 1980s sound quite removed from anything produced before. The two Trevors had come together to make a fresh musical statement on behalf of the band. While Rabin's brilliant writing and fresh, distinctive sound had changed Yes' whole approach, Horn's careful production gave the final product a more contemporary feel. Tracks such as 'Changes', 'Owner of a Lonely Heart' and 'Hearts' became classics of the eighties Yes sound.

For Yes, the album was fundamentally different from anything that preceded it: as much a change from *Drama* as *Time and a Word* had been from *Relayer*. 'City of Love' is probably the most un-Yes like track ever recorded by Yes, evocative of both Def Leppard and Styx! At the same time, 'Cinema' was one of the strangest pieces of music ever recorded by Yes, and one of their shortest songs: recorded live with a fast and furious guitar leading over a thunderous drum and bass backing. 'It Can Happen' and 'Leave It' were also radically different, whilst 'Hearts' was the most traditional sounding Yes track on the whole album.

Eddie Jobson (left) pictured with Yes during his brief time with the band.

But the key track on the album, 'Owner of a Lonely Heart', became Yes' finest commercial moment. It contained a terrific guitar opening that grabbed the listener from the start, soaring high vocals and a phenomenally clean, crisp sound. It became Yes' only number 1 single in the US and elicited a huge response – both within and outside the band.

Chris Squire said, 'What I learned from "Owner" is the wonderful thing of people going, "Is that Yes? Really?" I like that. It's especially good for all the fans who stuck with Yes for the right reasons – people who'd been written off by others who'd say, "Oh, he's into that old Yes shit." When "Owner" came out, those same people could finally say, "Have you heard my band's new single?"' Bill Bruford said, 'I didn't hear any Yes material at all after *Close to the Edge* until *ABWH*, with the sole exception of "Owner of a Lonely Heart". Which was impossible to avoid and I liked it a lot. I thought it was really, really good. I didn't think it could be Yes, I thought it had to be Trevor Horn. It was one guy's vision, that song. It was very good.' Trevor himself commented, 'It was imperative, coming back after such a load of shit, that Yes have a single. I would have killed to get that. That song was our best shot, so I made sure that it was as right as I could get it.'

Most Yes members, past and present, liked the album. Alan White said, 'The enthuasism that we all felt for Cinema was really what you were listening to when you heard *90125*. We spent eight months rehearsing all of that material. A lot of the success of that album came from dedication to a new kind of sound.' But not everyone was convinced. When he first heard the album, Steve Howe said, 'This isn't Yes. I could hear Jon a bit, and I hear Chris, which often fundamentally is very Yes but I just didn't feel that same kind of . . . the quality wasn't missing because I was missing, it was missing in a way the kind of work that we've done couldn't be repeated. And therefore, I thought, "Oh well, that's change."'

Released on Atlantic Records' Atco label on 7 November 1983, the album became a huge hit on the back of 'Owner of a Lonely Heart'. The album made the Top Twenty in the UK charts, where it spent six months, whilst the single made the Top Thirty in the UK. *90125*, the most atypical album Yes ever recorded, became their biggest seller of all time, much to the surprise of the music press, the music industry and the long-term fans. Within the first few months of release, the album had gone platinum. In 1984, two more singles were released from *90125*, 'Leave It' and 'It Can Happen', both of them charting in the UK and US. Surprisingly, Yes also had hits with excellent remixes of 'Owner' in the dance and R&B charts.

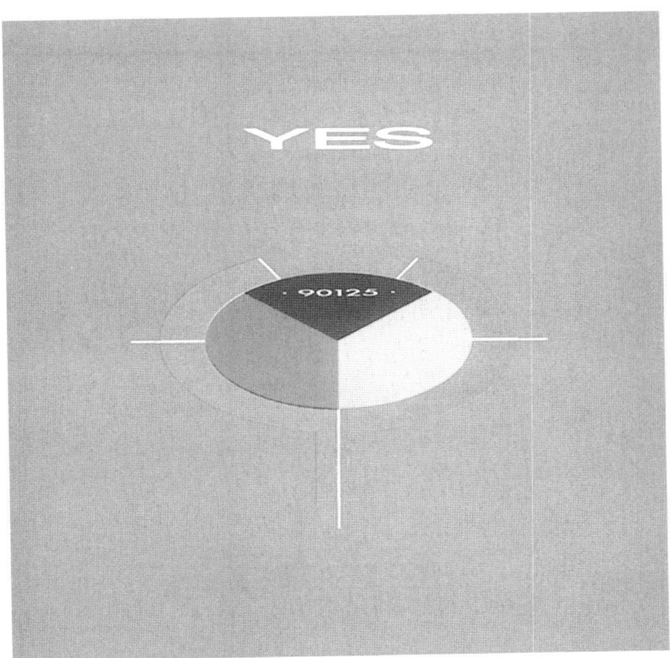

Cinema in the studio, prior to being re-named Yes.

With *90125* achieving massive sales worldwide, it was time for the band to reinforce their success with a tour. Virtually the whole of the remaining year would be spent on tour, starting in America during February, crossing the Atlantic for European and UK dates, then a stint in Japan, ending back in the US in October. It seemed as if there were no limits to what they could achieve – Yes were a global band again, and for the second time.

Yes chose to redefine their image: dispensing, for the second time, with Roger Dean, and embracing a new design style based on computer graphics. The 1980s Yes utilised a new updated Yes logo and released only their second promotional video in sixteen years, a live recording of their tour. The young filmmaker Steve Gottenburg produced *9012Live* for the Charlex Company, using state-of-the-art video technology – incorporating over 60 stunning visual effects. Nominated for various awards, *9012Live* provides an accurate portrait of the reformed band.

With a massive hit album and a number one single, the finances were available to put on a big show. To complement their new sound, Roger Dean's eerie landscapes were replaced by starker, but still spectacular lasers and computer graphics. Playing only in large arenas on this tour, the stage was multi-levelled, and sparse, its high-tech design reflecting the new album cover. The front of the stage sloped down to the audience while the rear sloped upwards, all band members on the same level except for Alan, whose drum pedestal was raised above the rest.

The new Yes began the evening's entertainment with a Bugs Bunny cartoon show, rather than their traditional orchestral overture. In the show proper, dry ice, lasers, strobe lights and spotlights were combined to stunning effect. During 'Hearts', the laser images of two hearts were projected onto the arena walls, whilst in the solos by Trevor and Tony, the cone laser light was used to great effect. After the climax of 'Starship Trooper', as the band went offstage, awaiting their call for an encore, lasers projected the word 'Yes' onto screens above the audience – encouraging the crowd to chant the band's name until they returned.

The world tour concluded in February 1985, in South America, final performances included the massive Rock in Rio festival which drew a crowd of 250,000. That same month, Yes won a Grammy award for best rock instrumental

CHRIS SQUIRE TONY KAYE TREVOR RABIN JON ANDERSON ALAN WHITE

performance for the track 'Cinema', from *90125*.

Preparation for the next album had been an ongoing project between Jon and Trevor, most of the composition taking place on the world tour. Regarding *90125* as more of the embryonic Cinema than of Yes, the individual band members took a well-earned break after the gruelling tour schedule and before any further group activity.

While Trevor Rabin's plans for a solo album were put back due to the recording schedule for the next Yes album – commencing in September 1985 for release in January or February of the next year, according to Atlantic Records – in December 1985, Jon Anderson released his solo album *Three Ships*, which reached number 81 in the charts.

Fans say Yes to reborn band

By Dennis Hunt
Los Angeles Times

HOLLYWOOD — The old Yes would have snootily turned up its nose at *90125*, the new band's current album, and certainly wouldn't have been caught dead playing "Owner of a Lonely Heart," the band's recent hit single. Not only was the single number one, it was a favorite in discos.

But the resurrected Yes, which will appear tomorrow and Monday nights at the Spectrum, is having the last laugh. *90125* has sold more than 2.5 million. Only one of the old Yes albums even cracked the million mark — and not by much. Also, there's the matter of the number one "Owner of a Lonely Heart," the first single by the new band. In 11 years, the old band didn't even have one Top 10 single. Its most popular single was "Roundabout," which went to number 13 in 1972.

Yes died four years ago, a victim of mediocre albums and fan disinterest — fans tired of the group's brand of grandiose, pretentious rock. Judging from the last few albums, the band was tired of the music, too. The parade of personnel changes — keyboard player Rick Wakeman even joined and dropped out twice — didn't help either.

The person largely responsible for the Yes rebirth is Trevor Rabin, 29, a singer, songwriter and guitarist from South Africa. He was barely into adolescence when bassist Chris Squire, singer Jon Anderson, drummer Bill Bruford, guitarist Peter Banks and keyboards player Tony Kaye formed Yes in the late '60s.

Two-and-a-half years ago, two yea after the band's demise, Squire a drummer Alan White, remnants the final edition of Yes, were looki to start a new band. "I got a call fro Chris [Squire], who was in Londo

(See YES on 5-C)

Yes members are (from left) Trevor Rabin, Alan White, Chris Squire, Jon Anderson and Tony Kay

At the start of 1986, the new Yes album still seemed far off on the horizon. The success of *90125* had become a millstone around their necks as fan expectation for the new album reached unrealistic levels – and created tensions within the group. The record company was spreading rumours about similarities between the album and Pink Floyd's multi-million selling *Dark Side Of The Moon*, which only added to the pressure, aggravated by the band's constant switching between recording locations.

In the meantime, March saw the release of *9012live The Solos*. A live album representing the solo works from the *90125* tour, it featured solo tracks by each member of the band, plus two Yes songs recorded live – 'Hold On' and 'Changes'.

The album hit the UK charts on 26 March, where it spent three weeks and reached number 44. The cover artwork continued the modern design theme of the studio album and tour merchandise, but the album itself didn't really represent a Yesshow at all. Looking back at the live albums recorded throughout their career, such as *Yessongs* and *Yesshows*, *9012live The Solos* was a cold, almost emotionless album, as if the record company was trying to squeeze the last profits out of a pre-existing album and tour, rather than truly trying to represent a Yes as a live band of the 1980s. Compared to the innovative video, the live album was a complete let-down.

In May, Jon followed his work on Mike Oldfield's album *Crises* by contributing vocals on to a track entitled 'Loved by the Sun' on *Tangerine Dream*'s soundtrack to the film *Legend*.

WORLD'S MOST OFF THE WALL GUITARS
Guitar Player
SEPT. '86
FREE POSTER
GTR
STEVE HOWE
STEVE HACKETT
LARRY CARLTON
DARRYL JONES
'86 READERS POLL BALLOT
WIN A FREE PAUL REED SMITH BASS
US $2.95
Canada $3.95 UK £2.35

Big Generator, the next album, had not been easy to record: studio sessions took place in various countries over a long

period of time, with more than one producer. Following Trevor Rabin's suggestion, some of the recording took place in a castle on an Italian hillside, with views reminiscent of a Roger Dean painting. But it did not go according to plan, as Trevor remembers: 'The reason I suggested going to Italy was I felt the band really needed to bond together. People were living in different places in the world and I thought we should almost be forced to be together to create music. This place in Italy was a luxurious castle, a beautiful old place for us to record. We weren't there to save money, the reason for going was purely because I felt it would bind us, or bond us together. But it turned out that there was too much partying going on and we didn't click and Trevor Horn said rightly after three months, "This is not working here. Let's get back to London."'

Due to the inordinate delay in producing the album, Yes suffered the loss of both money and record label support. With hindsight, perhaps they should have stayed in one place, as Chris Squire suggested: 'I realised – but certain people didn't – that going to Italy to save money was the start of doing it wrong. Inevitably when you try to do anything to save money, it ends up that because it's cheaper, it's not the best place to be – and therefore you end up re-doing it somewhere else. So we had to re-do stuff in London, and other people weren't happy with Trevor Horn doing it either, so we ended up doing it in L.A.! The most sensible thing in the world would've been if we'd never left here [L.A.] in the first place; then the album would've been finished a year ago.'

The band carried on with Rabin as producer and, later, Paul De Villiers. Although Horn would be (partly) credited for the production work on *Big Generator*, it appeared that Trevor Rabin was the man in control. He had now become the creative force behind Yes, his influence extending across the songwriting, production, orchestral arrangements, vocals, guitar and keyboards to the actual mixing of the album. However, the winning formula Yes locked into with *90125* was difficult to re-create. With two talented, but ultimately stubborn producers, who worked in very different ways, something had to give – culminating in the departure of Trevor Horn.

Big Generator was finally released in September 1987. While it failed to match the success of 90125, it sold well over a million copies and reached number seventeen in the UK charts, staying there for five weeks. Over the next year, three singles were released from the album: and although none of them had the impact of 'Owner of a Lonely Heart', the third single, 'Love Will Find a Way', made the lower fringes of the UK charts and, in October and November respectively, reached the US Top Thirty.

Big Generator maintained the eighties Yes sound pioneered on *90125*, with shorter songs and a more direct approach. Experimenting with many styles, they finally arrived at a mixture of radio-friendly tracks and spacey sixties rock, with fine Hammond playing from Tony Kaye, Jon's more spiritual sound, and a surprisingly eclectic range of influences, such as the vocal harmonies of the Beach Boys. Plenty of the classic Yes signatures remained – Jon's trademark lyrics in 'Holy Lamb', Chris's driving bass lines over Alan's solid drumming – with the additional augmentation of a brass section arranged by Trevor. The imagery for the album cover and merchandise came from design company Assorted Images. With a completely new logo and computer graphics, it was a million miles away from the classic hippie Yes logo.

The Big Generator promotional tour ran from

Trevor Rabin and Chris Squire.

November 1987 through to April 1988, by which time around 70 dates had been played. On 14 April 1988, Yes were invited to perform at the Atlantic Records 40th Anniversary party at Madison Square Gardens in New York, as part of an amazing line-up which included the re-grouped Led Zeppelin with John Bonham's son on drums.

The success of Trevor Rabin's singer-songwriter skills had seen Jon Anderson's dominant role as the front man gradually reduced over the last four years and he realised that he just wasn't enjoying himself anymore. Moreover, it was reported that he felt he lacked the control he once had and was further disenchanted with accountants and management making crucial decisions on the band's future and musical output. All of this was compounded by Jon and Chris suffering personal problems that had built up over the years, the fraught recording sessions for *Big Generator,* and its long, arduous corresponding tour. Everything had taken its toll on Jon, and, disillusioned at the end of the tour, he decided to leave the band for the second time.

'I enjoyed working with the guys on the last couple of albums very much,' Jon was still able to assert. 'My participation was very strong – it was just one of those things. You feel a turning point in your career . . . I wanted to make something more of an experience in music – a continuum of

what I believe really . . . I wasn't really creating that with Trevor and the guys.'

Once again Yes were thrown into crisis. Having achieved a remarkable comeback – while completely re-defining their musical and visual sensibilities – they were now faced with losing the vocal talent that defined the Yes sound, the man who epitomised the spirit of Yes music. Once again, the remaining members of Yes found themselves facing an uncertain future.

With the departure of Jon Anderson, Chris, Alan, Trevor and Tony continued to press on with new material they had written – effectively a return to the Cinema line-up and sound. Searching for a new band vocalist, they were intent on producing the next album by the end of 1988.

Meanwhile, Jon Anderson was formulating plans for the future – effectively working on a Yes Mark Two. In January, the press began to report rumours of a collaboration between four former Yes men under the name of Anderson Bruford Wakeman and Howe (ABWH). However, the members of the 'official' Yes were horrified by the situation, seeing ABWH as a rival who would steal thunder from the 'genuine' item.

There were effectively two Yeses, but only one that could legally use the name and the situation become fraught, long-term friendships became strained. Rick Wakeman commented in the *Close to Yes* fanzine that 'it was a funny situation, the fact that the line-up who wrote, recorded and performed all the classic Yes material could not use the name. If you've got Jon Anderson, Steve Howe, Bill Bruford and myself on stage, performing 'Roundabout', what are you going to call us?'

In the US, Yes launched a legal battle against ABWH in May 1988, attempting to stop them using the Yes name on any merchandising, tour posters or flyers on the basis that it could confuse the public as to who the real Yes were. The dispute soon spiralled into a nightmarish situation, although Chris Squire went on record saying, 'I don't regard them as rivals, I can't see that what they are doing has anything to do with Yes – it's Jon Anderson's solo thing.'

Inevitably, though, the inclusion of the other three ex-Yesmen soon put paid to any idea of the project being solely Jon's vision. Through Brian Lane, they struck a record deal with Arista and began recording straight away. After rehearsals in Paris, they all flew out to the island of Montserrat in February 1989 to record at the famous Air Studios owned by George Martin. Over the next four months the album slowly came together, with Bill drafting in Tony Levin, his bass-playing colleague from King Crimson.

'I've always said that I'm waiting for a group to come along and shock me,' explained Jon. 'And I said, "Hey, nothing's happening. I've got to do it myself. I've got to get together with the guys." The first one that I saw was Bill, and he shocked me. His computer drumming is extraordinary. His playing and his attitude were marvelous, and the same with Rick, the same with Steve. He brought some great songs along and it all seemed to fall into place. I decided that it would be a good thing to spend five weeks in an appropriate place like Paris, developing the initial songs, the music. Put it down. Then come to Montserrat, which is an extraordinarily beautiful place. There are beautiful people on the island. It was a great album to make here – you feel the energy.'

'For some unknown reason, this particular combination of musicians is quite frightening.' Rick recalled. 'It's weird, because Jon, Bill, Steve and I only actually played together for two and a half years. But during that period, we were four-fifths responsible for *Fragile*, *Close to the Edge* and a considerable

Rick rehearsing with ABWH on tour in the US.

Bill rehearsing with ABWH in the US.

amount of *Yessongs*. That's pretty terrifying. We were also aware that when Jon, Bill, Steve and I did some things together in the latter years of the seventies, something special was going to come out. So when we started this project, however people might accept it, we knew that this strange chemistry was going to produce something that would excite us.'

However, not everyone agreed. Chris Squire and Alan White were both fairly unimpressed by the album, eponymously titled Anderson Bruford Wakeman Howe. Trevor Rabin claimed to have enjoyed it but explained that Arista were worried about his solo album and *ABWH* battling for chart positions. The official Yes continued to develop material, but were without a lead singer or any plans to tour. When asked whether he would go and see the ABWH tour, Chris replied, 'I'll go and see them, and if they sell some back catalogue, I won't complain.' He went on to say that Jon suffered from 'Lead Singer's Disease' and was 'not irreplaceable'.

Following months of legal discussion and debate, a verdict was reached. In New York, the US district judge declared that ABWH could refer to their Yes heritage in the promotional material for the tour. And so, under the banner of 'ABWH: An Evening Of Yes Music Plus . . .', the tour began in July 1989 and continued through to March 1990, with the album, launched on 25 June at the Pall Joey Club in Soho, London.

The ABWH show was basically a Yes concert under a different name. To most of their old fans, ABWH *were* Yes. In a further nod to the band's history, the classic Roger Dean designs were re-introduced for the band logo, merchandising and album cover. In live performance the multi-levelled stage was stunning: with stairways leading up to two levels occupied by the two session players and Tony Levin on bass, and Jon in the centre. At the back, a rear projection screen gave the impression of a rock formation in silhouette, split into many parts. In front of this was a huge Roger and Martyn Dean-designed fibreglass spider creation that provided a multi-coloured light show from within, changing its glowing to resemble an animal or a machine.

ABWH opened their show with an excerpt from Benjamin Britten's Young Person's Guide to the Orchestra as once used by Yes, an uplifting piece that culminated in Jon's entrance, walking down the aisle and through the audience to the stage, singing the opening lines of 'Time and a Word'. The performance matched any Yesshow from the past, and the band were taken aback by the intensity of the crowd's reaction.

The album did well, spending six weeks in the charts, reaching number fourteen in the UK and 30 in the US. Rick remembers, 'The *ABWH* album was tremendous, Jon at his best. He had a musical vision and when Jon has that, he's at his best. There was also melody back in the fold and I like that. When we started writing for the second album there seemed to be a tremendous excitement in the air although suddenly when we came to start recording in France most of the original chosen material was ditched. The album recording was not going well and that formed the basis for the *Union* tour and album. Undoubtedly my best memories of recording are *Fragile* and *Close To The Edge*. The best tour was undoubtedly the *Union* tour. I just loved that tour and genuinely shed a tear in my hotel room when it finished. Second best tour would be the *ABWH* tour.'

Meanwhile, over in California, as Yes hadn't finalised the material for their next album, Trevor Rabin took the opportunity to work on his next solo album. Following the release of the album *Can't Look Away*, he undertook his first solo tour of small venues in the USA and Canada, throughout November and December 1989. By the end of the year, the 'official' Yes did not have any material ready for release and were not ready to perform live – in contrast to ABWH who had sold 750,000 copies of their album, to great public and critical acclaim.

Steve rehearsing while on tour in the US with ABWH.

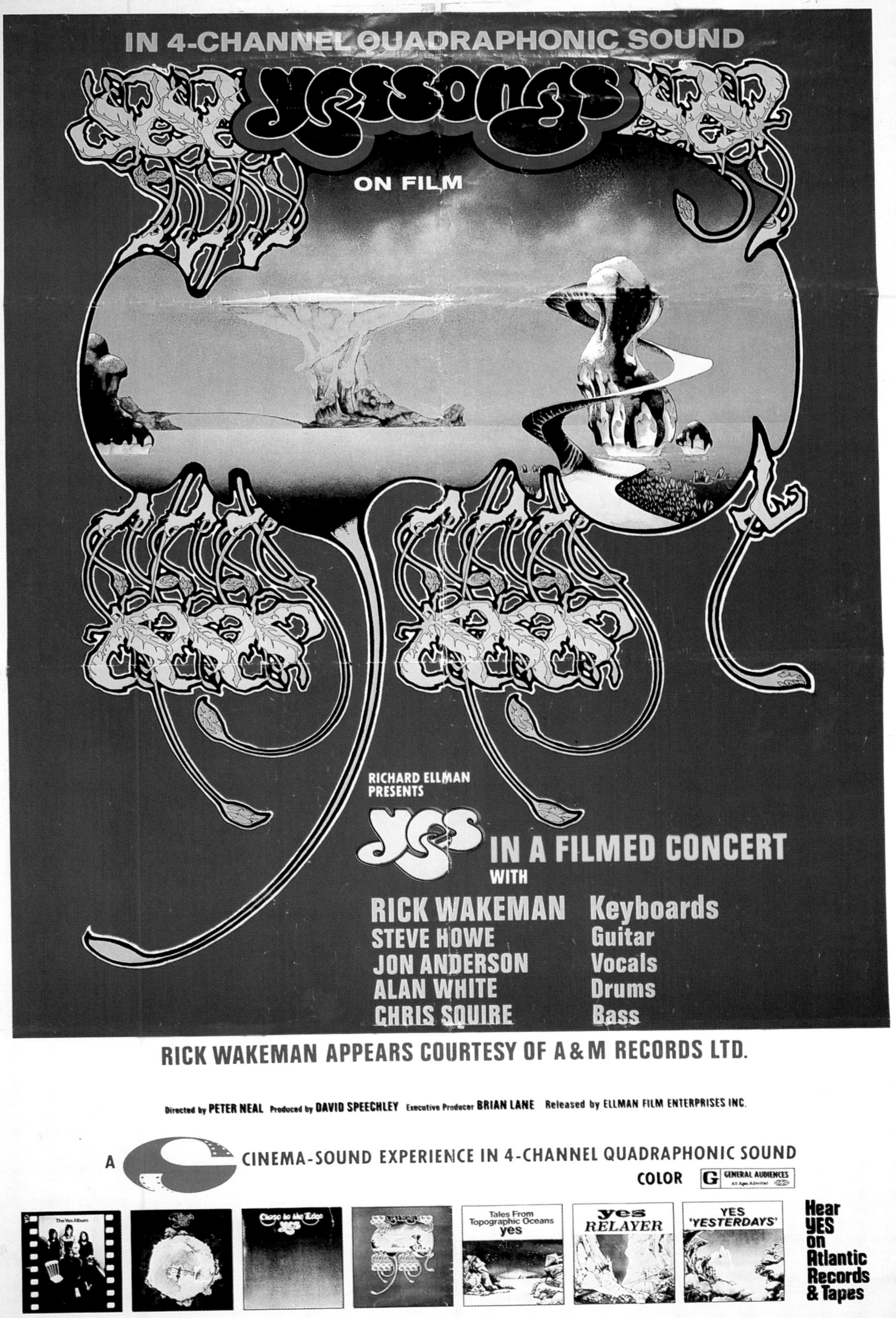

IN 4-CHANNEL QUADRAPHONIC SOUND

yessongs

ON FILM

RICHARD ELLMAN PRESENTS

yes IN A FILMED CONCERT

WITH

RICK WAKEMAN	Keyboards
STEVE HOWE	Guitar
JON ANDERSON	Vocals
ALAN WHITE	Drums
CHRIS SQUIRE	Bass

RICK WAKEMAN APPEARS COURTESY OF A & M RECORDS LTD.

Directed by PETER NEAL Produced by DAVID SPEECHLEY Executive Producer BRIAN LANE Released by ELLMAN FILM ENTERPRISES INC.

A  CINEMA-SOUND EXPERIENCE IN 4-CHANNEL QUADRAPHONIC SOUND

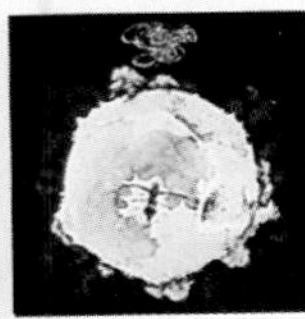

Hear YES on Atlantic Records & Tapes

Above: Roger Dean's 'Yellow City', as featured on the Yesyears *box set cover, 1991.*
Below: Roger Dean's 'The Guardians', used on the cover of the 1991 Union *album.*

Above: Roger Dean's 'Awakening', as featured in the multi-fold-out of Yessongs, *1973.*
Below: Roger Dean's 'Pathways', as featured on the cover of Yessongs, *1973.*

Above: Roger Dean's classic Yes logo, as used on Tales from Topographic Oceans *album cover in 1973. Dean's original logo drawings and artwork are now held at the Victoria and Albert Museum in London. Below: Roger Dean's artwork used on the cover of* Yesterdays *in 1976, here in poster format.*

A promotional poster for Yesterdays, *featuring Roger Dean's artwork from the album cover of* Time And A Word.

The Ladder *album cover,1999, featuring Roger Dean's artwork and incorporating his new Yes logo.*

ENDLESS DREAMS

1990 – 94

FOR THE FIRST three months of the new decade, ABWH played to sell-out audiences worldwide. Once the tour had finished, they started work on their second album, recording at Mirabelle Studios in the South of France.

However, problems soon sprang up over the direction the next album would take – Arista Records already urging ABWH to record material more redolent of Yes. However, the tradition of musicians from superstar bands going into the studio separately to lay down tracks, as established in the seventies, was not greatly conducive to igniting the creative spark necessary for Yesmusic.

The tentative release date for *ABWH 2* was October. Things turned upside-down overnight however, and the album changed into a completely different project. Conventional wisdom at the record company suggested that ABWH and Yes should pool their efforts – to create one Yes album instead of two! In theory, this would cancel out commercial competition between the two bands, and would culminate in a mooted package tour where the ultimate Yes line-up performed all their new material on stage. Arista approached Atlantic and agreed a one album record deal.

Jon performing with ABWH on their US tour.

Prior to this surprising development, Yes – whose legal representatives, only months earlier, had litigated against ABWH in court – had still been in the process of finding a singer to replace Jon Anderson, in order to complete their much-delayed album. Two new names had been linked with the vocal spot, Roger Hodgson of Supertramp, and Billy Sherwood of World Trade – a lesser-known name, perhaps, but one that would become an unofficial member while other options were reviewed, (principally, whether management felt they could lure Jon back into the fold). But, despite his vocal resemblance to Anderson, nothing came of Hodgson's short-lived collaboration with the band, and general uncertainty was compounded by rumours that Tony Kaye had left once again.

In the autumn of 1990, Jon and Chris met in Los Angeles to discuss the merger between Yes and ABWH. While Arista had instigated the project, little consideration had been given as to whether the two camps might gel creatively. Failing to communicate their thoughts adequately to the bands, the resulting album, *Union*, was a strained effort due to deep reservations on both sides, and increasing interference by the record company. 'The powers that be decided that in order to get sales higher than three quarter of a million it had to be a Yes album,' recalled Bill. 'The Californian Yessers would be kind of sellotaped onto the album. The whole thing would become a huge mess. There would then be eight members of the band. This whole ghastly mishmash would be produced by a guy called Jonathan Elias and the album was going to be called *Union*.'

The Jon-Chris rivalry was observed by Trevor Rabin: 'They are so totally different. You would never think they would be in a band together, because they are so different. Chris goes to bed at seven in the morning and Jon gets up at nine, so their clocks are totally different. And Jon's cosmic, if you like, for want of a better expression, and

Chris likes to party. In a lot of bands, they are a tight unit and everyone does the same things, they go to the same parties. That's really *not* how this band is . . . '

Steve recalls, 'Bill and I were particularly surprised that we were going to change midstream and become Yes. We had this group ABWH, which was on the up and up, and Yes were kind of – well, we didn't know where they were. In a way, Bill and I were surprised anybody lost faith in us at that point, but in comparison, releasing a record called Yes had more potential exposure. It was commerical thinking, which once again doesn't help a group like us.'

Linking the material together took producer Jonathan Elias around eight months of work as the band members travelled back and forth across the Atlantic to put tracks down and pull it all together by the end of January 1991. The proposed title for the album was initially *Dialogue* – with hindsight a more apt title than *Union* since it was hardly a unified project! During the lengthy production, the two camps fragmented further into a number of solo activities: including Rick Wakeman touring the UK from 29 May-30 September, and Geoff Downes working with Asia.

After years without an official Yes album, 1991 saw the April release of *Union.* Swiftly followed by the promotional Around the World in Eighty Dates tour. *Union* is a strange affair – unlike anything that preceded it in the Yes canon. Although it sported a Roger Dean cover and contained contributions from eight outstanding musicians who were all, theoretically at least, of Yes both present and past, its uneven compromise is the legacy of a build-up of jealousies and rivalries. It would also seem, from press reports of the time, that producers and session men had made various changes that were not sanctioned by the band. Although both the band and their fans gave the album a fair reception, the final

Chris captured live at Wembley Arena, 1991.

product was almost certainly watered down.

The band's own reaction was extreme: Trevor said, 'I think everyone will say that *Union* is a black mark on the band.' Rick explained, 'I call it the Onion album, because everytime I hear it, it brings tears to my eyes. I never listen to the *Union* album. It has nothing to do with Yes. Most of my stuff was removed or altered by the "producer". I don't own a copy of the album and would refuse to own one. I have been told they make great beer mats or coasters for hot chocolate though.' And Bill expressed further distaste: 'I thought that *Union* was a terrible record. Absolutely awful, an embarrassing record. It costs way too much money. There was no direction at all. It was just a record company thing where they were screwing the band rotten. All egos colliding. It was the most awful album to make.'

The one saving grace for Yes was the tour where all eight members performed on stage. The opening nights, at the 18,000 seater Philadelphia Spectrum, sold out in less than four hours, while the tickets for dates in Atlanta sold out in 35 minutes. The extended band were granted the collected privilege of playing before some of the largest audiences Yes had ever had – even if a small contingent were doubtless curious to see whether the musicians could rise above their internal soap opera and and wear a smile for the crowd.

The tour, which played from April through to August, was a massive success and, for some of the band, the best Yes tour ever. For a few of the Yes band members it would be the first time they had ever met: Wakeman and Kaye, or Howe and Rabin, had obviously occupied the postition of keyboard player or lead guitarist respectively at separate times. However, a fine balancing act was achieved by fitting each other's style into the overall set-list: Howe, for example, played on the classic seventies songs while Rabin dealt with recent Yessongs from the eighties (and nineties). Alan White said of his 'pairing up' with Bill Bruford, 'I thought it was going to be a lot more difficult than it has been. Bill and I are getting along extremely well, especially considering the different styles.' Bill saw it slightly differently. 'The eight-man line-up wasn't much fun. I was there for decorative purposes only. One critic put it very well, I thought: He said Alan White was the meat and I was the hollandaise sauce.'

Despite the various personal and logistical difficulties, Jon Anderson recalls the Around the World tour as an altogether more transcendental event, relating to one key performance: 'With 'Awaken', we let go of our egos . . . I remember doing the Forum in L.A. and it was playing the best I have ever heard in my life. And I tell you no word of lie, that a light came right through the ceiling into that auditorium and covered the band and audience with pure energy. It was the most extraordinary experience of my whole career. To do 'Awaken' and to get to that point where that chord comes at the end, and to put my hands up like that [gesturing], and a beam of light hit me right there. And I just couldn't move. I was shaking. I never do that on stage. I was totally immersed in energy. Whoever was there that night saw it, felt it and experienced it. That was the true union of this band. And I can never let that go. Till the end of my career. I'll remember – that's why we got together.'

From the sublime to the ridiculous: the rest of the band tended to direct their energies into tour pranks. 'Chris gets a

Steve Howe at Wembley, 1991.

terrible cringe on his face whenever he hears about anything to do with cuts on a hand – he goes nuts!' explains Trevor. 'So what we did on the last show of the *Union* tour was Alan got one of those trick blades that you put on your finger and it looks like it's almost cut off. We got some tomato sauce for it and it looked really authentic. I went up to Chris and said, "Where's Benny?" – who was our tour manager. And he asked why and I just acted really anxious, saying, "We need Benny, RIGHT NOW!" And he said, "But what's wrong?" I told him, "I'm not going to tell you, because you'll freak out. I've got to get back to the dressing room." So he followed me curiously and walked in and then saw Alan with his finger cut up, Chris didn't even make a sound, he just left the room white in the face. I ran out to him and said, "Hey, we're only joking," and he shouted, "You bastard!" He got me back later by injecting water into the seat I used when I played my guitar solo. So, when I sat down, my butt was completely wet! I had to keep playing, but it did kind of screw up the performance. It was difficult to focus when suddenly your pants are wet.'

As usual in Yesworld, by the end of the tour there were rumours of dissatisfaction among the band. In December 1991, when Bill toured Japan with Earthworks he was asked in an interview about the possible dates Yes were planning to play there in March. He knew nothing about them – as a testament to the incredible success of the most recent Yesshows, the Japanese dates had been added at the last moment without informing everyone in the band. Advertisements for the gigs began to appear in Japan, omitting Bill's name and photograph. But, despite appearances there was nothing overtly ominous about it – as Bill's Earthworks were playing six gigs in Germany from 21- 26 February, it was assumed he would have very little time to re-join Yes and rehearse. As soon as it was confirmed Bill would actually be in the line-up, the advertisements were changed.

After the Japanese tour ended, a meeting between group and management in L.A. came to the conclusion that a line-up of Trevor, Jon, Tony, Chris, Alan and Rick was the way forward, leaving Steve Howe and Bill Bruford free to pursue their own ventures.

Bill's departure was not surprising. He seemed uncomfortable in the extended line-up near the end of the tour and his aspirations with Yes were never long-term – King Crimson and Earthworks were his real passions.

The boxed set *Yesyears*, a near-comprehensive retrospective on the band, had been released by Atlantic Records in August 1991 – a truncated edition (reduced from four compact discs to two) entitled *Yesstory* was released the following month. With a Roger Dean cover and an excellent booklet that depicted the inside story of Yes, *Yesyears* was compiled from both studio and live recordings and was the first complete anthology of the band's material.

Despite the band retaining two keyboard players, Steve Howe also opted out of being a second guitarist. As part of this period of change, Arista Records – who had aggrieved the band by trying to dictate musical policy – declined to renew their album-by-album deal with Yes. Fortuitously, long-term enthusiast Phil Carson heard about their restlessness and, with his newly formed label, Victory, he approached the band with a deal.

The recording of the new album took place in Trevor Rabin's studio in the little town of San Clement in southern California, where he and Jon would spend a great deal of time, working together in ensuring that the next Yes album was a true collaboration of combined writing talents. But the overall process proved to be a long and drawn-out affair so the remaining *Union* line-up continued to perform solo shows.

In July 1992 Rick Wakeman toured with his Gospels show's while Chris Squire recorded some pieces of music for his album with Billy Sherwood, both of them fronting the Chris Squire Experiment for a short tour of California in August.

In July/August of 1992, the rumours emerged that Tony

Trevor Rabin in the US during the Union tour.

Kaye had left Yes, unhappy with the way the next album was progressing. This time, however, the rumours were well-founded. Tony's position in Yes had always seemed tentative, many fans regarding him as a passenger in the band rather than as a key figure – although his Hammond playing in the Cinema era will always be greatly admired.

In an interview conducted in November, Rick Wakeman confirmed that he was still an active member of Yes and that he would be going to the US for further keyboard work on the album.

Following the *Union* fiasco and the strain of the subsequent tour, the new album was proving difficult to kick-start. As hard as Jon and Trevor were working on the project, even they had to take time out to work on solo material and alleviate the stresses and strains of making a Yes record. The distance between Rick Wakeman – a prolific solo artist and, consequently, a member with a decreasing level of control over band material – and the rest of the band brought matters to a head on 26 March, 1993, when a press statement announced that he too was no longer a member of Yes.

Finally on 23 April, 1993, Victory announced that five tracks from the album were completed. At this time, Jon Anderson was touring South America – his current tour having included a special 27 March show in Pasadena, California for subscribers to the official Yes Magazine, which featured a Latin-influenced version of 'And You and I' – to promote his forthcoming album *The Power of Silence.*

Affirmative: Yes Solos Family Album came out in 1993, filling the void in the absence of a new Yes album, anthologising band members solo tracks from the 1970s and 1980s. The album *Symphonic Music of Yes* was also released, an orchestral album of covers of Yes classics compiled by Steve and Bill, with additional vocals by Jon to complement performances by the London Gospel Choir, the London Chamber Orchestra and the London Philharmonic Orchestra. Produced by Alan Parsons and mixed in the clear, bold tones of Dolby Surround Sound, it's truly a different kind of Yes music.

Released just before Christmas 1993 by Fragile Records, *ABWH: An Evening Of Yes Music Plus* is a double CD live recording from 1989. Beautifully packaged with a Roger Dean cover, it is probably the best representation of the 'un-official' Yes line-up. (A limited edition two-CD package with a video was also released, which is now very collectable.)

Speculation was now mounting over the new Yes album and whether it would have the AOR feel of *Union*, or whether it would emphasise Jon Anderson's more spiritual dimension, with bias toward longer, more expressive tracks. As Jon explains, 'Basically we make an album to take on stage rather than make an album just to sit around. You create music that you can perform, so it can get better and you can get more involved. When you make an album, it's the birth of the music which you then take on the road. This brings life to the album and to the songs. Some songs you just want to play thirty years later.'

The album went under a number of working titles, including *Blueprint* and *History of the Future,* before the band settled on *Talk*. Released in March 1994, it had taken Yes almost three years to complete, and expectations ran very high. Victory's early New Year announcement of a promotional tour in April seemed precarious when, in February, Jon Anderson suffered the recurrence of a slipped-disc injury in his back, caused by a fall on the 90125 tour years earlier – although he recovered just in time for the first dates.

Instead of using Roger Dean to produce the artwork, Yes opted for the well respected creative designs of modernist Peter Max. His brief was simply to provide a new Yes logo and not a full cover design. Resulting in a starkly modern, white album cover with *Talk* in a small, multi-coloured typeface centred on the plain white background, it was simply too

different for the fans to accept, and unfortunately it was not to be a long association between Yes and Peter Max.

The record company released the first Yes CD-ROM in November, a US limited edition entitled *Yes Active*. Featuring music and interviews from the *Talk* album and tour, it was an excellent look into the studio and behind the scenes.

Talk made number twenty in the UK and the Top 30 in the US. The single 'The Calling' also did well, reaching number 2 in the R&R Airplay chart and number 3 on the *Billboard* rock chart. By 8 March, it had made most US radio stations' play lists, three days later, it was the most played track on FM radio stations in America, reaping rewards for the promotional treadmill on which Victory had set the band.

With its clean and uncluttered content, it would seem that *Talk* was a Trevor Rabin solo project in all but name, as he commandeered composition, production and the overall feel of the album. Using the most up-to-date technology, Trevor worked fifteen-hour days until he had logged a total of 13,000 working hours. His perfectionist approach ensured that everything, from the production to the cover design, was free from the crazy excesses of *Union*.

Yes decided on seven tracks for the album's final cut, giving them a chance to mix radio-friendly tunes with Yes-style epics. The overall sound was darker and heavier in tone and more rock-based, Trevor's guitar at the centre of the mix. The record company hailed the album as the high point of his career as a composer, performer and producer.

Jon commented on this when he said. 'It's a special album. A couple of months ago, I was thinking, "How far does Yes go?" Obviously to me and a lot of people around the world, this album has really touched a nerve. The more I hear the album, the more I appreciate Trevor's work.' However, as an outsider, Steve Howe felt differently about the album, 'I listened to it and I found that it was very uncharacteristic to me. The approach wasn't very Yessish. In most respects, it's a good record, except to the point of being a Yes record. It doesn't seem to be a Yes record.'

On the 78-date promotional tour, beginning in the US in June and running through to October, Billy Sherwood became an associate member of the band, on rhythm guitar and backing vocals. Despite positive feelings within Yes about their new music, however, the core fan base, as reflected by both the official and un-official fan magazines, was dissatisfied with both the album and the live dates. Many fans remarked that, over the last few years, Yes had drifted far away from their own unique style of songs and epic musical structure that had made them so successful. Although *Talk* sold a few hundred thousand copies worldwide, it paled against the millions of copies sold of *90125* and *Big Generator*. The slide needed to be addressed. However comfortable individual members of Yes had been with their Rabin-dominated line-up and music, it was clearly not what the fans wanted anymore.

After much procrastination, they decided to take a break and then look long and hard at their future options. The band were now exhausted mentally and physically after a series of long tours and the massive effort involved in keeping the Yes machine on track.

Left: Jon Anderson on stage during the Talk tour.
Above: Trevor Rabin and Chris Squire during the Talk tour.

ONWARD

1995 – 97

JON ANDERSON'S SOLO albums, *Change We Must* and *Deseo* were released close together. Working together with various musicians in different countries, he produced some of his best work in years. Meanwhile, Yes would concentrate exclusively on solo projects. From external appearances, they seemed to lack inspiration, and their last album had been a relative failure in commercial terms: something had to give. Jon would come to realise that the current Rabin-based approach was unlikely to fulfil his dream of taking the band into the 21st century, while Trevor himself commented on numerous occasions that he thought *Talk* was the creative pinnacle of Yes and that he personally felt he had reached his creative limits within the band.

Eight months of stagnation followed. By 23 May 1995, an announcement was made that Yes were splitting once again. Both Trevor and Tony were to leave: Trevor to contribute to the musical soundtracks of films such as *The Glimmer Man*, *Armageddon* and *Enemy of the State;* Tony was quitting the music business completely to run a restaurant in California. Meanwhile, Jon Anderson had fallen in love with a sunny town in California called San Luis Obispo where he now began to plan the future of Yes.

Towards the summer of '95, Jon rang Steve Howe to gauge his opinion on whether the time was right for bringing back the classic 1970s Yes line-up. Steve concurred immediately with Jon's vision as did the rest of the band. This was a brave decision given that predominant musical trends were grunge and rap. Yes would have to rely on their older stalwart fans to buy their albums and attend their concerts.

Things moved very quickly. After a July meeting took place in Los Angeles, the classic line-up of Jon, Chris, Steve, Alan and Rick committed to recording a new album in a Californian studio that soon became known as Yesworld. Renewed interest in the band was further fed by the release, on August 22, of a CD called *Tales From Yesterday.* Packaged in a Roger Dean cover, this album consisted of bold new interpretations of classic Yessongs. On 23 October, the reformed Yes started rehearsing together in San Luis Obispo (SLO). In December, as the rehearsals were picking up momentum, Steve Howe was quoted as saying, "Yes are winding up the big machinery".

At this time, Tony Kaye also commented on the re-building of Yes: 'There's a lot of damage control to be done. Yes had to go back to the seventies line-up. I don't think there was any other way to go. There were too many complications and too many manipulations going on in the eighties line-up. It was getting nowhere fast. My advice to the band was that the manipulations had to stop. Yes had to take control of what they wanted to do. Managing the band is a different role for me and is something that I have wanted to do for a number of years. I've heard nothing negative about this line-up from the fans or from anyone. It's what people want to hear. It became obvious to me during the *Union* tour. There was so much fantastic music from the Yes of the seventies, but not a lot which could be classic from the eighties . . . I don't think we could be playing 'Love Will Find a Way' for too long – certainly not for the next five years. Even 'Owner' was getting a bit thin. But the real Yes fans wanted to hear those older songs. I think they were feeling a little let down after *Talk* . . . There is a lot of music from the sixties and seventies, and really the whole history of the band, that should be performed again.'

Jon signalled his clear intentions for the future: 'I'm not going to let myself down musically. I had a really tough time in the eighties trying to please everyone. No more. From now on, I will please myself first. Yes is going to carry on into the year 2000. We're still a good band, and we've been messed around by managers who just make money, and don't really care about the people in the band. They don't care about the music. They don't know what the music is. I have made a plan into the 21st century, and I am hoping that everyone in the band gets involved in that. Without reservation, I have pride in my work, and respect for the people that love the work I do, and the fans. We are not going to play the singles market. We are just going to make music. I still believe in what Yes represents, musically. I still believe in art. And I still believe in working with good musicians.'

It was all systems go in the Yes camp. On 29 January, 1996, Rick flew in to California to spend a few weeks in rehearsal with the band. They were in a celebratory mood, re-introducing their masterworks to the set and moving away from the chart material of recent years.

The proposed set-list for the San Luis Obispo gigs.

The first live dates would feature the seventies numbers alongside new pieces in a similar style, including the eighteen-minute 'That That Is'. (Live recordings of the shows would be released on the Castle/Alliance label, who won out in the race to strike a deal over Yes's old stable, Atlantic!) The first two shows were booked at short notice to be played in SLO. The concert venue was a surprise: the small, beautifully-restored, 1940s Fremont Movie Theatre on 1025 Monterey Street, with a decorative ceiling in classic Art Deco style and period artwork on the walls.

On February 16, tour dates were announced on the internet, ticket sales restricted exclusively to Yes fan clubs. This gave fans precisely ten days notice before the first gig – as the Fremont Theatre only held 700 people, and, with interest from all over the world, demand far outstretched supply. Tickets priced at $55 went on sale and sold out within minutes. The shows, recorded and released as a double CD set and video, were simply classic Yes. Between the opening of *The Firebird Suite* and the finale, the classic 'Starship Trooper', they performed 'Close to the Edge', 'Awaken', 'America', 'The Revealing Science of God' and 'Turn of the Century' with a renewed vigour.

On stage, Jon reflected aloud on how comfortable all of the band felt being back together at the gig. In a typical Yes/Jon Anderson moment, he had had souvenir t-shirts printed with the legend: 'Ascension of the Spirit is the Reality of our True Being. We all made this Agreement to be here in this world at this Moment.'

For six months after the shows, Steve worked hard on the compilation and mixing of live recordings for album release. 'I tried to make the live material sound like I thought the guys would want. Obviously I didn't receive any income during this period and didn't get any appreciation for it either. But that's the kind of group it is . . . vague. I thought if I sit here long enough I'll make an impression! I could see how Trevor Rabin got left with *Talk* and in a way I got left with *Keys to Ascension*. I just helped bring in some continuity but after it was over I thought, "Wow, never again. Don't call me with a project like that."'

Only a short time after the concerts, solo activities resumed. Jon played a 70-minute solo set on 12 May in an outdoor marquee, performing 'And You and I' and 'Children of Light'. Rick played a solo tour of the UK from April to June. After a gig at Buxton Opera House, he met up with Chris Squire and discussed the new album's title – Rick claimed it should have been called 'the political nightmare continues'. As much as he enjoyed the SLO reformation gigs, Rick was not known for his appreciation of managerial affairs, nor the intrigues of internal band politics – 'issues' remained that contributed to his love/hate relationship with Yes.

28 October 1996 saw the release of *Keys to Ascension*, by Castle Records in the UK, a double CD containing the classic Yessongs and two brand new compositions, 'That That Is' and 'Be The One'. Jon remembers, 'We were rehearsing *Keys to Ascension*, Steve said "Let's do 'Revealing'", and I said "Well, shall we edit it?" and he said, "No" and I said, "Well, OK". So we rehearsed and we rehearsed and after we had rehearsed it, we realised that with this new technology we were sounding so good. That's why we did 'That That Is' and we started to do long pieces of music, realising that long-form music is not a dead art form. So on the new album [*The Ladder*, the second studio album by the reformed seventies line-up] we were able to do 'Homeworld' and 'New Language' as longer pieces of music, and not have the fear that we would get heavily criticised for being who we are.'

Playing an unconventional tour to promote the live album, Yes eschewed huge concerts in mammoth venues in favour of a back-to-basics feel, playing small intimate venues where fans

Jon performing at the San Luis Obispo gigs.

were offered closer contact with the band – as well as a public signing at the HMV record store.

On 22 October, Yes held a press conference at the Pigalle restaurant in Paris to launch the album, then returned to the studio to begin electing and mixing tapes for *Keys To Ascension 2.* Around this time, problems arose when Castle Records expressed concern about the likelihood of Rick continuing to tour with the band. As a small company it was felt that any subsequent studio album by Yes would not be financially viable without an accompanying promotional tour. It also seemed that the magical mood of intimacy created by the SLO gigs ultimately added up to a missed opportunity – instead of touring extensively to ensure their international legion of fans shared the experience, it would be the preserve only of a lucky few. It was an echo of the lack of foresight and bad financial planning that prevented some members of the band becoming as financially secure as their fans would have expected them to be – a common complaint among rock performers of the 1960s/70s. And now, the moment to recreate the intimacy of those small scale reunion concerts had passed: Rick Wakeman, fed up with management politics, had resolved to quit Yes for the third time in his career.

The Yes camp was at war again. In a 7 March 1997 interview in the UK *Revealing Yes* fanzine, Rick spoke about disagreements over the release of *Keys 2*. After much discussion, he was overruled and the album went ahead as planned. Rick had become progressively isolated from both his fellow band members and the group's management. Lack of communication had compounded the offence, when no-one bothered to check the upcoming tour schedule with the keyboard player – causing him to drop out when tour dates clashed with previous solo committments. When the video of *Keys* was recalled to the manufacturers within two days of its 25 February release, on account of poor tape quality, it seemed a bad omen of future disagreements over Yes product – cementing Rick's monumental decision to leave.

From May to July 1997, confusion arose over who was actually still in the band. Steve Howe was still officially the band's guitarist, but, long-time fans could be forgiven for wondering, given the continual state of flux Yes appeared to be in, how long would it be before he left to make way for the return of Trevor Rabin? The scheduled tour was cancelled, leaving a bitter taste in everyone's mouth. Band members who had worked hard to complete Keys 2, now had no promotional duties around which to coalesce. Chris drifted away to write some material with Billy Sherwood. Steve and Jon worked on solo projects, and Jon took a little time out to marry Jane Luttenberger on 28 May.

Billy Sherwood was rapidly establishing himself in the band, influencing writing, recording and production – confirmation of him as an official band member, announced in a press release on 27 August. Hailing from Las Vegas, Billy's early influences came from his musical family: his mother sang and played

Signing at HMV Manhattan, 29th October, 1996.

percussion, his father was a big band leader, and his older brother played the piano. Billy sang in a choir from the tender age of four before moving onto the piano aged five and developing an early taste for soul performers Earth, Wind and Fire and the Ohio Players.

Billy was introduced to rock music when his brother became interested in Yes around 1973; the infatuation extending to Billy himself. His first band, Logic, formed with his brother, were signed to A & M Records for one album, *Nomadic Sounds,* in 1986. After Logic, Billy formed a new band called World Trade, whose debut album was released by Polydor in 1989. Billy supplemented his career with the band by using his multiple talents as a producer, songwriter, mixing engineer and multi-instrumentalist to contribute to soundtracks.

In 1989, while Yes were not playing together as a unit, 24-year-old Billy was introduced to Chris, who admired his work. This two-man mutual admiration society began writing together, with Billy recruited to work on Chris's solo album and tour with the Chris Squire Experiment. A small club tour of California cemented what was becoming a great friendship, then between 1989 and 1991, Billy began to work with the other members of Yes on various projects.

At that stage, Yes were on hold, paralysed by the legal ramifications of the ABWH/Yes case, and it wasn't until Yes finally came together on the studio album *Union* that Billy Sherwood's writing contribution came to fruition with the song 'The More We Live Let Go'. Fully integrated into Yes world, Billy provided rhythm guitar and backing vocals accompaniment for the *Talk* album promotional tour, and was also involved with the production of the albums *Keys 1 & 2.*

Familiar names in the running to replace Rick Wakeman as keyboard player included Geoff Downes (ex Yes/Asia), Eddie Jobson (ex

Billy Sherwood.

Igor Khoroshev, Yes' new star keyboardist.

Yes/UK) and Patrick Moraz (ex Yes/Moody Blues). During his travels around the world, however, Jon Anderson had been passed many musical/demo tapes and it was from one of these unsolicited tapes that he made the discovery of a brilliant unknown.

Russian-born Igor Petrovich Khoroshev grew up in Moscow in the 1960-70s. His musical training began at the age of four, when he started learning the piano. He focused on orchestration, composing and conducting, a virtuoso talent demonstrated by his love of the keyboards and his ability to play the guitar, horn, bass and trombone.

His key influence was classical music, partly due to its virtuosity but also because Khoroshev was restricted in his choice of western music. When he finally heard *Relayer* and discovered Yes, at the age of fifteen, he was completely overwhelmed, deciding that he had to expand his musical knowledge and style and ultimately, decamp to the West.

Arriving in the US in 1991, he began looking for an opening. Initially he took menial employment before beginning to play as a church organist in New York. Later, he joined a band and moved to Boston, where the music scene was particularly vibrant. He worked industriously, both playing with bands and performing sessions for the likes of Charlie Farren of Fahrenheit, Philip Byone, Brad Delp (ex Boston) and Benjamin Orr, formerly of The Cars.

Igor also found work at IBM, hired to create music for computer games by a man named Carl Jacobson, who shared his interest in progressive rock bands like Rush and Yes. Carl was doing some work for Jon Anderson at the time and thought that Jon should hear this new, exciting keyboard talent. Jacobson passed Jon a tape of Igor's performance, but it was only when Yes needed a new keyboard player that he actually listened to it. Realising Igor had potential, Jon invited him to audition. The Russian played the whole of 'The Revealing Science of God', then broke into more Yes tracks before the band stopped him in full flight. His sheer skill and flamboyance struck everyone immediately, and Igor was inaugurated as the new keyboard player in time for the recording of the next album *Open Your Eyes* and the promotional tour that followed in September 1997. Fans accepted him into the fold straight away, struck by his talent.

Open Your Eyes – originally announced under its working titles of Universal Garden, or just plain Yes – was originally a joint project of Chris and Billy, effectively a Chris Squire Experiment album. However, as the project slowly came together, everyone was asked to participate and it gradually transformed into the next Yes album.

The album was a more commercial venture than anything Yes had ever released before. All eleven tracks were seen as potential single releases. The 'big' production, with its profusion of overdubs, sounded like a fusion of the West Coast fell of *Big Generator* and the upbeat *Union*. Highlights included 'From the Balcony', 'Universal Garden', 'The Solution' and 'Open Your Eyes' – the title track that the record label, Eagle, hope would provide the first Yes hit single in the thirteen years since 'Owner of a Lonely Heart'. Hopes were dashed, however, when neither the single nor the album – which sold respectably, in excess of 200,000 copies – proved to be a runaway commercial success. Added to this, the feelings of Jon and Steve regarding the merits (or otherwise) of converting a solo album into a Yes album at breakneck speed have been well-documented – their contributions were added late, and it showed.

Billy Sherwood later commented, 'All of the tracks are written by us. I don't know if it has been that way in Yes for a long time. I thought that the best way to do it would be to get everyone's involvement, and have everyone participate. The album is produced by Yes as well, and not by one individual. It's a collective effort. I'm happy to be involved with it on that level because I believe that this band should be rocking.'

Though *Open Your Eyes* was seen as a filler album by many, the subsequent promotional tour was a definite high point – concentrating on vintage Yes classics, more than the new album, and selling out medium-sized (3-5000-seater) venues every night. Jon recalls, 'To perform 'The Revealing' on stage was like, "Take a deep breath guys, we are going to do it," and it sounded great. *Topographic Oceans* was damn good. It was amazing and I felt so proud that we could turn round 25 years later and perform that piece and say this is good music. I don't care what anybody said at that time, I don't care what Rick said, I don't care what management said, I don't care what record companies said, this was good music. It still holds together today.'

For Igor, his first Yes tour was a deeply emotional experience of a very personal kind, 'It's been very weird. I would be playing some song, like 'Soon' and I would be crying as I'm playing it. Because I remember my mother and I listening to it in Moscow, without even knowing what the song is about. So there are many many strings attached to this particular band and the music itself, and it is really a very, very magical touch for me. It's very special for me to be in this band – I'm in paradise.'

REJOICE, MILLENNIUM YEARS

1998–2001

1998 began with the Canadian leg of the *Open Your Eyes* tour, and the release, in the UK, of *Something's Coming*, a double CD featuring Yes sessions recorded at the BBC in 1969/70. Compiled as a labour of love by original Yes guitarist Peter Banks, it included vintage Yes tracks that had been available only on bootlegs for years in a new, technically-enhanced format, plus the previously unreleased 'For Everyone'. Presenting the band in their early days, full of energy and enthusiasm, it allowed a timely comparison with the revitalised line-up of the late 1990s.Tickets for the European leg of the tour, which ran through to the spring, were selling very well indeed. It had been seven years since Yes had last played in the UK and the excitement was tangible. Although the venues were on a smaller scale than previously, more shows had to be added to the sell-out dates to meet demand. The first gig on the UK tour, at the Manchester Apollo, was received very well and was particularly memorable because of a special appearance on the keyboards by Rick Wakeman's son Adam, who had tentatively been penned in to replace Igor on the keyboards, had the Russian not solved his UK visa problems at the last minute. Instead, to cushion Adam's disappointment, he joined Igor for their last number of the show, Starship Trooper. Geoff Downes went to see Yes playing in Cardiff and while impressed, expressed mixed feelings. 'Jon Anderson's voice had hardly changed at all and Chris Squire was still great on bass. In fact they were all playing well, although I don't think they are making any attempt with their most recent albums to make any serious advances. They've consolidated their position and have their audience of die-hard fans who will turn up and see them.'

The European tour proved to be a huge success as they continued to add dates and sell out venues. The Yesshows staging at this time was a lot simpler, with the focus definitely on the music. As it was the 30th anniversary year, the band tried to arrange a one-off celebration concert at the Royal Albert Hall, playing with the Royal Philharmonic Orchestra. This would be similar to the 'early years' gig when *Time and a Word* was released. Unfortunately, due to time constraints, it was not possible.

Steve Howe enjoyed what was effectively a 30th anniversary tour! 'When we started and did Manchester, Newcastle and Glasgow, that was like Yes coming back home to its very beginning. They sensed it was a rare opportunity to have Yes in their town. There was some great enthusiasm . . . I like thinking about England. Returning to Manchester and Birmingham

Bournemouth International Centre, UK, 1998.

Billy and Alan in discussion at Yestival, May, 1998.

was like going back to our roots. I suppose it's true of Yes travelling anywhere in England – I just can't help feeling we are going back to our grass roots of Yes. It was quite special.'

It was during this tour that Chris Squire demonstrated how richly he deserved his reputation for lateness, Alan White takes up the story: 'We were on a private plane in Vienna, or somewhere like that, we got up and were all waiting for Chris at the hotel and we were waiting in the limos and heard that Chris was still in the bathtub. So we left and waited on the plane for another half hour again. We sat there and finally made the decision to just leave him. So we flew to Rotterdam and got there, but apparently Chris was only ten minutes behind us when we took off. He then had to take a flight with some of the higher-up roadies – lighting guys and stuff like that. They had to make the same journey and they were on a small Cessna plane and it was the worst flight of the whole tour. Chris had to spend an hour and a half to two hours with all these roadies bouncing up and down all over the sky. He got to the other end and he was just furious. But he was never late on the tour again. He was there before anyone else.'

A special Surround Sound edition of *Open Your Eyes* was released, featuring the new technology that Yes would be the first to utilise live on stage on during the US leg of the tour, as pioneered by Alan Parsons and Clair Brothers sound systems. The press launch of the special CD, at the Hard Rock Cafe in New York City on 28 April coincided with an award presented by the music industry for sales totalling 30 million albums.

In June, a compilation CD was released by Eagle Records entitled *Yes, Friends and Relatives*, to commemorate the band's 30th anniversary. Featuring only two band tracks ('America' and 'Close to the Edge'), the CD's remaining seventeen cuts consisted of individual members' solo efforts, such as Jon's version of 'Owner of a Lonely Heart'. Long-time Yes stable Atlantic also honoured the occasion with the re-release of five classic albums – *Fragile, Close To The Edge, Yessongs, Tales From Topographic Oceans* and *Relayer* – as beautifully packaged CDs which became instant collector's items.

Immediately afterwards Steve Howe returned to work on his tribute album to Bob Dylan. Rick Wakeman was presented with the big red book on *This is Your Life* (a weekly UK TV show that celebrates the life of a noted celebrity). In February, Rick was recovering from serious illness, and on his recovery he started to work once more on his major project *Return To The Centre of The Earth* whilst Chris Squire finalised a deal for his solo work along with Billy Sherwood, although his overriding priority was with Yes. Meanwhile Steve Howe released *Pulling Strings*, the live recordings from his 1994 solo

Steve playing tunes at Yestival.

tour. March 1999 was a busy month: Billy Sherwood awaited the release of his latest solo project *The Big Peace*; ex Yes-man Trevor Rabin continued his work on film scores; while Alan White followed the lead of new recruit Igor Khoroshev by creating the musical soundtrack for computer games.

The next album began recording in Vancouver, Canada, with producer Bruce Fairbairn, who had just finished work with Aerosmith and had built up a good track record with Loverboy, AC/DC, Kiss, The Cranberries and Bon Jovi.

The hectic schedule of studio sessions continued throughout the months of April and May. These broke off abruptly, however, following the sudden death of Bruce Fairbairn in his sleep, aged 49, from natural causes. As a producer, Fairbairn had been an excellent motivator to Yes, a straight talker who had drawn out the true essence of the Yes sound. His untimely death was extremely sad, but, paradoxically, also acted as a powerful incentive for the band to forge ahead with some of the best music in their recent career. At Bruce's memorial service held on 24 May in Vancouver, Jon and Steve performed 'Nine Voices' from the forthcoming album, the finished album itself would be dedicated to Bruce's memory.

Their millennial album, *The Ladder*, was released in September, just after the 30th anniversary of the release of their first album *Yes*. Truly a band album, it was immediately embraced by the fans as a return to form. 'After a year and a half touring, we went straight into the studios to start rehearsing, so we were already working as a complete band' explains Jon. 'That's why we were able to make *The Ladder* more of a complete album because everybody had so much energy to perform together. It was a lot easier than putting together an album with Trevor Rabin, who would say, "this is what you're playing, this is what you're singing, this is the way I want it", etc. For the first time in maybe twenty years, we were together as a group in order to make a proper album. You know, in the eighties, it was the producers and record companies controlling the finances. They would say that you have to do what the producer says, and then you're given the money to make an album. For the last fifteen years, the band have been held together by accountants and record companies.'

The Ladder featured the instant classic 'Homeworld', which combined the styles of classic 1970s Yes and 'Hearts' one of the more successful 1980s recordings. Other prominent tracks that found favour with the audience included 'Lightning Strikes' which was released as a single, Bob Marley tribute 'The Messenger' and 'New Language', which, with its incorporation of all the traditional Yes hallmarks, was the latterday equivalent to the classic 'All Good People'. Many miles away, stylistically speaking, from the unrepresentative *Open Your Eyes*, *The Ladder* sent interest in the band soaring and reached number 36 in the album charts.

The 1999 world tour began in September in Rio De Janeiro. The main focus of the stage set for the South American tour was a huge square Yes logo, designed by Roger Dean, in the

From left: Billy Sherwood, Steve Howe, Jon Anderson, Chris Squire, Alan White and Igor Khoroshev.

Yes on the Ladder tour in the US.

middle of a back-projection screen. The 'carved rock' design was once again placed on the front of Alan White's drum riser, whilst Jon's harp stood at the back of the stage awaiting its use in 'Awaken'. Cosmic symbols were prominent on stage, while a simple light show projected images around tented screens, creating an otherworldly atmosphere. As Jon elaborated, 'We always have had excellent equipment and it's looking good, but we don't have finances like U2 who took the Zoo TV on the road, which was amazing.'

As Jon points out, nothing can ever be taken for granted in Yes. 'People working in groups can sometimes feel that they don't want to be in the group anymore. Like Rick, saying "I don't want to be in the band anymore, it's frustrating," eventually you say okay. You never know what's going to happen, we are going on tour soon and you don't know how life is going to be. I'm just so happy that we were able to make *The Ladder* because it completes a really good cycle, we have been on a 30-year cycle and we have got back to where we really should be musically.'

In December, the world tour wound up in Philadelphia, climaxing the musical career of Yes in the twentieth century.

The new millennium was another milestone for Yes. Still on the road and making albums 32 years on from their inception, they flew back to the UK to prepare for the European leg of *The Ladder* Tour.

At the time, Steve expressed his anxiety about the grand expectations they were expected to fulfil. 'We are under so much pressure in 2000 to perform . . . we all have, however unrealistic, expectations for what we are doing as we build ourselves up for something and it's a constant battle between money and artistic restraints. Our expectation of the end result can be too high. We are hoping we can produce a great album, one that turns fans on like *The Ladder*. It's not easy but we got closer with *The Ladder* this time, we want to do the best for everyone with the best show.'

The European tour started in February in Dublin, Ireland. (However the ferry from Ireland to England carrying the equipment was cancelled due to inclement weather, resulting in the cancellation of the Birmingham Symphony Hall gig). The rest of the tour mostly ran to schedule, although in Italy Jon became ill and three gigs were cancelled.

As each show began, Igor and Alan were raised on central tiers while the screen backdrop was spread across the whole stage. Projected onto the screen was retrospective film footage of the band spanning all of the Yesyears, giving the fans a truncated audio-visual history. Fantastic computer-generated images were also projected onto the back screen, dancing formations that moved in time to the music. During the new favourite 'Homeworld', graphics from the Homeworld computer game appeared on the screen, while during the all-time classic, 'Awaken', ticker tape fluttered down from the roof of the arena, illuminated by spotlights, giving the surrealistically beautiful impression of butterflies floating in the air.

One of the major highlights of the tour was Yes playing at the Royal Albert Hall for the first time since 1971. The set list comprised not only classics like Perpetual Change and Awaken but also many tracks from the current hit album *The Ladder*. 'It's a wonderful hall,' Steve commented, 'unlike anywhere else, with that ceiling and setting.' On the afternoon of the second show at the Royal Albert Hall, Yes gave their first full signing session at the HMV record store in Oxford Circus in central

London. The organisers, expecting a turnout of around 300-400 (the average), were shocked when 1,500 fans turned up.

After the tour, some of the band went back to working on solo projects for a few months whilst others took a break. After many years of planning, March saw the long-awaited second solo album from Chris Squire, in partnership with Billy Sherwood, called *Conspiracy*. Featuring great bass work and strong vocals, it had more of a passing resemblance in sound to *Open Your Eyes* than any other work.

In April, Yesworld announced dates for the next American tour, with Kansas as support band – an unusual arrangement, in that Yes had played a two-hour set with no support for years. The world tour would have the collective title of Masterworks, and would be based upon a rare instance of performer-audience democracy: Yesworld set up a poll whereby fans could vote for the tracks that they would most like the band to play. 'This has been a long time coming,' remarked Jon, 'our audience has been asking for this for years. We want to honour their passion and loyalty.'

In April, Steve Howe released *Homebrew 2* and re-released *Homebrew 1*, offering the opportunity for fans to see how the songs grew and evolved into either a Yessong or a solo offering. Steve, remaining as busy as ever, continued his work on his new anthology CD project-set due out in 2001.

In May, rumours circulated on the internet that Billy Sherwood had left the band. Official sources were initially reticent, but, on 14 June, a band statement was released via the official Yesworld website: 'It was officially announced today that Billy Sherwood, a member of Yes since 1997, is departing the group to focus on other creative endeavours. Billy's departure is on amicable terms with the group and his exit was agreed by mutual consent. According to the band, "We support Billy in his decision and wish him all the best in the future." Yes will tour with the classic line-up of Jon Anderson, Chris Squire, Steve Howe, and Alan White, who are once again joined by Igor Khoroshev.'

Above and below: Steve Howe and Igor Khoroshev in the US during the Ladder tour.

Billy's departure came just weeks before the Masterworks tour. Though the extent of his creative input may have been a factor in Billy's decision to depart, most fans agree that, whatever their relative merits, Billy Sherwood made major contributions to the *Talk* tour and the *Union*, *Keys* and *Open Your Eyes* albums.

When the US tour began on 20 June in Reno, Nevada, the fan-polls three most requested songs were the epic 'The Gates of Delirium', 'Ritual' and 'Close to the Edge'. Fans went wild at hearing these momentous pieces of music, performed live, alongside other pieces from *Relayer*, *Tales From Topographic Oceans* and *Close To The Edge* that had been lying, temporarily, dormant due to commercial pressures from record companies and radio stations.

In contrast to recent tours, the stage sets were minimalistic, with just a basic lighting rig, and large, translucent white sheets all around the stage and on the roofing of the lighting rig. Although initially spartan in its effect, the wash of coloured lights that hit the sheeting created a sense of openness and space on the stage. Fireworks were used at many shows, exploding during 'Roundabout' and filling the sky to

Chris Squire during the Ladder tour.

climax another spectacular Yesshow.

A few days into the tour, the official website advertised an innovative exclusive offer – allowing the fans to create their own Yes live CD with the help of imix.com. Choosing from over 140 minutes of material, the fan could then select exclusive cover art by Roger Dean and the current Yes logo on one of four different coloured backgrounds. Yesworld and various radio stations collaborated on a link-up to the Masterworks CD page, with a track listing of up to fifteen titles on a double CD (lasting two hours and twenty minutes or a shorter set on a single disc (70 minutes)).

The official release of the eagerly awaited first DVD, *House of Yes: Live from the House of Blues*, was released in July 2000 – featuring a bonus 'Homeworld' single, a virtual tour book with interviews and photographs, interactive menus, a video press kit and a version of Yesworld. Making use of consumer technology, Yes may possibly have begun to kill off the bootlegging industry that has fed on their output for years.

Despite his contributions to two albums and tours, Igor's status with the band remained that of a freelance musician and not a contracted member of the band. At the completion of the Masterworks tour, Igor concentrated on his solo projects, leaving the remaining members of Yes to work on their next album venture.

During the winter of 2000/2001, Jon, Chris, Alan and Steve embarked upon a huge undertaking for their next album. Working with producer Tim Weidner and conductor Larry Groupe, they collaborated with orchestral musicians to provide symphonic backing to replace Igor on keyboards. Having spent eight months working on the album in Santa Barbara, the band released *Magnification* in August 2001. Quite unlike any other Yes album and tour, YesSymphonic/*Magnification* took the band one step beyond the Masterworks tour, employing a fifty piece orchestra with every show. No band had undertaken such a task since Yes's friends and rivals, ELP, had toured in the seventies with their legendary *Works*. The YesSymphonic tour started in the US in July 2001 and was due to end in early September, with a short break before the European leg of the tour at the beginning of October in Austria.

There can be no doubt that for Yes, the YesSymphonic tour had been a life-long ambition, not without its challenges. Would this be Yes' crowning moment? Would they once again surprise their devoted fans by surpassing the stunning Masterworks tour? Only time would tell. One thing can be sure, the Yes story will continue as the band endeavour to create more music and perform to delighted fans all over the world.

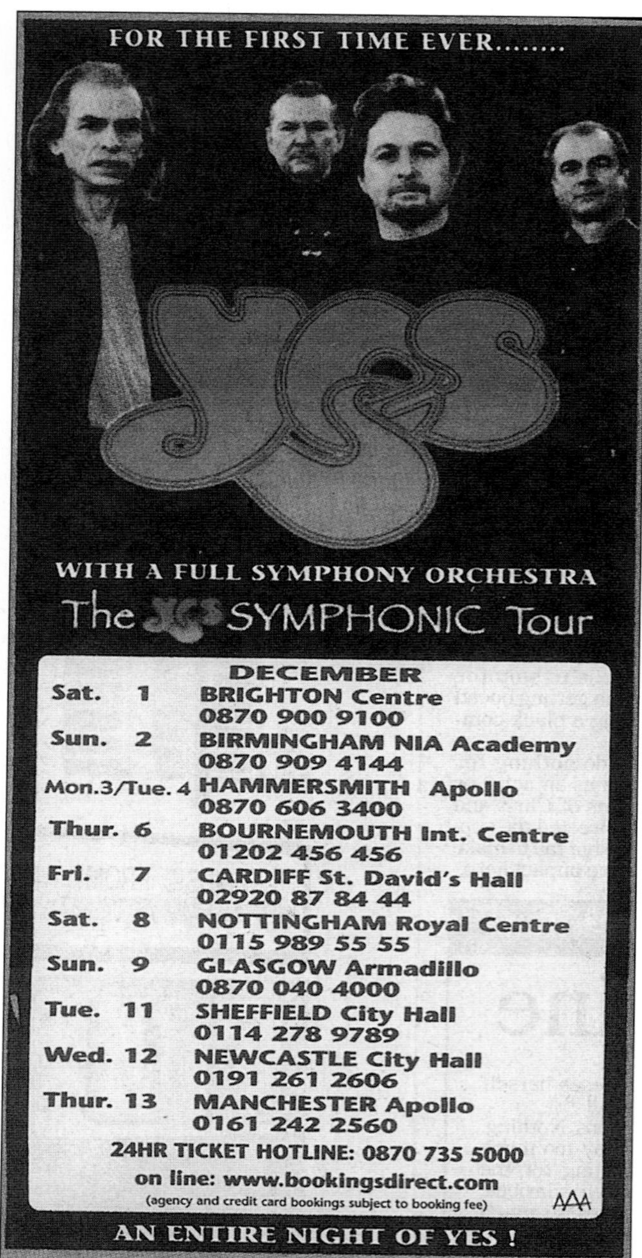

APPENDIX

JON ANDERSON'S *True You True Me* collaborative project with Igor Khoroshev was due for release in 2001, available exclusively via the internet. He was also hoping to finish his next solo album, *Millennium Child,* for a 2001 release, and hinted that another project, based on global tribal music should be completed.

CHRIS SQUIRE had plans for a third solo album,which was not expected for release until 2003. Further solo plans included a collaboration between Chris, Billy Sherwood and possibly Trevor Rabin.

STEVE HOWE had a number of plans in the pipeline, including a handpicked compilation album; anthologising highlights of his career from his early, pre-Yes bands, through the Yesyears and his solo projects. The UK tour, In The Groove ran from September to November 2000 plus dates in Europe and an extensive tour of North America. Steve released his accoustic solo album *Natural Timbre* in the UK in May 2001 on Eagle Records.

ALAN WHITE continues to create music for video games, in partnership with Reek Havoc in a joint business venture entitled Sounds Amazing. As a subsidiary arm of Sounds Amazing, Crash and Bang was launched to specialise in music for computer games and CD-Roms.

BILLY SHERWOOD was in discussion with various film studios who were interested in commissioning him, and his brother Michael, to create soundtracks. While completing his solo CD, *No Comment,* in October 2000, he also signed up with advertising company Elias and Associates to produce TV scores and jingles.

IGOR KHOROSHEV may follow the Jon Anderson collaboration *True You True Me* working for Cakewalk software in the US. He plans to record an album in 2001 with the Tibetan musician MAO Inhibitor, to be called *Culture of One.* Igor has been approached by a number of movie directors to write soundtracks.

RICK WAKEMAN reformed the English Rock Ensemble in 2000, they have released three albums, *Now and Then, Out of the Blue* and *Out There.* Rick continues to make numerous television appearances and hosts *The Rock Show* on BBC Digital Radio. Rick performed the premiere of Return to the Centre of the Earth in Canada in 2001 accompanied by a full orchestra and choir.

TREVOR RABIN continues to work on film soundtracks. Films that have featured his music include *Texas Rangers, Remember the Titans, Metal God* and *Whispers.*

BILL BRUFORD remained busy with Earthworks, touring and recording throughout 2001. Bill planned to form a new band in 2002 who would release an album and then tour.

PATRICK MORAZ released an album, *Resonance,* of his piano compositions late in the year 2000. His next solo project was going to be called ESP and a percussion album was also in the pipeline. Added to this Moraz was collaborating with ex-Renaissance singer Annie Haslam.

GEOFF DOWNES played with Asia on their new album *Aura*, released in January 2001, with a stunning Roger Dean cover. Steve Howe guests on a number of tracks, but did not join the band's US and European tour.

PETER BANKS continues to be active with contributions to Ant-Bee, Superfox. He was also working on a solo album during 2001, entitled *Production.* His autobiography was due for publication sometime in 2001.

TONY KAYE, whose whereabouts since leaving Yes are extremely sketchy, was last reported to be involved in a restaurant in California. Other rumours have mentioned him working on a film soundtrack.

TREVOR HORN was planning to release a collection of his material from the last twenty years, called *The Trevor Horn Archive Collection.* He continues to produce work with Art Of Noise.

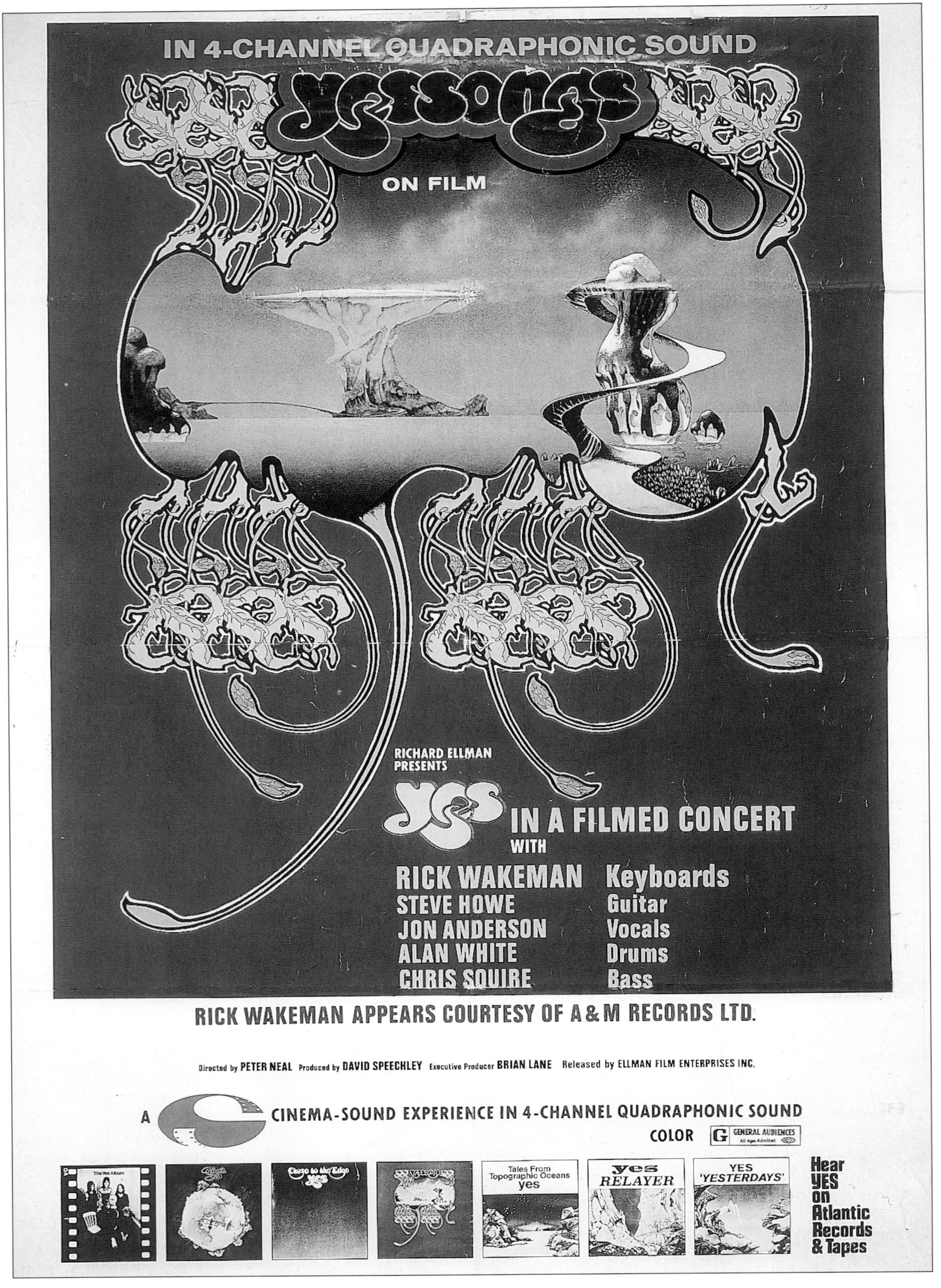

IN 4-CHANNEL QUADRAPHONIC SOUND

YESSONGS

ON FILM

RICHARD ELLMAN PRESENTS

YES IN A FILMED CONCERT WITH

RICK WAKEMAN	Keyboards
STEVE HOWE	Guitar
JON ANDERSON	Vocals
ALAN WHITE	Drums
CHRIS SQUIRE	Bass

RICK WAKEMAN APPEARS COURTESY OF A & M RECORDS LTD.

Directed by PETER NEAL Produced by DAVID SPEECHLEY Executive Producer BRIAN LANE Released by ELLMAN FILM ENTERPRISES INC.

A 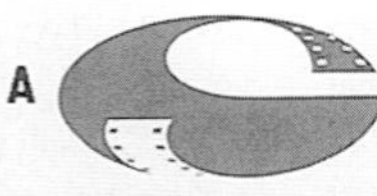 CINEMA-SOUND EXPERIENCE IN 4-CHANNEL QUADRAPHONIC SOUND

COLOR 

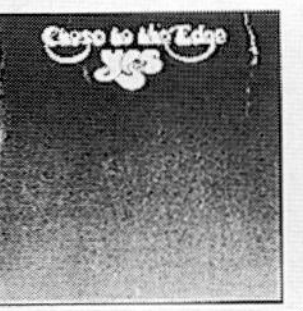

Hear YES on Atlantic Records & Tapes

TOUR DATES

1960

WARRIORS

ACCRINGTON, ENGLAND
Playing venues such as the Imperial Ballroom Nelson for the next few years on a monthly basis as support to Little Richard, Bill Hayley and the Comets and Gene Vincent. Playing also with all the top British acts of the time between 1963-65 at the Liverpool Cavern club and other such prestigious venues.

1963

WARRIORS

DECEMBER

ENGLAND, SOUTHERN SPORTING CLUB
The head of Decca Records Dick Rowe goes to see them perform.

1964

WARRIORS

JANUARY

13 LONDON, ENGLAND, DECCA RECORDS
The Warriors travel to London for auditions at Decca at Studio Two.

FEBRUARY

26-27

LONDON, ENGLAND, DECCA RECORDS
More auditions at Studio Two.

MANCHESTER, ENGLAND, MANCHESTER CATHEDRAL
Back up to Manchester, England, to perform the only pop music service ever at the Cathedral, arranged to celebrate the 21st anniversary of the student Christian movement within schools.

APRIL

7 LONDON, ENGLAND, DECCA RECORDS
The Warriors travel down to London to see their manager and agent Phil Solomon in Wardour street and discuss a movie role for the band.

8 LONDON, ENGLAND, DECCA RECORDS
The band go to Shepperton film studios for filming of the pop music movie *Just For You*.

DECEMBER

ACCRINGTON, ENGLAND, ANTLEY CHURCH

31 BOLTON, ENGLAND, NEVADA DANCE HALL

1965

SELFS

MARCH

LONDON, ENGLAND, KINGSBURY, ST. ANDREWS CHURCH HALL, THE GRAVEYARD CLUB
This is the earliest known gig for Chris Squire.

20 LONDON, ENGLAND, ROE GREEN CHURCH HALL
Dance night on Saturday at 7.45pm.

DECEMBER

31 LONDON, ENGLAND, KINGSBURY TOWN HALL

1966

WARRIORS

JANUARY

8 WORSLEY, ENGLAND, CIVIC HALL

17 BLACKBURN, ENGLAND, PALAIS

26 LEIGH, ENGLAND, BEACHCOMBER CLUB

27 BOLTON, ENGLAND, BOLTON PALAIS

FEBRUARY

1 MANCHESTER, ENGLAND, BAMBOO CLUB
Notes from a fan's diary: -'They seem to have a new organist tonight, Brian. John ruined the first half with his showing off! They only got £10 for tonight, I think they're going down the drain'.

5 ROCHDALE, ENGLAND, FIRE STATION
A local fan said they sang three new songs.

9 LONDON, ENGLAND, PHILLIPS RECORD COMPANY
Accompanied by their manager at the time, Don Reed, the Warriors attend a recording session for their next single Run To Me.

13 MANCHESTER, ENGLAND, JIGSAW CLUB
A fashion conscious fan noted that they were wearing their grey jackets with new red leather buttons and half belts.

17 BOLTON, ENGLAND, CASINO

26 LEIGH, ENGLAND, BEACHCOMBER CLUB

MARCH

1 LEIGH, ENGLAND, BEACHCOMBER CLUB

By March 25th the Warriors single You Came Along had sold 10,000 copies.

SYN

LONDON, ENGLAND, KINGSBURY, COUNTY GRAMMAR SCHOOL
Supported by Plum Nellie.

WARRIORS

MAY

16 **BOLTON, ENGLAND, BOLTON PALAIS**
They had by now been given a spot every Monday & Thursday night. It was noted in a diary for this night that they were being watched by a manager from a club in Hamburg who seemed very impressed. Throughout the summer of 1966, the Warriors had regular appearances at the Bolton Palais & Leigh Beachcomber Clubs, Withinshaw Sporting Club and the Longsight Club, all in and around Bolton.

JUNE

27 **COLOGNE, GERMANY, STORYVILLE CLUB**
This show was on the very day that England won the World Cup, 'They think it's all over, it is now'! The evening shows were reportedly played from 6pm till 2am with a break of five minutes each hour. Two shows were played and the victory, they celebrated well into the night.

SYN

JUNE

Interesting to note that just as Syn were preparing to play the famous Marquee Club in London, the likes of David Bowie and the Buzz were also playing every Sunday afternoon between 3 – 6pm.

AUGUST

26 **LONDON, ENGLAND, MARQUEE CLUB**
With two other acts, Gary Farr and the T-Bones (featuring Keith Emerson).

SEPTEMBER

12 **LONDON, ENGLAND, MARQUEE CLUB**
Supported by the VIP's.

23 **LONDON, ENGLAND, MARQUEE CLUB**
Supported by the Action.

29 **LONDON, ENGLAND, MARQUEE CLUB**
Supported by the Move. (Marquee Club membership was 2/6d [12 pence/7 cents approx] the opening times 7.30 – 11pm. Admission was 5/- members and 7/6d [37 pence/20 cents approx] non-members).

OCTOBER

10 **LONDON, ENGLAND, MARQUEE CLUB**
The Alan Brown Set also performed.

marquee
London W.1
90 Wardour Street

Thursday, December 29th (7.30-11.0)
★ THE PINK FLOYD
★ SYN
Friday, December 30th (7.30-11.0)
★ LONG JOHN BALDRY
with ALAN WALKER, BLUESOLOGY
with STUART A. BROWN
★ THE GOOD-GOODS
Saturday, December 31st (7.30-12.30)
NEW YEAR'S EVE RAVE
★ JIMMY JAMES,
★ COUNT PRINCE MILLER
and the VAGABONDS
★ THE BUNCH
★ THE NEAT CHANGE
(Members: 10/-. Non-members: 12/6 available in advance or at the door)
Sunday, January 1st CLOSED

Monday, January 2nd (7.30-11.0)
★ THE MONDAY NIGHT DATE WITH
★ THE HERD
★ THE NITE PEOPLE
Tuesday, January 3rd (7.30-11.0)
★ MARQUEE SURFIN' NIGHT
★ TONY RIVERS
and the CASTAWAYS
★ SYN
Wednesday, January 4th (7.30-11.0)
★ SPECIAL FOLK MUSIC SESSION
with STAR GUESTS
Thursday, January 5th (7.30-11.0)
★ THE PINK FLOYD
★ EYES OF BLUE

marquee artists Agency and Management 18 Carlisle Street, W.1 GER 6601

NOVEMBER

28 **LONDON, ENGLAND, MARQUEE CLUB**
The Alan Brown Set also performed.

DECEMBER

6 **LONDON, ENGLAND, MARQUEE CLUB**
Supported by Jimmy James and the Vagabonds.

13 **LONDON, ENGLAND, MARQUEE CLUB**
Supported by Eric Burdon and the Animals.

20 **LONDON, ENGLAND, MARQUEE CLUB**
Supported by the Spencer Davis Group.

29 **LONDON, ENGLAND, MARQUEE CLUB**
Supported by Pink Floyd.

WARRIORS

DECEMBER

COLOGNE, GERMANY, STORYVILLE CLUB
Played throughout December.

JANUARY

FRANKFURT, GERMANY
Played from New Year to February 1967.

1967

SYN

JANUARY

3 **LONDON, ENGLAND, MARQUEE CLUB**
Supported by Tony Rivers and the Castaways.

17 **LONDON, ENGLAND, MARQUEE CLUB**
Supported by Zoot Money's Big Roll Band.

24 **LONDON, ENGLAND, MARQUEE CLUB**
Support to Jimi Hendrix.

31 **LONDON, ENGLAND, MARQUEE CLUB**
Supported by Jimmy James and the Vagabonds.

FEBRUARY

7 **LONDON, ENGLAND, MARQUEE CLUB**
Supported by Spencer Davis Group.

14 **LONDON, ENGLAND, MARQUEE CLUB**
Supported by Tony Rivers and the Castaways.

21 **LONDON, ENGLAND, MARQUEE CLUB**
Supported by Cat Stevens, George Bean and the Runners.

28 **LONDON, ENGLAND, MARQUEE CLUB**
Supported by Alan Brown Set.

WARRIORS

FEBRUARY

DENMARK, COPENHAGEN, CAROUSEL CLUB
The Warriors spent a whole month here playing this small club in the middle of the red light district.

MARCH

1 **COLOGNE, GERMANY, STORYVILLE CLUB**
Once again, they find themselves at the Storyville Club playing for a whole month.

SYN

MARCH

16 **LONDON, ENGLAND, 100 CLUB**
Supported by Cliff Bennet & the Rebel Rousers, Ronnie Jones & the Bluejays.

APRIL

1 **LONDON, ENGLAND, MARQUEE CLUB**
Supported by the Footprints.

8 **LONDON, ENGLAND, MARQUEE CLUB**
Supported by the Love Affair.

15 **LONDON, ENGLAND, MARQUEE CLUB**
Supported by C-Jam Blues.

22 **LONDON, ENGLAND, MARQUEE CLUB**
Supported by the Stalkers.

WARRIORS

22 **COLOGNE, GERMANY, STORYVILLE CLUB**
Playing here for a week.

29 **MUNICH, GERMANY, P.N. HIT HOUSE**

SYN

29 **LONDON, ENGLAND, MARQUEE CLUB**
Supported by Skip Bifferty.
On the front page of the Marquee Club Flyer it announces that Syn, who have built a strong following after their Tuesday evening residency, take over the Saturday evening sessions this month.

TOMORROW (Steve Howe)

29 **LONDON, ENGLAND, ALEXANDRA PALACE**
While Syn play to a regular crowd in the centre of London Steve Howe is on stage with Tomorrow at the 14 – Hour Technicolor Dream hippy extravaganza with other bands such as Pink Floyd.

AUGUST 1967 **PROGRAMME** AUGUST 1967

Tue. 1st
THE ACTION
The Time-Box
(Members' Tickets 7/- in advance from July 25th)

Wed. 2nd
ROY GUEST presents
THE NEW SONGS
AL STEWART . THE PICADILLY LINE

Thur. 3rd
MARMALADE
Studio Six

Fri. 4th
THE CREATION
John Evan Smash

Sat. 5th
THE TRIBE
The Third Eye

Sun. 6th
SYN
and Support Group

Mon. 7th
THE FAMILY
Cock-a-Hoop

Tue. 8th
ERIC BURDON
and the ANIMALS
The Time Box
(Members' Tickets 7/6 in advance from Aug. 1st)

Wed. 9th
ROY GUEST presents
THE NEW SONGS
AL STEWART . THE PICADILLY LINE

Thur. 10th
MARMALADE
BLOSSOM

Fri. 11th
ROBERT HIRST
and the Big Taste
The Taste

Sat. 12th
THE TRIBE
and Support Group

Sun. 13th
One Appearance Only
direct from Belgium
ADAMS RECITAL

Mon. 14th
THE LONG JOHN BALDRY SHOW
with Stuart Brown, Marsha Hunt, and
Bluesolcgy
Jimmy Powell

Tue. 15th
Marquee debut:
PETER GREEN'S FLEETWOOD MAC
(Direct from the Windsor Festival)
The Chicken Shack
(Members' Tickets 7/- in advance from Aug. 8th)

Wed. 16th
ROY GUEST presents
THE NEW SONGS
AL STEWART . THE PICADILLY LINE

Thur. 17th
MARMALADE
The Love Affair

Fri. 18th
TONY RIVERS and the CASTAWAYS
TEN YEARS AFTER
in an Evening of Contrasted Musical Styles

Sat. 19th
THE TRIBE
The Darlings

Sun. 20th
SYN
and Support Group

Mon. 21st
The Crazy World of ARTHUR BROWN
Studio Six

Tue. 22nd
ALAN BOWN
The Time Box
(Members' Tickets 7/- in advance from Aug. 15th)

Wed. 23rd
ROY GUEST presents
THE NEW SONGS
AL STEWART . THE PICADILLY LINE

Thur. 24th
MARMALADE
The Iveys

Fri. 25th
TERRY REID with
PETER JAY and the JAYWALKERS
The Mud

Sat. 26th
THE TRIBE
The Third Eye

Sun. 27th
Coasting on Sunday
A Wonderful New Sound
THE PLAYGROUND

Mon. 28th
JOHN MAYALL'S BLUES BREAKERS
TEN YEARS AFTER

Tue. 29th
First Appearance at the Marquee
THE AMEN CORNER SHOW
The Time Box
(Members' Tickets 7/- in advance from Aug. 22nd)

Wed. 30th
ROY GUEST presents
THE NEW SONGS
AL STEWART . THE PICADILLY LINE

Thur. 31st
MARMALADE
The Love Affair

All Programmes are subject to alteration and the Management canno be held responsible for non appearance of artistes.

Printed by Richard Moore & Leslie Ltd. 57 Poland Street, W.1.

SYN

MAY

6 **LONDON, ENGLAND, MARQUEE CLUB**
Supported by We Three Kings.

13 **LONDON, ENGLAND, MARQUEE CLUB**
Supported by the Stalkers.

20 **LONDON, ENGLAND, MARQUEE CLUB**
Supported by the Darlings.

21 **LONDON, ENGLAND, UFO CLUB**
Supported by Tomorrow (SH) and by the Crazy World of Arthur Brown.

27 **LONDON, ENGLAND, MARQUEE CLUB**
Supported by the Bluesyard.

The famous meeting place of Jon Anderson and Chris Squire, the La Chasse Club opens its doors to the public.

JUNE

1 The Beatles release *Sergeant Pepper's Lonely Hearts Club Band.*

10 **LONDON, ENGLAND, MARQUEE CLUB**
Supported by the Stalkers.

17 **LONDON, ENGLAND, MARQUEE CLUB**
Supported by the Love Affair.

TOMORROW

18 LONDON, ENGLAND, THE ELECTRIC GARDEN

24 LONDON, ENGLAND, MARQUEE CLUB
Supported by C-Jam Blues.

SYN

JULY

17 LONDON, ENGLAND, MARQUEE CLUB
Supported by the Darlings.

TOMORROW

29 LONDON, ENGLAND, ALEXANDRA PALACE, LONDON LOVE-IN
With Pink Floyd, the Animals and The Crazy World of Arthur Brown plus others.

AUGUST

TOMORROW

3 LONDON, ENGLAND, TILES CLUB

SYN

6 LONDON, ENGLAND, MARQUEE CLUB

SYN & TOMORROW

11-13 WINDSOR, ENGLAND, THE 7TH NATIONAL JAZZ & BLUES FESTIVAL
Situated in Balloon Meadow, Windsor, a short drive from London. Three members of the future Yes play at the event on the 11th. The main acts were The Small Faces, the Move and the Animals.

TOMORROW

18 LONDON, ENGLAND, UFO CLUB
The Chris McGregor Quintet also played.

SYN

20 LONDON, ENGLAND, MARQUEE CLUB

TOMORROW

26–28 WOBURN ABBEY, ENGLAND, FESTIVAL OF FLOWER CHILDREN
The gig is shortened due to a stage fire caused by some fireworks.

SEPTEMBER

TOMORROW

1 LONDON, ENGLAND, UFO FESTIVAL, THE ROUNDHOUSE
Also on the bill were Pink Floyd, The Crazy World Of Arthur Brown, Fairport Convention and the Nack.

SYN & MABEL GREER'S TOYSHOP

7 LONDON, ENGLAND, HAPPENING 44 CLUB (MGT)

7 LONDON, ENGLAND, MARQUEE CLUB (SYN)
Syn were supported by Studio Six.
Both Syn and Mabel Greer's Toyshop had adverts for gigs on the same day! Inexplicably both Syn & Mabel Greer's Toyshop seem to be running simultaneously. Mabel Greer's Toyshop also played the following venues from September – December 1967, no dates can be confirmed.

MABEL GREER'S TOYSHOP

LONDON, ENGLAND, ELECTRIC GARDEN
Supported by The Crazy World of Arthur Brown.

LONDON, ENGLAND, ELECTRIC GARDEN
Supported by Eire Apparent.

LONDON, ENGLAND, ELECTRIC GARDEN
Supported by Tomorrow (SH).

LONDON, ENGLAND, BRUNEL UNIVERSITY

LONDON, ENGLAND, LONDON LSE

LONDON, ENGLAND, HEREFORD CORN EXCHANGE

TOMORROW

9 CHELMSFORD, ENGLAND, THE CORN EXCHANGE

10 SHEFFIELD, ENGLAND, LOON MOJO CLUB

16 MIDDLESEX, ENGLAND, HOUNSLOW RICKY TICK CLUB

23 BELGIUM, HOLLAND, TV SHOW APPEARANCE

25 LONDON, ENGLAND, MARQUEE CLUB
Supported by the Chris Shakespear Movement.

SYN

OCTOBER

12 LONDON, ENGLAND, MARQUEE CLUB
Supported by the Third Eye.

NOVEMBER

2 LONDON, ENGLAND, MARQUEE CLUB
Supported by the Quik.

16 LONDON, ENGLAND, MARQUEE CLUB
Supported by the Love Affair.

TOMORROW (SH)

18-19 PARIS, FRANCE, PALAIS DES SPORTS
Supported by Soft Machine, Spencer Davis Group, Cat Stevens and others.

MABEL GREER'S TOYSHOP

25 LONDON, ENGLAND, MIDDLE EARTH CLUB

DECEMBER

TOMORROW

2 LONDON, ENGLAND, THE UPPER CUT
Supported by the Breakthrough.

MABEL GREER'S TOYSHOP

9 LONDON, ENGLAND, MARQUEE CLUB
Supported by Neat Change.

22 LONDON, ENGLAND, MIDDLE EARTH CLUB

23 LONDON, ENGLAND, MARQUEE CLUB
Supported by Army, Mint Tulip, Pandamonium, Magic Mixture, Wilson's Transaxion, Dr. Marigold's Prescription, Katch 22 and Geranium Pond.

TOMORROW

22 LONDON, ENGLAND, OLYMPIA, CHRISTMAS ON EARTH
A major musical gathering showcasing many of the top artists of the day. Featured Jimi Hendrix, Pink Floyd, the Who, Soft Machine and others.

1968

MABEL GREER'S TOYSHOP

JANUARY

1 LONDON, ENGLAND, MARQUEE CLUB
Supported by the Nice.

SYN

7 LONDON, ENGLAND, CAT BALOU CLUB

MABEL GREER'S TOYSHOP

20 LONDON, ENGLAND, MARQUEE CLUB
Supported by the Gods.

FEBRUARY

2 LONDON, ENGLAND, MIDDLE EARTH CLUB
Supported by the Action, Odyssey and Jeff Dexter.

MARCH

30 LONDON, ENGLAND, MARQUEE CLUB
The Who also played.

APRIL

3 LONDON, ENGLAND, BBC RADIO JOHN PEEL SHOW 'NIGHT RIDE'

JON ANDERSON & THE GUN

6 LONDON, ENGLAND, MARQUEE CLUB
Supported by Family (JA not a confirmed appearance).

MAY

MABEL GREER'S TOYSHOP

2 LONDON, ENGLAND, MARQUEE CLUB
Supported by the Nice.

LONDON, ENGLAND, HIGHGATE ARCHWAY
Supported by Action (who changed their name to Mighty Baby). The last Mabel Greer's Toyshop gig with Bob Hagger (alias Alexander Belmont) although others were advertised, Jon Anderson was the vocalist on this night.

JUNE

7 DEPTFORD, ENGLAND, RACHEL MACMILLAN'S COLLEGE
Bill Bruford's first gig with MGT (almost Yes). The band was paid £11.

9 LONDON, ENGLAND
The band spend time rehearsing.

13 LONDON, ENGLAND
Jon Anderson rehearses in the daytime with MGT and in the evening joins the Gun.

JON ANDERSON & THE GUN

13 LONDON, ENGLAND, MARQUEE CLUB
Supporting Marmalade, a confirmed gig. It has also been recorded that they supported the Who.

JUNE

MABEL GREER'S TOYSHOP

14 LONDON, ENGLAND
The band spend time rehearsing at the Lucky Horseshoe Café in Shaftesbury Avenue, at a cost of £4 a day.

19 LONDON, ENGLAND
The band spend time rehearsing.

24 LONDON, ENGLAND
The band spend time rehearsing.

29 LONDON, ENGLAND
The band spend time rehearsing.

JULY

1-5 LONDON, ENGLAND
The band spend time rehearsing.

7-12 LONDON, ENGLAND
The band spend time rehearsing.

12 LONDON, ENGLAND
Peter Banks' band Neat Change's single is released.

15 LONDON, ENGLAND
The band spend time rehearsing.

MAY 1968 **PROGRAMME** MAY 1968

Thur. 2nd
THE NICE
Mabel Greer's Toyshop
Members 6/- Non Members 8/6

Fri. 3rd
Blues Night
JETHRO TULL
The New Nadir

Sat. 4th
THE TIME BOX
The Spirit of John Morgan

Mon. 6th
THE NITE PEOPLE
Breakthru

Tue. 7th
MANFRED MANN
The Glass Menagerie
(Members' Tickets available in advance.
Non-Members 12/6 on evening)

Thur. 9th
THE GODS
Granny's Intentions

Fri. 10th
Blues Night
AYNSLEY DUNBAR RETALIATION
Tramline

Sat. 11th
DICK MORRISSEY UNIT
CLOUDS

Mon. 13th
THE NEAT CHANGE
The Exception

Tue. 14th
TRAFFIC
with STEVIE WINWOOD
By Popular Demand: Ireland's Top Blues Group
The Taste
(Member's Tickets 10/- available in advance.
Non-Members 12/6 on evening)

Thur. 16th
JOE COCKER (is coming)
Granny's Intentions

Fri. 17th
Blues Night
JETHRO TULL
THE TASTE

Sat. 18th
THE TIME BOX
Circus

Mon. 20th
THE NITE PEOPLE
Rivers Invitation

Tue. 21st
TO BE ANNOUNCED
Dick Morrissey Unit
(Members' Tickets available in advanc
Non-members on evening)

Thur. 23rd
MARMALADE
Granny's Intentions
(Members 6/- Non-members 8/6)

Fri. 24th
Blues Night
TEN YEARS AFTER
Duster Bennett

Sat. 25th
THE TIME BOX
and Support Group

Mon, 27th
SPOOKY TOOTH
Rivers Invitation

Tue. 28th
JOHN MAYALL'S
BLUES BREAKERS
Tramline
(Members' Tickets 7/6 available in advan
Non-Members 10/- on evening.)

Thur. 30th
THE GODS
Juniors Eyes

Fri. 31st
Blues Night
JETHRO TULL
The Spirit of John Morgan

EVERY WEDNESDAY
STUDENTS' NIGHT
Union Cards MUST be presented
Admission : 4/6

EVERY SUNDAY
"WHOLE LOTTA SOUL"
featuring
RADIO ONE DJ STUART HENR
and the best in recorded "Soul mus
also live groups
Members : 5/- **Guests :**

All Programmes are subject to alteration and the Management cannot be held respo
for non appearance of artistes.

Printed by Richard Moore & Leslie Ltd. 57 Poland Street, W.1.

16 **LONDON, ENGLAND**
Peter Banks leaves Neat Change to rejoin MGT.

17-19 **LONDON, ENGLAND**
The band spend time rehearsing.

20 **KINGSTON, ENGLAND, KINGSTON MARKET HALL**
It is not clear if Peter or Clive played at this gig or whether it was cancelled.

22-24 **LONDON, ENGLAND**
The band spend time rehearsing.

26 **BRACKNELL, ENGLAND, BRACKNELL SPORTS CENTRE**
Reportedly, the actual date Peter Banks joined MGT, unclear if it went ahead.

27 **NEWMARKET, ENGLAND, MUNICIPAL HALL**
Unclear if it went ahead.

31 **LONDON, ENGLAND**
The band spend time rehearsing.

YES LIVE

Jon Anderson, Chris Squire, Bill Bruford, Peter Banks, Tony Kaye.
In a number of cases in the tour dates lists through the earlier years 1968–72, alternatives for some venues and dates have appeared from different sources. Where this occurs, this list shows Bill Bruford's diary entries unless there are overwhelming reports otherwise.

AUGUST

1-2 **LONDON, ENGLAND**
The band spends time rehearsing at the Lucky Horseshoe Café in Shaftesbury Avenue.

3 **EAST MERSEA, ESSEX, ENGLAND, EAST MERSEA YOUTH CAMP**
The first Yes gig which has been the subject of controversy, since the date is debatable as has the spelling of the venue. Bill Bruford & Peter Banks both record August 3rd as the first Yes gig in their separate diaries and not August 4th as previously documented in some Yes histories.

5 **LONDON, ENGLAND, MARQUEE CLUB**
Supported by the Nite People (First gig billed as Yes! Playing two shows). Yes' first Monday night at the Marquee Club, London. Yes have to pay the support band their fee of £15 for the gig. Only 30 people turn up for the night due to bad weather.

8 **LONDON, ENGLAND**
The band spend time rehearsing.

9 **BRACKNELL, ENGLAND, SPORTS CENTRE**

10 **WALSALL, ENGLAND, RED LION**

11 **OMBERSLEY, ENGLAND, WHARF HOTEL** *

12 **CIRENCESTER, ENGLAND, CORN HILL** *

13-14 **LONDON, ENGLAND**
The band spend time rehearsing.

16 **LONDON, ENGLAND**
The band spend time rehearsing.

17 **LONDON, ENGLAND, MARQUEE CLUB**
Supported by Neat Change (Two shows).

23 **STOKE-ON-TRENT, ENGLAND, THE PLACE**

30 **LONDON, ENGLAND, WELWYN GARDEN CITY, CIVIC HALL**

31 **LONDON, ENGLAND, BLACKSHEEP CLUB PICCADILLY**

SEPTEMBER

6 **LONDON, ENGLAND, MARQUEE CLUB**
Supported by Joe Cocker & the Grease Band.

8 **KINGS LYNN, ENGLAND, MAIDSHEAD**

10 **LONDON, ENGLAND, MARQUEE CLUB**

12 **LONDON, ENGLAND**
Recording in the studio.

13 **MARLOW, ENGLAND, CROWN HOTEL**

14 **BECKINGHAM, ENGLAND**
(Venue unknown)

15 **LONDON, ENGLAND, BLAISE'S CLUB**
Replace Sly And The Family Stone at very short notice.

18 **LONDON, ENGLAND, BLAISE'S CLUB**

19 **LONDON, ENGLAND, MARQUEE CLUB**
Supported by the Nice.

20 **EDMINGTON, ENGLAND, COOK'S FERRY INN**
(Cancelled)

21-22 **MARGATE, ENGLAND, WEST END CLUB**
Possibly the date that Bill Bruford went to Leeds University.

28 **LONDON, ENGLAND, MARQUEE CLUB***
Supported by Dream Police.

OCTOBER

5 **HITCHIN, ENGLAND, HERMITAGE BALLROOM** *

13 **LONDON, ENGLAND, BLAISES** *
Yes go to Blaises for photographic session.

14 **LONDON, ENGLAND, REVOLUTION** *

15 **LONDON, ENGLAND, ROYAL ALBERT HALL Czechoslovakia benefit** *

17 **LONDON, ENGLAND, PHEASNTRY** *

22 **LONDON, ENGLAND, BLAISES** *

25 **LEICESTER, ENGLAND, GRANBY HALLS** *

26 **LONDON, ENGLAND, MIDDLE EARTH** *

30 **LONDON, ENGLAND, BLAISES** *
*Tony O'Riley, the Koobas drummer, stood in as the Yes drummer from 28 September to 23 November while Bill Bruford spent some time at Leeds University. Total of sixteen gigs. Ian Wallace also stood in for Bill Bruford for one gig, the date was most likely one of the following London dates: October 13,14,15,17, 22, 26,30, or November 2,13.

NOVEMBER

2 **LONDON, ENGLAND, MARQUEE CLUB** *
Supported by Dream Police.

8 **LONDON, ENGLAND, GRANADA** *
Supported by the Who, Joe Cocker & the Grease Band, The Crazy World of Arthur Brown, and the Mindbenders.

13 **LONDON, ENGLAND, MARQUEE CLUB** *
Supported by the Love Sculpture.

15 **LONDON, ENGLAND, ROUNDHOUSE***
An all night show supported by the Who, Joe Cocker & the Grease Band, Small Faces, The Crazy World of Arthur Brown, Mindbenders.

18 **NEWCASTLE, ENGLAND, CITY HALL** *
An all night show along with the Who, Joe Cocker & the Grease Band, Small Faces, The Crazy World of Arthur Brown, Mindbenders. (The Leeds University gig at which Bill decided to rejoin Yes would have been most likely between the 17th – 23rd November).

24 **LONDON, ENGLAND, BLAISE'S**
Bill rejoined Yes for this warm-up gig and to practise for the big show on the 26th November at The Royal Albert Hall.

25 **LONDON, ENGLAND, REVOLUTION CLUB**
With Bill again back in the driving seat.

26 **LONDON, ENGLAND, ROYAL ALBERT HALL**
Cream play their farewell concert. The event captured on film and recorded saw the end of the wonderful talent that was Clapton, Bruce and Baker. No film has ever appeared of Yes on the day. Cream were supported by Rory Gallagher, Taste and John Hiseman's Colosseum and at the bottom of the bill, a very nervous Yes.

AUGUST 1968 — PROGRAMME — AUGUST 1968

Thur. 1st
THE BEATSTALKERS
The Groop

Fri. 2nd
Blues Night:
SAVOY BROWN BLUES BAND
Gordon Smith

Sat. 3rd
NEAT CHANGE
and Supporting Group

Mon. 5th
THE NITE PEOPLE
Yes!

Tue. 6th
THE CRAZY WORLD OF ARTHUR BROWN
East of Eden
(Members' Tickets 7/6 available in advance from July 30th. Non-members 10/- on evening).

Wed. 7th
SPOOKY TOOTH
Clouds

Thur. 8th
THE NICE
The Glass Menagerie
(Members 7/6. Non-members 10/-)

Fri. 9th
Blues Night:
JETHRO TULL
Black Cat Bones

Sat. 10th
NEAT CHANGE
The Boots

Mon. 12th
Blues Night:
THE TASTE
Keef Hartley

Tue. 13th
JOHN MAYALL'S

Fri. 16th
Blues Night:
TEN YEARS AFTER
Tramline

Sat. 17th
NEAT CHANGE
Yes!

Mon. 19th
THE NITE PEOPLE
The Cortinas

Tue. 20th
TONY RIVERS and the CASTAWAYS
The Glass Menagerie
(Members' Tickets 7/- available in advance from Aug. 13th. Non-members 8/6 on evening)

Wed. 21st
The Fantastic
JOE COCKER
The Open Mind

Thur. 22nd
THE NICE
East of Eden
(Members 7/6. Non-Members 10/-)

Fri. 23rd
Blues Night:
JETHRO TULL
Duster Bennett

Sat. 24th
NEAT CHANGE
Young Blood

Mon. 26th
Blues Night:
THE TASTE
Tramline

Tue. 27th

27 LONDON, ENGLAND, MARQUEE CLUB
Supported by Van Der Graaf Generator.

30 LONDON, ENGLAND, RONNIE SCOTTS

DECEMBER

6 WOOD GREEN, ENGLAND, FISHMONGERS ARMS

7 BRISTOL, ENGLAND, BRISTOL UNIVERSITY

8 LONDON, ENGLAND, BLAISES

12 LONDON, ENGLAND, THE REVOLUTION

13 LONDON, ENGLAND, SPEAKEASY
Opening night for the club.

16 LONDON, ENGLAND, THE REVOLUTION

17 LONDON, ENGLAND, MARQUEE CLUB
The Who's Christmas Party supported by others.

19 LONDON, ENGLAND, ROYAL ALBERT HALL
Janis Joplin was the main act.

24 LONDON, ENGLAND, SPEAKEASY

26 LONDON, ENGLAND, BLAISES

31 LONDON, ENGLAND, BBC TV MAGPIE SHOW
(Daytime)

31 LONDON, ENGLAND, SPEAKEASY
(Evening)

1969

JANUARY

1 LONDON, ENGLAND, MARQUEE CLUB

7 LONDON, ENGLAND, BBC STUDIOS JOHN PEEL'S TOP GEAR SHOW

8 LONDON, ENGLAND, MARQUEE CLUB
Supported by Toast.

12 LONDON, ENGLAND, BBC SESSIONS
Top Gear with John Peel.

15 LONDON, ENGLAND, MARQUEE CLUB
Supported by Procession.

18 SOUTHAMPTON, ENGLAND, COLLEGE OF EDUCATION
On this occasion, the youthful Phil Collins offered his services as a roadie for the evening, he was a big fan. This gig also offers the earliest known Yes ticket stub.

22 LONDON, ENGLAND, MARQUEE CLUB
Supported by Village.

23 WOLVERHAMPTON, ENGLAND, LAFAYETTE CLUB

24 PLYMOUTH, ENGLAND, VAN DYKE CLUB

29 LONDON, ENGLAND, MARQUEE CLUB
Supported by Clouds.

FEBRUARY

1 BOURNEMOUTH, ENGLAND, THE RITZ

5 LONDON, ENGLAND, MARQUEE CLUB
Supported by Caravan.

9 LONDON, ENGLAND, MARQUEE CLUB
Supported by the Spirit of John Morgan.

11 LONDON, ENGLAND
Recording in the studio.

12 LONDON, ENGLAND, MARQUEE CLUB
Supported by Octopus.

13 DORKING, ENGLAND, PIER BALLROOM

14 BATTERSEA, LONDON, (Venue unknown) or GUILDFORD, SURREY UNIVERSITY

15 LONDON, ENGLAND, KENSINGTON QUEEN ELIZABETH COLLEGE

16 SUNDERLAND, ENGLAND, PETERLEE JAZZ CLUB

17 WOLVERHAMPTON, ENGLAND, THE CATACOMB

19 LONDON, ENGLAND, MARQUEE CLUB

23 LONDON, ENGLAND, BBC
Top Gear with John Peel.

24 SHEFFIELD, ENGLAND, DOWN BROADWAY

25 CAMBRIDGE, ENGLAND, GUILDHALL

26 LONDON, ENGLAND, MARQUEE CLUB
Supported by Clouds.

27 LONDON, ENGLAND, SPEAKEASY

28 LONDON, ENGLAND, RICHMOND ATHLETIC GROUND

MARCH

1 CHESTERFIELD, ENGLAND, EMPIRE BALLROOM

5 LONDON, ENGLAND, MARQUEE CLUB
Supported by Circus.

7 YORK, ENGLAND, UNIVERSITY OF YORK

8 SUNDERLAND, ENGLAND, EMPIRE THEATRE

9 KIDDERMINSTER, ENGLAND, FRANK FREEMANS CLUB

12 LONDON, ENGLAND, MARQUEE CLUB
Supported by Killing Floor.

15 SOUTHAMPTON, ENGLAND, SOUTHAMPTON UNIVERSITY

17 LONDON, ENGLAND, BBC
Sunday show sessions.

16 LONDON, ENGLAND, THE COUNTRY CLUB

19 LONDON, ENGLAND, MARQUEE CLUB
Supported by Clouds.

21 WOLVERHAMPTON, ENGLAND, CIVIC HALL

22 BRIXTON, ENGLAND, COLLEGE OF BUILDING

24 LONDON, ENGLAND, RECORDING AT ADVISION STUDIOS

25 LONDON, ENGLAND, MADAME TUSSAUD'S HALL OF KINGS

26 LONDON, ENGLAND, MARQUEE CLUB
Supported by Procession, in the evening, detailed on a Marquee flyer.

27 LONDON, ENGLAND, RECORDING AT ADVISION STUDIOS

28 LONDON, ENGLAND, RECORDING AT ADVISION STUDIOS
(Day)

28 LONDON, ENGLAND, LYCEUM BALLROOM
(Evening)

29 LONDON, ENGLAND, BARNET COLLEGE

APRIL (EUROPE)

2 LONDON, ENGLAND, MARQUEE CLUB
Supported by Harsh Reality.

3 ESSEX, ENGLAND, HARROW FIELD YOUTH CENTRE

4 LONDON, ENGLAND, SPEAKEASY

8 LONDON, ENGLAND, RECORDING AT ADVISION STUDIOS

9 LONDON, ENGLAND, MARQUEE CLUB
Supported by Elastic Band.

14 LONDON, ENGLAND, MARQUEE CLUB
Supported by Peter Cooper.

16 LONDON, ENGLAND, RECORDING AT ADVISION STUDIOS

16 LONDON, ENGLAND, MARQUEE CLUB
Supported by Kippington Lodge in the evening, detailed on a Marquee flyer.

17 LONDON, ENGLAND, UNIVERSITY COLLEGE

21 LONDON, ENGLAND, ROYAL ALBERT HALL
Supporting Janis Joplin.

23 LONDON, ENGLAND, TRIDENT STUDIOS RECORDING

LONDON, ENGLAND, MARQUEE CLUB
Supported by Leviathan.

24 MONTREUX, SWITZERLAND, THE CASINO – GOLDEN ROSE TV FESTIVAL
Yes first met Patrick Moraz, jamming at his villa, he later watched the show.

25 MONTREUX, SWITZERLAND, THE CASINO – GOLDEN ROSE TV FESTIVAL

26-27 GODDELALL, GERMANY, THE TANZCLUB

28 LONDON, ENGLAND, MARQUEE CLUB
Supported by Maddening Crowd.

30 LONDON, ENGLAND, MIXING AT ADVISION STUDIOS

LONDON, ENGLAND, MARQUEE CLUB
Supported by Hard Meat; details from a Marquee Flyer.

MAY

1 LONDON, ENGLAND, MIXING AT ADVISION STUDIOS

2 PLYMOUTH, ENGLAND, VAN DYKE CLUB

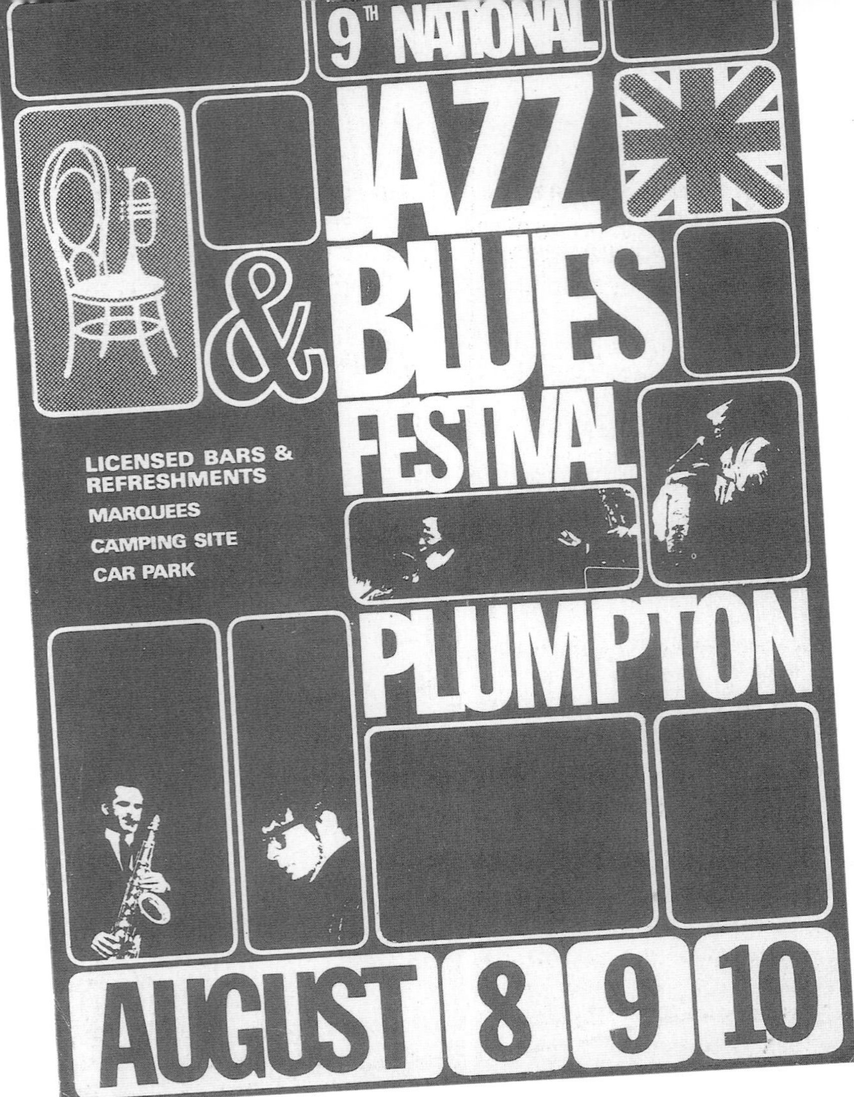

3 **LONDON, ENGLAND, CHELSEA COLLEGE OF ART**
Supported by Clouds.

4 **LONDON, ENGLAND, MARQUEE CLUB**
Supported by Peter Cooper.

8 **SCARBOROUGH, ENGLAND, THE PENTHOUSE**

10 **EXETER, ENGLAND, UNIVERSITY**

11 **KIDDERMINSTER, ENGLAND, FRANK FREEMAN'S CLUB**

14 **LONDON, ENGLAND, MARQUEE CLUB**

16 **LONDON, ENGLAND, LYCEUM 'MIDNIGHT COURT'**
Supported by John Mayall, Hard Meat and Gypsy.

17 **LONDON, ENGLAND, UNIVERSITY COLLEGE**

18 **LONDON, ENGLAND, CAMDEN FESTIVAL**
Many other bands on the bill.

21 **LONDON, ENGLAND, HARRODS THE WAY INN**
Supported by Sharon Tandy.

22 **LONDON, ENGLAND, RADIO ONE CLUB**
Supported by Sharon Tandy.

24 **SOUTHEND, ENGLAND, COLLEGE OF TECHNOLOGY**

25 **LONDON, ENGLAND, PARLIAMENT HILL FREE CONCERT**
Supported by Procol Harum, Soft Machine, Third Ear, Blossom Toes.

26 **WOLVERHAMPTON, ENGLAND, LAFAYETTE CLUB**

28 **LONDON, ENGLAND, MARQUEE CLUB**

29 **PLYMOUTH, ENGLAND, VAN DYKE CLUB**
Also on the bill King Crimson and five other acts.

31 **BRIGHTON, ENGLAND, COLLEGE OF TECHNOLOGY**

JUNE (EUROPE)

2 **LONDON, ENGLAND, MARQUEE CLUB**
Supported by Andromeda.

5 **SCARBOROUGH, ENGLAND, THE PENTHOUSE**

6 **HULL, ENGLAND, THE FAIRGROUND**

9 **LONDON, ENGLAND, MARQUEE CLUB**
Supported by Hard Meat.

11 **LONDON, ENGLAND, MARQUEE CLUB**
Supported by Sweet Marriage.

13 **LEICESTER, ENGLAND, COLLEGE OF ART**

14 **LONDON, ENGLAND, BBC STUDIOS**
Session for the Johnny Walker Show.

15 **KIDDERMINSTER, ENGLAND, FRANK FREEMAN'S CLUB**

16 **LONDON, ENGLAND, SCOTCH OF ST. JAMES**

17 **CANTERBURY, ENGLAND, THE UNIVERSITY OF KENT**

20 **LONDON, ENGLAND, MARQUEE CLUB**
Supported by Mandrake and Paddle Streamer.

21 **ANTWERP, BELGIUM, POP FESTIVAL**

23 **LONDON, ENGLAND, MARQUEE CLUB**
Supported by Leviathan.

25 **LONDON, ENGLAND, MARQUEE CLUB**

27 **HOLLAND 'JAM' TV PROGRAMME**

28 **BIRMINGHAM, ENGLAND, THE FACTORY**

29 **REDCAR, ENGLAND, JAZZ CLUB**
Supported by Queen.

30 **SUNDERLAND, ENGLAND, BAY HOTEL**

LONDON, ENGLAND, MARQUEE CLUB
Both dates recorded in separate places, the London Marquee Club date was supported by Hard Meat.

JULY

1 **LONDON, ENGLAND, RONNIE SCOTTS**
Press reception in the afternoon.

2 **LONDON, ENGLAND, MARQUEE CLUB**
Supported by Andromeda.

3 **LONDON, ENGLAND**
Yes play a private society party for Prince Lowenstein.

4 **BARNSTAPLE, ENGLAND, QUEENS HALL**

5 **HAVERFORDWEST, ENGLAND, MARKET HALL**

6 **LONDON, ENGLAND, ICA ROUNDHOUSE , THE MALL**
Supported by Juggernaut.

7 **LONDON, ENGLAND, MARQUEE CLUB**

8 **LONDON, ENGLAND, INSTITUTE OF CONTEMPORARY ARTS**
Also reported as a Birmingham, England gig supported by Mothers.

9 **LONDON, ENGLAND, MARQUEE CLUB**
Supported by Hard Meat.

10 **PENZANCE, ENGLAND, WINTER GARDENS**

11 **LONDON, ENGLAND, LYCEUM 'MIDNIGHT COURT' CONCERT**
Supported by the Nice, Keith Relf's Renaissance, Peter Cooper and Peter Hammill.

12 **NOTTINGHAM, ENGLAND, RACE COURSE**
12 Hour Happiness Concert, supported by the Nice, Eclection, Caravan, King Crimson, Juniors Eyes, Edgar Broughton

Band, Idle Race, Status Quo.

13 **LONDON, ENGLAND, WEMBLEY POOL OXFAM CHARITY**

14 **LONDON, ENGLAND, MARQUEE CLUB**
Supported by Samson.

15 **LONDON, ENGLAND, 'GROOVE' WEEKEND TV STUDIOS**

16 **LONDON, ENGLAND, MARQUEE CLUB**
Supported by Kippington Lodge.

18 **BELFAST, NORTHERN IRELAND, ULSTER HALL**
Supported by the Nice and the Bonzo Dog Band.

19 **DUBLIN, (REPUBLIC OF) IRELAND, NATIONAL BOXING STADIUM**
Supported by the Nice and the Bonzo Dog Band.

20 **CORK, IRELAND, FOOTBALL STADIUM**
Supported by the Nice and the Bonzo Dog Band. (Cancelled)

23 **LONDON, ENGLAND, MARQUEE CLUB**
Supported by Leviathan.

25 **SOUTH SHIELDS, ENGLAND, NEW CELLAR CLUB**

26 **KIRKLEVINGTON, ENGLAND, COUNTRY CLUB**

27 **BRIDGEND, WALES, KEE CLUB**

28 **BRISTOL, ENGLAND, OLD GRANARY CLUB**

30 **LONDON, ENGLAND, MARQUEE CLUB**
Supported by Hard Meat.

AUGUST

2 **ISLE OF WIGHT, ENGLAND, THE MUSIC BOX**

3 **LONDON, ENGLAND, BBC STUDIOS**
Yes record for the Dave Cash Show. BB records.

4 **LONDON, ENGLAND, BBC STUDIOS**
Yes record for the Stuart Henry Show. BB records.

6 **LONDON, ENGLAND, HARRODS WAY INN**

7 **LONDON, ENGLAND, MARQUEE CLUB**
Supported by Leviathan.

8 **BIRMINGHAM, ENGLAND, MOTHER'S**

9 **PLUMPTON RACE COURSE, ENGLAND, THE 9th NATIONAL JAZZ POP BALLADS & BLUES FESTIVAL**
Festival running 8/9/10 featuring Peter Hammill, Jigsaw, Breakthru, the Strawbs, Roy Harper, the Bonzo Dog Band, the Who, Chicken Shack, Fat Mattress, John Surman, Aynsley Dunbar, the Spirit of John Morgan, Groundhogs, King Crimson, Idle Race, Breakthru, Cuby's Blues Band, Dry Ice.

10 **LONDON, ENGLAND, MARQUEE CLUB**

13 **TOLWORTH, ENGLAND, TOBY JUG**

14 **LONDON, ENGLAND, MARQUEE CLUB**
Supported by Samson.

15 **BARNSTAPLE, ENGLAND, QUEENS HALL**

16 **PLYMOUTH, ENGLAND, VAN DYKE CLUB**

20-21
HAMBURG, GERMANY, STAR CLUB

22-23
LCKKERKERK, HOLLAND, CLUB ELAND

24 **MAASTRICHT, HOLLAND, ZEELAND CLUB**

26 **WIESBADEN, GERMANY, BIG APPLE CLUB**
German TV appearance.

27 **GODDELAU, GERMANY, TANZCLUB**

28-31
MUNICH, GERMANY, BLOW-UP CLUB

SEPTEMBER (EUROPE)

1-7
MUNICH, GERMANY, BLOW-UP CLUB

8-11
PARIS, FRANCE, ILE-DE-FRANCE
All gigs not confirmed.

12 **SHEFFIELD, ENGLAND, PENTHOUSE**

13 **KIRKLEVINGTON, ENGLAND, COUNTRY CLUB**

14 **BISHOP AUCKLAND, ENGLAND, QUEENS HOTEL**

15 **ROMFORD, ENGLAND, KING HALL**

20 **HAVERFORDWEST, ENGLAND, MARKET HALL**

21 **KIDDERMINSTER, ENGLAND, FRANK FREEMAN'S CLUB**

26 **BRISTOL, ENGLAND, COLLEGE OF TECHNOLOGY**

27 **MALVERN, ENGLAND, WINTER GARDEN**
Supported by Caravan.

28 **HARROGATE, ENGLAND, OPERA HOUSE**
Supported by the Nice.

OCTOBER (EUROPE)

3 **PLYMOUTH, ENGLAND, VAN DYKE CLUB**
LONDON, ENGLAND, MARQUEE CLUB
Supported by Time Box. Both dates advertised on separate flyers.

4 **BRISTOL, ENGLAND, UNIVERSITY**
After Yes's gig at Bristol University, Pete Townshend of The Who spoke favourably about Yes' performance to the audience. The Who had loaned Yes their PA system for the show.

9 **ESSEN, GERMANY, GRUGENHALLE, FIRST GERMAN BLUES FESTIVAL**
Fleetwood Mac, Pretty Things, Spooky Tooth, Keef Hartley, Warm Dust, Free, Hard Meat.

11 **NEWCASTLE, ENGLAND, NEWCASTLE UNIVERSITY**

12 **REDCAR, ENGLAND, JAZZ CLUB**

14-15
BELGIUM TV APPEARANCE

17 **ROMFORD, ENGLAND, KINGS HEAD**

18 **CHESTERFIELD, ENGLAND, VICTORIA BALLROOM**

20 **SUNDERLAND, ENGLAND, BAY HOTEL**

22 **BREMEN, GERMANY, BEAT CLUB TV**

24 **NOTTINGHAM, ENGLAND, UNIVERSITY**

25 **CARDIFF, ENGLAND, CARDIFF UNIVERSITY**

27 **TOURNAI, BELGIUM, 'ACTUEL THE FIRST PARIS MUSIC FESTIVAL' ARNOUGIES POP FESTIVAL.**
Pretty Things, Chicken Shack, Sam Apple Pie, Frogeaters, David Allen Group, Keith Tippett Group, Pharoah Sanders, Dave Burrell, John Surman, Clifford Thornton, Sonny Sharrock, Acting Trio.

28 **BRUSSELS, BELGIUM, 140 THEATRE**

30 **LONDON, ENGLAND, MARQUEE CLUB**
Supported by Samson.

31 **SWANSEA, ENGLAND, SWANSEA UNIVERSITY**

NOVEMBER

1 **MANCHESTER, ENGLAND, U.M.I.S.T.**
Supported by Anton Farmer.

2 **LONDON, ENGLAND, LYCEUM 'SUNDAY LYCEUM'**
Supported by Deep Purple, the Divine, Vivian Stanshall, Griffin and the Grope.

LONDON, ENGLAND, MARQUEE CLUB
Supported by Dream Police (Detailed on a Marquee flyer one of these dates for the 2nd must have been cancelled.)

3-4 **PARIS, FRANCE, A PARIS TV SHOW**

FIRST GERMAN BLUES FESTIVAL
KONRAD MALLISON
IN CONJUNCTION WITH
PLANNED ENTERTAINMENTS
PRESENT THE ESSEN POP AND BLUES
AT THE GRUGA - HALLE - ESSEN - W. GERMANY

Thursday, 9th October, 1969 — 7 p.m. till 3 a.m.
FLEETWOOD MAC
PRETTY THINGS • SPOOKY TOOTH • YES
KEEF HARTLEY • WARM DUST • FREE • HARD MEAT

Friday, 10th October, 1969 — 7 p.m. till 3 a.m.
MUDDY WATERS • ALEXIS KORNER
CHAMPION JACK DUPREE
AYNSLEY DUNBAR RETALIATION • TASTE
KEEF HARTLEY
STEAM HAMMER • HARDIN AND YORK • AMON DUUL II

Saturday, 11th October, 1969 — 6 p.m. till 3 a.m.
NICE • PINK FLOYD • DEEP PURPLE
AYNSLEY DUNBAR RETALIATION • TASTE
KEEF HARTLEY
HARDIN AND YORK • AMON DUUL II • CUBY'S BLUES BAND
LIVIN' BLUES • BRAIN BOX

Tickets 30/- per day or 70/- for all three days

For advance tickets send stamped addressed envelope and P.O. to PLANNED ENTERTAINMENTS, 548-560 High Road, Chiswick, W.4
Phone 01-994 3526/7

13 **LONDON, ENGLAND, MARQUEE CLUB**
Supported by Love Sculpture.

14 Conflicting venues have been found for the 14th, one being an appearance in a London television show called *Late Night Line-up* and the other appearance in Newcastle, England at the Newcastle City Hall.

15 **FOLKESTONE, ENGLAND, MARINE PAVILION**

19 **LONDON, ENGLAND, ADVISION STUDIOS RECORDING**

21 **LONDON, ENGLAND, ADVISION STUDIOS RECORDING**

26 **BASLE, SWITZERLAND, BASLE THEATRE**

27 **GENEVA, SWITZERLAND, TV SHOW**
(Day)
BERNE, SWITZERLAND, CHIKITO CLUB
(Evening)

28 **GERLAFINGEN, SWITZERLAND, GRUNAU RESTAURANT**

29 **MONTREUX, SWITZERLAND, THE CASINO**

30 **LONDON, ENGLAND, ROUNDHOUSE 'POLYTECHNIC ARTS FESTIVAL'**
Supported by Manfred Mann, Chapter III, Deep Purple, Brian Auger Trinity, Atomic Rooster, Free, Village and Liverpool Scene. There is speculation that they may have also played at the Locamo Rex Cinema as well.

DECEMBER (EUROPE)

1 **ZURICH, SWITZERLAND, TV SPECIAL**

2 **MONTREUX, SWITZERLAND, THE CASINO**

5 **STOKE, ENGLAND, STOKE-ON-TRENT ART COLLEGE**

6 **WESTON -SUPER-MARE, ENGLAND, WINTER GARDENS**

7 **CROYDON, ENGLAND, GREYHOUND**
Supported by Stray.

9 **HARROWFIELD, ENGLAND, YOUTH CENTRE**
Supported by Professor Trange and a Disco.

11 **LEICESTER, ENGLAND, LEICESTER POLYTECHNIC**
Supported by Lucas & the Mike Cotton Sound, Zoot Money, Medicine Head and a Disco.

12 **NEWPORT, ENGLAND, IN-PLACE**

13 **LONDON, ENGLAND, IMPERIAL COLLEGE**

14 **REDCAR, ENGLAND, JAZZ CLUB**

18 **LONDON, ENGLAND, ADVISION STUDIOS RECORDING**

19 **HARROWFIELD, ENGLAND, YOUTH CENTRE**

21 **SHEFFIELD, ENGLAND, KINGSTONE HOTEL**
Supported by Gracious.

24 **SOUTHALL, ENGLAND, NORTH COTE ARMS**
Supported by Farx Club and Nexus.

26 **LONDON, ENGLAND, MARQUEE CLUB**
Supported by Jon Hendricks and Man.

27 **KIRKLEVINGTON, ENGLAND, COUNTRY CLUB**

28 **BIRMINGHAM, ENGLAND, MOTHER'S**

1970

JANUARY (EUROPE)

5-6 **LONDON, ENGLAND, ADVISION STUDIOS RECORDING**

8 **LONDON, ENGLAND, ADVISION STUDIOS RECORDING**

10-11 **PARIS, FRANCE, OLYMPIA**

13-14 **LONDON, ENGLAND, ADVISION STUDIOS RECORDING**

16 **LONDON, ENGLAND, ADVISION STUDIOS RECORDING**

17 **BRADFORD, ENGLAND, UNIVERSITY**

19 **LONDON, ENGLAND, BBC STUDIOS**
Recording for Dave Lee Travis radio show.

23 **STOKE-ON-TRENT, ENGLAND, THE KINGS HALL**

24 **SOUTHAMPTON, ENGLAND, SOUTHAMPTON UNIVERSITY**

25 **CROYDON, ENGLAND, GREYHOUND**

27 **LLANELLI, WALES, GLEN BALLROOM**

29 **BOSTON, ENGLAND, STARLIGHT ROOM**

31 **UXBRIDGE, ENGLAND, BRUNEL UNIVERSITY**
Supported by Liverpool Scene.

FEBRUARY (EUROPE)

1 **SUNDERLAND, ENGLAND, EMPIRE THEATRE**
Supported by the Nice.

7 **LONDON, ENGLAND, FESTIVAL HALL**
Supported by the Nice.

8 **OXFORD, ENGLAND, POLYTECHNIC**
Supported by the Nice.

14 **CANTERBURY, ENGLAND, UNIVERSITY OF KENT**

19 **DENMARK, COPENHAGEN, REVOLUTION**
Supported by Small Faces and the Edgar Broughton Band.

20 **GOTHENBURG, SWEDEN, CUE CLUB**
Supported by Small Faces and the Edgar Broughton Band.

21 **STOCKHOLM, SWEDEN, THE UNIVERSITY**
Supported by Small Faces and the Edgar Broughton Band.

22 **OSLO, NORWAY, CLUB SEREN**
Supported by Small Faces and the Edgar Broughton Band.

23 **BREMEN, GERMANY, BEAT CLUB TV**

24 **BREMEN, GERMANY, BEAT CLUB**
Supported by Small Faces and the Edgar Broughton Band.

27 **PLYMOUTH, ENGLAND, VAN DYKE CLUB**

28 **LONDON, ENGLAND, IMPERIAL, COLLEGE**
Supported by Web.

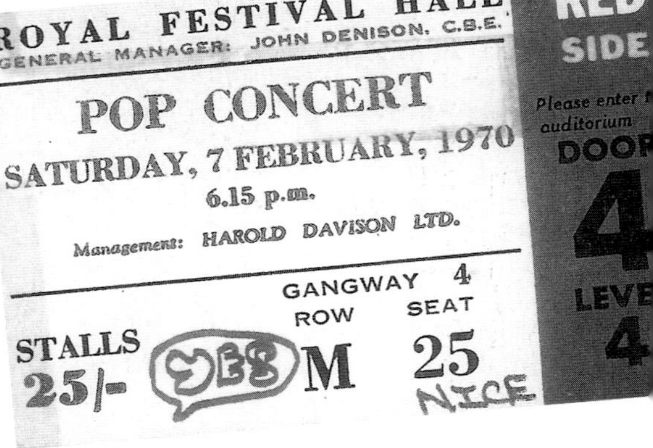

MARCH (EUROPE)

6 **BINGLEY, ENGLAND, YORKSHIRE COLLEGE**

7 **LEEDS, ENGLAND, UNIVERSITY OF LEEDS**

9 **DARLINGTON, ENGLAND, CIVIC THEATRE**

16 **DUSSELDORF, GERMANY, MUSIC FESTIVAL**
Supported by Hardin & York.

17 **LONDON, ENGLAND, BBC STUDIOS**
Sunday show sessions.

12 **LONDON, ENGLAND, BBC STUDIOS**
Studio recording for John Peel's Sunday radio show.

13 **GLOUCESTER, ENGLAND, GUILDHALL**
Supported by Fresh.

14 **CROYDON, ENGLAND, TECHNICAL COLLEGE**
Supported by Easy Leaf, Dwarf, a disco and lights.

20 **SALFORD, ENGLAND, UNIVERSITY**

21-22 **LONDON, ENGLAND, QUEEN ELIZABETH HALL**
Supported by Royal College of Music Youth Orchestra.

24 **LONDON, ENGLAND, DISCO TWO TV SHOW**

28 **SALISBURY, ENGLAND, ALEX DISCO CLUB**
Supported by the New Era Jazz Band and a disco.

29 **BIRMINGHAM, ENGLAND, MOTHER'S**

30 **BARNSTAPLE, ENGLAND, QUEEN'S HALL**

31 **BRUSSELS, BELGIUM, TV SHOW**

APRIL

1 **BRUSSELS, BELGIUM, TV SHOW**

3 **COLOGNE, GERMANY, SPORTSHALLE**

4 **ERLINGEN, GERMANY, ERLINGEN UNIVERSITY**

5 **MAINSCHAFF, GERMANY, MAINHALLE**
(Day and Evening shows)

7 **LONDON, ENGLAND, BBC RADIO SESSIONS**
For the Mike Harding *Sounds Of The 70s* Show.

10 **LONDON, ENGLAND, MARQUEE CLUB**
Supported by Slade & Trevor Billmuss.

11 **LONDON, ENGLAND, BBC TV *NOT ONLY BUT ALSO* RECORDING**

14 **SURBITON, ENGLAND, ASSEMBLY ROOM**
Supported by Julian Treatment.

16 **WEYMOUTH, ENGLAND, WEYMOUTH PAVILION**

17 **SURBITON, ENGLAND, POPERAMA DEVIZES**

18 **LUTON, ENGLAND, LUTON COLLEGE**
Supported by Mighty Baby and Tiny Clanger. Peter Banks' final Yes gig. All planned gigs for the next two months were cancelled due to the lack of a guitarist.

JULY

17 **LONDON, ENGLAND, LYCEUM**
Steve Howe's first Yes gig. Supported by Black Sabbath, Uriah Heep, Clark Hutchinson and Big Lil.

18 **BIRMINGHAM, ENGLAND, MOTHER'S**

19 **REDCAR, ENGLAND, JAZZ CLUB**

26 **CROYDON, ENGLAND, GREYHOUND**

31 **PLYMOUTH, ENGLAND, VAN DYKE CLUB**

AUGUST

2 **CROYDON, ENGLAND, GREYHOUND**
Supported by Supertramp.

9 **PLUMPTON, ENGLAND, THE 10th NATIONAL JAZZ, POP, BALLADS & BLUES FESTIVAL**
Supported by Deep Purple, John Hiseman's, Colosseum, Juicy Lucy, Chris Barber, Caravan, Audience, Fat Mattress, Hard Meat, Van Der Graaf Generator, Wishbone Ash, Da Da & Trevor Billmuss.

14 **LEYTONSTONE, ENGLAND, CHEZ CLUB**

16 **KRUMLIN, BARKISLAND, HALIFAX ENGLAND, - THE YORKSHIRE FOLK, BLUES & JAZZ FESTIVAL**
Also on the large bill: Ginger Baker's Airforce, Pink Floyd, Mungo Jerry, Taste, Edgar Broughton, Quintessence, Steamhammer, Mike Westbrook, Concert Orchestra, National Head Band, Their Heavy Friends, Greatest Show On Earth, Jan Dukes De Grey and Choir.

18 **LONDON, ENGLAND, MARQUEE CLUB**

21 **BARNSTAPLE, ENGLAND, MAGIC CIRCUS**

22 **DAGENHAM, ENGLAND, VILLAGE**
Supported by Nosher Brown.

29 **LINCOLN, ENGLAND, BASTON BAR BQ**

31 **REDCAR, ENGLAND, JAZZ CLUB**

SEPTEMBER

1-4 **BELGIUM, FILMING**

5 **HUY, BELGIUM, HUY FESTIVAL**

6 **DORTMUND, GERMANY, FANTASIO**

10 **SWANSEA, WALES, BRARNWYGH TOWN HALL**

11 **SWANSESA, WALES, TOWN HALL**

12 **COLCHESTER, ENGLAND, CORN EXCHANGE**

18 **ELTHAM, ENGLAND, AVERY HILL COLLEGE**
Supported by Uriah Heep, Information, and Amazing Grace.

19 **BISHOPS STORTFORD, ENGLAND, RHODES CENTRE**
Supported by Gin.

20 **NOTTINGHAM, ENGLAND, BOAT CLUB**

22 **BIRMINGHAM, ENGLAND, MAYFAIR ROOMS**

23 **CARDIFF, WALES, BARRY MEMORIAL HALL**
Supported by Gypsy Universe.

26 **MARGATE, ENGLAND, DREAMLAND**

27 **CROYDON, ENGLAND, GREYHOUND**

28 **ABERYSTWYTH, WALES, UNIVERSITY OF SOUTH WALES**

OCTOBER

1 **SCARBOROUGH, ENGLAND, SCENE ONE AND TWO**

2 **LEICESTERSHIRE, ENGLAND, LOUGHBOROUGH UNIVERSITY**
Supported by Mayfields Mule and Purple Gang.

3 **WATFORD, ENGLAND, COLLEGE OF TECHNOLOGY**
Supported by Band of Roadies.

9 **STRATFORD, ENGLAND, WEST HAM COLLEGE**
Supported by Noir.

10 **LONDON, ENGLAND, QUEEN MARY, COLLEGE**
Supported by Edgar Broughton Band and Mandrake.

15 **DUNDEE, SCOTLAND, DUNDEE UNIVERSITY**

16 **NEWCASTLE, ENGLAND, CITY HALL**

17 **MALVERN, ENGLAND, WINTER GARDENS**
Supported by the Keef Hartley Band.

20 **LONDON, ENGLAND, BBC STUDIOS**
Recording for the *Sounds of the 70s* show by Mike Harding.

21 **LONDON, ENGLAND, ADVISION STUDIOS RECORDING**

23 **LEEDS, ENGLAND, LEEDS POLYTECHNIC**
Supported by Curved Air.

24 **MANCHESTER, ENGLAND, MANCHESTER UNIVERSITY**

26 **ROMFORD, ENGLAND, KING'S HEAD**
Supported by Canary Hunt.

27-29
LONDON, ENGLAND, ADVISION STUDIOS RECORDING

30 **GUILDFORD, ENGLAND, SURREY UNIVERSITY**

31 **LONDON, ENGLAND, QUEEN ELIZABETH HALL**
Supported by Da Da.

NOVEMBER (EUROPE)

2-3 **DUNSTABLE, ENGLAND, CIVIC HALL**
The Dunstable gig is cancelled so Yes work in Advision Studios, London.

5-6 **BERNE, SWITZERLAND, CHIKITO CLUB**

7 **LIVERPOOL, ENGLAND, LIVERPOOL UNIVERSITY**

10 **MUNICH, GERMANY, BLOW-UP CLUB**

12 **LONDON, ENGLAND, ADVISION STUDIOS**

13 **LONDON, ENGLAND, JOHN CASS COLLEGE**
Supported by Jan Dukes and De Grey.

14 **BRADFORD, ENGLAND, BRADFORD UNIVERSITY**

16-19
LONDON, ENGLAND, ADVISION STUDIOS

20 **LANCASTER, ENGLAND, LANCASTER POLYTECHNIC**

21 **OXFORD, ENGLAND, OXFORD POLYTECHNIC**

22 **PLYMOUTH, ENGLAND, VAN DYKE CLUB**
Supported by Clark Hutchinson.

24 **BRADFORD, ENGLAND, BRADFORD UNIVERSITY**
(Cancelled)

25 **CAMBRIDGE, ENGLAND, CORN EXCHANGE**

27 **SOUTHEND, ENGLAND, TECHNICAL COLLEGE**
Supported by Surly Bird and Tank.

28 **BOSTON, ENGLAND, STARLIGHT ROOM**
Supported by Jan Dukes and De Grey.

DECEMBER

1 **LONDON, ENGLAND, MARQUEE CLUB**
(Cancelled)

2 **MANCHESTER, ENGLAND, COLLEGE OF ART**
(Cancelled)

3 **LONDON, ENGLAND, ADVISION STUDIOS**

4 **LANCASTER, ENGLAND, LANCASTER UNIVERSITY**
The Lancaster gig is cancelled so Yes work in Advision Studios, London.

5 **LIVERPOOL, ENGLAND, LIVERPOOL STADIUM**
The Liverpool gig is cancelled so Yes work in Advision Studios, London.

7 **LONDON, ENGLAND, ADVISION STUDIOS**

8 **NEWCASTLE, ENGLAND, CITY HALL**
Supported by Hardin & York.

9 **HULL, ENGLAND, HULL UNIVERSITY**
Supported by the Strawbs.

10 **MIDDLESBOROUGH, ENGLAND, TEESSIDE POLYTECHNIC**

11 **WARRINGTON, ENGLAND, PADDGATE COLLEGE**

12 **LONDON, ENGLAND, ADVISION STUDIOS**

13 **BROMLEY, ENGLAND, NEW THEATRE**
Supported by Trader Horne, the show was cancelled, Yes moved into Advision Studios in London for a rehearsal and recording session.

14 **DUNSTABLE, ENGLAND, DUNSTABLE CIVIC HALL**

18 **LONDON, ENGLAND, LYCEUM**
Yes Xmas Party with Da Da, Clark Hutchinson and Blitzkrieg. Yes were reportedly playing their set at 2am!

19 **FOLKESTONE, ENGLAND, HEATHCLIFF HALL**

20 **CLEETHORPES, ENGLAND, WINTER GARDENS**

22 **SHREWSBURY, ENGLAND, MUSIC HALL**

26 **BRIGHTON, ENGLAND, THE BIG APPLE**
Cancelled, billed as THE YES! with an exclamation mark.

1971

JANUARY (EUROPE)

Supported by Iron Butterfly.
At the insistence of Yes, all ticket prices for the forthcoming tour with Iron Butterfly were priced at 10s (50p/$1).

3 **CROYDON, ENGLAND, GREYHOUND**

8 **EINDHOVEN, NETHERLANDS, STADSTNOUWBURG**

9 **AMSTERDAM, NETHERLANDS, GEBOUW**

10 **ROTTERDAM, HOLLAND, DOELEN**

13 **LONDON, ENGLAND, THE ROYAL ALBERT HALL**
Supported by Iron Butterfly and Da Da.

14 **NEWCASTLE, ENGLAND, NEWCASTLE CITY HALL**
Supported by Iron Butterfly and Da Da.

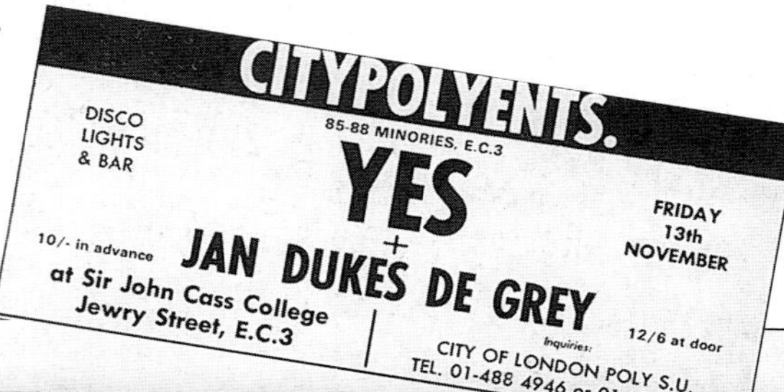

Page 22—MELODY MAKER, November 7, 1970

CAUGHT IN THE ACT

Oh, Yes..

INCREDIBLE Yes! One of the finest bands in Britain marched on to maturity with two splendid shows at London's Queen Elizabeth Hall on Saturday.

After the changes that have taken place in the band, some Yes fans felt that the band might be in danger of losing some of their established identity. Not so. With Steve Howe, Yes have reached a new peak.

The guitarist proved something of a show stealer with his unaccompanied acoustic tour de force, "The Clap." He ranged over a whole gamut of country rag licks and it was done with such audacious speed and aplomb — he gained an ovation.

But that was only part of the story. Yes are such a musical band they can entertain on many levels. And there are not many bands one could watch twice on the same evening and enjoy both.

The second show was however, the better. "Astral Traveller" long a Yes favourite opened followed by John Anderson's beautiful new work "Yours Is No Disgrace." "All Good People" featured Steve's mandolin and the vocal choir of Anderson, Howe and Squire.

Chris Squire and Steve took part in a phenomenal battle of the bass guitars in what Chris called "A Bass Odyssy" showing how the rock bass can become an exciting lead instrument.

The climax of the show was their dramatic arrangement of Simon and Garfunkel's "America" which opened with a strangely "1930 in Berlin" theme played by Tony Kay on organ and Steve, leading in to John's simple but emotive vocal.

Bill Bruford's drumming was the proverbial tower of strength throughout and he lead into the final encore with a tom tom and cymbals cross rhythm reminiscent of Art Blakey.

Opening each show of their tour are Da Da, a band much improved on their initial showing, who feature a heavy brass front line, the vocal talents of Elkie Brooks and new singer Robert Palmer. — CHRIS WELCH.

YES: a new peak

The Return of
A Midnight Court
&
LEGS LARRY SMITH
at
YES' XMAS PARTY
with
DA DA
CLARK HUTCHINSON
BLITZKREIG
LYCEUM, STRAND
FRIDAY, DECEMBER 18th
All-nighter, midnight till dawn
Tickets 20/- from Lyceum & Computicket

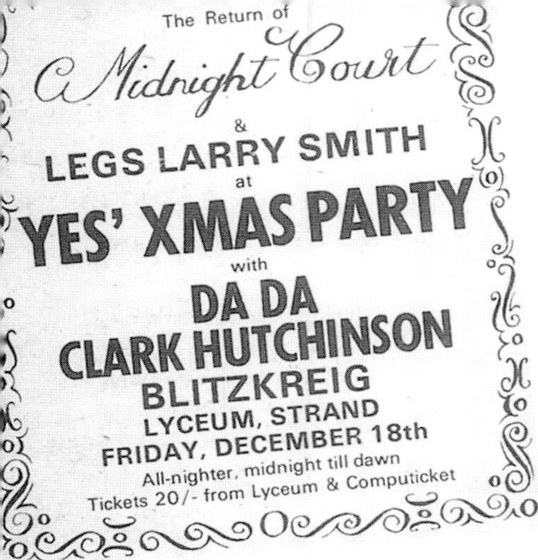

15 **LANCASTER, ENGLAND, LANCASTER UNIVERSITY**
Supported by Iron Butterfly and Da Da.

16 **SOUTHSEA, ENGLAND, PORTSMOUTH POLYTECHNIC**
Supported by Iron Butterfly and Da Da.

17 **BRISTOL, ENGLAND, COLSTON HALL**
Supported by Iron Butterfly and Da Da.

18 **GLASGOW, SCOTLAND, GREENS PLAYHOUSE**

19 **BIRMINGHAM, ENGLAND, MOTHER'S**

20 **LONDON, ENGLAND, BBC TV DISCO 2**

21 **SOUTHAMPTON, ENGLAND, GUILDHALL**

23 **AARHUS, DENMARK, VEJLBY RISKUVHALLEN DEN**

24 **GOTHENBURG, SWEDEN, GOTEBORGS CONCERT HALL**

25 **COPENHAGEN, DENMARK, FALKENER THEATRE CENTRE**

28 **BREMEN, GERMANY**
(Venue unknown, possibly cancelled)

29 **LILLE, FRANCE**
(Venue unknown, possibly cancelled)

30 **LYONS, FRANCE**
(Venue unknown, possibly cancelled)

31 **BRUSSELS, BELGIUM**
(Venue unknown, possibly cancelled)

FEBRUARY (EUROPE)

1-2 **PARIS, FRANCE, PALAIS DES SPORTS**
Supported By Iron Butterfly, Soft Machine, Kevin Ayers & Gong. (Cancelled due to riots!)

4 **BORDEAUX, FRANCE, ALHAMBRA THEATRE**

5 **BARNSTAPLE, ENGLAND, QUEENS HALL**

6 **CARDIFF, WALES, LLANDAFF TECHNICAL COLLEGE**
(Cancelled)

7 **REDCAR, ENGLAND, JAZZ CLUB**
(Cancelled due to a car crash)

8 **LIEGE, FRANCE**
(Cancelled)

9 **BRUSSELS, BELGIUM**
(Cancelled)

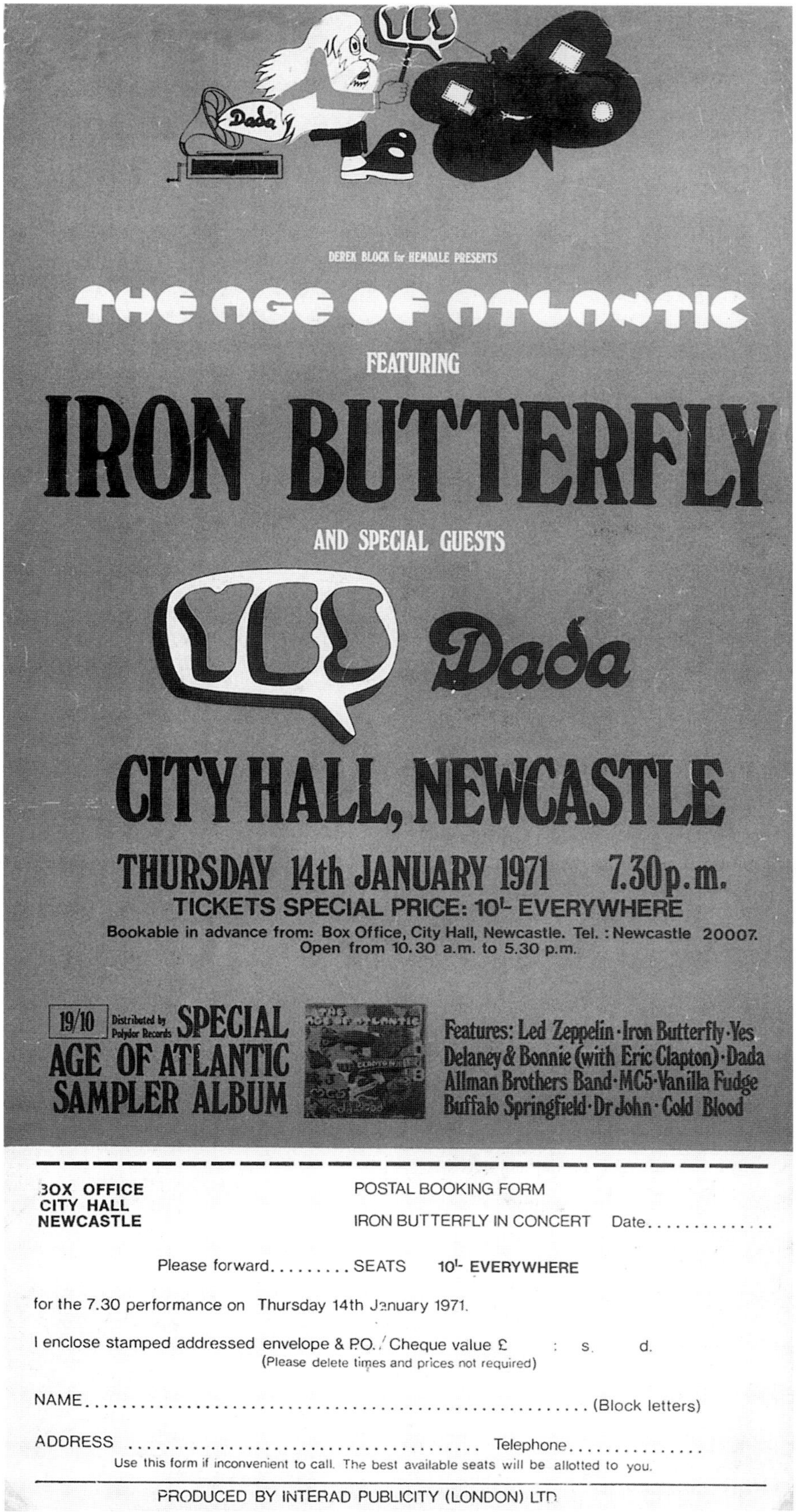
YES
Dada
DEREK BLOCK for HEMDALE PRESENTS
THE AGE OF ATLANTIC
FEATURING
IRON BUTTERFLY
AND SPECIAL GUESTS
YES Dada
CITY HALL, NEWCASTLE
THURSDAY 14th JANUARY 1971 7.30p.m.
TICKETS SPECIAL PRICE: 10/- EVERYWHERE
Bookable in advance from: Box Office, City Hall, Newcastle. Tel.: Newcastle 20007.
Open from 10.30 a.m. to 5.30 p.m.
19/10 Distributed by Polydor Records SPECIAL AGE OF ATLANTIC SAMPLER ALBUM
Features: Led Zeppelin · Iron Butterfly · Yes Delaney & Bonnie (with Eric Clapton) · Dada Allman Brothers Band · MC5 · Vanilla Fudge Buffalo Springfield · Dr John · Cold Blood
BOX OFFICE CITY HALL NEWCASTLE
POSTAL BOOKING FORM
IRON BUTTERFLY IN CONCERT Date..............
Please forward......... SEATS 10/- EVERYWHERE
for the 7.30 performance on Thursday 14th January 1971.
I enclose stamped addressed envelope & P.O./Cheque value £ : s. d.
(Please delete times and prices not required)
NAME.. (Block letters)
ADDRESS .... Telephone...............
Use this form if inconvenient to call. The best available seats will be allotted to you.
PRODUCED BY INTERAD PUBLICITY (LONDON) LTD

12 LONDON, ENGLAND, SCHOOL OF ECONOMICS
Supported by the Tremeloes, Southern Comfort, Alan Bown & Adge Cutler.

13 LONDON, ENGLAND, HOLBORN THEATRE LSE

19 LEEDS, ENGLAND, LEEDS UNIVERSITY

20 KINGSTON, ENGLAND, POLYTECHNIC COLLEGE
Supported by Queen.

27 DAGENHAM, ENGLAND, ROUNDHOUSE

MARCH (EUROPE)

4 LIVERPOOL, ENGLAND, LIVERPOOL STADIUM
Supported by Jonathan Swift.

5 DONCASTER, ENGLAND, TOP RANK BALLROOM
Supported by Egg.

6 BRIGHTON, ENGLAND, THE BIG APPLE
Supported by Wicked Nun.

7 REDCAR, ENGLAND, JAZZ CLUB

9 BIRMINGHAM, ENGLAND, TOWN HALL
Supported by Jonathan Swift.

10 BOURNEMOUTH, ENGLAND, WINTER GARDENS
Supported by Jonathan Swift.

12 CARDIFF, WALES, LLANDAFF COLLEGE
Supported by Jonathan Swift.

14 BLACKBURN, ENGLAND, ST. GEORGE'S HALL
Supported by Jonathan Swift.

15 GUILDFORD, ENGLAND, CIVIC HALL
Supported by Jonathan Swift.

16 NOTTINGHAM, ENGLAND, ALBERT HALL
Supported by Jonathan Swift.

18 BELFAST, NORTHERN IRELAND, BELFAST UNIVERSITY

19 STIRLING, SCOTLAND, STIRLING UNIVERSITY

20 AVIEMORE, SCOTLAND, SKI CENTRE

21 DUNFERMLINE, SCOTLAND, KINEMA

22 GLASGOW, SCOTLAND, CITY HALL

DONCASTER JOINT STUDENTS' COMMITTEE
(Colleges of Technology and Education)
present on Friday, March 5, 8 p.m.-2 a.m.
YES · IF
EGG
TOP RANK SUITE, DONCASTER
Booked by Cabin Agency, 01-749 1121 (4 lines)
April 16: PINK FLOYD

27-28 BERLIN, GERMANY, ARTS FESTIVAL, DEUTSCHLANDHALLE

30 WOLVERHAMPTON, ENGLAND, CITY HALL

31 LONDON, ENGLAND, BBC TV CENTRE
For the only live appearance of Yes on the famous UK music show *Top Of the Pops*. Featured in the album slot Yes played a shortened version of Yours Is No Disgrace.

APRIL

4 HEMEL HEMPSTEAD, ENGLAND, HEMPSTEAD PAVILION

6 MANCHESTER, ENGLAND, MANCHESTER FREE TRADE HALL
Supported by Lancaster and Highly Inflammable.

8 LEEDS, ENGLAND, TOWN HALL
Supported by Lancaster and Highly Inflammable.

10 SURBITON, ENGLAND, CORN EXCHANGE
Another venue with the same gig date was also advertised, being at the Poperama Devizes.

12 LONDON, ENGLAND, BBC STUDIOS
To record *Sounds of the 70s* with Alan Black.

16 STUTTGART, GERMANY, BOBLINGEN SPORTSHALLE

17 SAARBRUCKEN, GERMANY, SAARLANDHALLE

18 HAMBURG, GERMANY, MUSIKHALLE

19 BREMEN, GERMANY, BEAT CLUB

24 NELSON, ENGLAND, IMPERIAL

25 LONDON, ENGLAND, CHALK FARM ROUNDHOUSE
Camden Arts Festival along with many other acts.

30 LUTON, ENGLAND, RECREATION CENTRE
Supported by Lancaster.

CIVIC HALL
WOLVERHAMPTON
YES
STALLS
70p
A 3
Tues. Mar. 30
at 7.45 p.m.
NO MONEY BE REFUNDED
TO BE RETAINED

MAY

1 DAGENHAM, ENGLAND, POLYTECHNIC COLLEGE
Supported by Satisfaction.

2 STOKE, ENGLAND, TRENTHAM GARDENS

7 CHATHAM, ENGLAND, CENTRAL HALL
Supported by the Mick Abraham Band.

8 OXFORD, ENGLAND, TOWN HALL
Supported by the Mick Abraham Band.

9 ROME, ITALY, BRANCACCIO

10 MILAN, ITALY, TEATRO CENTRAL LYRICO

11 ROME, ITALY, TEATRO DI BRANCACCIO DI ROMA

14 BIRMINGHAM, ENGLAND, BIRMINGHAM UNIVERSITY

15 NORWICH, ENGLAND, LADS CLUB
Supported by Groundhogs and Da Da.

16 LEICESTER, ENGLAND, DE MONTFORT HALL

21 STRATHCLYDE, SCOTLAND, GLASGOW UNIVERSITY

22 MANCHESTER, ENGLAND, MANCHESTER UNIVERSITY

23 HARROGATE, ENGLAND, OPERA HOUSE

29 EXETER, ENGLAND, EXETER COLLEGE
(Cancelled)
Yes announce tour dates for South America, Mexico City 31 May – 5 June, a nine-day trip to Australia and Japan. All of which are later cancelled due to other commitments.

JUNE (GERMANY & USA)

4 CLACTON, ENGLAND, PRINCESS THEATRE
(Cancelled)

5 BERLIN, GERMANY, SPORTPALAST
(Cancelled)

18 SOUTHPORT, ENGLAND, FLORAL HALL
(Cancelled)

26 SHEFFIELD, ENGLAND, SHEFFIELD UNIVERSITY
(Cancelled)

YES' FIRST NORTH AMERICAN TOUR

24 EDMONTON, CANADA, EDMONTON GARDENS
First gig outside of Europe. Supported by Jethro Tull.

25 VANCOUVER, CANADA, P – M – E , COLISEUM
Supported by Jethro Tull.

26 SEATTLE, WASHINGTON, SEATTLE COLISEUM
Supported by Jethro Tull.

27 SACRAMENTO, CALIFORNIA, MEMORIAL AUDITORIUM

28-29
LOS ANGELES, CALIFORNIA, WHISKY A GO GO
Supported by Jethro Tull, there is speculation that they might actually have played at Kansas City Auditorium.

30 OKLAHOMA CITY, OKLAHOMA, STATE FAIRGROUNDS
Supported by Jethro Tull.

31 BOSTON, MASSACHUSETTS, STARLIGHT ROOM
(Cancelled)

JULY (USA)

1 SAN ANTONIO, TEXAS, MUNICIPAL AUDITORIUM
Supported by Jethro Tull.

2 DALLAS, TEXAS, MEMORIAL COLISEUM
Supported by Jethro Tull.

3 HOUSTON, TEXAS, HOUSTON COLISEUM
Supported by Jethro Tull.

4 NEW ORLEANS, LOUISIANA, THE WAREHOUSE
Supported By Jethro Tull.

5 INDIANAPOLIS, INDIANA, NATIONAL GUARD ARMOURY

6 INDIANAPOLIS, INDIANA, ROBERTS STADIUM

7 DE LAND, FLORIDA, SPORTS STADIUM

8 HAMPTON BEACH, NEW HAMPSHIRE, THE BEACH CASINO
Supported by Jethro Tull.

9 PHILADELPHIA, PENNSYLVANIA, CONVENTION CTR
Supported by Jethro Tull. Jon, Steve and Bill record a ten minute radio interview with DJ Ed Skiaky.

10 ASBURY PARK, NEW JERSEY, CONVENTION HALL

11 ALEXANDRIA BAY, N.Y. ROLLER RINK

13 OXON HILL, MARYLAND (Venue unknown)

14-15
PORTCHESTER, NEW YORK, N.Y. CAPITOL THEATRE

16-17
DETROIT, MICHIGAN, EASTTOWN THEATRE

19 OTTAWA, CANADA, AUDITORIUM

23 BRONX, NEW YORK, N.Y. GAELIC PARK

24 NEW HAVEN, CONNECTICUT, YALE BOW
Supported by Grand Funk Railroad.

31 LONDON, ENGLAND CRYSTAL PALACE GARDEN PARTY II
On the bill with Elton John and four other acts in this outdoor arena with a lake on front of it. Tony Kaye's final gig with the band, until his return some 13 years later.

AUGUST

11-13 LONDON, ENGLAND, ADVISION STUDIOS RECORDING

16-17
LONDON, ENGLAND, ADVISION STUDIOS RECORDING

20 LONDON, ENGLAND, ADVISION STUDIOS RECORDING

23-25
LONDON, ENGLAND, ADVISION STUDIOS RECORDING

27-29
LONDON, ENGLAND, ADVISION STUDIOS RECORDING

SEPTEMBER

3-5 LONDON, ENGLAND, ADVISION STUDIOS

24 BARNSTAPLE, ENGLAND, QUEENS HALL

25 DEVIZES, ENGLAND, TOWN HALL

30 LEICESTER, ENGLAND, DE MONTFORD HALL
Supported by Jonathan Swift.

OCTOBER

Supported by Jonathan Swift.

1 MANCHESTER, ENGLAND, FREE TRADE HALL

2 BRADFORD, ENGLAND, ST. GEORGE'S HALL

3 HEMEL HEMPSTEAD, ENGLAND, PAVILION

4 ABERDEEN, SCOTLAND, MUSIC HALL

6 GLASGOW, SCOTLAND, GREENS PLAYHOUSE

8 LONDON, ENGLAND, ROYAL FESTIVAL HALL

9 EDINBURGH, SCOTLAND, EMPIRE THEATRE
Cancelled due to non-arrival of band's equipment, the fans are offered a free poster for their trouble.

10 DUNDEE, SCOTLAND, CAIRED HALL

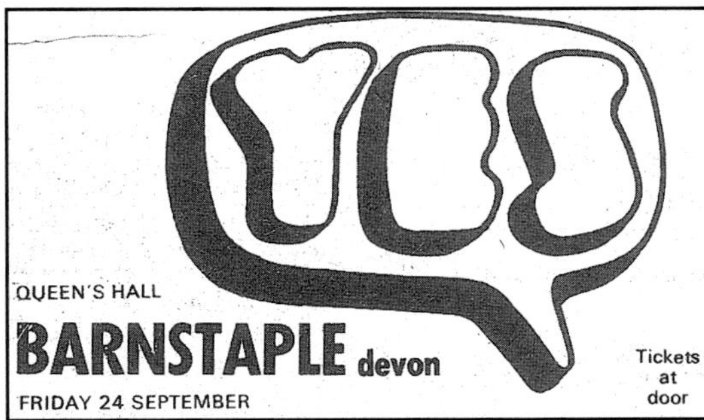

11 WOLVERHAMPTON, ENGLAND, CIVIC HALL

12 BRISTOL, ENGLAND, COLSTON HALL

13 SHEFFIELD, ENGLAND, CITY HALL

15 STOCKTON, ENGLAND, A.B.C

16 NEWCASTLE, ENGLAND, CITY HALL

17 STOKE , ENGLAND, TRENTHAM GARDENS

18 BIRMINGHAM, ENGLAND, TOWN HALL

21 COVENTRY, ENGLAND, WARWICK UNIVERSITY

22 LEEDS, ENGLAND, LEEDS UNIVERSITY

23 EDINBURGH, SCOTLAND EMPIRE THEATRE

25 CHATHAM, ENGLAND, CENTRAL HALL

26 LIVERPOOL, ENGLAND, LIVERPOOL STADIUM

28 SOUTHAMPTON, ENGLAND, GUILD HALL

31 AMSTERDAM, HOLLAND, CONCERTGEBOUW

NOVEMBER (USA)

2 OAKLAND, CALIFORNIA, COLISEUM
Cancelled. PA equipment is stolen shortly after the band's tour commences.

3 LOS ANGELES, CALIFORNIA, WHISKY A GO GO
Supported by Ten Years and Mary Wells.

YES CANCEL

YES had to cancel their sell-out midnight concert at the Empire Theatre, Edinburgh, last Saturday (9), when their equipment failed to turn up — but they have promised to return to the same theatre on Saturday, October 23!

Said Yes's management: "We want to kill rumours that Yes failed to turn up! They did — but a fantastic run of bad luck saw the van carrying four tons of equipment from the Royal Festival Hall the night before, break down at Birmingham."

"Incredibly — so did two more sent to replace it. This is the first time that Yes have failed to appear for a gig on schedule, since they formed three years ago."

Two thousand fans can either hold on to their tickets, or have their money refunded. Yes want to "keep face" and promise that every customer on October 23, will receive a free poster.

4-7 **LOS ANGELES, CALIFORNIA, WHISKY A GO GO**
Supported by Ten Years After.

8 **SAN FRANCISCO, CALIFORNIA, CALIFORNIA WINTERLAND**
Supported by Ten Years After.

9 **SAN DIEGO, CALIFORNIA, SPORTS, COLISEUM**

10 **INGLEWOOD, CALIFORNIA, GREAT WESTERN FORUM**

11 **HOLLYWOOD, CALIFORNIA, FORUM**
Supported by Ten Years After and the J. Geils Band.

12 **PHILADELPHIA, PENNSYLVANIA, THE SPECTRUM ARENA**

13 **PHILADELPHIA, PENNSYLVANIA, THE SPECTRUM ARENA**
Supported by Emerson Lake and Palmer.

14 **CHICAGO, ILLINOIS, ILLINOIS AMPHITHEATRE**
Supported by Emerson Lake and Palmer.

15-16
DETROIT, MICHIGAN, EASTTOWN THEATRE

17 **ELYRIA, OHIO, ELYRIA CATHOLIC HIGH SCHOOL**

19 **WILLIAMSBURG, VIRGINIA, WILLIAM MARY COLLEGE**

20 **DURHAM, NORTH CAROLINA, DUKE UNIVERSITY**

21 **BALTIMORE, MARYLAND (Venue unknown)**

22 **ATLANTA, GEORGIA, MUNICIPAL AUDITORIUM**
Supported by Emerson Lake and Palmer.

23 **DE LAND, FLORIDA, STETSON UNIVERSITY - THE PIT**

24-25
NEW YORK, N.Y., ACADEMY OF MUSIC
Supported by King Crimson.

26 **YORKTOWN, N.Y., STRUTKERS HIGH SCHOOL**

27 **NEW YORK, N.Y., STATEN, RITZ THEATRE**

28 **NEW YORK, N.Y., STONY BROOK, S.U.N.Y.**

30 **NEW YORK, N.Y., GENESIO COLLEGE**

DECEMBER (USA)

Steve Howe's guitar is destroyed in transit, he borrows a guitar from a student at a gig to perform 'Clap'.

1 **HARTFORD, CONNECTICUT, WATERBURY PALACE THEATRE**

2 **CINCINNATI, OHIO, OHIO REFLECTION**

3 **AKRON, OHIO, CIVIC THEATRE**

4 **GETTYSBURG, PENNSYLVANIA, GETTYSBURG COLLEGE**

5 **NEW YORK, N.Y., PLATTSBURG, S.U.N.Y.**

9 **RHODE ISLAND, N.Y., SMITHFIELD, BRYANT COLLEGE GYM**
Supported by the Blues Project.

10 **CARLISLE, PENNSYLVANIA, PENN DICKINSON COLLEGE**

11 **GARDEN CITY, NEW YORK, N.Y. NASSAU COLLEGE**

12 **NEWARK, NEW JERSEY, STATE COLLEGE**

14 **BOSTON, MASSACHUSETTS, OPRPHLEUM THEATRE**

15 **CLEVELAND, OHIO, ALLEN THEATRE**

16 **PITTSBURG, PENNSYLVANIA, SYRIA MASQUE**

17 **SKADY, GAITHESBURG, GROVE MUSIC FAIR**

18 **NEW ORLEANS, LOUISIANA, LOUISIANA WAREHOUSE**

Yes for Rainbow

YES are to make their first British concert appearances of 1972 at London's new Rainbow Theatre on January 14 and 15 . . . and these are to be the group's only shows in this country before late April, when a ten day British concert tour is planned.

An appearance at the Rainbow on December 24 will not now take place.

The group left for their second American tour on Tuesday, and return on December 12. They will take a month's holiday prior to the Rainbow concerts.

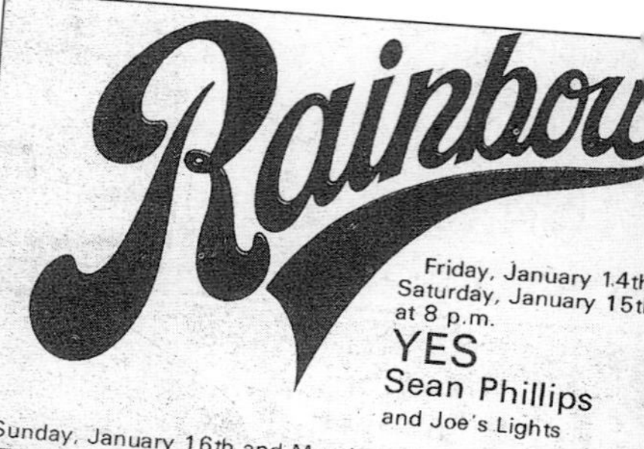

1972

JANUARY (EUROPE)

14-15
LONDON, ENGLAND, RAINBOW THEATRE
Supported by Shawn Philips.

19 **LEUVEN, BELGIUM, UNIVERSITY OF LEUVEN**

20 **ANTWERP, BELGIUM, CINEMA ROMA**

21 **DOELEN, ROTTERDAM, HOLLAND, HET CONCERTGEBOUW**
Doelen taken from Bill Bruford's records, the other location advertised for the 21st was Amsterdam.

23 **BREDC, TERSCHIP HALL**
Bill Brufords records show in Bredc but it has also been reported as being in Rotterdam, Netherlands from.

28 **BRISTOL, ENGLAND, TOP RANK SUITE**

29 **BOSTON, ENGLAND, GLYDERROME STARLIGHT ROOM**

31 **MANCHESTER, ENGLAND, FREE TRADE HALL**

FEBRUARY (USA)

1-2 **LONDON, ENGLAND, ADVISION RECORDING**

10 **LONDON, ENGLAND, TRIDENT STUDIOS**
Bill Bruford's records show that he and Rick Wakeman spend some time recording.

14 **NEW YORK, N.Y. PLATTSBURGH, MEMORIAL HALL**

15 **PROVIDENCE, RHODE ISLAND, UNIVERSITY OF RHODE ISLAND**

18 **BETHANY, WEST VIRGINIA, BETHANY COLLEGE**

19 **NEW YORK, N.Y., ACADEMY OF MUSIC**

21 **ASBURY PARK, NEW JERSEY, SUNSHINE INN**

22 **PRINCETON, NEW JERSEY, THE UNIVERSITY**

23 **NEW YORK, N.Y., ACADEMY OF MUSIC**

24 **BURLINGTON, VERMONT, UNIVERSITY OF VERMONT**

25 **PROVIDENCE, RHODE ISLAND, UNIVERSITY OF RHODE ISLAND**

26 **PASSAIC, NEW JERSEY, CAPITAL THEATRE**

27 **WATERBURY, VERMONT, PALACE THEATRE**

28 **BUFFALO, WYOMING, KLEINHANS AUDITORIUM**

29 **STATEN ISLAND, NEW YORK, RITZ THEATRE**

MARCH (USA)

1 **ROCHESTER, N.Y., WAR MEMORIAL AUDITORIUM**

2 **SYRACUSE, N.Y., WAR MEMORIAL AUDITORIUM**

3 COLUMBIA, SOUTH CAROLINA, TOWNSHIP AUDITORIUM

4 SALEM, VIRGINIA, CIVIC CENTRE

5 NORFOLK, VIRGINIA, THE DOME

6 WILMINGTON, CAROLINA, UNIVERSITY OF CAROLINA

7 KUTZTOWN, PENNSYLVANIA, STATE COLLEGE

8 SHIPPENSBURO, PENNSYLVANIA, STATE COLLEGE

YES GOLD IN U.S.?

YES have jumped a further six places in the American LP chart with their "Fragile" album which is now at number 11. Sales of the LP have now topped 370,000 and Atlantic Records in America estimate that both "Fragile" and "The Yes Album" will attain Gold Disc status by the time the group arrive in New York to start their third US tour on February 17.

Yes are to record their version of Paul Simon's "America" — one of the highlights of their stage act. The nine-minute track is likely to be released as part of a special all-star Kinney album later this year, and Led Zeppelin are also understood to be recording new material for this album.

9 LAKELAND, FLORIDA, CIVIC CENTRE

10-11 SAN FRANCISCO, CALIFORNIA, WINTERLAND

12 LAS VEGAS, NEVADA, LAS VEGAS CONVENTION CENTRE

13 DENVER, COLORADO, DENVER COLISEUM

14 WASHINGTON, WASHINGTON D.C., SPOKANE COLISEUM

15 LOS ANGELES, CALIFORNIA, HOLLYWOOD FORUM

16 TUCSON, ARIZONA, COMMUNITY CENTRE

17 SAN BERNADINO, CALIFORNIA, SPORTS ARENA

18 SAN DIEGO, CALIFORNIA, SPORTS ARENA

19 LAS VEGAS, NEVADA, CONVENTION CENTRE

21 CHICAGO, ILLINOIS, ARIE CROWN THEATRE

22 DETROIT, MICHIGAN, COBO HALL

23 CINCINNATI, OHIO, MUSIC HALL

24 SOUTH-BEND, INDIANA, MORRIS CIVIC AUDITORIUM

25 COLUMBUS, OHIO, MEMORIAL HALL

FREE TRADE HALL (Peter Street) MANCHESTER

WARNING
Official Programmes & Posters sold INSIDE Hall only. Beware of pirate sellers operating outside

CHRYSALIS presents—
YES
in Concert

MONDAY, 31st JANUARY, 1972
at 7-30 p.m.

BALCONY - 50p (10/-)
A 11

26 CLEVELAND, OHIO, LAKELAND COMMUNITY COLLEGE

27 BOSTON, MASSACHUSETTS, AQUARIUS THEATRE
Supported by King Crimson, Bill Bruford's last gig with Yes until he rejoined for the Union album in the 1990s.

APRIL

5 SESSIONS FOR BILL BRUFORD

13 SESSIONS FOR BILL BRUFORD

27 SESSIONS FOR BILL BRUFORD

MAY (EUROPE)

No concerts for Yes, the band rehearses *Close To the Edge*. *Billboard* magazine in the US awards Yes the Number 1 spot for their mid-year award for Top Group On Album.

27 Jon Anderson and Steve Howe perform at the Great Western Express Festival in the Netherlands.

JUNE

1-8 LONDON, ENGLAND, ADVISION RECORDING CLOSE TO THE EDGE

11-18 LONDON, ENGLAND, ADVISION RECORDING CLOSE TO THE EDGE

25-29 LONDON, ENGLAND, ADVISION RECORDING CLOSE TO THE EDGE

JULY (USA)

19 Bill Bruford leaves Yes to join King Crimson.

26 EDWARDSVILLE, ILLINOIS, EDWARDSVILLE AMPHITHEATRE
(Cancelled)

27 LOUISVILLE, KENTUCKY, COMMONWEALTH CONVENTION CENTRE

28 MEMPHIS, TENNESSEE, MID-SOUTH COLISEUM
Supported by the Eagles, it has been reported that both 28th-29th were cancelled, and also that they went ahead with Alan White playing as the drummer in residence.

29 LITTLE ROCK, ARKANSAS, BARTON COLISEUM
(Cancelled)

30 DALLAS, TEXAS, MEMORIAL AUDITORIUM
Alan White officially joins Yes.

31 HOUSTON, TEXAS, HOFHEINZ PAVILION

AUGUST (USA & CANADA)

1 OKLAHOMA CITY, OKLAHOMA, FAIRGROUNDS ARENA

3 DENVER, COLORADO, DENVER COLISEUM

4 LONG BEACH, CALIFORNIA, LONG BEACH ARENA
Supported by the Eagles & Edgar Winter.

5 BERKELEY, CALIFORNIA, BERKELEY COMMUNITY THEATRE

6 PORTLAND, OREGON, MEMORIAL COLISEUM

7 VANCOUVER, BRITISH COLUMBIA, PACIFIC COLISEUM

8 SEATTLE, WASHINGTON, SEATTLE CENTRE

9 DAYTONA, OHIO, HARA ARENA

11 AKRON, OHIO, RUBBER BOWL

12 ASBURY PARK, NEW JERSEY, CONVENTION HALL

13 COLUMBIA, MARYLAND, MERRIWEATHER POST PAVILION

14 HARTFORD, CONNECTICUT, DILLON STADIUM
Supported by the Eagles, Edgar Winter.

15 PHILADELPHIA, PENNSYLVANIA, THE SPECTRUM ARENA

16 BRONX, N.Y., GAELIC PARK

21 ST. LOUIS, MISSOURI, KIEL AUDITORIUM

SEPTEMBER (UK & USA)

2 LONDON, ENGLAND, CRYSTAL PALACE, THE 3RD GARDEN PARTY
Supported by Lindisfarne, Mahavishnu Orchestra, Gary Wright's Wonderwheel & Capability Brown.

4-5 GLASGOW, SCOTLAND, KELVIN HALL

9 BRISTOL, ENGLAND, COLSTON HALL

10 MANCHESTER, ENGLAND, BELVUE STADIUM

12 NEWCASTLE, ENGLAND, CITY HALL

15 MIAMI, FLORIDA, MIAMI BASEBALL STADIUM

16 TAMPA, FLORIDA, CURTIS HIXON HALL

17 JACKSONVILLE, FLORIDA, MISSISSIPPI COLISEUM

20 INDIANNAPOLIS, INDIANA, COLISEUM
In an unusual event for Yes, serious crowd problems were reported which nearly lead to a riot. The problems seemed to stem from a lack of ticket availability.

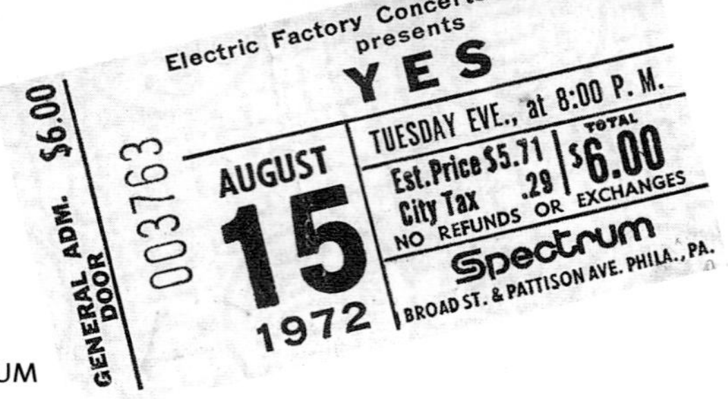

21 DETROIT, MICHIGAN, COBO HALL

22-23 CHICAGO, ILLINOIS, ARIE CROWN THEATRE
Supported by the Eagles.

24 MILWAUKEE, WISCONSIN, UPTOWN THEATRE

25 HARTFORD, CONNECTICUT, DILLON STADIUM

27 LONG BEACH, CALIFORNIA, LONG BEACH ARENA

28 NEW ORLEANS, LOUISIANA, LOUISIANA CITY AUDITORIUM

29 ATHENS, GEORGIA, UNIVERSITY OF GEORGIA

30 ATLANTA, GEORGIA, MUNICIPAL AUDITORIUM
Supported by the Eagles.

OCTOBER (USA & CANADA)

1 TUSCALOOSA, ALABAMA, MEMORIAL COLISEUM

2 COLUMBIA, SOUTH CAROLINA, CAROLINA COLISEUM

3 CHARLOTTE, NORTH CAROLINA, THE COLISEUM

28 MILLERSVILLE, PENNSYLVANIA, SPORTS ARENA

30 KITCHENER, ONTARIO, UNIVERSITY OF WATERLOO

31 TORONTO, ONTARIO, MAPLE LEAF GARDENS

NOVEMBER (USA & CANADA)

1 OTTOWA, ONTARIO, NATIONAL THEATRE

7 PITTSBURG, PENNSYLVANIA, PITTSBURG CIVIC ARENA
Supported by J. Geils.

9 NORFOLK, VIRGINIA, SCOPE THEATRE
Supported by Tranquility.

10 ROANOKE, VIRGINIA, ROANOKE CIVIC CENTRE COLISEUM

11 DURHAM, NORTH CAROLINA, DUKE UNIVERSITY
Supported by Tranquility.

14 SOUTH BEND, INDIANA, NOTRE DAME A.C.C

15 KNOXVILLE, TENNESSEE, KNOXVILLE CIVIC AUDITORIUM

17 TERRE HAUTE, INDIANA, STATE UNIVERSITY - TILSON AUDITORIUM

20 UNIONDALE, N.Y., NASSAU VETERANS MEMORIAL COLISEUM

DECEMBER

15-16 LONDON, ENGLAND, RAINBOW THEATRE
Supported by Badger, recording used for the Yessongs film.

17 MANCHESTER, ENGLAND, HARDROCK
Supported by Badger who had the ex-Yes guitarist Peter Banks and the Warriors

bass player David Foster, their album was on a Yes label and the beautiful album cover was by Roger Dean. The cover was later used as the front design for Steve Howe's vegetarian food shop Brownies in Hampstead, London.

1973

FEBRUARY

Yes have £2,500 worth of equipment stolen. An informant, who remains nameless, pocketed £500 reward.

MARCH (JAPAN, AUSTRALIA & NEW ZEALAND)

8 TOKYO, JAPAN, KOSEINENKIN KAIKAN

9-10 TOKYO, JAPAN, SHIBUYA KOUKAIDOU

11 NAGOYA, JAPAN, NAGOYASHI KOHKAIDO

12 OSAKA, JAPAN, SHIBUYA KOSEINENKIN KAIKAN

14 KYOTO, JAPAN, KYOTOKAIKAN

17 SYDNEY, AUSTRALIA, HORDEN PAVILION
Or as sometimes reported the R.A.S show ground's grandstand.

19 BRISBANE, AUSTRALIA, FESTIVAL HALL
Both Rick Wakeman and Steve Howe fit in brief renditions of Waltzing Matilda and Tie Me Kangaroo Down Sport!

21 ADELAIDE, AUSTRALIA, APOLLO STADIUM

23 MELBOURNE, AUSTRALIA, FESTIVAL HALL
Or reported as VFL park.

26 SYDNEY, AUSTRALIA, HORDEN PAVILION

29 AUCKLAND, NEW ZEALAND, WESTERN SPRINGS
(Cancelled)

30 WELLINGTON, NEW ZEALAND, ATHLETIC PARK
(Cancelled)

31 CHRISTCHURCH, NEW ZEALAND, TOWN HALL
(Cancelled)

APRIL (USA)

4 SAN DIEGO, CALIFORNIA, SPORTS PALACE

5 LOS ANGELES, CALIFORNIA, THE L.A. FORUM

6 LAS VEGAS, NEVADA, CONVENTION CENTRE

7 SAN FRANCISCO, CALIFORNIA, WINTERLAND
Focus and Poco also on the bill.

8 ALBUQUERQUE, NEW MEXICO, UNIVERSITY OF NM – JOHNSON GYM
Supported by Poco.

9 PHOENIX, ARIZONA, (Venue unknown)

11 BLOOMINGTON, NEW MEXICO, METROPOLITAN SPORTS CENTRE

12 OKLAHOMA CITY, OKLAHOMA, FAIRGROUNDS ARENA

14 HOUSTON, TEXAS, HOFHEINZ PAVILION

15 DALLAS, TEXAS, MEMORIAL AUDITORIUM

16 KANSAS CITY, MISSOURI, KEIL OPERA HOUSE
Poco also on the bill.

17 ST. LOUIS, MISSOURI, KEIL OPERA HOUSE
Poco also on the bill.

18 NASHVILLE, TENNESSEE, MUNICIPAL AUDITORIUM

19 ATLANTA, GEORGIA, ALEXANDER MEMORIAL COLISEUM
Supported by Poco and Les Moore.

20 SAVANNAH, GEORGIA, CIVIC CENTRE

21 TAMPA, FLORIDA, TAMPA STADIUM
Supported by Poco.

22 WEST PALM BEACH, FLORIDA, CORAL SKY AMPHITHEATRE

SOUTH AMERICAN TOUR

MAY

1 ACAPULCO, MEXICO, SALLE UNIVERSITY
(Cancelled)

5 SOUTH AMERICAN TOUR VENUES NEVER RELEASED
(Cancelled)

TALES FROM TOPOGRAPHIC OCEANS

NOVEMBER

1 LONDON, ENGLAND, BBC SESSIONS
For *Tales From Topographic Oceans*.

16-17 BOURNEMOUTH, ENGLAND, WINTER GARDEN

18 BRISTOL, ENGLAND, HIPPODROME

19 PORTSMOUTH, ENGLAND, GUILDHALL

20-24 LONDON, ENGLAND, RAINBOW THEATRE

25 OXFORD, ENGLAND, NEW THEATRE

26 LEICESTER, ENGLAND, DE MONTFORT HALL

27 SHEFFIELD, ENGLAND, CITY HALL

28-29 MANCHESTER, ENGLAND, FREE TRADE HALL

30 LIVERPOOL, ENGLAND, LIVERPOOL EMPIRE

DECEMBER

1 CARDIFF, WALES, CAPITOL THEATRE

2 STOKE, ENGLAND, TRENTHAM GARDENS

3-4 BIRMINGHAM, ENGLAND, HIPPODROME

6-7 GLASGOW, SCOTLAND, APOLLO CENTRE

8-9 NEWCASTLE, ENGLAND, CITY HALL

10 EDINBURGH, SCOTLAND, EMPIRE

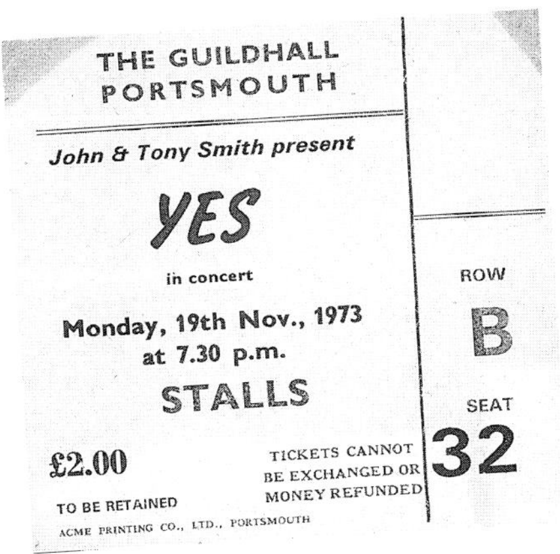

1974

FEBRUARY (USA & CANADA)

7 GAINSVILLE, FLORIDA, UNIVERSITY OF FLORIDA

8 MIAMI, FLORIDA, MIAMI STADIUM

9 TAMPA, FLORIDA, TAMPA STADIUM

10 COLUMBIA, SOUTH CAROLINA, UNIVERSITY OF SOUTH CAROLINA

11 ATLANTA, GEORGIA, GEORGIA TECH

12 ROANOKE, VIRGINIA, CIVIC CENTRE

13 BALTIMORE, MARYLAND, CIVIC CENTRE
John Martyn also on the bill.

14 UNIONDALE, N.Y., NASSAU COLISEUM
(Two shows)

15 NEW HAVEN, CONNECTICUT, NEW HAVEN COLISEUM

16 PHILADELPHIA, PENNSYLVANIA, THE SPECTRUM ARENA
(Two shows)

18 NEW YORK, N.Y., MADISON SQUARE GARDEN

20 NEW YORK, N.Y., MADISON SQUARE GARDEN

21 PITTSBURG, PENNSYLVANIA, CIVIC ARENA

22 TORONTO, ONTARIO, MAPLE LEAF GARDENS
Supported by John Martyn.

23 BINGHAMPTON, N.Y., BROOME COUNTY ARENA

24 ITHACA, N.Y., CORNELL UNIVERSITY

25 MONTREAL, QUEBEC, FORUM
Supported by John Martyn.

26 BOSTON, MASSACHUSETTS, BOSTON GARDENS

27-28
DETROIT, MICHIGAN, COBO HALL

MARCH (USA)

1 HERSHEY, PENNSYLVANIA, HERSHEY ARENA

2 LOUISVILLE, KENTUCKY, CONVENTION CENTRE

3 CINCINNATI, OHIO, CINCINNATI GARDENS

5 MINNEAPOLIS, MINNESOTA, MET SPORTS CENTRE

6-7 CHICAGO, ILLINOIS, INTERNATIONAL AMPHITHEATRE

8 ST. LOUIS, MISSOURI, KIEL AUDITORIUM

10 MEMPHIS, TENNESSEE, COOK CONVENTION CENTRE

11 OKLAHOMA CITY, OKLAHOMA, FAIRGROUNDS ARENA

12 WICHITA, KANSAS, CENTURY II CIVIC CENTRE

13 ALBUQUERQUE, NEW MEXICO, UNIVERSITY OF NEW MEXICO

15-16
SAN FRANCISCO, CALIFORNIA, CALIFORNIA WINTERLAND
Supported by Charlie Starr.

17 SACRAMENTO, CALIFORNIA, MEMORIAL AUDITORIUM

18 LOS ANGELES, CALIFORNIA, FORUM

19 LONG BEACH, CALIFORNIA, ARENA

20 FRESNO, CALIFORNIA, SELLAND ARENA

21 SAN DIEGO, CALIFORNIA, SPORTS ARENA

23 SAN ANTONIO, TEXAS, SAN ANTONIO CIVIC CENTRE

25 DALLAS, TEXAS, MEMORIAL AUDITORIUM

26 BATON ROUGE, LOUISIANA, STATE UNIVERSITY

APRIL (EUROPE)

11 FRANKFURT, GERMANY, KONGRESHALLE

12-13
MUNICH, GERMANY, OLYMPIAHALLE

14 LUDWIGSHAFEN, GERMANY, FRIEDRICH EBERT HALLE

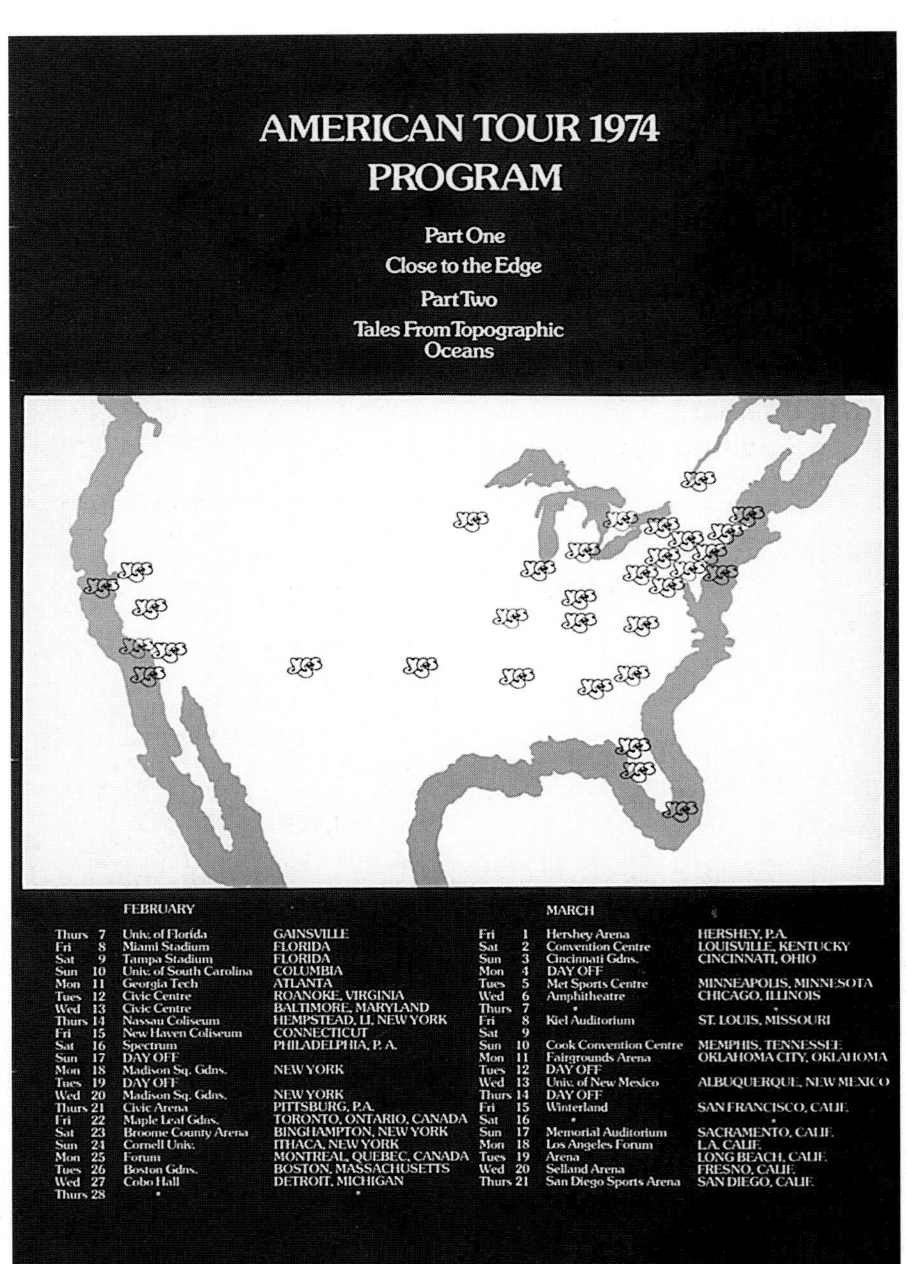

AMERICAN TOUR 1974
PROGRAM

Part One
Close to the Edge
Part Two
Tales From Topographic Oceans

FEBRUARY

Thurs	7	Univ. of Florida	GAINSVILLE
Fri	8	Miami Stadium	FLORIDA
Sat	9	Tampa Stadium	FLORIDA
Sun	10	Univ. of South Carolina	COLUMBIA
Mon	11	Georgia Tech	ATLANTA
Tues	12	Civic Centre	ROANOKE, VIRGINIA
Wed	13	Civic Centre	BALTIMORE, MARYLAND
Thurs	14	Nassau Coliseum	HEMPSTEAD, LI, NEW YORK
Fri	15	New Haven Coliseum	CONNECTICUT
Sat	16	Spectrum	PHILADELPHIA, P. A.
Sun	17	DAY OFF	
Mon	18	Madison Sq. Gdns.	NEW YORK
Tues	19	DAY OFF	
Wed	20	Madison Sq. Gdns.	NEW YORK
Thurs	21	Civic Arena	PITTSBURG, P.A.
Fri	22	Maple Leaf Gdns.	TORONTO, ONTARIO, CANADA
Sat	23	Broome County Arena	BINGHAMPTON, NEW YORK
Sun	24	Cornell Univ.	ITHACA, NEW YORK
Mon	25	Forum	MONTREAL, QUEBEC, CANADA
Tues	26	Boston Gdns.	BOSTON, MASSACHUSETTS
Wed	27	Cobo Hall	DETROIT, MICHIGAN
Thurs	28	•	•

MARCH

Fri	1	Hershey Arena	HERSHEY, P.A.
Sat	2	Convention Centre	LOUISVILLE, KENTUCKY
Sun	3	Cincinnati Gdns.	CINCINNATI, OHIO
Mon	4	DAY OFF	
Tues	5	Met Sports Centre	MINNEAPOLIS, MINNESOTA
Wed	6	Amphitheatre	CHICAGO, ILLINOIS
Thurs	7	•	•
Fri	8	Kiel Auditorium	ST. LOUIS, MISSOURI
Sat	9		
Sun	10	Cook Convention Centre	MEMPHIS, TENNESSEE
Mon	11	Fairgrounds Arena	OKLAHOMA CITY, OKLAHOMA
Tues	12	DAY OFF	
Wed	13	Univ. of New Mexico	ALBUQUERQUE, NEW MEXICO
Thurs	14	DAY OFF	
Fri	15	Winterland	SAN FRANCISCO, CALIF.
Sat	16	•	•
Sun	17	Memorial Auditorium	SACRAMENTO, CALIF.
Mon	18	Los Angeles Forum	L.A. CALIF.
Tues	19	Arena	LONG BEACH, CALIF.
Wed	20	Selland Arena	FRESNO, CALIF.
Thurs	21	San Diego Sports Arena	SAN DIEGO, CALIF.

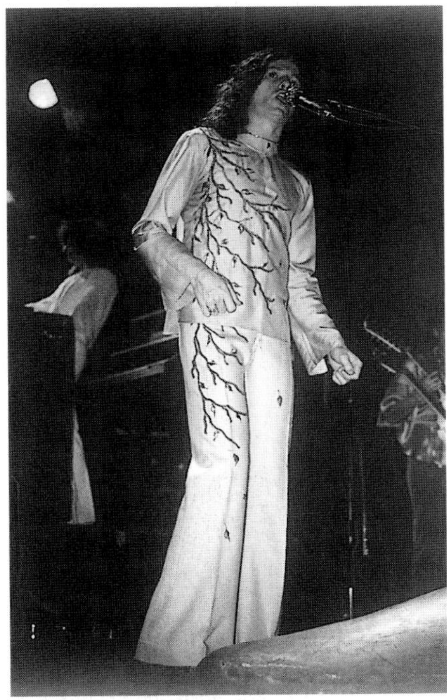

Jon on the Relayer tour.

15 STUTTGART, GERMANY, SINDELDINGEN NEUE MESSEHALLE

16 DORTMUND, GERMANY, WESTFALENHALLE

17 ROTTERDAM, HOLLAND, AHOY-HALLE
Rick Wakeman breaks his leg!

19 PARIS, FRANCE, PALAIS DES SPORTS
700 forged concert tickets cause a riot in Paris.

21 ZURICH, SWITZERLAND, HALLENSTADION

23 ROME, ITALY, TEATRO DI BRANCACCIO DI ROMA

MAY

18 Rick Wakeman quits Yes on his 25th birthday.

AUGUST

Patrick Moraz joins Yes.
Rick Wakeman is hospitalised suffering from nervous and physical exhaustion.

NOVEMBER (USA)

8 COLUMBUS, OHIO, STATE UNIVERSITY
Supported by Gryphon.

13 MADISON, WISCONSIN, DANE COUNTY COLISEUM

14 SOUTH BEND, INDIANA, NOTRE DAME UNIVERSITY

15 INDIANAPOLIS, INDIANA, CONVENTION CENTRE

16 NORMAL, ILLINOIS, STATE UNIVERSITY

17 ST. LOUIS, MISSOURI, KEIL AUDITORIUM

18 DETROIT, MICHIGAN, COBO HALL

20 NEW YORK, N.Y., MADISON SQUARE GARDEN

21 BUFFALO, N.Y., MEMORIAL AUDITORIUM

22 RICHFIELD, OHIO, RICHFIELD COLISEUM

23 CHARLESTON, WEST VIRGINIA, CHARLESTON CIVIC CENTRE

24 GREENSBORO, NORTH CAROLINA, GREENSBORO COLISEUM

25 KNOXVILLE, TENNESSEE, CIVIC COLISEUM

28 MIAMI, FLORIDA, MIAMI JAI ALAI FRONTON

29 LAKELAND, FLORIDA, LAKELAND CIVIC CENTRE

30 ATLANTA, GEORGIA, OMNI COLISEUM

DECEMBER (USA)

1 BATON ROUGE, LOUISIANA, PETER MARAVICH ASSEMBLY CENTRE

2 HOUSTON, TEXAS, HOUSTON ASTRODOME

4 FORT WORTH, TEXAS, TARRANT COUNTY CONVENTION CENTRE

5 TULSA, OKLAHOMA, CIVIC CENTRE

6 LAWRENCE, KANSAS, ALLEN FIELDHOUSE

7 IOWA CITY, IOWA, UNIVERSITY OF IOWA

8 LOUISVILLE, KENTUCKY, FREEDOM HALL

10 NEW HAVEN, CONNECTICUT, VETERANS MEMORIAL COLISEUM

11 BOSTON, MASSACHUSETTS, BOSTON GARDENS

12 BALTIMORE, MARYLAND, CIVIC CENTRE

13 PITTSBURG, PENNSYLVANIA, CIVIC CENTRE

14 PHILADELPHIA, PENNSYLVANIA, THE SPECTRUM ARENA
Supported by Carmen.

15 CINCINNATI, OHIO, OHIO GARDENS

16 CHICAGO, ILLINOIS, ILLINOIS AMPHITHEATRE

continued from p47

YES, 5,000 Frenchmen can't be wrong!

Fragile, but this is still in the talking stage. "There are a couple of people we know we'd happily have on our own label," said Jon. "People whose music we admire immensely, and we think anybody into Yes would like to hear."

"But the most artists we would handle would be three or four. It would not be just a business thing, but the creation of a musical environment. Well, I suppose it is a business trip for a group to start its own label — but we'd really like to put some good music out."

What else were the Yesmen planning? "Well I'm producing Clive Muldoon who I've known for six or seven years, and was with me in Bodast," said Steve, "and I'm opening my own guitar shop . . . in fact why don't I open my own radio station and a boutique?" Steve laughed, but Jon said most firmly: "Well, I'm going home, to watch the World Cup on TV."

AT the Palais des Sports, the road crew were busy with the equipment. Thousands of empty seats gaped down on the stage where the gantry waited its injection of gas to lift up the group's own lighting system.

There were Alan White's drums, under the green canopy designed by Roger Dean. There were the boxes of tools, wires, transistors, dry ice (for smoke) wet ice (for drinks), brown rice (for Steve) and Watneys (for Rick). Microphones, junction boxes, huge steel lined packing cases (dented), all scattered about in that forbidden land — backstage.

While two of the American roadies took time off for an impromptu wrestling match, Rick looked worried, tinkered with his keyboards.

"I'm really in trouble. They promised me a Hammond organ man. He'll be here all day they said. No Hammond man. And where's the food? Look at all that brown rice. I wouldn't give it to my dog!"

"Come on — let's find our seats," said an optimistic Keith Goodwin, the group's PR. Five thousand fans had poured into the huge domed arena by now and none of them were going to budge an inch. All available space was taken, including the gangways.

No British jobsworth would have allowed it, and from a fire regulation view, he would have been right. Struggling through to the non-existant seats with Jenny, Jon's wife, it became worrying when the black jackets suddenly burst upon us, shoving all aside, and streaking towards the stage that had taken 12 hours to make ready.

As the boarders were repelled, the gendarmes began furiously unrolling a fire hose and water began to spray out through the doors, being held against a struggling mass outside.

"Ooh, I'm frightened," giggled Jenny, but she battled on, down the 100 feet of steeply sloping gangway, jammed with bodies. The reserved seats had long been snatched. Local security men began a desperate tussle to oust the occupants, who resisted manfully.

You couldn't blame them. After all, they had paid to see the show. When one of them pulled a knife on a startled Keith Goodwin, the wives and Brian Lane decided to retreat backstage.

I knelt on a spare patch of sawdust, and despite an urgent desire to find the pissoir, and flee this shambles, was rewarded by magic notes of "Siberian Khatru." Mercifully, Yes weren't going to hang about. It was on with the show, and the music was so mesmerising, the aches of knee and bladder melted away. See Grasshopper. When strings are plucked and cymbals beat, then shall mind triumph over pees, pins and needles.

"And You And I," "Close To The Edge," the music swelled and roared and faded with immense, controlled power.

All the dented packing cases and busted Moogs were forgotten, as once again Yes locked together and became . . . an orchestra. As smoke began to pour from the tunnel at the side of the stage, the band seemed frozen, immobile while blue light bathed them in an eerie glow, and ethreal chords held time in abeyance.

Then Jon sang "I get up, I get down," Rick's church organ effects roared, and "Close To The Edge," stepped back from the brink. Girls screamed after this as if they had been raped.

"We'd like to carry on with some music from an LP called 'Tales From Topographic . . .'" "WAH!" A fan bellowed his approval just above my head. I thought someone had trodden on his Gaulloise.

"The Revealing Science Of God," chanted in, and stars from distant galaxies were projected onto giant "ears" that opened out over Alan's drums. He look if he was inside the ja a monster. Next came Ancient" (side three o album) and "Ritual" (f

The band played such fire and attack, work became a living . . . and with the pru of the original score, n its musical intentions n plainer.

Steve Howe played extraordinary fero during "The Ancient," the contrast with the ac tic passages was all more effective. The cussion section dur "Ritual" was much m organised than when f launched, with Jon a Chris on tom-toms a tympani contributing r and useful power to Alar explosive and dynamic lan slide.

The whole piece mai tained a much faster an firmer tempo than befor and where there had been surfeit of good ideas, nov each section of this labou of love was made to count The finale and most effec tive burst of smoke of the evening came as Alan wound up his drum solo.

The Roger Dean settings, the glowing red organ pipes above Rick's keyboard complex, and the ever changing lights somehow made a far more cohesive effect than even the Pink Floyd's exceptional visuals. For this was an integral part of the music, as the drums roared to a cataclysmic finale.

Then it all faded back to peace and tranquility, leaving Jon, frail and whiteclad singing "nous somme du soleil," strumming his old acoustic, Steve tracing delicate patterns, Rick caressing the grand piano. It was a beautiful, masterly touch.

The crowd went ape, as they say in showbiz. They seemed to be yelling, "oompah, oompah!" "This means they want another. They are receptive to the music," translated a kindly local who observed my hesistant ballpoint.

"Roundabout" was the encore, stomping and swirling, Ricardo drawing fire with a dazzling Hammond solo, and then before the houselights went up, "Starship Trooper." Good grief, the lighting gantry suddenly dropped two or three feet, threatening to nut Stephen during his most tumultuous solo.

The gas was running low, inside the arena — and out. Cheers ringing in their ears, the group stole away into the night blissfully unaware of the forged tickets and mayhem.

For them the important matter was having projected themselves and their music, another night, in another city and another country.

Said Jon, tired, his voice reduced to a whisper. "After everything that's been said about the act and the music — I don't regret one bit of it."

Five thousand Frenchmen weren't wrong — either.

Yes' Steve Howe: delighted

17 **ST. PAUL, MINNESOTA, CIVIC CENTRE**
Supported by Gryphon. Yes jam with the support band Gryphon on the last day of tour and play 'South Side of the Sky' together.

1975

FEBRUARY

28 Steve Howe performs at the Guitarists All Stars Concert with John Williams, Kevin Peak and Juan Martin.

APRIL

15-17 **NEWCASTLE, ENGLAND, CITY HALL**

18-19 **GLASGOW, SCOTLAND, APOLLO**

20-21 **EDINBURGH, SCOTLAND, USHER HALL**

23 **PRESTON, ENGLAND, GUILDHALL**

24-25 **LEICESTER, ENGLAND, DE MONTFORT HALL**

27-28 **LIVERPOOL, ENGLAND, LIVERPOOL EMPIRE**

29-30 **MANCHESTER, ENGLAND, PALACE THEATRE**

MAY

2-3 **CARDIFF, WALES, CAPITOL THEATRE**

5-7 **BRISTOL, ENGLAND, COLSTON HALL**

10 **LONDON, ENGLAND, QUEEN'S PARK RANGERS FOOTBALL GROUND**
Supported by Gryphon, Ace, Seals & Crofts, filmed and used for TV, released on Video, Laser Disc and bootlegged many times. One of the very few occasions this spectacular tour was captured on film.

12-14 **SOUTHAMPTON, ENGLAND, GAUMONT**

17 **STOKE, ENGLAND, STOKE CITY FOOTBALL GROUND**
Supported by Gryphon, Ace and The Sensational Alex Harvey Band.

JUNE (USA & CANADA)

17 **DENVER, COLORADO, DENVER COLISEUM**
Supported by Ace.

18 **SALT LAKE CITY, UTAH, SALT PALACE**

19 **LAS VEGAS, NEVADA, CONVENTION CENTRE**

20 **TUCSON, ARIZONA, CONVENTION HALL**

21 **LOS ANGELES, CALIFORNIA, HOLLYWOOD BOWL**

22 **TEMPE, ARIZONA, FEYLINE FIELDS STATE UNIVERSITY**

23 **LONG BEACH, CALIFORNIA, ARENA**

24 **SAN DIEGO, CALIFORNIA, SPORTS ARENA**

25 **SAN FRANCISCO, CALIFORNIA, COW PALACE**

27 **VANCOUVER, CANADA, COLISEUM**

28 **SEATTLE, WASHINGTON, SEATTLE CENTRE**

29 **PORTLAND, OREGON, COLISEUM**

JULY (USA & CANADA)

2 **LINCOLN, NEBRASKA, PERSHING MUNICIPAL AUDITORIUM**

3 **KANSAS CITY, MISSOURI, MUNICIPAL AUDITORIUM**

4 **CHICAGO, ILLINOIS, CHICAGO STADIUM**

5 **EVANSVILLE, ILLINOIS, ROBERTS MEMORIAL STADIUM**

6 **MEMPHIS, TENNESSEE, MID SOUTH COLISEUM**

7 **LITTLE ROCK, ARKANSAS, BARTON COLISEUM**

8 **NASHVILLE, TENNESSEE, WAR MEMORIAL**

9 **ST. LOUIS, MISSOURI, RIVER FESTIVAL EDWARDSVILLE**

10 **INDIANAPOLIS, INDIANA, MARKET SQUARE ARENA**

11 **CLEVELAND, OHIO, CLEVELAND STADIUM**
Michael Stanley Band, Ace and Joe Walsh also on the bill.

12 **BUFFALO, N.Y., BUFFALO STADIUM**

13 **JERSEY CITY, NEW JERSEY, ROOSEVELT STADIUM**
Cancelled and moved to 24th July.

15 **FORT WAYNE, INDIANA, MEMORIAL COLISEUM**
Recording at KMET Hollywood, 110 minutes, broadcast on 30 October 1976.

16 **MILWAUKEE, WISCONSIN, ARENA**

18 **MONTREAL, QUEBEC, MONTREAL STADIUM**

19 **TORONTO, ONTARIO, MAPLE LEAF GARDENS**

20 **YPSILANTI, MICHIGAN, RYMEARSON STADIUM**

21-22 **PHILADELPHIA, PENNSYLVANIA, THE SPECTRUM ARENA**

23 **PROVIDENCE, RHODE ISLAND, CIVIC CENTRE**

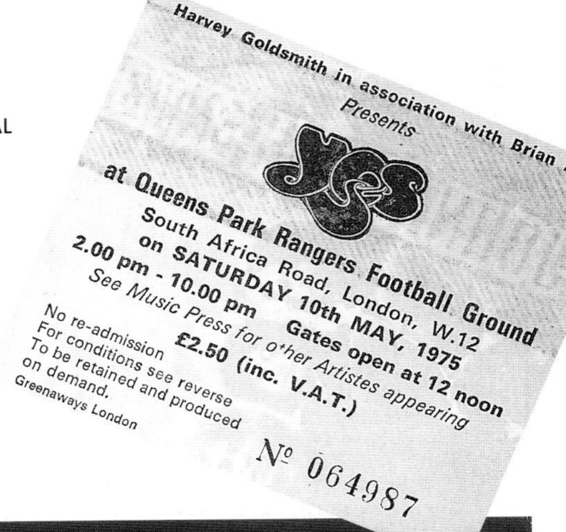

The Barnacle stage set at the Reading Festival, UK, 1975.

STEVE HOWE

YES tour

CHRIS SQUIRE

FULL DETAILS were announced this week of the extensive spring tour by Yes, plans for which were exclusively revealed by NME three weeks ago. They will be playing a total of 20 indoor concerts — including three in Newcastle and two at each of eight other venues — plus two major outdoor soccer-stadium gigs. There is a distinct possibility of further dates being added, and Gryphon will be the support act throughout the tour.

The two open-air events will be at the Queen's Park Rangers ground in West London on Saturday, May 10, and at Stoke City's Victoria Road ground the following Saturday (17). These two shows will run from 2 to 10 p.m. and will include at least two additional acts, and there is a possibility that one of these will be current U.S. chart star Minnie Riperton.

A 25,000 crowd limit has been set for the football-ground shows, and discussions are taking place with a view to British Rail running special trains from key centres. A spokesman said that the gigs will go ahead in overcast conditions or drizzle, but in the event of a complete wash-out they would be switched to the following day. The QPR concert will be filmed, although the purpose of this exercise is not yet clear.

Tickets for all venues go on sale next week. Meanwhile, mail orders will be accepted provided they are accompanied by a stamped addressed envelope. Each applicant will be limited to four tickets, in an attempt to eradicate touting. The complete Yes itinerary, together with ticket prices, is as follows:

NEWCASTLE City Hall (April 15, 16 and 17; £2.20, £1.80 and £1.40); GLASGOW Apollo Centre (April 18 and 19; £2.25, £1.75, £1.25 and £1); EDINBURGH Usher Hall (April 20 and 21; £2.20, £1.80 and £1.40); PRESTON Guildhall (April 23 only; £2.20, £1.80 and £1.40); LEICESTER De Montfort Hall (April 24 and 25; £2.20, £1.80, £1.45 and £1.25); LIVERPOOL Empire (April 27 and 28; £2.20, £1.80, £1.40 and £1.20); MANCHESTER Palace (April 29 and 30; £2.20, £1.80, £1.40 and £1.20); CARDIFF Capitol (May 2 and 3; £2.20, £1.80 and £1.40); BRISTOL Colston Hall (May 5 and 6; £2.20, £1.80 and £1.40); LONDON Queen's Park Rangers FC (May 10; £2.50 only); SOUTHAMPTON Gaumont (May 12 and 13; £2.20, £1.80, £1.50 and £1.20); STOKE City FC (May 17; £2.50 only).

All indoor concerts will last from 2½ to three hours. Yes will be featuring material from all their albums, and at least one track from Steve Howe's upcoming solo album. The band will be using the same stage set as in America, including a 48-feet lighting gantry, and they will be travelling with 20 tons of equipment. The tour will mark the live debut in Britain of new Yes keyboards man Patrick Moraz, who replaced Rick Wakeman last year.

At present, Steve Howe has almost completed work on his solo set, while Chris Squire has just started on his — and Jon Anderson is in the planning stages of a huge concept album. The band leave for a four-week American tour on June 20, then return to London to begin a collective studio album. Because of these commitments, plans for tours of Japan and Australia have been postponed until next year.

● Yes' first full-length feature film had its world premiere in America—at Madison, Wisconsin — last Wednesday (12), and is now being screened throughout the States. The movie is a mixed-media presentation of music and animation, featuring Yes (when Rick Wakeman was still a member) performing and recording "Yessongs", which is also the title of the picture. It was produced by the band's manager Brian Lane in association with Al "OK" Films of London. There are plans for it to be seen in this country later in the year.

24 JERSEY CITY, NEW JERSEY, ROOSEVELT STADIUM

AUGUST

23 READING, ENGLAND, THE READING FESTIVAL
Supported by Mahavishnu Orchestra, Zebra, Ozark Mountain, Daredevils, Supertramp, Thin Lizzy, Snafu and 18 others.

1976

MAY (USA)

26-27 ROANOKE, VIRGINIA, CIVIC CENTRE
(Rehearsal - tracks included 'The Remembering', 'Flight of the Moorglad' and 'I'm Down')

28 ROANOKE, VIRGINIA, CIVIC CENTRE

29 HAMPTON ROADS, VIRGINIA, HAMPTON COLISEUM

30 CHARLESTON, WEST VIRGINIA, CIVIC CENTRE

31 JOHNSON CITY, TENNESSEE, FREEDOM HALL

JUNE (USA)

1 NASHVILLE, TENNESSEE, MUNICIPAL AUDITORIUM

3 ATLANTA, GEORGIA, OMNI

4 MEMPHIS, TENNESSEE, MID-SOUTH COLISEUM

5 JACKSON, MISSISSIPPI, COLISEUM

6 HUNTSVILLE, ALABAMA, VAN BRAUN CIVIC CENTRE

8 CINCINNATI, OHIO, RIVERFRONT COLISEUM

9 **BINGHAMPTON, N.Y., CIVIC CENTRE**
This venue replaces the original one advertised as Hershey, Pennsylvania.

10 **PROVIDENCE, RHODE ISLAND, CIVIC CENTRE**

12 **PHILADELPHIA, PENNSYLVANIA, JFK STADIUM**
Supported by Pousette-Dart Band, Gary Wright, The Mummers, Peter Frampton, a truly spectacular Yes Gig with over 110,000 people in attendance.

13 **WASHINGTON, D.C., RFK STADIUM**
Supported by Pousette-Dart Band, Ace, Gary Wright and Peter Frampton.

16 **UNIONDALE, N.Y., NASSAU COLISEUM**
This venue replaces the Jersey City, New Jersey show advertised and changed.

17 **JERSEY CITY, NEW JERSEY, ROOSEVELT STADIUM**
Supported by Pousette-Dart Band.

18 **BOSTON, MASSACHUSETTS, BOSTON GARDENS**

19 **HARTFORD, CONNECTICUT, COLT PARK**

20 **ROCHESTER, N.Y., MEMORIAL AUDITORIUM**

21 **KALAMAZOO, MICHIGAN, WING STADIUM**

22 **PITTSBURG, PENNSYLVANIA, CIVIC ARENA**

24 **COLUMBIA, SOUTH CAROLINA, UNIVERSITY OF S C**

25 **SAVANNAH, GEORGIA, CIVIC CENTRE**

26 **TAMPA, FLORIDA, TAMPA STADIUM**

JULY (USA & CANADA)

17 **ANAHEIM, CALIFORNIA, ANAHEIM STADIUM**
Supported by Gary Wright, Gentle Giant & Peter Frampton.

18 **SAN DIEGO, CALIFORNIA, BALBOA STADIUM**

20 **DALEY CITY, CALIFORNIA, COW PALACE**
Supported by Gentle Giant, this is the rearranged venue replacing Oakland, California.

22 **VANCOUVER, BRITISH COLUMBIA, COLISEUM**

23 **SEATTLE, WASHINGTON, SEATTLE CENTRE**

24 **SPOKANE, WASHINGTON, COLISEUM**

25 **PORTLAND, OREGON, COLISEUM**

27 **SALT LAKE CITY, UTAH, SALT PALACE**

28 **DENVER, COLORADO, AUDITORIUM ARENA**
Supported by Gentle Giant.

30 **EL PASO, TEXAS, COLISEUM**

31 **PHOENIX, ARIZONA, COLISEUM**

AUGUST (USA)

1 **LAS VEGAS, NEVADA, ALADDIN THEATRE**

3 **FRESNO, CALIFORNIA, SELLAND ARENA**

4 **CORPUS CHRISTI, TEXAS (Venue unknown)**
(Cancelled)

6 **SAN ANTONIO, TEXAS, CIVIC CENTRE**

7 **FORT WORTH, TEXAS, S.M.U. MOODY COLISEUM**

8 **HOUSTON, TEXAS, HOLFHEINZ PAVILION**

10 **OKLAHOMA CITY, OKLAHOMA, MYRIAD**
(Cancelled)

11 **ST. LOUIS, MISSOURI, KIEL AUDITORIUM**

12 **LOUISVILLE, KENTUCKY, FREEDOM HALL COLISEUM**

13 **COLUMBUS, OHIO, ST. JOHN'S ARENA**

14 **CICERO, ILLINOIS, HAWTHORNE RACE TRACK**
Peter Frampton, Gary Wright, Lynyrd Skynyrd also on the bill, rescheduled from the cancelled original venue of Comisky Park, Chicago, Illinois.

15 **ST. PAUL, MINNESOTA, CIVIC AUDITORIUM**

16 **MILWAUKEE, WISCONSIN, AUDITORIUM**

17-19 **DETROIT, MICHIGAN, COBO HALL**

20 **TOLEDO, OHIO, TOLEDO SPORTS ARENA**

21 **RICHFIELD, OHIO, RICHFIELD COLISEUM**

22 **FORT WAYNE, INDIANA, WAR MEMORIAL COLISEUM**

1977

JULY (USA)

Supported by Donovan.

LITITZ, PENNSYLVANIA
The band spend time rehearsing.

30 **TOLEDO, OHIO, TOLEDO SPORTS ARENA**

31 **WHEELING, WEST VIRGINIA, CIVIC CENTRE**

AUGUST (USA)

1 **HAMPTON ROADS, VIRGINIA, HAMPTON ROADS COLISEUM**

2 **PHILADELPHIA, PENNSYLVANIA, THE SPECTRUM ARENA**

3 **PHILADELPHIA, PENNSYLVANIA, THE SPECTRUM ARENA**

5-7 **NEW YORK, N.Y., MADISON SQUARE GARDEN**

7-9 **NEW HAVEN, CONNECTICUT, COLISEUM**

10 **SPRINGFIELD, MASSACHUSETTS, CIVIC CENTRE**

12-13 **BOSTON, MASSACHUSETTS, BOSTON GARDENS**

14 **PORTLAND, MAINE, CUBERLAND COUNTY CIVIC CENTRE**

15 **PROVIDENCE, RHODE ISLAND, CIVIC CENTRE**

16 **LANDOVER, MARYLAND, CAPITOL CENTRE**
Supported by Donovan, Elvis dies on this day and Donovan plays a tribute to him.

17-18 **RICHFIELD, OHIO, RICHFIELD COLISEUM**

19 **PITTSBURG, PENNSYLVANIA, CIVIC ARENA**

20 **BUFFALO, N.Y., RICH STADIUM**

SPECIAL GUEST
Donovan
SAT. AUGUST 27, 7PM
Nashville Municipal Auditorium
Tickets: $7.50 Reserved, $6.00 General Admission
Now on sale at Sound Seventy, Port O'Call (Harding Mall & Madison), Morris Sound (100 Oaks & R'Gate Pl.), Discount Records (Ellison Pl.), Headquarters (Bowling Gr.), Citizens Central & M'Boro Music Center (M'Boro), Other Side (Dickson), Tapes & Threads (Clarksville), Tribal Sounds (Gallatin), & Variety Records (Columbia). 25c handling charge per ticket at all outside locations.
Mail Orders Accepted! Send cashier's check or M.O. payable to Sound Seventy, to Yes, c/o Sound Seventy, 1719 West End Ave., Nashville, Tn. 37203. Enclose self-addressed stamped env. & 25c handling charge.
A Sound Seventy Production

22-23 DETROIT, MICHIGAN, COBAL HALL
25 ATLANTA, GEORGIA, OMNI
26 BIRMINGHAM, ALABAMA, JEFFERSON CIVIC CENTRE
27 NASHVILLE, TENNESSEE, MUNICIPAL AUDITORIUM
28 LOUISVILLE, KENTUCKY, FREEDOM HALL COLISEUM
29 CINCINNATI, OHIO, RIVERFRONT COLISEUM
30 INDIANAPOLIS, INDIANA, MARKET SQUARE ARENA
31 MADISON, WISCONSIN, DANE COUNTY MEMORIAL COLISEUM

SEPTEMBER (USA & CANADA)

1 MILWAUKEE, WISCONSIN, DANE COUNTY MEMORIAL COLISEUM
2-3 CHICAGO, ILLINOIS, ILLINOIS INTERNATIONAL AMPHITHEATRE
17 VANCOUVER, BRITISH COLUMBIA, COLISEUM
18-19 SEATTLE, WASHINGTON, SEATTLE CENTRE
20 PORTLAND, OREGON, PORTLAND MEMORIAL COLISEUM
21-22 OAKLAND, CALIFORNIA, OAKLAND COLISEUM
23-24 LOS ANGELES, CALIFORNIA, L.A. FORUM
25 SAN DIEGO, CALIFORNIA, SPORTS ARENA
26 LONG BEACH, CALIFORNIA, LONG BEACH ARENA
27 LAS VEGAS, NEVADA, ALADDIN THEATRE
29 EL PASO, TEXAS, EL PASO COUNTY COLISEUM
30 ABILENE, TEXAS, ABILENE CIVIC CENTRE

OCTOBER

1 HOUSTON, TEXAS, SAM HOUSTON COLISEUM
2 DALLAS, TEXAS, REUNION ARENA
3 OKLAHOMA CITY, OKLAHOMA, MYRIAD ARENA
4-5 ST. LOUIS, MISSOURI, KIEL AUDITORIUM
6 KANSAS CITY, MISSOURI, KEMPER ARENA
7 MEMPHIS, TENNESSEE, MID SOUTH COLISEUM
8 JACKSON, MISSISSIPPI, MISSISSIPPI COLISEUM
9 NEW ORLEANS, LOUISIANA, MUNICIPAL AUDITORIUM
24-29 LONDON, ENGLAND, WEMBLEY ARENA

NOVEMBER (EUROPE)

2-4 STAFFORD, ENGLAND, NEW BINGLEY HALL
6-8 GLASGOW, SCOTLAND, APOLLO
Bootlegged on film, it is the best available example of a 1977 show.
11 OSLO, NORWAY, EKEBERGHALLEN
12 GOTHENBURG, SWEDEN, SCANDINAVIUM
13 COPENHAGEN, DENMARK, FOLKENER CENTRE
14 HANNOVER, GERMANY, MUSIKHALLE HANNOVER
15 DORTMUND, GERMANY, WESTFALENHALLE
16 DUSSELDORF, GERMANY, PHILIPSHALLE
18 FRANKFURT, GERMANY, FESTHALLE
19 NURENBERG, GERMANY, MESSEHALLE
20 ZURICH, SWITZERLAND, HALLENSTADION
21 HEIDELBERG, GERMANY, STADTHALLE
23 MUNICH, GERMANY, OLYMPIAHALLE

YES
The biggest gig in the entire history of the world

Jon Anderson: 'I feel eager to get on with new things. Not settle back. The new album is what's on our minds.'

Bicentennialand and rock's favourite vegetarians take Phil Sutcliffe by storm.

IT WAS Saturday morning and most of Yes were sat around the pool. They were waiting for their biggest gig ever, in fact the biggest non-festival gig in the entire history of the world. It was an official 105,000 sell-out at the JFK Stadium for the triple bill of Yes, Peter Frampton and Gary Wright.

Pictures: Chuck Pulin

(Clockwise from left) Peter Frampton, Steve Howe, teeming US hordes, Jon Anderson and young lady struggling to get her hands on those dishy Yes boys (yummy!).

24-25
ROTTERDAM, HOLLAND, AHOY-HALLE

26 ANTWERP, BELGIUM, SPORTSPALEIS

27 BREMEN, GERMANY, STADTHALLE

28 BERLIN, GERMANY, DEUTSCHLANDHALLE

29 COLOGNE, GERMANY, SPORTHALLE

DECEMBER (EUROPE)

1 ESSLINGEN, GERMANY, EBERHARD – BAUAR- HALLE

2 COLMAR, FRANCE, PARC DES EXPOSITIONS

4 LYON, FRANCE, LE TRANSPORTEUR DES LYON

5-6 PARIS, FRANCE, PAVILION DE PARIS

1978

YES' 10th ANNIVERSARY TOUR OF THE USA

AUGUST

28 ROCHESTER, N.Y., MEMORIAL AUDITORIUM

29 BUFFALO, N.Y., MEMORIAL AUDITORIUM

30-31
BOSTON, MASSACHUSETTS, BOSTON GARDENS

SEPTEMBER (USA)

1 PROVIDENCE, RHODE ISLAND, CIVIC CENTRE

2 SPRINGFIELD, MASSACHUSETTS, CIVIC CENTRE

3-4 NEW HAVEN, CONNECTICUT, COLISEUM

6-9 NEW YORK, N.Y., MADISON SQUARE GARDEN

10 LANDOVER, MARYLAND, CAPITOL CENTRE

11-12 PHILADELPHIA, PENNSYLVANIA, THE SPECTRUM ARENA

13 HAMPTON ROADS, VIRGINIA, COLISEUM

14 GREENSBORO, NORTH CAROLINA, COLISEUM

16 NASHVILLE, TENNESSEE, MUNICIPAL AUDITORIUM

17 MEMPHIS, TENNESSEE, MID-SOUTH COLISEUM

19 RICHFIELD, OHIO, RICHFIELD COLISEUM

20 CINCINNATI, OHIO, RIVERFRONT

21 DETROIT, MICHIGAN, OLYMPIC STADIUM

22 SOUTH BEND, INDIANA, NOTRE DAME

23-24
CHICAGO, ILLINOIS, AMPHITHEATRE

25 INDIANAPOLIS, INDIANA, CONVENTION CENTRE

27 KANSAS CITY, MISSOURI, KEMPER ARENA

28 ST. LOUIS, MISSOURI, CHECKERDOME

29 TULSA, OKLAHOMA, ASSEMBLY CENTRE

30 HOUSTON, TEXAS, SAM HOUSTON COLISEUM

OCTOBER (USA)

1 FT. WORTH, TEXAS, TARRANT COUNTY COLISEUM

3 LAS CRUCES, NEW MEXICO, PAN AMERICAN CENTRE

4 TEMPE, ARIZONA, STATE UNIVERSITY

5-6 INGLEWOOD, CALIFORNIA, GREAT WESTERN FORUM

TORMATO
WEMBLEY ARENA
28th Oct. 1978
Non Restricted
GUEST PASS

7-8 OAKLAND, CALIFORNIA, COUNTY COLISEUM
The Oakland R Cheerleaders join Yes.

OCTOBER

26-28
LONDON, ENGLAND, WEMBLEY ARENA
This turned out to be one of the greatest Yesshows recorded. It became the most widely bootlegged show ever. By public demand Yes played a matinee show at 3pm on the 28th

1979

APRIL (USA & CANADA)

6 KANSAS CITY, MISSOURI, KEMPER ARENA (Cancelled)

9 KALAMAZOO, MICHIGAN, WING STADIUM

10 BLOOMINGTON, INDIANA, INDIANA UNIVERSITY

11 PITTSBURG, PENNSYLVANIA, CIVIC ARENA

12 DAYTON, OHIO, UNIVERSITY OF DAYTON

13 LOUISVILLE, KENTUCKY, FREEDOM HALL

14 HUNTINGTON, WEST VIRGINIA, CIVIC CENTRE ARENA

16 OTTAWA, ONTARIO, CIVIC CENTRE

17 MONTREAL, QUEBEC, THE MONTREAL FORUM

18 QUEBEC CITY, QUEBEC, THE COLISEUM

20 TORONTO, ONTARIO, MAPLE LEAF GARDENS

21 DETROIT, MICHIGAN, OLYMPIC STADIUM

22 WEST LAFAYETTE, INDIANA, MACKAY ARENA

Right: Steve taking the applause after his solo spot on the 1979 'In the Round' tour.

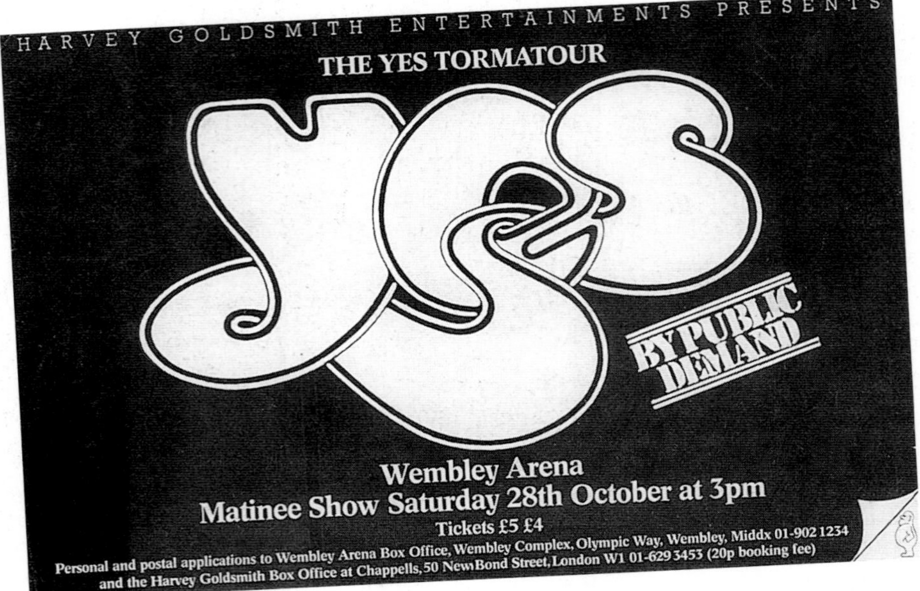

23 CHAMPAIGN, ILLINOIS, UNIVERSITY OF ILLINOIS

24 OMAHA, NEBRASKA, CIVIC CENTRE

25 CEDAR RAPIDS, IOWA, FOUR SEASONS ARENA

26 MILWAUKEE, WISCONSIN, MILWAUKEE ARENA

27 MADISON, WISCONSIN, DANE COUNTY COLISEUM

28 BLOOMINGTON, MINNEAPOLIS, METROPOLITAN SPORTS CENTRE

29 DULUTH, MINNESOTA, DULUTH ARENA

30 WINNIPEG, CANADA, WINNIPEG ARENA

MAY (USA & CANADA)

1 REGINA, SASKATCHEWAN, REGINA AGRIDOME

2 EDMONTON, ALBERTA, COLISEUM BOWL

3 CALGARY, ALBERTA, CALGARY CORRAL

5 VANCOUVER, BRITISH COLUMBIA, PACIFIC COLISEUM

6 SPOKANE, WASHINGTON, SPOKANE ARENA

7 PORTLAND, OREGON, MEMORIAL COLISEUM

8 SEATTLE, WASHINGTON, SEATTLE CENTRE

12 RIO DE JANEIRO, BRAZIL, MARACANANZINHO GYM (Cancelled)

18 SAO PAULO, BRAZIL, IBARAPUARA GYM (Cancelled)

24 FRESNO, CALIFORNIA, SELLAND ARENA

25-26 LONG BEACH, CALIFORNIA, LONG BEACH ARENA

27 SAN DIEGO, CALIFORNIA, SPORTS ARENA

29 DENVER, COLORADO, MC NICHOLES SPORTS ARENA

30 AMARILLO, TEXAS, CIVIC CENTRE

31 FORT WORTH, TEXAS, TARRANT COUNTY CONVENTION CENTRE

JUNE (USA)

1 AUSTIN, TEXAS, SPECIAL EVENTS CENTRE

3-4 HOUSTON, TEXAS, SAM HOUSTON COLISEUM

5 OKLAHOMA CITY, OKLAHOMA, MYRIAD ARENA

6 KANSAS CITY, MISSOURI, KEMPER ARENA (Cancelled)

7 ST. LOUIS, MISSOURI, THE ST. LOUIS ARENA

8-10 CHICAGO, ILLINOIS, INTERNATIONAL AMPHITHEATRE

12 UNIONDALE, N.Y., NASSAU VETERANS MEMORIAL COLISEUM

13-15 NEW YORK, N.Y., MADISON SQUARE GARDEN

16-17 NEW HAVEN, CONNECTICUT, MEMORIAL COLISEUM

18 SPRINGFIELD, MASSACHUSETTS, CIVIC EXHIBITION HALL

19 BOSTON, MASSACHUSETTS, BOSTON GARDENS

20-22 PHILADELPHIA, PENNSYLVANIA, THE SPECTRUM ARENA

23 LEXINGTON, KENTUCKY, RUPP ARENA

24 BIRMINGHAM, ALABAMA, JEFFERSON CIVIC CENTRE

25 ATLANTA, GEORGIA, OMNI

27 BATON ROUGE, RIVERSIDE CENTROPLEX AUDITORIUM

28 MOBILE, ALABAMA, CIVIC CENTRE (Cancelled)

29 LAKELAND, FLORIDA, LAKELAND CIVIC CENTRE ARENA

30 MIAMI, FLORIDA, HOLLYWOOD SPORTATORIUM

1980

AUGUST (CANADA)

29 TORONTO, ONTARIO, MAPLE LEAF GARDENS

30 MONTREAL, QUEBEC, MONTREAL FORUM

SEPTEMBER (USA)

1 HARTFORD, CONNECTICUT, CIVIC CENTRE

2 PORTLAND, MAINE, CUMBERLAND CIVIC CENTRE

4-6 NEW YORK, N.Y., MADISON SQUARE GARDEN
Yes sell out the venue all nights and break the record formerly held by Led Zeppelin.

7 UNIONDALE, N.Y., NASSAU COLISEUM

8 PROVIDENCE, RHODE ISLAND, CIVIC CENTRE

9 BOSTON, MASSACHUSETTS, BOSTON GARDENS

10 GLENS FALLS, N.Y., CIVIC CENTRE

11 LANDOVER, MARYLAND, CAPITOL CENTRE

12-13
PHILADELPHIA, PENNSYLVANIA, THE SPECTRUM ARENA

14 BINGHAMPTON, N.Y., BROOME, COUNTY ARENA

16 ROCHESTER, N.Y., WAR MEMORIAL

17 BUFFALO, N.Y., MEMORIAL AUDITORIUM

18 PITTSBURG, PENNSYLVANIA, CIVIC ARENA

19 DETROIT, MICHIGAN, JOE LOUIS ARENA

20 CLEVELAND, OHIO, RICHFIELD COLISEUM

21 CINCINNATI, OHIO, RIVERFRONT COLISEUM

22-23
CHICAGO, ILLINOIS, AMPHITHEATRE

25 ST. LOUIS, MISSOURI, CHECKERDOME

26 TULSA, OKLAHOMA, ASSEMBLY CENTRE

27 DALLAS, TEXAS, REUNION HALL

28 SAN ANTONIO, TEXAS, HEMISPHERE ARENA

29 HOUSTON, TEXAS, SUMMIT

OCTOBER (USA)

1 TEMPE, ARIZONA, UNIVERSITY ACTIVITY CENTRE

2 SAN DIEGO, CALIFORNIA, SPORTS ARENA

3-4 LOS ANGELES, CALIFORNIA, SPORTS ARENA

5 FRESNO, CALIFORNIA, SELLAND ARENA

6 DALEY CITY, CALIFORNIA, COW PALACE

7 OAKLAND, CALIFORNIA, COLISEUM

9 ST. PAUL, MINNESOTA, ST. PAUL CIVIC CENTRE

10 SOUTH BEND, INDIANA, JOYCE CENTRE

11 TERRE HAUTE, INDIANA, INDIANA STATE UNIVERSITY
(Cancelled)

12 CHAMPAIGN, ILLINOIS, UNIVERSITY OF ILLINOIS

13 LOUISVILLE, KENTUCKY, FREEDOM HALL

14 NASHVILLE, TENNESSEE, COLISEUM

16 MEMPHIS, TENNESSEE, MID-SOUTH COLISEUM

17 PHILADELPHIA, PENNSYLVANIA, THE SPECTRUM ARENA
Replaced Greensboro, North Carolina, which was cancelled.

18 HAMPTON ROADS, VIRGINIA, HAMPTON ROADS COLISEUM

19 HEMPSTEAD, N.Y., NASSAU COLISEUM

20 NEW HAVEN, CONNECTICUT, VETERAN MEMORIAL COLISIUM
(Cancelled)

NOVEMBER

16 BRISTOL, ENGLAND, HIPPODROME

17 OXFORD, ENGLAND, NEW THEATRE

19-20
BIRMINGHAM, ENGLAND, ODEON

22 DEESIDE, ENGLAND, LEISURE CENTRE

24-25
LEICESTER, ENGLAND, DE MONTFORT HALL

27 GLASGOW, SCOTLAND, APOLLO

29-30
EDINBURGH, SCOTLAND, PLAYHOUSE

DECEMBER

2-4 NEWCASTLE, ENGLAND, CITY HALL

6-7 MANCHESTER, ENGLAND, APOLLO

9-10 SOUTHAMPTON, ENGLAND, GAUMONT
Steve and Alan record an interview on BBC Radio One to discuss Drama, the band's split and the controversial Yesshows album release.

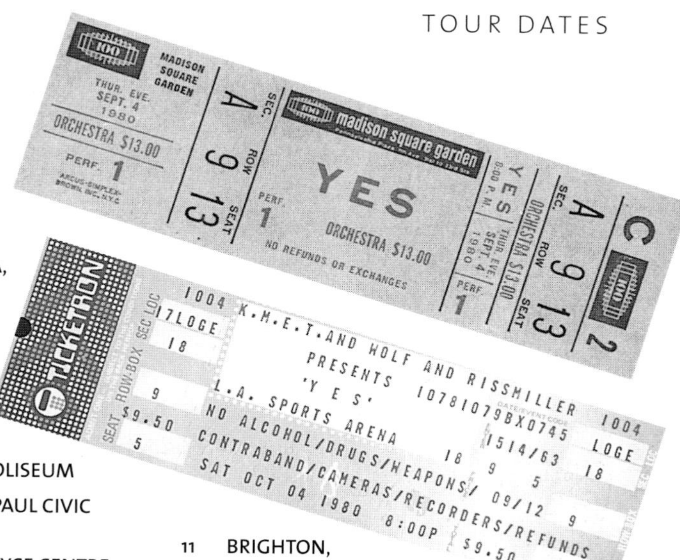

11 BRIGHTON, ENGLAND, BRIGHTON CENTRE

12 LEWISHAM, ENGLAND, ODEON

14-16
LONDON, ENGLAND, HAMMERSMITH ODEON

17-18
LONDON, ENGLAND, RAINBOW THEATRE

1980

JON ANDERSON SOLO TOUR

NOVEMBER

21 IPSWICH, ENGLAND, GAUMONT THEATRE

22 WOLVERHAMPTON, ENGLAND, CIVIC HALL

25 SOUTHAMPTON, ENGLAND, GAUMONT THEATRE

26 BRIGHTON, ENGLAND, THE DOME

28 BOURNEMOUTH, ENGLAND, WINTER GARDENS

29 OXFORD, ENGLAND, NEW THEATRE

DECEMBER

1 LONDON, ENGLAND, THE ROYAL ALBERT HALL

3 SHEFFIELD, ENGLAND, CITY HALL

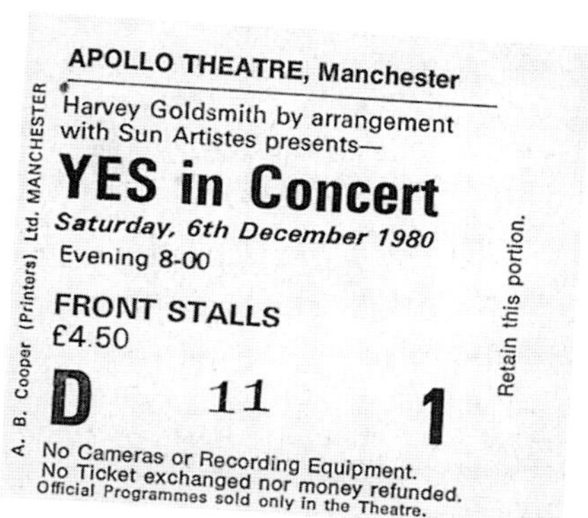

4 BIRMINGHAM, ENGLAND, ODEON
5 LIVERPOOL, ENGLAND, EMPIRE THEATRE
6 COVENTRY, ENGLAND, THEATRE
11 EDINBURGH, SCOTLAND, PLAYHOUSE
12 NEWCASTLE, ENGLAND, CITY HALL
13 GLASGOW, SCOTLAND, APOLLO THEATRE
15 LEICESTER, ENGLAND, DE MONTFORT HALL
16 MANCHESTER, ENGLAND, APOLLO

1982

ASIA TOUR

With no Yes, two of Yes' ex members, Steve Howe and Geoff Downes, launch Asia and tour with Carl Palmer and John Wetton.

APRIL

1 POTS DAM, N.Y., CLARKSON COLLEGE (Rehearsal)
22 POTS DAM, N.Y., CLARKSON COLLEGE
23 UTICA, N.Y., STANLEY THEATRE
24 FREDONIA, N.Y., S.U.N.Y. AUDITORIUM
25 PITTSBURG, PENNSYLVANIA, STANLEY THEATRE
27 NEW HAVEN, CONNECTICUT, YALE WOOLSEY HALL
28 OWINGS MILL, MARYLAND, PAINTERS MILL THEATRE
29 BOSTON, MASSACHUSETTS, ORPHEUM THEATRE
30 PASSAIC, NEW JERSEY, CAPITOL THEATRE

MAY

1 PHILADELPHIA, PENNSYLVANIA, TOWER THEATRE
2 NEW YORK, N.Y., CITY PALLADIUM
3 BUFFALO, N.Y., KLEINMANS THEATRE

5 ROCHESTER, N.Y., AUDITORIUM THEATRE
6 POUGHKEEPSIE, N.Y., MID HUDSON CIVIC CENTRE
7 MONTREAL, QUEBEC, VERDUN THEATRE
8 TORONTO, ONTARIO, UNIVERSITY OF WEST ONTARIO
10 AKRON, OHIO, E. J. THOMAS CENTRE
12 GRAND RAPIDS, MICHIGAN, GRAND CENTRE
13 DETROIT, MICHIGAN, ROYAL OAK THEATRE
14 CHICAGO, ILLINOIS, ILLINOIS AUDITORIUM THEATRE
15 AMES, IOWA, STATE UNIVERSITY
17 MINNEAPOLIS, MINNEAPOLIS, ORPHEUM THEATRE
18 MILWAUKEE, WISCONSIN, PERFORMING ARTS THEATRE
21-22 SAN FRANCISCO, CALIFORNIA, WARFIELD THEATRE
23 FRESNO, CALIFORNIA, WARNER THEATRE
24 STOCKTON, CALIFORNIA, FOX THEATRE
25 SANTA CRUZ, CALIFORNIA, CIVIC AUDITORIUM
27 SANTA BARBARA, CALIFORNIA, ARLINGTON THEATRE
28-29 SANTA MONICA, CALIFORNIA, CIVIC CENTRE
30 SAN DIEGO, CALIFORNIA, FOX THEATRE

JUNE

14 TOLEDO, OHIO, CENTENNIAL HALL
15-16 DETROIT, MICHIGAN, PINE KNOB MUSIC CENTRE
17 CHICAGO, ILLINOIS, ILLINOIS POPLAR CREEK
18 CUYAHOGA FALLS, OHIO, BLOSSOM MUSIC FESTIVAL
19 DAYTON, OHIO, HARA ARENA
21 COLUMBIA, OHIO, MERRIWEATHER POST
22 PHILADELPHIA, PENNSYLVANIA, THE SPECTRUM ARENA
23 SARATOGA SPRINGS, N.Y., PERFORMING ARTS CENTRE
25 NORFOLK, VIRGINIA, SCOPE ARENA
26 CHARLESTON, WEST VIRGINIA, CIVIC CENTRE
27 ATLANTA, GEORGIA, FOX THEATRE
29 NEW ORLEANS, LOUISIANA, LOUISIANA SAENGER THEATRE
30 HOUSTON, TEXAS, THE SUMMIT

JULY

1 AUSTIN, TEXAS, SPECIAL EVENTS CENTRE
2 DALLAS, TEXAS, REUNION ARENA
4 KANSAS CITY, MISSOURI, STARLIGHT THEATRE
5 OMAHA, NEBRASKA, CIVIC CENTRE
6 ST. LOUIS, MISSOURI, KIEL AUDITORIUM
8 DENVER, COLORADO, RED ROCKS THEATRE

OCTOBER

5 BRUSSELS, BELGIUM, FOREST NATIONAL
6 UTRECHT, NETHERLANDS, MUSIK CENTRUM
7-8 PARIS, FRANCE, PAVILION BALTARD
9 DUSSELDORF, GERMANY, PHILIPSHALLE
11 HAMBURG, GERMANY, KONGRESS CENTRUM
12-13 FRANKFURT, GERMANY, JAHRHUNDERTHALLE
14 LYON, FRANCE, BOURSE DU TRAVAIL

16 SAN SEBASTIAN, SPAIN, VELODROMA ANOETA
18 TURIN, ITALY, PALAZZO DELLO SPORT
19 ROME, ITALY, PALAZZO DELLO SPORT-PALAEUR
21 MUNICH, GERMANY, RUDI SEDLMAYER HALLE
22 MANNHEIM, GERMANY, ROSENGARTEN MOTZARTSAAL
23 WURZBERG, GERMANY, CARL DIEM HALLE
24 BASEL, SWITZERLAND, ST. JACOB SPORTHALLE
27-28 LONDON, ENGLAND, WEMBLEY ARENA

1984

JANUARY (USA)

26 NORTH FORT MYERS, FLORIDA, LEE CIVIC CENTRE
27 TALLAHASSEE, FLORIDA, LEON COUNTY CIVIC CENTRE
28 HOLLYWOOD, FLORIDA, HOLLYWOOD SPORTATORIUM
30 LAKELAND, FLORIDA, LAKELAND CIVIC CENTRE ARENA

31 JACKSONVILLE, FLORIDA, MEMORIAL COLISEUM

FEBRUARY (USA & CANADA)

2 ATLANTA, GEORGIA, THE OMNI COLISEUM

4 CHAPEL HILL, NORTH CAROLINA, DEAN SMITH CENTRE

5 HAMPTON, VIRGINIA, HAMPTON COLISEUM

7 PHILADELPHIA, PENNSYLVANIA, THE SPECTRUM ARENA

8 NEW HAVEN, CONNECTICUT, MEMORIAL COLISEUM

9 PORTLAND, MAINE, CUMBERLAND, COUNTY CIVIC CENTRE

10 WORCESTER, MASSACHUSETTS, CENTRUM CENTRE

12 LANDOVER, MARYLAND, CAPITOL CENTRE

13 ROCHESTER, N.Y., ROCHESTER WAR MEMORIAL

14 BUFFALO, N.Y., BUFFALO WAR MEMORIAL

16 UNIONDALE, N.Y., NASSAU MEMORIAL COLISEUM

17 EAST RUTHERFORD, NEW JERSEY, BRENDON BYRNE ARENA

20 TORONTO, ONTARIO, CANADIAN NEC

21 MONTREAL, QUEBEC, THE MONTREAL FORUM

22 OTTAWA, ONTARIO, LANDSDOWN PARK

23 QUEBEC CITY, QUEBEC, THE COLISEUM

25 NEW YORK, N.Y., MADISON SQUARE GARDEN

26 BETHLEHEM, PENNSYLVANIA, STABLER ARENA

27 PITTSBURG, PENNSYLVANIA, PITTSBURG CIVIC ARENA

28 MILLERSVILLE, PENNSYLVANIA, PUCILLO GYM & NATATORIUM

29 LEXINGTON, KENTUCKY, ADOLPH RUPP ARENA

MARCH (USA)

1 COLUMBUS, OHIO, EXHIBITION CENTRE COLISEUM

2 TOLEDO, OHIO, CENTENNIAL HALL

4 DETROIT, MICHIGAN, JOE LOUIS AUDITORIUM

5 CHAMPAIGN, ILLINOIS, UNIVERSITY OF ILLINOIS

6 CEDAR RAPIDS, IOWA, FIVE SEASONS CENTRE ARENA

7 ST. PAUL, MINNESOTA, ST. PAUL CIVIC CENTRE

8-9 ROSEMONT, ILLINOIS, ROSEMONT HORIZON

10 MILWAUKEE, WISCONSIN, MECCA ARENA

11 ST LOUIS, MISSOURI, THE ST. LOUIS ARENA

12 BONNER SPRINGS, KANSAS CITY, MISSOURI SANDSTONE AMPHITHEATRE

14 OKLAHOMA CITY, OKLAHOMA, MYRIAD ARENA

15 DALLAS, TEXAS, REUNION ARENA

16 HOUSTON, TEXAS, SUMMIT

17 AUSTIN, TEXAS, THE FRANK C. ERWIN JR. SPECIAL EVENTS CENTRE, UNIVERSITY OF TEXAS

20 DENVER, COLORADO, MC NICHOLS SPORTS ARENA

21 ALBEQUERQUE, NEW MEXICO, TINGLEY COLISEUM

22 PHOENIX, ARIZONA, VETERANS MEMORIAL COLISEUM

23 TUCSON, ARIZONA, MCKALE COMMUNITY CENTRE

24 LAS VEGAS, NEVADA, THOMAS AND MACK CENTRE

26 LOS ANGELES, CALIFORNIA, THE LOS ANGELES FORUM

27 SAN DIEGO, CALIFORNIA, SAN DIEGO SPORTS ARENA

28 LOS ANGELES, CALIFORNIA, THE LOS ANGELES FORUM

29 DALY CITY, CALIFORNIA, COW PALACE

30 DALY CITY, CALIFORNIA, COW PALACE

31 RENO, NEVADA, RENO HILTON AMPHITHEATRE

APRIL (USA & CANADA)

2 VANCOUVER, BRITISH COLUMBIA, PACIFIC COLISEUM

3 SEATTLE, WASHINGTON, SEATTLE CENTRE

4 PULLMAN, WASHINGTON, WALLIS BEASLEY P.A.C.

5 BOISE, IDAHO, BOISE STATE UNIVERSITY PAVILION

8 RAPID CITY, SOUTH DAKOTA, RUSHMORE ARENA PLAZA CIVIC CENTRE

10 ST. PAUL, MINNESOTA, ST. PAUL CIVIC CENTRE

11 MADISON, WISCONSIN, DANE COUNTY MEMORIAL COLISEUM

12 INDIANAPOLIS, INDIANA, MARKET SQUARE ARENA

13 CINCINNATI, OHIO, RIVERFRONT COLISEUM

15 NASHVILLE, TENNESSEE, MUNICIPAL AUDITORIUM

16 ATLANTA, GEORGIA, THE OMNI COLISEUM

TOUR NEWS

YES IT'S YES

YES are back on the road, touring Europe and England after a four year break. Sparkmatic Car Sounds presents a tour that takes in Sweden, Denmark, Norway, Austria, West Germany, Belgium and France starting on June 11th. One month later on July 11th, YES play Wembley Arena and on 14th July Birmingham N.E.C. Tickets are priced at £8.50 and £7.50 for Wembley and £7.50, £6.50 and £5.50 for Birmingham. Tickets for both the English gigs are available from the usual outlets but the Wembley date has tickets available by post too. Postal orders should be made payable to M.A.C. Promotions and should included a 30p booking fee per ticket. Send, together with SAE, to: YES, M.A.C. Promotions, P.O. Box 2BZ, London W1A 2BZ. Allow about fourteen days for a reply.

18-19 LAKELAND, FLORIDA, LAKELAND CIVIC CENTRE

20 NORTH FORT MYERS, FLORIDA, LEE CIVIC CENTRE

21 HOLLYWOOD, FLORIDA, SPORTATORIUM

22 JACKSONVILLE, FLORIDA, JACKSONVILLE VETERANS MEMORIAL COLISEUM

24 MEMPHIS, TENNESSEE, MID - SOUTH COLISEUM

25 LEXINGTON, KENTUCKY, ADOLPH RUPP ARENA

26 SOUTH BEND, INDIANA, JOYCE CENTRE NOTRE DAME

28 OXFORD, OHIO, UNIVERSITY OF OHIO MILLET HALL

29 ERIE, PENNSYLVANIA, ERIE CIVIC CENTRE

30 PHILADELPHIA, PENNSYLVANIA, THE SPECTRUM ARENA

MAY (USA)

1 PITTSBURG, PENNSYLVANIA, CIVIC ARENA

2 RICHFIELD, OHIO, RICHFIELD, COLISEUM

4-5 HARTFORD, CONNECTICUT, CIVIC CENTRE

7 EAST RUTHERFORD, NEW JERSEY, BRENDON BRYNE ARENA

8 PROVIDENCE, RHODE ISLAND, PROVIDENCE CIVIC CENTRE

9 BUFFALO, N.Y., BUFFALO MEMORIAL AUDITORIUM

10 ROCHESTER, N.Y., ROCHESTER WAR MEMORIAL

11 UNIONDALE, N.Y., NASSAU VETERANS MEMORIAL COLISEUM

12 WORCESTER, MASSACHUSETTS, WORCESTER CENTRUM CENTRE

14 NEW YORK CITY, N.Y., MADISON SQUARE GARDEN

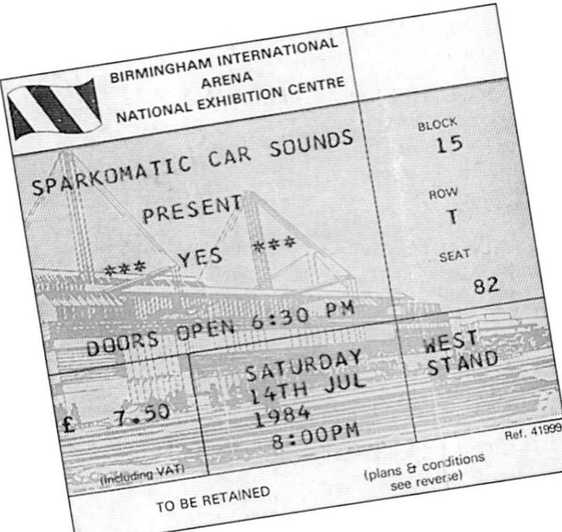

BIRMINGHAM INTERNATIONAL ARENA
NATIONAL EXHIBITION CENTRE
SPARKOMATIC CAR SOUNDS
PRESENT
*** YES ***
BLOCK 15
ROW T
SEAT 82
DOORS OPEN 6:30 PM
WEST STAND
£ 7.50
(including VAT)
SATURDAY 14TH JUL 1984 8:00PM
Ref. 41999
TO BE RETAINED
(plans & conditions see reverse)

15 LANDOVER, MARYLAND, CAPITOL CENTRE

JUNE (EUROPE)

11 STOCKHOLM, SWEDEN, SKELLEFTEA ISSTADION

13 COPENHAGEN, DENMARK, FALKONER THEATRE

15 GOTHENBURG, SWEDEN, VALKOMMEN TILL SCANDINAVIUM

16 DRAMMEN, NORWAY, DRAMMENSHALLEN

18 BERLIN, GERMANY, DEUTSCHLANDHALLE

19 HAMBURG, GERMANY, ERNST-MERCK HALLE

21 COLOGNE, GERMANY, SPORTHALLE

22 STUTTGART, GERMANY, HANNS MARTIN SCHLEYER HALL

24 DORTMUND, GERMANY, WESTFALEN-HALLE
Jimmy Page joins Yes on stage for the encore of 'I'm Down'.

25 MUNICH, GERMANY, BAYERN OLYMPIAHALLE

26 VIENNA, AUSTRIA, WIEN STADTHALLE

28 MANNHEIM, GERMANY, NORDRHEIN – WESTFALEN

29 FRANKFURT, GERMANY, FESTHALLE MESSE

30 WUERZBURG, GERMANY, CARL DIEM HALL

JULY (EUROPE)

1-2 ROTTERDAM, NETHERLANDS, AHOY HALLEN

3 BRUSSELS, BELGIUM, NATIONAL THEATRE

5 NANTES, FRANCE, LA STADE DE BEAUJOIRE

7-8 PARIS, FRANCE, PALAIS OMNISPORTS PARIS BERCY

11-12 LONDON, ENGLAND, WEMBLEY ARENA

14 BIRMINGHAM, ENGLAND, NEC

17 ZURICH, SWITZERLAND, HALLENSTADION ZURICH

18 MILAN, ITALY, PALASPORT DI SAN SIRO

20 NICE, FRANCE, STADE DE L'OUEST

21 BEZIERS, FRANCE (Venue unknown)

22 BIARRITZ, FRANCE, PARC DES SPORTS AGUILERRA

24 BARCELONA, SPAIN, PALACIO MUNICIPAL DE LOS DEPORTES

26 MADRID, SPAIN, PALICIO DE LOS DEPORTES DE LA COMUNIDAD DE MADRID

AUGUST (USA & CANADA)

9 OMAHA, NEBRASKA, OMAHA AUDITORIUM

11 EAST TROY, WISCONSIN, ALPINE VALLEY MUSIC THEATRE

13 CLARKSTON, MICHIGAN, PINE KNOB MUSIC CENTRE

15 LOUISVILLE, KENTUCKY, FREEDOM HALL COLISEUM

16 CINNCINATI, OHIO, OHIO RIVERFRONT

17 FORT WAYNE, INDIANA, ALLEN COUNTY WAR MEMORIAL COLISEUM

18 MICHIGAN, WYOMING, FT. WYOMING

20 OTTAWA, ONTARIO, LANDSDOWNE PARK EXHIBITION CENTRE

21 QUEBEC CITY, QUEBEC, LE COLISEE DE QUEBEC

22 MONTREAL, QUEBEC, LE FORUM DE MONTREAL

23 TORONTO, ONTARIO, CANADIAN NEC

24 CUYAHOGA FALLS, OHIO, BLOSSOM MUSIC FESTIVAL

25 ROCHESTER, N.Y., ROCHESTER WAR MEMORIAL

26 SYRACUSE, N.Y., COUNTY WAR MEMORIAL

27 SARATOGA SPRINGS, N.Y., SARATOGA PERFORMING ARTS CENTRE

29 FOREST HILLS, N.Y., FOREST HILLS TENNIS CENTRE

SEPTEMBER (USA)

1 HERSHEY, PENNSYLVANIA, HERSHEY PARK ARENA

2 SPRINGFIELD, MASSACHUSETTS, SPRING-FIELD CIVIC CENTRE EXHIBITION HALL

3 PORTLAND, MAINE, CUMBERLAND COUNTY CIVIC CENTRE

4 HOLMDEL, NEW JERSEY, GARDEN STATE ART CENTRE

6 COLUMBIA, MARYLAND, MERRIWEATHER POST PAVILION

7 BOSTON, MASSACHUSETTS, BOSTON GARDEN

8 HARTFORD, CONNECTICUT, HERSHEY PARK ARENA

9-10 PHILADELPHIA, PENNSYLVANIA, THE SPECTRUM ARENA

12 HAMPTON, VIRGINIA, HAMPTON COLISEUM

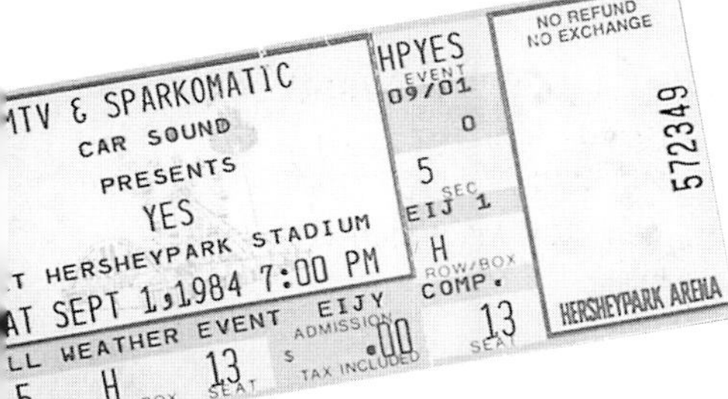

13 CHARLOTTE, NORTH CAROLINA, THE COLISEUM

14 GREENSBORO, NORTH CAROLINA, NORTH CAROLINA COLISEUM

16 ATLANTA, GEORGIA, THE OMNI COLISEUM

17 BONNER SPRINGS, KANSAS, SANDSTONE AMPHITHEATRE

18 BOULDER, COLORADO, CONFERENCE CENTRE

20 RENO, NEVADA, RENO HILTON AMPHITHEATRE

21-22 BERKELEY, CALIFORNIA, GREEK THEATRE

23 IRVINE, CALIFORNIA, IRVINE MEADOWS AMPHITHEATRE

25 SALT LAKE CITY, UTAH, SALT PALACE CONVENTION CENTRE

27 CALGARY, ALBERTA, SADDLEDOME

28-29 EDMONTON, ALBERTA, EDMONTON COLISEUM BOWL

1985

JANUARY (SOUTH AMERICA)

17 RIO DE JANEIRO, BRAZIL
Rock In Rio giant festival, Yes' biggest ever shows, performing to over 200 - 250,000 people the first night!

20 RIO DE JANEIRO, BRAZIL
Rock In Rio the second date, this was the biggest Yesshow ever, performing to 300 – 400,000 people! Yes were on top of the bill finishing both nights with fireworks and laser light shows. The other acts over the two days were Queen, AC/DC, Iron Maiden, Rod Stewart, Go Gos, Al Jarreau and Nina Hagen.

27 MALDONADO, URUGUAY, EL CAMPUS MUNICIPAL DE MALDONADO

FEBRUARY (ARGENTINA)

1-2 BUENOS AIRES, ARGENTINA, ESTADIO DEL FUBAL DE VELEZ SARSFIELD

9 BUENOS AIRES, ARGENTINA, ESTADIO DEL FUBAL DE VELEZ SARSFIELD

1987

NOVEMBER (USA)

14 OMAHA, NEBRASKA, CIVIC AUDITORIUM ARENA

19 SPRINGFIELD, ILLINOIS, CIVIC ARENA

20 KALAMAZOO, MICHIGAN, WING STADIUM

21 DETROIT, MICHIGAN, COBO HALL

22 LOUISVILLE, KENTUCKY, FREEDOM HALL

23 ST LOUIS, MISSOURI, THE ST. LOUIS ARENA CHECKERDOME

24 MILWAUKEE, WISCONSIN, MILWAUKEE ARENA

25 ROSEMONT, ILLINOIS, ROSEMONT HORIZON

26 BUFFALO, N.Y., WAR MEMORIAL (Cancelled)

27 PITTSBURG, PENNSYLVANIA, CIVIC ARENA

28 RICHMOND, VIRGINIA, RICHMOND COLISEUM

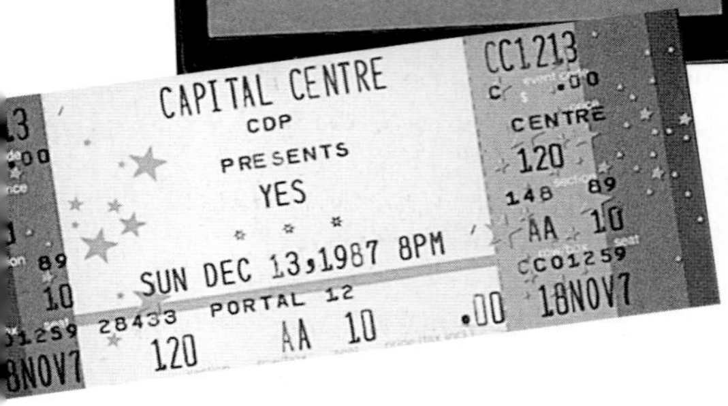

29-30
PHILADELPHIA, PENNSYLVANIA, THE SPECTRUM ARENA

DECEMBER (USA)

1 SYRACUSE, N.Y., ONONDAGA COUNTY WAR MEMORIAL

3 HARTFORD, CONNECTICUT, CIVIC CENTRE

4 BUFFALO, N.Y., BUFFALO MEMORIAL AUDITORIUM

5 ROCHESTER, N.Y., WAR MEMORIAL

6 OTTAWA, ONTARIO, LANDSDOWNE PARK

7 QUEBEC CITY, QUEBEC, THE QUEBEC COLISEUM

8 MONTREAL, QUEBEC, THE MONTREAL FORUM

9 TORONTO, ONTARIO, MAPLE LEAF GARDENS

10 PROVIDENCE, RHODE ISLAND, CIVIC CENTRE

11 WORCESTER, MASSACHUSETTS, CENTRUM CENTRE

12 ROCHESTER, N.Y., ROCHESTER WAR MEMORIAL

13 LANDOVER, MARYLAND, CAPITAL CENTRE

14 LARGO, MARYLAND, CAPITAL CENTRE

15 TROY, N.Y., RENNSSELAER POLYTECHNIC INSTITUTE FIELDHOUSE

16 NEW YORK CITY, N.Y., MADISON SQUARE GARDENS

17 PROVIDENCE, RHODE ISLAND, PROVIDENCE CIVIC CENTRE

18-19
EAST RUTHERFORD, NEW JERSEY, MEADOWLANDS

20 BETHLEHEM, PENNSYLVANIA, STABLER ARENA

21 WORCESTER, MASSACHUSETTS, WORCESTER CENTRUM CENTRE

1988

JANUARY (USA)

19 TALLAHASSEE, FLORIDA, LEON COUNTY CIVIC CENTRE

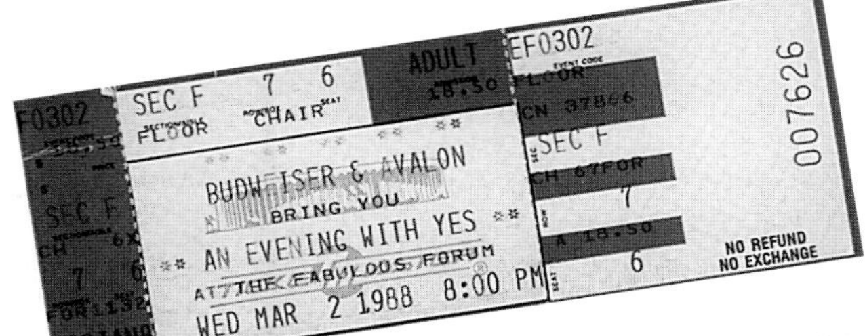

20 PENSACOLA, FLORIDA, CIVIC CENTRE

21 TALLAHASSEE, FLORIDA, FLORIDA STATE UNIVERSITY

22-23 TAMPA, FLORIDA, SUNDOME

24 HOLLYWOOD, FLORIDA, HOLLYWOOD SPORTATORIUM

25 JACKSONVILLE, FLORIDA, CIVIC CENTRE

28 KNOXVILLE, TENNESSEE, THOMPSON BOILER ARENA

29 COLUMBUS, OHIO, OHIO CENTRE

31 INDIANAPOLIS, INDIANA, MARKET SQUARE ARENA

FEBRUARY (USA)

5 UNIONDALE, N.Y., MEMORIAL COLISEUM

6 BINGHAMPTON, N.Y., BROOME COUNTY ARENA

7 PHILADELPHIA, PENNSYLVANIA, THE SPECTRUM ARENA

8 HERSHEY, PENNSYLVANIA, HERSHEY PARK ARENA

10 NASHVILLE, TENNESSEE, MUNICIPAL AUDITORIUM

12 ATLANTA, GEORGIA, THE OMNI COLISEUM

13 CHARLOTTE, NORTH CAROLINA, THE COLISEUM

14 CHAPEL HILL, NORTH CAROLINA, DEAN SMITH CENTRE NORTH CAROLINA UNIVERSITY

16 RICHFIELD, OHIO, RICHFIELD COLISEUM

17 CINCINNATI, OHIO, RIVERFRONT COLISEUM

19 HOUSTON, TEXAS, SUMMIT

20 LAFAYETTE, LOUISIANA, CAJUN DOME

23 AUSTIN, TEXAS, THE FRANK ERWIN CENTRE

24 TUCSON, ARIZONA, CONVENTION HALL

26 SACRAMENTO, CALIFORNIA, A.R.C.O. ARENA

27 OAKLAND, CALIFORNIA, COLISEUM ARENA

28 RENO, NEVADA, RENO HILTON AMPHITHEATRE

MARCH (USA)

2 LOS ANGELES, CALIFORNIA, INGLEWOOD GREAT WESTERN FORUM

3-5 COSTA MESA, CALIFORNIA, IRVINE MEADOWS AMPHITHEATRE

6 LAS VEGAS, NEVADA, ALADDIN THEATRE

8 SAN DIEGO, CALIFORNIA, SPORTS ARENA

9 TEMPE, ARIZONA, STATE UNIVERSITY

10 PHOENIX, ARIZONA, VETERANS MEMORIAL COLISEUM

11 ALBEQUERQUE, NEW MEXICO, TINGLEY COLISEUM

13 DENVER, COLORADO, MC NICHOL'S ARENA

30 HONOLULU, HAWAII, NEAL BLAISDEL ARENA

APRIL (JAPAN)

4-7 TOKYO, JAPAN, YOYOGI OLYMPIC POOL

9 KANAGAWA, JAPAN, YOKOHAMA BUNKA TAIIKUKAN

10 NAGOYA, JAPAN, AICHI-KEN NAGOYA, CONGRESS CENTRE

12-13 OSAKA, JAPAN, OSAKA-KU PERFECTURAL GYMNASIUM

14 NEW YORK, N.Y., MADISON SQUARE GARDENS
Atlantic Records 40th year celebrations marked this big celebrity event, many artists featured, the show was filmed and shown on TV. Yes performed one track.

DECEMBER

7 At 11.41am a massive earthquake hits Armenia, the music business pulls together to create *Rock Aid*, a charity record to aid the disaster. Chris Squire and Geoff Downes participate on the Deep Purple track 'Smoke On The Water'.

1989

ABWH

JULY (USA)

29 MEMPHIS, TENNESSEE, MUD ISLAND

30 ATLANTA, GEORGIA, CHASTAIN PARK

AUGUST (USA & CANADA)

1 HAMPTON ROADS, VIRGINIA, COLISEUM

2 HARRISBURG, PENNSYLVANIA, CITY ISLAND

3 PHILADELPHIA, PENNSYLVANIA, THE SPECTRUM ARENA

4 UNIONDALE, N.Y., VETERANS MEMORIAL, COLISEUM

5 COLUMBIA, MARYLAND, MERRIWEATHER POST

6 MANSFIELD, MASSACHUSETTS, GREATWOODS CENTRE FOR THE PERFORMING ARTS

8 MANCHESTER, NEW HAMPSHIRE, RIVERFRONT PARK

9 MIDDLETOWN, N.Y., ORANGE COUNTY FAIRGROUNDS

10 WANTAUGH, N.Y., JONES BEACH

11 HARTFORD, CONNECTICUT, CIVIC CENTRE

12 OLD ORCHARD BEACH, MAINE, SEASHORE PAC

13 HOLMDEL, NEW JERSEY, GARDEN STATE ARTS

15 PITTSBURG, PENNSYLVANIA, A. J. PALUMBO CENTRE

16 CUYAHOGA FALLS, OHIO, BLOSSOM MUSIC CENTRE

17 WEEDSPORT, N.Y., CAYUAGA COUNTY FAIRGROUNDS

18 DARIEN, N.Y., DARIEN LAKE PERFORMING ARTS CENTRE

19 CLARKSTON, MICHIGAN, PINE KNOB

20 HOFFMAN ESTATES, ILLINOIS, POPLAR CREEK

22 TORONTO, ONTARIO, C.N.E.C

23 OTTAWA, ONTARIO, CIVIC CENTRE

24 MONTREAL, QUEBEC, THE FORUM

25 QUEBEC CITY, QUEBEC, AGORA

28 HOUSTON, TEXAS, THE SUMMIT

29 DALLAS, TEXAS, STARPEX

31 BONNER SPRINGS, KANSAS, SANDSTONE AMPHITHEATRE

SEPTEMBER (USA)

1 MORRISON, COLORADO, RED ROCKS AMPHITHEATRE

2 UTAH CITY PARK, UTAH, WOLF MOUNTAIN AMPHITHEATRE

4 SAN DIEGO, CALIFORNIA, OPEN AIR THEATRE
Jeff Berlin substitutes for Tony Levin who is ill.

5 COSTA MESA, CALIFORNIA, PACIFIC AMPHITHEATRE

6-7 LOS ANGELES, CALIFORNIA, GREEK THEATRE

8 SANTA BARBARA, CALIFORNIA, COUNTY BOWL

9 MOUNTAIN VIEW, CALIFORNIA, SHORELINE AMPHITHEATRE

10 SACRAMENTO, CALIFORNIA, CALIFORNIA EXPO AMPHITHEATRE

OCTOBER

20 WHITLEY BAY, ENGLAND, WHITLEY BAY ICE RINK
Following his illness Tony Levin rejoins the band for the tour.

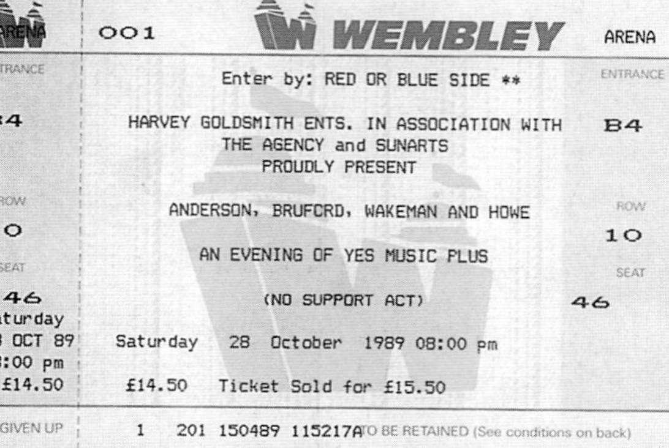

21-22 EDINBURGH, SCOTLAND, PLAYHOUSE

24-25 BIRMINGHAM, ENGLAND, NEC

28-30 LONDON, ENGLAND, WEMBLEY ARENA

NOVEMBER (EUROPE)

2 BRUSSELS, BELGIUM, VORST NATIONAL THEATRE

3 ROTTERDAM, NETHERLANDS, AHOY HALLEN

5 HAMBURG, GERMANY, SPORTHALLE

6 COPENHAGEN, DENMARK, FOLKENER CENTRE

8 STOCKHOLM, SWEDEN, ISSTADION

9 OLSO, NORWAY, SKEDSMOHALLEN

11 COLOGNE, GERMANY, SPORTHALLE

12 KASSEL, GERMANY, EISSPORTHALLE

13 MUNICH, GERMANY, RUDI SEDLMAYER-SPORTHALLE

14 STUTTGART, GERMANY, HANNS-MARTIN-SCHLEYER HALLE

16 FRANKFURT, GERMANY, FESTHALLE MESSE FRANKFURT

17 WUERZBERG, GERMANY, CARL-DIEM - HALLE

18 BASEL, SWITZERLAND, ST. JAKOBS HALLE

19 PARIS, FRANCE, PALAIS BERCY GENERAL SPORTS CENTRE

20 TURIN, ITALY, TORINO SPORTS PALACE

21 MILAN, ITALY, TEATRO DI PALATRUSSARDI

23 ROME, ITALY, PALAZZO DE PALAEUR DELLO SPORT

24 MODENA, ITALY, NUOVO PALASPORT

25 GRENOBLE, FRANCE, PALAIS DES SPORTS

26 MONTPELLIER, FRANCE, LE ZENITH

27 TOULOUSE, FRANCE, PALAIS DES SPORTS

29 BARCELONA, SPAIN, PALACIO MUNICIPAL DE LOS DEPORTES
(Cancelled)

30 MADRID, SPAIN, PALACIO DE LOS DEPORTES
(Cancelled)

1990

ABWH

FEBRUARY (SPAIN)

21 BARCELONA, SPAIN, PALACIO DE LOS DEPORTES

22 ZARAGOZA, SPAIN, PALACIO DE DEPORTES
Cancelled show moved to the 23rd.

23 MADRID, SPAIN, PALACIO DE LOS DEPORTES

MARCH (JAPAN, USA & CANADA)

1-3 TOKYO, JAPAN, NIHON HOHSOH KYOKAI

5 OSAKA, JAPAN, FESTIVAL HALL

7 YOKOHAMA, JAPAN, YOKOHAMA BUNKA TAIIKUKAN

8 TOKYO, JAPAN, NIKON HOHSOH KYOKAI

11 SEATTLE, WASHINGTON, SEATTLE CENTRE

12 VANCOUVER, BRITISH COLUMBIA, PACIFIC COLISEUM

13 SPOKANE, WASHINGTON, THE SPOKANE OPERA HOUSE

OREGON, EARLE A. CHILES CENTRE

18 RICHMOND ,VIRGINIA, MOSQUE THEATRE

19 PHILADELPHIA, PENNSYLVANIA, THE SPECTRUM ARENA

20 BOSTON, MASSACHUSETTS, WASHINGTON THEATRE

22 WASHINGTON, WASHINGTON D.C., D.A.R. CONSTITUTIONAL HALL

23 NEW YORK CITY, N.Y., MADISON SQUARE GARDEN

1991

YES

APRIL (USA & CANADA)

9 PENSACOLA, FLORIDA, CIVIC CENTRE

13 ATLANTIC CITY, NEW JERSEY, TAJ MAHAL HOTEL

14 E. ROTHERFORD, NEW JERSEY, MEADOWLANDS

16 PHILADELPHIA, PENNSYLVANIA, THE SPECTRUM ARENA

The Spectrum sells out within 4 hours.

17 WORCESTER, MASSACHUSETTS, CENTRUM

18 HARTFORD, CONNECTICUT, CIVIC CENTRE

19 FAIRFAX, VIRGINIA, PATRIOT CENTRE (Rescheduled from 12th April)

20 UNIONDALE, NEW JERSEY, NASSAU COLISEUM

22 QUEBEC CITY, QUEBEC, COLISEUM

23 TORONTO, ONTARIO, SKYDOME

24 MONTREAL, QUEBEC, FORUM

25 ALBANY, N.Y., KNICKERBOCKER ARENA

26 BUFFALO, N.Y., MEMORIAL AUDITORIUM

27 AUBURN HILLS, MICHIGAN, PALACE OF AUBURN HILLS

29 RICHFIELD, OHIO, RICHFIELD COLISEUM

MAY (USA & EUROPE)

1 ST. PAUL, MINNESOTA, CIVIC CENTRE

3 KALAMAZOO, MICHIGAN, WING STADIUM

4 DAYTON, OHIO, ERVINE J. NUTTER CENTRE

5 CHAMPAIGN, ILLINOIS, UNIVERSITY OF ILLINOIS

6 ROSEMONT, ILLINOIS, ILLINOIS ROSEMONT HORIZON

7 BLOOMINGTON, ILLINOIS, MYRIAD CENTRE

9 DENVER, COLORADO, MC NICHOLS ARENA

11 PHOENIX, ARIZONA, DESERT SKY

12 LAS VEGAS, NEVADA, THOMAS AND MACK CENTRE

14 SAN DIEGO, CALIFORNIA, SPORTS ARENA

15 LOS ANGELES, CALIFORNIA, THE FORUM

16 SACRAMENTO, CALIFORNIA, ARENA

17 OAKLAND, CALIFORNIA, OAKLAND COLISEUM

19 PORTLAND, OREGON, COLISEUM

20 VANCOUVER, BRITISH COLUMBIA, PNE

21 SEATTLE, WASHINGTON, SEATTLE CENTRE

29 FRANKFURT, GERMANY, FESTHALLE

30 MUNICH, GERMANY, OLYMPIAHALLE

31 STUTTGART, GERMANY, SCHLEYERHALLE

JUNE (EUROPE)

1 OLDENBURG, GERMANY, WESER- EMS-HALLE

2 COLOGNE, GERMANY, SPORTHALLE

3-4 PARIS, FRANCE, ZENITH

6 GRENOBLE, FRANCE, GRENOBLE SPORTS CENTRE

7 MARSEILLE, FRANCE, PALAIS DES SPORTS

8 TOULOUSE, FRANCE, PALAIS DES SPORTS

10 ZURICH, SWITZERLAND, ZURICH STADIUM HALL

12 MILAN, ITALY, TEATRO DI PALATRUSSARDI

13 ROME, ITALY, PALAEUR SPORTS PALACE

16 ATHENS, GREECE, ATHENS SPORTS PALACE

18 BRUSSELS, BELGIUM, GRADE SAJAM

19 ZAGREB, ZEMUN STADIUM

20 BUDAPEST, HUNGARY, NEP STADIUM

22 BRUSSELS, BELGIUM, FOREST NATIONAL

23 ROTTERDAM, HOLLAND, AHOYHALLEN

25-26 BIRMINGHAM, ENGLAND, NEC

28-30 LONDON, ENGLAND, WEMBLEY ARENA

JULY (USA)

5 TAMPA, FLORIDA, FAIRGROUND

6 MIAMI, FLORIDA, MIAMI AVENUS

7 ORLANDO, FLORIDA, ORLANDO ARENA

9 ATLANTA, GEORGIA, LAKEWOOD AMPHITHEATRE

10 RALEIGH NORTH, CAROLINA, WALNUT CREEK AMPHITHEATRE

12-13 PHILADELPHIA, PENNSYLVANIA, THE SPECTRUM ARENA

14 LAKE PLACID, N.Y., OLYMPIC ICE ARENA

15 NEW YORK CITY, N.Y., MADISON SQUARE GARDEN

16 HOLMDEL, NEW JERSEY, PNC BANK ARTS CENTRE

18 MANSFIELD, MASSACHUSETTS, GREAT WOODS ARTS CENTRE

19 CANANDAIGUA, N.Y., FINGER LAKES P.A.C.

20 LANDOVER, MARYLAND, CAPITAL CENTRE

21 WANNTAUGH, N.Y., JONES BEACH

22 MIDDLETOWN, N.Y., ORANGE COUNTY FAIRGROUNDS

24 BURGETTSTOWN, PENNSYLVANIA, STARLAKE AMPHITHEATRE

25 TINLEY PARK, ILLINOIS, NEW WORLD MUSIC THEATRE

26 EAST TROY, WISCONSIN, ALPINE VALLEY MUSIC THEATRE

27 MARYLAND HEIGHTS, MISSOURI, RIVERPORT AMPHITHEATRE

28 CINCINNATI, OHIO, RIVERFRONT COLISEUM

30 CLARKSTON, MICHIGAN, PINE KNOB MUSIC CENTRE

31 NOBLESVILLE, INDIANA, DEER CREEK MUSIC CENTRE

AUGUST (USA)

1 LAFAYETTE, LOUISIANA, CAJUN DOME

2 THE WOODLANDS, TEXAS, MITCHELL PAVILION

3 DALLAS, TEXAS, STARPLEX AMPHITHEATRE

6 COSTA MESA, CALIFORNIA, THE PACIFIC AMPHITHEATRE

7 CONCORD, CALIFORNIA, CONCORD PAVILION

8 MOUNTAIN VIEW, CALIFORNIA SHORELINE AMPHITHEATRE
The *Union* Tour Live video and laser disc is recorded at this venue, only distributed in Japan.

1992

FEBRUARY (JAPAN)

29 TOKYO, JAPAN, YOYOGI OLYMPIC POOL

MARCH (JAPAN)

2 OSAKA, JAPAN, CASTLE HALL

3 NAGOYA, JAPAN, CONGRESS CENTER CENTURY HALL

4 YOKOHAMA, JAPAN, YOKOHAMA BUNKA TAIIKUKAN

5 TOKYO, JAPAN, BUDOKAN HALL
The Union tour ends making it the last show for Bill Bruford.

1994

JUNE (USA)

16 NEW YORK, N.Y., MADISON SQUARE GARDEN
(Cancelled)

18 BINGHAMPTON, N.Y., BROOME COUNTY ARENA

19 CANADAIGUA, N.Y., FINGER LAKE PERFORMING ARTS CENTRE

21 ALLENTOWN, PENNSYLVANIA, ALLENTOWN FAIRGROUNDS

23 DAYTON, OHIO, ERVINE J. NUTTER CENTRE

24 COLUMBUS, OHIO, POLARIS AMPHITHEATRE

25 CLARKSTON, MICHIGAN, PINE KNOB MUSIC CENTRE

26 NOBLESVILLE, INDIANA, DEER CREEK MUSIC CENTRE

28 MOLINE, ILLINOIS, THE MARK OF THE QUAD - CITIES

29 MARYLAND HEIGHTS, MISSOURI, RIVERPORT AMPHITHEATRE

30 MILWAUKEE, WISCONSIN, MARCUS AMPHITHEATRE

JULY (USA)

2 TINLEY PARK, ILLINOIS, NEW WORLD MUSIC THEATRE

3 MINNEAPOLIS, MINNESOTA, TARGET CENTRE

4 BONNER SPRINGS, MISSOURI, SANDSTONE AMPHITHEATRE

The eight man line-up on the Union tour.

6 MORRISON, COLORADO, RED ROCKS AMPHITHEATRE

7 PARK CITY, UTAH, WOLF MOUNTAIN AMPHITHEATRE

9 SALEM, OREGON, LB DAY AMPHITHEATRE

10 QUINCY, WASHINGTON, THE GORGE

13 CONCORD, CALIFORNIA, PAVILION

14 SACRAMENTO, CALIFORNIA, EXPO AND STATE FAIR

15 MOUNTAINVIEW, CALIFORNIA, CALIFORNIA EXPO

16 RENO, NEVADA, RENO HILTON AMPHITHEATRE

17 DEVORE, CALIFORNIA, GLEN HELEN BLOCKBUSTER PAVILION

19 FRESNO, CALIFORNIA, SELLAND ARENA

21-22 LOS ANGELES, CALIFORNIA, GREEK THEATRE

24 SANTA BARBARA, CALIFORNIA, S B COUNTY BOWL

26 SAN DIEGO, CALIFORNIA, STATE UNIVERSITY

27 LAS VEGAS, NEVADA, THOMAS AND MACK CENTRE

28 PHOENIX, ARIZONA, BLOCKBUSTER DESERT SKY PAVILION

30 DALLAS, TEXAS, STARPLEX AMPHITHEATRE

31 SAN ANTONIO, TEXAS, SEA WORLD

AUGUST(USA)

1 THE WOODLANDS, TEXAS, CYNTHIA WOODS MITCHELL PAVILION

3 OKLAHOMA CITY, OKLAHOMA, MYRIAD ARENA

5 NEW ORLEANS, LOUISIANA, LOUISIANA LAKEFRONT ARENA

6 PENSACOLA, FLORIDA, PENSACOLA CIVIC CENTRE

7 ATLANTA, GEORGIA, LAKEWOOD AMPHITHEATRE

9 TAMPA, FLORIDA, SUN DOME UNIVERSITY OF SOUTH FLORIDA

10 MIAMI, FLORIDA, MIAMI ARENA

11 ORLANDO, FLORIDA, ARENA

12 JACKSONVILLE, FLORIDA, MEMORIAL COLISEUM

13 CHARLOTTE, NORTH CAROLINA, THE BLOCKBUSTER PAVILION

14 RALEIGH, NORTH CAROLINA, WALNUT CREEK AMPHITHEATRE

16 HUNTSVILLE, ALABAMA, VON BRAUN CIVIC CENTRE

17 LITTLE ROCK, ARKANSAS, J BRECKLING RIVERFRONT PARK

Live on the US leg of the Talk tour.

18 ANTIOCH, TENNESSEE, STARWOOD AMPHITHEATRE

19 MARRILLEVILLE, INDIANA, STAR PLAZA THEATRE

20 CUYAHOGA, OHIO, BLOSSOM MUSIC CENTRE

21 MIDDLETOWN, N.Y., ORANGE COUNTY FAIRGROUND

22 SARATOGA, N.Y., SARATOGA PERFORMING ARTS CENTRE

24 BURGETTSTOWN, PENNSYLVANIA, STARLAKE AMPHITHEATRE

25 SYRACUSE, N.Y., THE STATE FAIR

26 PHILADELPHIA, PENNSYLVANIA, THE SPECTRUM ARENA

27 RICHMOND, VIRGINIA, STRAWBERRY HILL AMPHITHEATRE

28 COLUMBIA, MARYLAND, MERRIWEATHER POST PAVILION

29 MANSFIELD, MASSACHUSETTS, GREAT WOODS

31 TORONTO, ONTARIO, KINGSWOOD MUSIC THEATRE

SEPTEMBER (USA, CANADA & SOUTH AMERICA)

1 MONTREAL, QUEBEC, MONTREAL FORUM

2 QUEBEC CITY, QUEBEC, COLISEUM

3 PORTLAND, MAINE, CUMBERLAND COUNTY CIVIC CENTRE

7 HOLMDEL, NEW JERSEY, PNC BANK ARTS CENTRE

8 WANNTAUGH, N.Y., JONES BEACH THEATRE

9 NEW HAVEN, CONNECTICUT, VETERANS MEMORIAL COLISEUM

10 NEW YORK CITY, N.Y., MADISON SQUARE GARDEN

14 RIO DE JANEIRO, BRAZIL, THE METROPOLITAN

15-16 SAO PAULO, BRAZIL, OLYMPIA

18 VINA DEL MAR, CHILE, QUINTA VERGARA AMPHITHEATRE

20 SANTIAGO, CHILE, METROPOLITAN

21 SANTIAGO, CHILE, METROPOLITAN

22 BUENOS AIRES, ARGENTINA, THE BROADWAY THEATRE

23 BUENOS AIRES, ARGENTINA, CLUB OBRAS SANITARIAS

24 BUENOS AIRES, ARGENTINA, OBRAS STADIUM

29 OSAKA, JAPAN, OSAKA CASTLE HALL (Cancelled)

30 TAKAMATSU, JAPAN, KENMIN HALL

OCTOBER (JAPAN)

1 KOKURA, JAPAN, KOSEI NENKIN HALL

4-5 TOKYO, JAPAN, BUDOKEN HALL

Above and right: the classic Yes line-up at San Luis Obispo, March, 1996.

6 SENDAI, JAPAN, SUN PLAZA HALL

10 NAGOYA, JAPAN, RAINBOW HALL

11 HIROSHIMA, JAPAN, KOSEI NENKIN HALL
Trevor Rabin and Tony Kaye's final Yes gig.

1996

THE MASTERWORKS OF YES RECORDINGS AND SHOWS, SAN LUIS OBISPO MARCH (USA)

4-6 SAN LUIS OBISPO, CALIFORNIA, THE FREMONT THEATRE
The great reunion of the classic Yes line-up including Rick Wakeman on keyboards, the three shows were attended by Yes fans from all over the world, making this a very special event in the Yes calendar. The shows were recorded and filmed for CD, video and DVD releases.

OCTOBER

22 MOULIN ROUGE, PARIS, PIGALLE RESTAURANT
The *Keys To Ascension* promotional tour took the classic Yes line-up along with the sixth Yesman, Roger Dean, to Paris. Yes get plastered for the Wall Of Hands' at Rock Circus, London.

28 MANHATTAN, N.Y., HOWARD STONE RADIO SHOW WXRK
An early Monday morning start for Yes for their madcap interview with the infamous Stone, Yes played 'Roundabout' and 'All Good People' which were aired, 'Long Distance Runaround' was rehearsed but not aired.

29 MANHATTAN, N.Y., FOX'S TV SHOW, *FOX AFTER BREAKFAST*
(Day) Performing on Fifth Avenue in the open air on a crisp Tuesday morning 9.30am, Yes played edited versions of 'America' and 'Roundabout'.

29 HMV MUSIC STORE SIGNING, NEW YORK

NOVEMBER

20 SUNSET BOULEVARD, LOS ANGELES, TOWER RECORDS
Yes play live to 500 people . Although they played these few open air, mini gigs and made some signing appearances, the final Yesshow for Rick and the fans is commonly considered the San Luis Obispo show back in March.

1997

KEYS TO ASCENSION USA TOUR

JUNE

12 HARTFORD, CONNECTICUT, MEADOWS
(Cancelled)

13 MANSFIELD, MASSACHUSETTS, GREAT WOODS CENTRE
(Cancelled)

17-18
NEW YORK, N.Y., BEACON THEATRE
(Cancelled)

20 HOLMDEL, NEW JERSEY, PNC BANK ARTS CENTRE
(Cancelled)

JULY

1 CINCINNATI, OHIO, RIVERBEND MUSIC CENTRE AMPHITHEATRE
(Cancelled)

21 SAN DIEGO, CALIFORNIA, HOSPITALITY POINT
(Cancelled)

25 IRVINE, CALIFORNIA, IRVINE MEADOWS AMPHITHEATRE
(Cancelled)

26-27
UNIVERSAL CITY, CALIFORNIA, UNIVERSAL AMPHITHEATRE
(Cancelled) The ill-fated tour with Rick Wakeman, it never went ahead due to too many personnel and managerial problems.

1997 OPEN YOUR EYES TOUR

OCTOBER

17 HARTFORD, CONNECTICUT, MEADOWS

18 BOSTON, MASSACHUSETTS, ORPHEUM THEATRE

19 NEW BRUNSWICK, NEW JERSEY, TATE THEATRE

21 ALBANY, N.Y., PALACE THEATRE

22 FAIRFAX, VIRGINIA, PATRIOT CENTRE

24-26 PHILADELPHIA, PENNSYLVANIA, TOWER THEATRE

28 HERSHEY, PENNSYLVANIA, HERSHEY PARK ARENA

29-31 NEW YORK, N.Y., BEACON THEATRE

NOVEMBER

2 PITTSBURG, PENNSYLVANIA, PALUMBO THEATRE

3 DETROIT, MICHIGAN, FOX THEATRE

5 GRAND RAPIDS, MICHIGAN, NI VAN ANDEL ARENA

6 TORONTO, CANADA, MASSEY HALL

7 QUEBEC, CANADA, COLISÉE

8 TORONTO, ONTARIO, LANDMARK THEATRE

9 POUGHKEEPSIE, N.Y., MID-HUDSON CIVIC CENTRE

10 BUFFALO, N.Y., SHEAS PAC

12 CLEVELAND, OHIO, OHIO MUSIC HALL

13 MERRILLVILLE, INDIANA, STATE THEATRE

14 CHICAGO, ILLINOIS, ROSEMONT THEATRE

15 MILWAUKEE, WISCONSIN, RIVERSIDE THEATRE

18 MINNEAPOLIS, MINNESOTA, STATE THEATRE

20 INDIANAPOLIS, INDIANA, MURAL THEATRE

21 LOUISVILLE, KENTUCKY, PALACE THEATRE

22 CINCINNATI, OHIO, TAFT THEATRE

23 COLUMBUS, OHIO, VETERAN'S MEMORIAL

25 ST LOUIS, MISSOURI, FOX THEATRE

26 TULSA, OKLAHOMA, BRADY THEATRE

28 DALLAS, TEXAS, BRONCO ARENA

29 HOUSTON, TEXAS, BAYOU PLACE

30 SAN ANTONIO, TEXAS, MAJESTIC THEATRE

The band pictured at Fox After Breakfast *TV show in New York.*

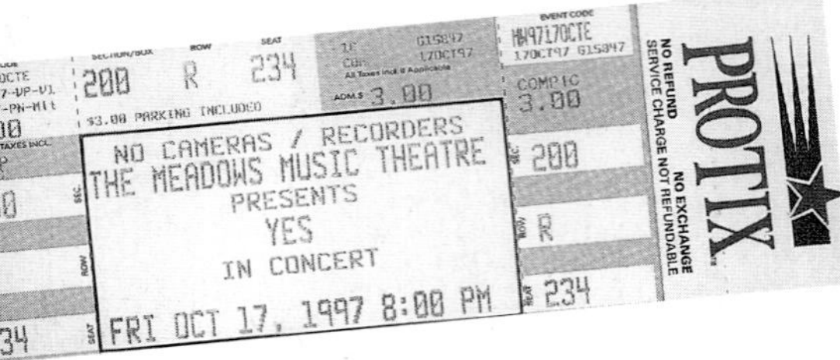

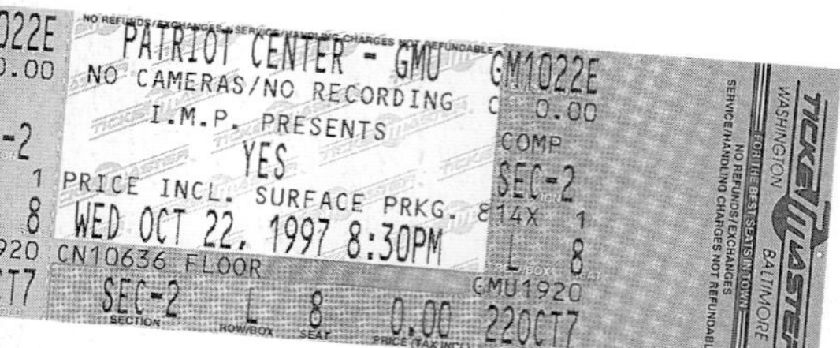

DECEMBER

2-3 DENVER, COLORADO, BUELL AUDITORIUM

5 PHOENIX, ARIZONA, UNION HALL

6 LAS VEGAS, NEVADA, HARD ROCK CAFÉ - THE JOINT

7 LOS ANGELES, CALIFORNIA, UNIVERSAL AMPHITHEATRE
The show was recorded for a later radio broadcast.

8 FRESNO, CALIFORNIA, WARNOR'S THEATRE

9 SAN DIEGO, CALIFORNIA, CIVIC THEATRE

11 SACRAMENTO, CALIFORNIA, MEMORIAL AUDITORIUM

12-13 SAN FRANCISCO, CALIFORNIA, WARFIELD THEATRE

14 SAN JOSE, CALIFORNIA, CENTRE FOR PERFORMING ARTS

1998

JANUARY (USA & CANADA)

2 PORTLAND, OREGON, CIVIC AUDITORIUM
(Cancelled)

3-4 SEATTLE, WASHINGTON, PARAMOUNT THEATRE
(Cancelled)

5 VANCOUVER, BRITISH COLUMBIA, QUEEN ELIZABETH THEATRE
(Cancelled)

8 EDMONTON, ALBERTA, JUBILEE AUDITORIUM
(Cancelled)

9 CALGARY, ALBERTA, JUBILEE AUDITORIUM
(Cancelled)

10 SASKATOON, SASKATCHEWAN, (Venue unknown)
(Cancelled)

REGINA, SASKATCHEWAN, (Venue unknown)
(Cancelled)

11 WINNIPEG, MANITOBA, (Venue unknown)
(Cancelled)

FEBRUARY

26 MANCHESTER, ENGLAND, APOLLO
The keyboard player Igor had problems getting a passport and documents through on time for the first gig in the UK, Rick Wakeman's son Adam is on stand-by all day and learns the whole show just in case Igor doesn't turn up. Igor made it just in time, so Adam was invited to play on the encore of 'Starship Trooper'.

27 NEWCASTLE, ENGLAND, CITY HALL

28 GLASGOW, SCOTLAND, CLYDE AUDITORIUM

MARCH (EUROPE)

1 NOTTINGHAM, ENGLAND, ROYAL CONCERT HALL

3 BOURNEMOUTH, ENGLAND, INTERNATIONAL CENTRE

4-5 LONDON, ENGLAND, HAMMERSMITH APOLLO
Yes play a song to thank the road crew. Jon and Steve are joined on stage at one of the Hammersmith shows by a cellist from a London orchestra. They played the track From The Balcony.

6 PARIS, FRANCE, PALAIS DE\ CONGRES

8-9 UTRECHT, NETHERLANDS, MUZICKCENTRUM VREDENBURG

10 FRANKFURT, GERMANY, JAHRHUNDERTHALLE

11 DUSSELDORF, GERMANY, PHILIPSHALLE

13 ZURICH, SWITZERLAND, KONGRESSHAUS

14 MILAN, ITALY, LINCO THEATRE

16 BERLIN, GERMANY, I.C.C. BERLIN

17 DRESDEN, GERMANY, KULTURPALAST DRESDEN

18 MANNHEIM, GERMANY, MOZARTSAAL IM ROSENGARTEN

19 GENEVA, SWITZERLAND, ARENA

20 STUTTGART, GERMANY, LIEDERHALLE

22 HAMBURG, GERMANY, CONGRESS CENTER HALL 1

23 HANNOVER, GERMANY, MUSIKHALLE HANNOVER

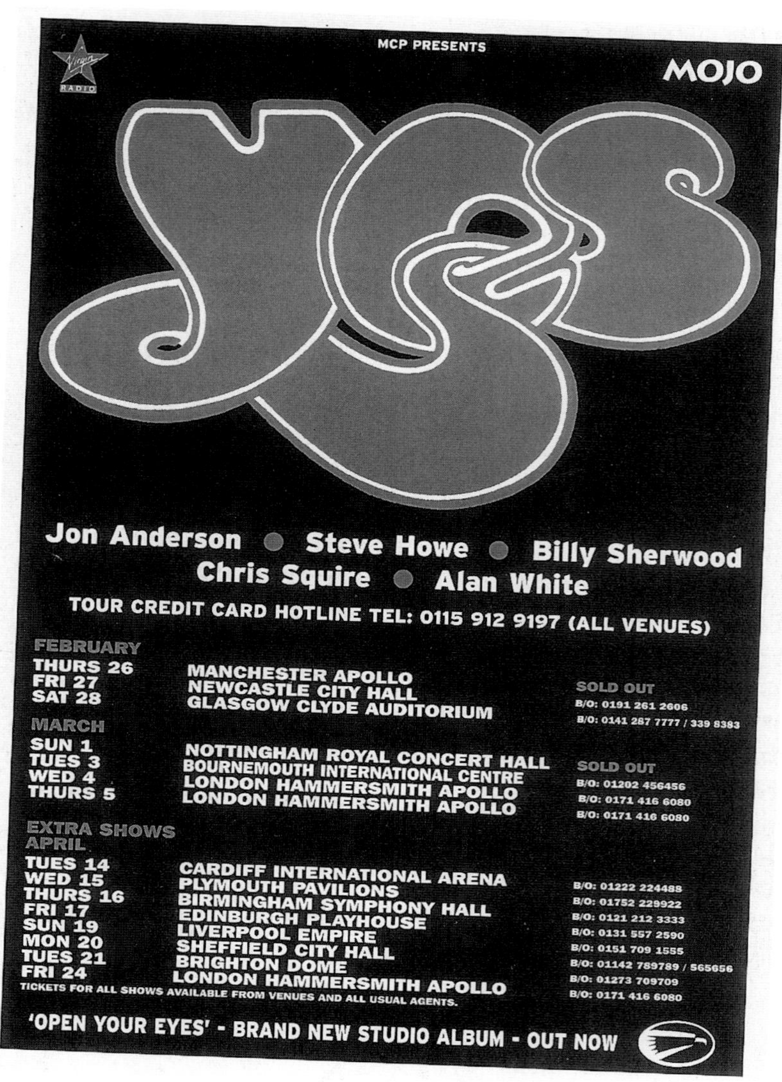

24 BAYREUTH, GERMANY, OBERTRANKENHALLE

26 WARSAW, POLAND, SALA KONGRESOWA
The Warsaw gig is broadcast on the internet.

27 KATOWICE, POLAND, SPODEK

28 PRAGUE, CZEHOSLOVAKIA, MALA SPORTOVNI HALA

29 POZNAN, POLAND, SALA ARENA HALL

31 BUDAPEST, HUNGARY, SPORTCSARNOK

APRIL (EUROPE)

Yes have their press launch at the Hard Rock Café in New York.

1 TRIESTE, ITALY, PALASAPORT DI CHIARBOLA

2 VIENNA, AUSTRIA, MUSIC HALL LIBRO

3 MUNICH, GERMANY, CIRCUS KRONE-BAU

4 RAVENSBURG, GERMANY, OBERSCHWABENHALLE
(Cancelled)

6 BRUSSELS, BELGIUM, VOREST NATIONAL THEATRE

7 LILLE, FRANCE, ZENITH ARENA

8 DIFFERDANGE, LUXEMBOURG, THE SPORT HALL

10 GRONNGEN, NETHERLANDS, MARTINI HALL

11 EINDHOVEN, NETHERLANDS, PHILIPS MUZICKCENTRUM

13 BIRMINGHAM, ENGLAND, SYMPHONY HALL

14 CARDIFF, WALES, INTERNATIONAL CENTRE

Labatt's APOLLO HAMMERSMITH
Queen Caroline Str.
WED 4th MAR'98 7:30 PM £30.00
Virgin Radio Presents
YES
STALLS BLOCK 23 G27

15 PLYMOUTH, ENGLAND, THE PAVILION

16 BIRMINGHAM, ENGLAND, SYMPHONY HALL

17 EDINBURGH, SCOTLAND, PLAYHOUSE

19 LIVERPOOL, ENGLAND, EMPIRE

20 SHEFFIELD, ENGLAND, CITY HALL

21 BRIGHTON, ENGLAND, DOME

22 CROYDON, ENGLAND, FAIRFIELD HALL

24 LONDON, ENGLAND, HAMMERSMITH APOLLO

MAY (SOUTH AMERICA)

7-9 SAO PAULO, BRAZIL, OLYMPIA

10 BELO HORIZANTE, BRAZIL, THE SHOPPING AREA

12 RIO DE JANEIRO, BRAZIL, THE METROPOLITAN

14-16
BUENOS AIRES, ARGENTINA, ESTADIO OBRAS

19 PORTO ALEGRE, BRAZIL, BAR OPINIAO

20 CURITIBA, BRAZIL, THE FORUM
(Cancelled)

21 SANTIAGO, CHILE, MONUMENTAL EL TEATRO

25-26
MEXICO CITY NATIONAL AUDITORIUM

28 MONTERREY, MEXICO, COCA COLA AUDIROTIO

27-28
Yestival, the Yes fan convention in Cherry Hill, New Jersey.

THE 30th ANNIVERSARY TOUR

Support act Alan Parsons and his band.

JUNE (USA & CANADA)

18 TORONTO, ONTARIO, MOLSON AMPHITHEATRE

19 MONTREAL, QUEBEC, PARC DES ILES – FESTIVAL

20 QUEBEC CITY, QUEBEC, HIPPODROME DE QUEBEC – FESTIVAL

22 VIRGINIA BEACH, VIRGINIA, GTE VIRGINIA BEACH AMPHITHEATRE

23 WASHINGTON, WASHINGTON D.C., NISSAN PAVILION AT STONE RIDGE

24 PITTSBURG, PENNSYLVANIA, IC LIGHT AMPHITHEATRE

26 HOLMDEL, NEW JERSEY, GARDEN STATE

27 CAMDEN, NEW JERSEY, BLOCKBUSTER/SONY ENT CENTRE

28 SCRANTON, NEW JERSEY, MONTAGE MOUNTAIN PERFORMING ARTS CENTRE

30 BOSTON, MASSACHUSETTS, HARBOR LIGHTS PAVILION

JULY (USA & CANADA)

1 WALLINGFORD, CONNECTICUT, OAKDALE MUSIC THEATRE

2 WANTAUGH, N.Y., JONES BEACH AMPHITHEATRE

4 ROCHESTER, N.Y. FINGER LAKES PERFORMING ARTS CENTRE

5 CLARKSTON, MICHIGAN, PINE KNOB MUSIC CENTRE

6 CINCINNATI, OHIO, RIVERBEND AMPHITHEATRE

7 CUYAHOGA FALLS, OHIO, BLOSSOM MUSIC CENTRE

9 CHICAGO, ILLINOIS, ILLINOIS WORLD MUSIC THEATRE

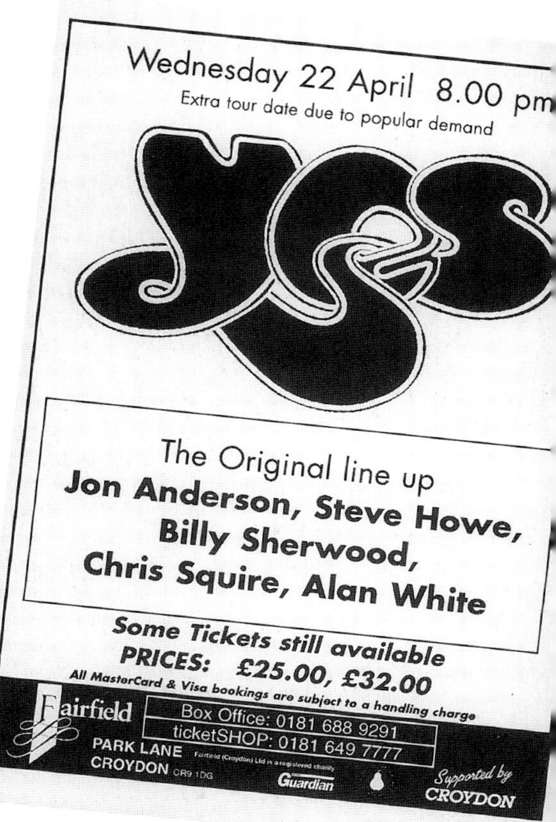

10 WALKER, MINNESOTA, MOON DANCE RANCH FESTIVAL

11 MILWAUKEE, WISCONSIN, MARCUS AMPHITHEATRE

12 INDIANAPOLIS, INDIANA, DEER CREEK AMPHITHEATRE

14 DENVER, COLORADO, FIDDLER'S GREEN AMPHITHEATRE

15 SALT LAKE CITY, UTAH, WEST VALLEY CENTRE

17 VANCOUVER, BRITISH COLUMBIA, GENERAL MOTORS PLACE

18 WOODINVILLE, WASHINGTON, CHATEAU STE MICHELLE WINERY

20 RENO, NEVADA, RENO HILTON AMPHITHEATRE

21 CONCORD, CALIFORNIA, CONCORD PAVILION

22 SAN DIEGO, CALIFORNIA, OPEN AIR THEATRE

Montage Mountain Performing Arts Center, Scranton, New Jersey, 28th June, 1998.

24 LOS ANGELES, CALIFORNIA, UNIVERSAL AMPHITHEATRE
Yes appear live on VH1 USA. They were joined on stage by the local school choir to perform 'No Way We Can Lose'.

25 LAS VEGAS, NEVADA, HARD ROCK CAFE/THE JOINT

26 PHOENIX, ARIZONA, BLOCKBUSTER DESERT SKY PAVILION

27 EL PASO, TEXAS, ABRAHAM-CHAVEZ THEATRE

28 SANTA FE, NEW MEXICO, PAOLO SOLERI AMPHITHEATRE

30 DALLAS, TEXAS, STARPLEX AMPHITHEATRE

31 HOUSTON, TEXAS, WOODLANDS

AUGUST (USA)

1 AUSTIN, TEXAS, BACKYARD

2 SAN ANTONIO, TEXAS, MUNICIPAL AUDITORIUM

4 MEMPHIS, TENNESSEE, MUD ISLAND

5 NASHVILLE, TENNESSEE, STARWOOD AMPHITHEATRE

6 ATLANTA, GEORGIA, CHASTAIN PARK

7 TAMPA, FLORIDA, THEATRE OF THE PERFORMING ARTS

8 WEST PALM BEACH, FLORIDA, CORAL SKY AMPHITHEATRE

OCTOBER

5 ANCHORAGE, ALASKA, SULLIVAN ARENA
(Cancelled)

8-9 TOKYO, JAPAN, SHIBUYA KOKAIDO

11 KAWSQUCHI, JAPAN, LILIA MAIN HALL

13 NAGOYA, JAPAN, NAGOYA - SHI KOKAIDO

14 OSAKA, JAPAN, KOUSEI NENNKIN KAIKAN

1999

MAY

Yes are named the 33rd most collectible group out of the 500 entered in the annual *Record Collector* magazine poll, UK.

SEPTEMBER (SOUTH AMERICA)

6 RIO DE JANEIRO, BRAZIL, TEATRO DE CANECAO

8-9 SAO PAULO, BRAZIL, OLYMPIA

12 BUENOS AIRES, ARGENTINA, LUNA PARK STADIUM

14 SANTIAGO, CHILE, ESTADIO CHILE
(Cancelled)

16 LIMA, PERU, MUELLO UNO

18 SAN PEDRO, COSTA RICA, ALAMEDA DEL PLANETA

21-22 CARACAS, VENEZUELA, CONPLEJO CULTURAL DE TERESA CARENO
Supported by Tempano.

24 MEXICO, MEXICO CITY, SPORTS PALACE

OCTOBER (NORTH AMERICA)

15 MYRTLE BEACH, SOUTH CAROLINA, HOUSE OF BEACH

16 ATLANTA, GEORGIA, THE TABERNACLE

18-19 TAMPA, FLORIDA, CAROL MORSANI HALL

21 MIAMI, FLORIDA, SUNRISE MUSIC THEATRE

22 ORLANDO, FLORIDA, LAKE BUENA VISTA, HOUSE OF BLUES, WALT DISNEY WORLD

23 JACKSONVILLE, FLORIDA, JACKSONVILLE THEATRE

25 NEW ORLEANS, LOUISIANA, LOUISIANA HOUSE OF BLUES

26 HOUSTON, TEXAS, ARIAL THEATRE

29 PHOENIX, ARIZONA, UNION HALL

30 ANAHEIM, CALIFORNIA, SUN THEATRE

31 LAS VEGAS, NEVADA, HOUSE OF BLUES
The show is filmed for the release *House of Yes*.

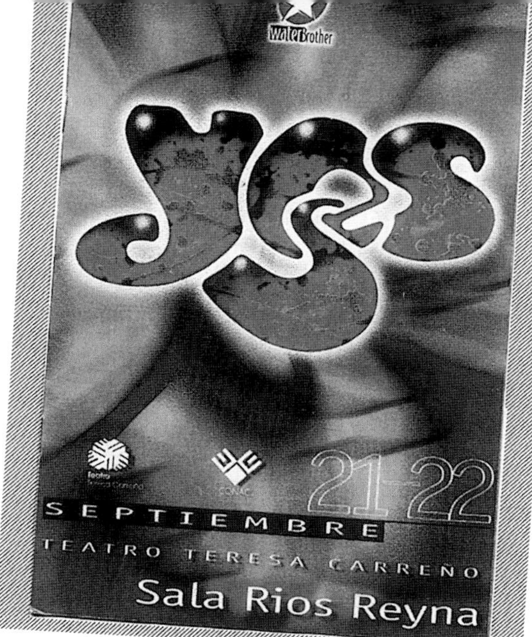

NOVEMBER (NORTH AMERICA)

1 LOS ANGELES, CALIFORNIA, KLOS RADIO STATION *JIM LADD'S LIVING ROOM SHOW*

2-2 LOS ANGELES, CALIFORNIA, HOUSE OF BLUES

6-7 SAN FRANCISCO, CALIFORNIA, THE WARFIELD

9 SEATTLE, WASHINGTON, PARAMOUNT THEATRE

12 MINNEAPOLIS, MINNESOTA, ORPHEUM THEATRE

13 MILWAUKEE, WISCONSIN, AUDITORIUM THEATRE

15-17 CHICAGO, ILLINOIS, RIVIERA THEATRE

19 MICHIGAN, ROYAL OAK MUSIC THEATRE

20 TOLEDO, OHIO, SEAGATE CENTRE

21 CINCINNATI, OHIO, TAFT THEATRE

23 ROCHESTER, N.Y., AUDITORIUM THEATRE

24 CLEVELAND, OHIO, AGORA THEATRE

26 NEW BRUNSWICK, NEW JERSEY, STATE THEATRE

27 MASHUNTUCKET, CONNECTICUT, FOX CASINO AND THEATRE

28 WALLINGFORD, CONNECTICUT, OAKDALE THEATRE

30 WILKES-BARRE, PENNSYLVANIA, KIRBY CENTRE
Ex Yes man Rick Wakeman gets the shock of his life when *This is Your Life*, a UK biographical TV programme, visit him. The TV show was broadcast at a later date. Yes appeared on film wishing Rick well.

DECEMBER (NORTH AMERICA)

1 PITTSBURG, PENNSYLVANIA, PALUMBO THEATRE

2 MT PLEASANT, MICHIGAN, SOARING EAGLE CASINO

4 TORONTO, ONTARIO, MASSEY HALL

7-9 NEW YORK, N.Y., BEACON THEATRE

11 BOSTON, MASSACHUSETTS, ORPHEUM THEATRE

12-13 UPPER DARBY, PENNSYLVANIA, TOWER THEATRE

2000

FEBRUARY

6 DUBLIN, IRELAND, NATIONAL CONCERT HALL

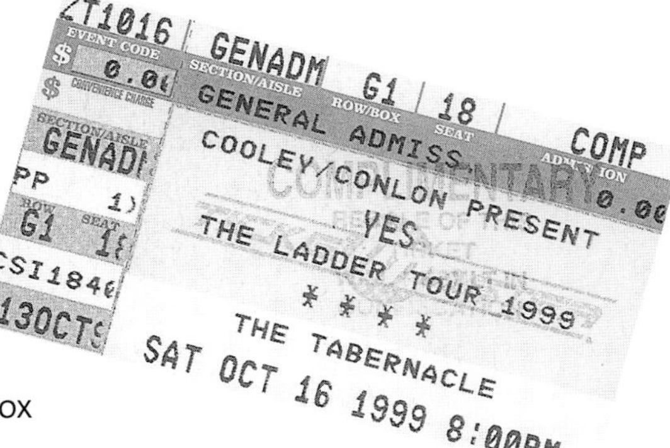

7 BIRMINGHAM, ENGLAND, SYMPHONY HALL
Bad weather causes the ferry from Ireland to be cancelled so no equipment reached the mainland. Birmingham Symphony Hall gig was cancelled.

8 BIRMINGHAM, ENGLAND, SYMPHONY HALL

10 SHEFFIELD, ENGLAND, CITY HALL

11 CARDIFF, WALES, CARDIFF INTERNATIONAL ARENA

12 BOURNEMOUTH, ENGLAND, INTERNATIONAL CENTRE

13 MANCHESTER, ENGLAND, APOLLO THEATRE

14 LIVERPOOL, ENGLAND, THE EMPIRE THEATRE

16 NOTTINGHAM, ENGLAND, ROYAL CONCERT HALL

17 GLASGOW, SCOTLAND, CLYDE AUDITORIUM S.E.C.C.

19-20 LONDON, ENGLAND, THE ROYAL ALBERT HALL
Yes play Royal Albert Hall, London, for two nights, the last time was in the early 1970s. Jon and Steve's sons join Yes on stage for the final 'Roundabout'.

(EUROPE)

23 PORTO, PORTUGAL, COLISEU DO PORTO

24 LISBON, PORTUGAL, ATLANTICO PAVILHAO

25 MADRID, SPAIN, LA RIVIERA

26 BARCELONA, SPAIN, EL TEATRO ZELESTE

28 PARIS, FRANCE, THE OLYMPIA THEATRE

29 BRUSSELS, BELGIUM, VORST NATIONAL THEATRE

MARCH

1-2 UTRECHT, NETHERLANDS, MUZIECKCENTRUM VREDENBURG

4 BOLOGNA, ITALY, PALASAVENA

5 PALAZZOLO SULL'OGLIO, ITALY, PALA-US (Cancelled)

6 MILAN, ITALY, PALVOBIS (Cancelled)

7 FLORENCE, ITALY, TEATRO VERDI (Cancelled)

9 ZURICH, SWITZERLAND, KONGRESSHAUS

11 OFFENBACH, GERMANY, STADTHALLE

12 KOLN, GERMANY, PALLADIUM

13 STUTTGART, GERMANY, LIEDERHALLE

15 LEIPZIG, GERMANY, HAUS AUENSEE

16 BERLIN, GERMANY, COLUMBIAHALLE

17 FURTH, GERMANY, STADTHALLE

19 VIENNA, AUSTRIA, LIBRO MUSIC HALL

20 LLUBLJANA, SLOVENIA, HALA TIVOLI

23 SOFIA, BULGARIA, NATIONAL PALACE OF CULTURE

25 BUCHAREST, ROMANIA, SALA PALATULUI
Billy Sherwood's final show. Chris Squire and Billy Sherwood's new album released in the UK.

APRIL

13 The repeat broadcast of the November 2nd 1999 show aired on pay per view Hob.com. *Record Collector* magazine in

the UK runs a seven-page article on Yes' live shows.

2000 MASTERWORKS TOUR
Supported by Kansas.

JUNE (NORTH AMERICA)

20 RENO, NEVADA, RENO AMPHITHEATRE

21 CONCORD, CALIFORNIA, CONCORD PAVILION

23 LOS ANGELES, CALIFORNIA, UNIVERSAL AMPHITHEATRE

24 DEVORE, CALIFORNIA, BLOCKBUSTER PAVILION

25 PHOENIX, ARIZONA, DESERT SKY PAVILION

27 ALBUQUERQUE, NEW MEXICO, MESA DEL SOL

28 DENVER, COLORADO, FILMORE AUDITORIUM

30 ST. LOUIS, MISSOURI, RIVERPORT AMPHITHEATRE

JULY (NORTH AMERICA)

1 BONNER SPRINGS, KANSAS, SANDSTONE AMPHITHEATRE

2 DALLAS, TEXAS, STARPLEX AMPHITHEATRE

5 BURGETTESTOWN, PENNSYLVANIA, STAR LAKE AMPHITHEATRE

6 CUYAHOGA FALLS, OHIO, BLOSSOM MUSIC CENTRE

7 COLUMBUS, OHIO, POLARIS AMPHITHEATRE

8 CHICAGO, ILLINOIS, TASTE OF CHICAGO

11 DETROIT, MICHIGAN, PINE KNOB MUSIC CENTER

12 CINCINNATI, OHIO, RIVERBEND AMPHITHEATRE

13 INDIANAPOLIS, INDIANA, DEER CREEK AMPHITHEATRE

15 WANTAUGH, N.Y., JONES BEACH AMPHITHEATRE

16 SARATOGA, N.Y., SPRINGS SPAC

18 CAMDEN, NEW JERSEY, BLOCKBUSTER-SONY CENTER

19 HOLMDEL, NEW JERSEY, PNC BANK ARTS CENTRE

21 BOSTON, MASSACHUSETTS, BANC BOSTON

22 HARTFORD, CONNECTICUT, HARTFORD MEADOWS

23 WASHINGTON, WASHINGTON D.C., NISSAN PAVILION

25 VIRGINIA, BEACH GTE AMPHITHEATRE

27 RALEIGH, NORTH CAROLINA, ALTEL PAVILION

28 CHARLOTTE, NORTH CAROLINA, BLOCKBUSTER PAVILION

29 NASHVILLE, TENNESSEE, FIRST AMERICAN MUSIC CENTRE

30 ATLANTA, GEORGIA, LAKEWOOD AMPHITHEATRE

AUGUST (NORTH AMERICA)

1 WEST PALM BEACH, FLORIDA, MARS MUSIC AMPHITHEATRE

3 INDIANAPOLIS, INDIANA, DEER CREEK AMPHITHEATRE

4 CINCINNATI, OHIO, RIVERBEND AMPHITHEATRE

2001

YESSYMPHONIC TOUR

JULY (NORTH AMERICA)

25 SAN DIEGO, CALIFORNIA, NAVY PIER
With the San Diego Symphony Orchestra

28 KELSEYVILLE, CALIFORNIA, KONOCTI FIELD AMPHITHEATRE
With the Santa Rosa Symphony Orchestra.

30 LOS ANGELES, CALIFORNIA, HOLLYWOOD BOWL
With the Hollywood Bowl Orchestra

31 LOS ANGELES, CALIFORNIA, CONCORD CHRONICLE PAVILION
With the Yes Symphony Orchestra

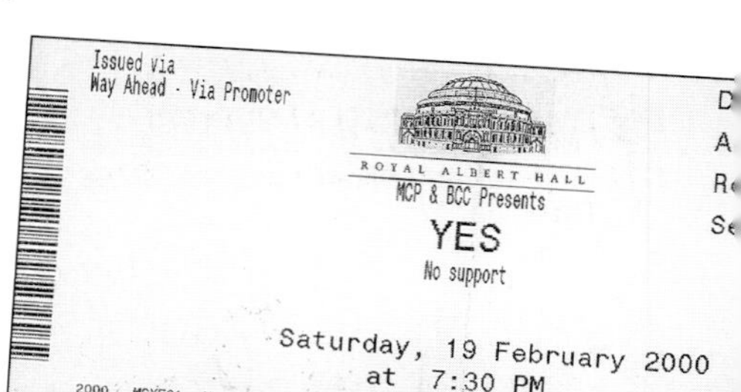

The stage set of the Homeworld tour at the Royal Albert Hall, London, February, 2000.

AUGUST (NORTH AMERICA)

2 VANCOUVER, BRITISH COLUMBIA, QUEEN ELIZABETH THEATRE
With the Vancouver Symphony Orchestra

3 WOODINVILLE, WASHINGTON, CHATEAU ST. MICHELLE WINERY

5 ENGLEWOOD, COLORADO, FIDDLER'S GREEN AMPHITHEATRE

7 MINNEAPOLIS, MINNESOTA, STATE THEATRE

8 CHICAGO, ILLINOIS, THE ARIE CROWN THEATRE

10 CUYAHOGA FALLS, OHIO, BLOSSOM MUSIC CENTRE

11 COLUMBUS, OHIO, THE AUDITORIUM

12 CLARKSTON, MICHIGAN, DTE ENERGY CENTRE
With orchestral musicians from Northern Michigan

14 INTERLOCHEN, MICHIGAN, INTERLOCHEN CENTRE

15 MILWAUKEE, WISCONSIN, RIVERSIDE THEATRE

16 KETTERING, OHIO, FRAZE PAVILION, LINCOLN PARK
With musicians from Dayton Philharmonic Orchestra

18 ATLANTA, GEORGIA, CHASTAIN AMPHITHEATRE
With the Atlanta Symphony Orchestra

19 PORTSMOUTH, VIRGINIA, HARBOR CENTRE
With the Virginia Symphony Summer Pops Orchestra

21 PHILADELPHIA, PENNSYLVANIA, MANN MUSIC CENTRE
With the Mann Festival Orchestra

22 LEWISTON, NEW YORK, N.Y. ARTPARK

24 VIENNA, VIRGINIA, WOLF TRAP FARM PARK
With the Wolf Trap Symphony Orchestra

25 UNCASVILLE, CONNECTICUT, MOHEGAN SUN RESORT

26 QUEBEC CITY, QUEBEC, L AGORA DU VIEUX PORT

28 TORONTO, ONTARIO, MOLSON AMPHITHEATRE

29 MONTREAL, QUEBEC, MOLSON CENTRE

SEPTEMBER

1 WALLINGFORD, CONNECTICUT, OAKDALE THEATRE

2 SARATOGA SPRINGS, NEW YORK, N.Y. SARATOGA PERFORMING ARTS CENTRE

3 DANBURY, CONNECTICUT, CHARLES IVES CENTRE

OCTOBER

25 VIENNA, AUSTRIA, BANK AUSTRIA HALL

26 KATOWICE, POLAND, SPODEK HALL

27 POZNAN, POLAND, TOWAR HALL

29 RHIGA, LATVIA, ARENA

31 MOSCOW, RUSSIA, KREMLIN PALACE

NOVEMBER

2 TALIN, ESTONIA, SAKU SUURHALL

3 ST. PETERSBERG, RUSSIA, OKTYABRSKY CONCERT HALL

4 HELSINKI, FINLAND, HARTWELL

6 STOKHOLM, SWEDEN, THE CIRCUS

7 OSLO, NORWAY, THE CONCERT HOUSE

9 BERLIN, GERMANY, ICCI

10 LEIPZIG, GERMANY, GEWANDHAUS

11 PRAGUE, CZECH REPUBLIC, INDUSTRIAL PALACE

12 BERLIN, GERMANY, STADTHALLE MADGEBURG

14 FRANKFURT, GERMANY, ALTE OPER

15 STUTTGART, GERMANY, LIEDERHALLE

16 ZURICH, SWITZERLAND, KONGRESSHAUS

17 MILAN, ITALY, PALAVOBIS

19 BERLIN, GERMANY, COLUMBRIAHALLE HOUSE

20 DUSSELDORF, GERMANY, PHILIPSHALLE

21 AMSTERDAM, THE NETHERLANDS, HEINEKIN MUSIC HALL

22 AMSTERDAM, THE NETHERLANDS, HEINEKIN MUSIC HALL

24 ANTWERP, BELGIUM, SPORTAPALEIS

26 PARIS, FRANCE, OLYMPIA THEATRE

28 DUBLIN, IRELAND, THE POINT THEATRE

DECEMBER

1 BRIGHTON, ENGLAND, INTERNATIONAL CENTRE

2 BIRMINGHAM, ENGLAND, NATIONAL INDOOR ARENA ACADEMY

3 LONDON, ENGLAND, HAMMERSMITH APOLLO

4 LONDON, ENGLAND, HAMMERSMITH APOLLO

6 BOURNEMOUTH, ENGLAND, INTERNATIONAL CENTRE

7 CARDIFF, WALES, ST. DAVIDS HALL

8 NOTTINGHAM, ENGLAND, ROYAL CONCERT HALL

9 GLASGOW, SCOTLAND, CLYDE AUDITORIUM

11 SHEFFIELD, ENGLAND, SHEFFIELD CITY HALL

12 NEWCASTLE, ENGLAND, NEWCASTLE CITY HALL

13 MANCHESTER, ENGLAND, APOLLO THEATRE

GUIDE TO GIGS

Year	Number of shows
1968	55
1969	203
1970	125
1971	17
1972	105
1973	52
1974	82
1975	58
1976	52
1977	88
1978	41
1979	60
1980	68
1981	0
1982	0
1983	0
1984	156
1985	6
1986	0
1987	33
1988	46
1989	67
1990	18
1991	83
1992	5
1993	0
1994	79
1995	0
1996	3
1997	45
1998	104
1999	51
2000	64
2001	64
Total Number of shows	1830

SET LISTS

1959–68 WARRIORS
Everly Brothers songs – Cathy's Clown, Bye Bye, Love/Walk Right Back – I'm Down, Twist and Shout and I Won't Be Long (3 x Beatles), Don't Make me Blue (Dave Foster's first ever song), You Came Along, I Found You (sessions only), It Won't Be Long (Beatles), Hey Good Lookin' (Bo Diddley), Blowing in the Wind (Bob Dylan), Not Fade Away (Rolling Stones), Goldfinger (Shirley Bassey) and Hold On I'm Coming (Sam & Dave).

1966–8 SYN
Various Motown Covers, I'll Be There, Dancing in the Streets, 14 Hour Technicolor Dream, Flowerman, Illusion, Heatwave, Created by Clive, Flower Man Rock Opera, The Gardener and the Flowers, Gangster Opera, Mr White's Flying Machine, Grounded.

1967–8 MABEL GREER'S TOYSHOP
Beyond and Before, Electric Funeral, Get Yourself Together, Midnight Sleigh Ride, Images of Me and You, Eight Miles High, In The Midnight Hour (extended), Jeanetta, I See You (Byrds), So You Want To Be A Rock and Roll Star (Byrds), Light My Fire (Doors), extended solos (Peter Banks), I Can Take You To The Sun (Misunderstood), various 12 bar blues songs.

1968/9 YES
In The Midnight Hour, Carpet Man (Fifth Dimension), Paper Cup (Fifth Dimension), Eleanor Rigby (The Beatles), I See You (The Byrds), No Opportunity, Heaven Is In Your Mind (Traffic), Dear Father, Every Little Thing (Beatles), It's Love, Number 14 Bus! (PB acoustic solo), You Keep Me Hanging On (Supremes), I can Hear the Grass Grow, Paper Cup (5th Dimension), Wish That Could Happen, Something's Coming (Leonard Bernstein), Eight Miles High, Mr Fantasy (Traffic), Heaven Is In Your Mind (Traffic), I'm Only Sleeping (The Beatles).

1970 TIME AND A WORD TOUR
No Opportunity Necessary, Astral Traveller, Yours Is No Disgrace, Everydays, Something's Coming, I've Seen All Good People, Clap, Every Little Thing, A Bass Odyssey (early fish), The Prophet, Clear Days, I See You, America, Time and a Word, Then.

1971 THE YES ALBUM TOUR
Opening: Also Sprach Zarathustra (2001 movie theme), Yours Is No Disgrace, I've Seen All Good People, Clap, Classical Gas, Perpetual Change, It's Love, Everydays, Astral Traveller, America, Heart of the Sunrise.

1972 FRAGILE, CLOSE TO THE EDGE TOUR
Firebird Suite, I've Seen All Good People, Heart Of The Sunrise, Mood For A Day, Colours Of The Rainbow (JA solo), And You And I, Siberian Khatru, Close to the Edge, Sakura Sakura (tour song), Long Distance Runaround, The Fish, Perpetual Change, Clap, Yours Is No Disgrace, Wakeman solo, Roundabout, South Side of the Sky, Starship Trooper, America.

1973–4 TALES FROM TOPOGRAPHIC OCEANS TOUR
Firebird Suite, Siberian Khatru, And You And I, Heart of the Sunrise, Close to the Edge, I've Seen All Good People, The Revealing Science Of God, The Ancient, The Remembering, Ritual, Roundabout, Starship Trooper, Yours Is No Disgrace.

1974-75 RELAYER TOUR
Firebird Suite, Sound Chaser, Close To The Edge, To Be Over, The Gates Of Delirium, Your Move, Mood For A Day, Long Distance Runaround, Moraz piano solo, Clap, And You And I, Ritual, Awaken excerpt, Yours Is No Disgrace, Roundabout, South Side Of The Sky, Sweet Dreams.

1975-76 GROUP + SOLO TOUR
Firebird Suite, Siberian Khatru, Sound Chaser, I've Seen All Good People,Hold Out Your Hand (CS), You By My Side (CS), And You And I, Break Away From It All (SH), Beginnings (SH), Clap (SH), Ram (SH), One Way Rag (SH), Australia (instrumental) (SH), The Gates Of Delirium, Alan solo, Long Distance Runaround, Moraz solo, Close To The Edge, Heart Of The Sunrise, Anderson harp solo, Song of Innocence (AW), Ritual, Roundabout, I'm Down, Sweet Dreams, Starship Trooper.

1977 GOING FOR THE ONE TOUR
Firebird Suite, Parallels, I've Seen All Good People, Close To The Edge, Wondrous Stories, Colours Of The Rainbow, Turn Of The Century, Tour Song, Ritual excerpt, And You And I, Ram, Yours Is No Disgrace, Going For the One, Awaken, Starship Trooper, Roundabout.

1978 TORMATO TOUR
Close Encounters Film Soundtrack, Siberian Khatru, Heart Of The Sunrise, Circus Of Heaven, Future Times Rejoice, Time And A Word, Long Distance, Runaround, The Fish, Perpetual Change, Soon, Don't Kill The Whale, Clap, Release Release, Parallels, Starship Trooper, Madrigal, On The Silent Wings Of Freedom, Abilene, Wakeman solo, Awaken, Going For The One, I've Seen All Good People, Roundabout, The Midnight Hour.

1979 USA TOUR
Firebird Suite, Siberian Khatru, Heart Of The Sunrise, Close To The Edge, Future Times – Rejoice, Circus of Heaven, Time And A Word, Long Distance Runaround, The Fish, Perpetual Change, Sound Chaser, The Gates Of Delirium, Soon, The Ancient excerpt, Don't Kill The Whale, Clap, And You And I, Starship Trooper, On the Silent Wings Of Freedom, Wakeman's solo, Awaken, Tour Song, I've Seen All Good People, Roundabout.

1980 USA/UK DRAMA TOUR

Firebird Suite, Does it Really Happen? Yours Is No Disgrace, Into the Lens, Clap, And You And I, Go Through This, Man In The White Car Suite, Parallels, We Can Fly From Here, Tempus Fugit, Fish, Amazing Grace, Machine Messiah, Starship Trooper, Roundabout.

1982 ASIA

Time Again, One Step Closer, Without You, The Ancient (SH), Ram (SH), Clap (SH), Midnight Sun, Only Time Will Tell, The Smile Has Left Your Eyes, Cutting It Fine, Wildest Dreams, Here Comes The Feeling, Drum solo Sole Survivor, Heat Of The Moment.

1984 90125

Cinema / Leave It, Yours Is No Disgrace, Hold On, Perpetual Change, Hearts, I've Seen All Good People, Solly's Beard, Changes, Our Song, And You And I, Soon, Ritual excerpt, Make It Easy intro / Owner Of A Lonely Heart, It Can Happen, Long Distance Runaround, White Fish, Amazing Grace, City Of Love, Awaken (excerpt), Starship Trooper, Roundabout, I'm Down + Jimmy Page, Gimme Some Lovin, Sweet Dreams.

1987-8 BIG GENERATOR TOUR

Almost Like Love, Rhythm of Love, Final Eyes, I'm Running, Hold On, Heart Of The Sunrise, Big Generator, Changes, Shoot High Aim Low, Holy Lamb, Solly's Beard, Make It Easy intro, Owner Of A Lonely Heart, Yours Is No Disgrace, Ritual excerpt (AW), Amazing Grace (CS), And You And I, Starship Trooper, Love Will Find A Way, I've Seen All Good People, Roundabout, Donguri Koro Koro (Japan only).

1989/90 ABWH US/EUROPEAN

Evening Of Yes Music Plus Tour, Time And A Word, Owner Of A Lonely Heart, Teakbois, Clap (SH), Mood For A Day (SH), Madrigal & Merlin the Magician, Wakeman solo, Long Distance Runaround, Bruford solo, Birthright, And You And I, Soon, I've Seen All Good People, Themes, Bruford/Levin duet, Close To The Edge, The Meeting, Brother Of Mine, Heart Of The Sunrise, The Order Of The Universe, Roundabout, Starship Trooper, Sweet Dreams, The Ancient excerpt, Quartet, Let's Pretend, Zou-San (Japan only).

1992 US/EUROPEAN UNION TOUR

Firebird Suite, Yours Is No Disgrace, Rhythm Of Love, City Of Love, Shock To The System, Heart Of The Sunrise, The Ancient excerpt (SH solo), Clap, Ram, All's A Chord, Mood For A Day, Make It Easy intro / Owner Of A Lonely Heart, And You And I, Bruford & White solo duet, Hold On, Trevor's solo Solly's Beard, Etoile Noir, Take The Water To The Mountain, Soon, Long Distance Runaround, Saving My Heart, White Fish (CS solo), Amazing Grace, Lift Me Up, Tombo No Megane, Wakeman solo, Awaken, Roundabout, Starship Trooper, Gimme Some Lovin', Close To The Edge.

1994-5 TALK TOUR US/JAPAN

Keyboard taped Intro, Perpetual Change excerpt, The Calling, I Am Waiting, Rhythm Of Love, Real Love, Changes, Heart Of The Sunrise, Hearts, Cinema, City of Love, Where Will You Be?, Owner Of A Lonely Heart, And You And I, I've Seen All Good People, Walls, Endless Dream, Roundabout, It Can Happen, Ouma No Oyako (JA solo), Hold On.

1997 US OPEN YOUR EYES TOUR

Firebird Suite, Rhythm Of Love, Siberian Khatru, America, Open Your Eyes, And You And I, No Way We Can Lose, Heart Of The Sunrise, Second Initial (SH), The Valley Of Rocks (SH), Arrada (SH), Masquerade (SH), Mood For A Day (SH), Ram (SH), Valley Of Rocks (SH), Clap (SH), The Ancient excerpt (Leaves Of Green), Children Of Light, Khoroshev's solo, Long Distance Runaround, Whitefish CS solo, Sound Chaser excerpt, Tempus Fugit excerpt, White solo, Owner Of A Lonely Heart, Wondrous Stories, Soon, From the Balcony, The Revealing Science Of God, I've Seen All Good People, Roundabout, Starship Trooper.

1998 OPEN YOUR EYES – 30TH ANNIVERSARY UK/JAPAN/US SURROUND SOUND

Intro music pre-show– Final ambient Yes track from OYE album, Firebird Suite, Rhythm Of Love, Siberian Khatru, America, Open Your Eyes, Yours Is No Disgrace, No Way We Can Lose, Heart Of The Sunrise, Second Initial (SH solo), The Valley Of Rocks (SH), Arrada (SH), Masquerade (SH), Mood For A Day (SH), Ram (SH), Valley of Rocks (SH), Clap (SH), The Ancient excerpt, Children Of Light, Khoroshev's solo, Close To The Edge, Long Distance Runaround, The Fish (CS solo), Sound Chaser excerpt (CS), Tempus Fugit excerpt (CS), White solo, Owner Of A Lonely Heart, Wondrous Stories, Soon, From the Balcony, The Revealing Science Of God, I've Seen All Good People, Roundabout, Starship Trooper.

1999 NORTH AMERICA LADDER TOUR

Firebird Suite or Benjamin Britten's Young Person's Guide To The Orchestra, Yours Is No Disgrace, Time and a Word, America, Lightening Strikes, To Feel Alive, New Language, The Messenger, Face To Face, Ritual excerpts – Nous Sommes Du Soleil (JA), And You And I, Ram (SH), Cactus Boogie (SH), Mood For A Day (SH), Australia (SH), Surface Tension (SH), Meadow Rag (SH), Valley of the Rocks (SH), Clap (SH), Homeworld, Nine Voices, It Will Be A Good Day, Long Distance Runaround, Perpetual Change, White solo, Awaken, Hearts, Close To The Edge, Sweet Dreams, If Only You Knew, Roundabout, Rocking The House Of Blues, I've Seen All Good People, Cinema, Owner of a Lonely Heart, Thank you jam (for various venues).

1999 SOUTH AMERICA LADDER TOUR

Firebird Suite or Benjamin Britten's Young Person's Guide To The Orchestra, Yours Is No Disgrace, Time And A Word, America, Lightening Strikes, To Feel Alive, New Language, Ritual excerpts-Nous Sommes Du Soleil, Soon (excerpt), And You And I, Mood For A Day (SH), Clap (SH), Homeworld, Nine Voices, It Will Be A Good Day (SH), Long Distance Runaround, Perpetual Change, White solo, Awaken, Owner Of A Lonely Heart, Survival, Hearts, Close To The Edge, I've Seen All Good People, Sweet Dreams, If Only You Knew, Thank you (various cities) songs /jam, Roundabout.

2000 UK/EUROPEAN LADDER TOUR

Firebird Suite, Yours Is No Disgrace, Time and a Word, Homeworld, Perpetual Change, Lightening Strikes, The Messenger, Nous Sommes Du Soleil, Ritual excerpts, And You And I, It Will Be A Good Day, Face To Face, Hearts, Awaken, I've Seen All Good People, Clap (SH), Cinema, Owner Of A Lonely Heart, Roundabout, Thank you all jam.

2000 MASTERWORKS TOUR

Benjamin Britten's Young Person's Guide To The Orchestra (opening), Close To The Edge, Starship Trooper, Gates Of Delirium, Mood For A Day (SH small part), The Ancient, Leaves Of Green section, Heart Of The Sunrise, Ritual (Nous Sommes Du Soleil), I've Seen All Good People / Your Move (encore), Roundabout (encore).

2001 YESSYMPHONIC TOUR

Overture, Close to the Edge, And You and I, Don't Go, In The Presence Of, Gates of Delerium, Wondrous Stories, Perpetual Change, Long Distance Runaround, Ritual, Starship Trooper, Roundabout.

COLLECTORS GUIDE

Collecting memorabilia is a passion! Some people regard it as an investment, and others even elevate it to the status of art collecting, but, whatever the motivation, Yes is one of the most interesting subjects for keen collectors.

Interest in the rock and pop collectibles market has reached an all-time high in recent years, with Beatles memorabilia in particular selling for record sums at auction houses. While the Beatles have always been considered the most collectible of bands, the 2000 readers' poll in the UK magazine, *Record Collector*, rated Yes among the top thirty in the world. Three decades of visually spectacular history are not only represented by Roger Dean's vivid fantasies, but also by numerous photographs, video recordings of the most memorable shows, concert programmes and posters. All of these items, whether they hold financial or sentimental value for the collector, combine to create the rich tapestry of Yes experience.

For the first time, presented in this book, is an overview of the memorabilia that has been produced and collected over the past thirty year; a catalogue of Yes collectibles. Articles have not been priced, since prices are variable: any item, however rare, is only worth what someone is willing to pay for it on the day. What is a treasure to one person is not always of interest to another.

With 30 years of material to choose from, there is tremendous scope for amassing an ever-increasing collection of Yes artefacts. The average lifespan of most bands is only four years, so collectible material is often limited. Yes, however, are one of the rare exceptions, who, thanks to their dedicated fan base, carry on as strong as ever today, in the new millennium, three decades after their original debut.

YES ALBUMS

The official Yes albums have been released in many different formats over the years. What follows is a listing of the variations.

12" VINYL ALBUM	LP
8 TRACK CASSETTE	8T
CASSETTE TAPE	CT
COMPACT DISC	CD
VIDEO CASSETTE	VC
LASER DISC	LD
DAT TAPE	DT
CD REMASTERED	CDR
DVD	DVD
CD MINI ALBUM LTD	CDA
MINI DISC	MD
REEL TO REEL	RR
GOLD SPECIAL EDITION	GSE

Yes 1969/LP/CT/CD/CDR
Time And A Word 1970/LP/CT/CD/CDR
The Yes Album 1971/LP/CT/CD/CDR
Fragile 1971/LP/CT/CD/CDR/8T/CDA/GSE
Close To The Edge 1972/LP/CT/CD/CDR/8T/CDA
Yessongs 1973/LP/CT/CD/CDR/8T/CDA
Tales From Topographic Oceans 1973/LP/CT/CD/CDR/8T/CDA/RR
Relayer 1974/LP/CT/CD/CDR/8T/CDA
Yesterdays 1975/LP/CT/CD/CDR
Going For The One 1977/LP/CT/CD/CDR
Tormato 1978/LP/CT/8T/CD/CDR
Drama 1980/LPCT/CD/CDR
Yesshows 1980/LP/CT/CD/CDR
Classic Yes 1982/LP/CT/CD/CDR
90125 1983/LP/CT/CD
9012live 1985/LP/CT/CD/VC
Big Generator 1985/LP/CT/CD
Union 1991/LP/CT/CD/CDR
Yesyears box set 1991/CD/CT/VC
Yesstory 1991/LP/CT/CD
Talk 1994/LP/CT/CD/CD-ROM
Keys To Ascension 1996/CD/CT/VC/DVD
Keys To Ascension 2 1997/CD/CT/VC/DVD
Open Your Eyes 1997/CD/CT
Keys To Ascension box set vol 1 & 2 1998/CD
Open Your Eyes Surround Sound 1998/CD
The Ladder 1999/CD/LP (list below)
House of Yes: Live From The House of Blues 2000/DVD/CD/VC/CDA

DISCOGRAPHY

YES ALBUM DISCOGRAPHY

COUNTRIES OF ORIGIN
A = Austria **AR** = Argentina **AU** = Australia **B** = Brazil **BE** = Benelux **BEL** = Belgium **C** = Canada **CZ** = Czechoslovakia **D** = Denmark **EG** = East Germany **F** = France **G** = West Germany **GR** = Greece **H** = Holland **I** = Italy **IS** = Israel **J** = Japan **K** = South Korea **M** = Mexico **MA** = Malaysia **N** = Netherlands **NZ** = New Zealand **P** = Portugal **PO** = Poland **RO**= Romania **RU** = Russia/USSR **S** = Spain **SC** = Scotland **SA** = South Africa **SW** = Sweden **SZ** = Switzerland **T** = Taiwan **TH** = Thailand **UK** = Great Britain **US** = United States **V** = Venezuela **Y** = Yugoslavia

Yes (Atlantic)
Beyond And Before, I See You, Yesterday And Today, Looking Around, Harold Land, Every Little Thing, Sweetness, Survival
LP: Atlantic 588-190 (UK) 25 July 1969, reissued as Atlantic K 40034 (UK) 1972, Atlantic SD 8243 (US)(C) 15 October 1969, Atlantic MLP 15341 (G) Atlantic 40 034-Z (G) 1975, Atlantic 50 870 (G) 1975, Atlantic HATS 421-242 (S) Nippon Grammophon MT-1098 (J) Atlantic P-8287A (J), Atlantic P 6522A (J)
CD: Atlantic K (UK), Atlantic SD 8243-2 (US), Atlantic 7567-81447-2/8243-2 (US) October 1989, Atlantic 7567-82680-2 (US) 18 August 1994 remastered, Atlantic (G), Atlantic 18P2-2881(J) 10 August 1989, Atlantic AMCY 360 (J)

Time And A Word (Atlantic)
No Opportunity Necessary No Experience Needed, Then, Everydays, Sweet Dreams, The Prophet, Clear Days, Astral Traveller, Time And A Word
LP: Atlantic 2400 006 (UK) July 1970, Atlantic K 40085 (UK) 1972, Atlantic SD 8273 (US)(C) 11/02/70, Atlantic MLP 15 367 (G), Atlantic 40 085-Z (G), Atlantic 40.085 (G) 1975, Atlantic HATS 421-243 (S), Atlantic K 40085 (I), Atlantic P-8014A (J), Atlantic P 6523A (J), Atlantic MH 50-14.341 (Ar) Lyra (Gr) R60-00507 (Ru) 1991
CD: Atlantic 7567-81449-2/8273-2 (US) 10/89, Atlantic 7567-82681-2 (US) 18/8/94 remastered, Atlantic (G), Atlantic 18P2-2882 (J) 10 August 1989, Atlantic AMCY 361 (J)

The Yes Album (Atlantic)
Yours Is No Disgrace, Clap, Starship Trooper: a. Life Seeker, b. Disillusion, c. Wurm, I've Seen All Good People: a. Your Move, b. All Good People, A Venture, Perpetual Change
LP: Atlantic 2400 101 (UK) 29 January 1971, Atlantic K 40106 (UK) 1972, Atlantic SD 8283 (US)(C) 19 March 1971, Atlantic SD 19131 (US) 1978, Atlantic SD 8283 (C), Atlantic MLP 15 403 (G), Atlantic ATL 40 106-Z (G), Atlantic HATS 421-71 (S) 1972, Atlantic SD 8283 (I), Atlantic P-8079A (J), Atlantic P 6524A (J) Union TD 1746 (T), Atlantic (Ar) Lyra 0116 (Gr) Phonogram (Gr)
CD: Atlantic K 240106 (UK) July 1987, Atlantic SD 19131-2 (US) 1988, Atlantic 7567-82665-2 (US) 18 August 1994 remastered, Atlantic 240 106 (G) Atlantic 20P2-2112 (J) 25 October 1988, Atlantic AMCY 362 (J) IMMI CDE 119112 (Cz)

Fragile (Atlantic)
Roundabout, Cans And Brahms, We Have Heaven, South Side Of The Sky, Five Per Cent For Nothing, Long Distance Runaround, The Fish (Schindleria Praematurus), Mood For A Day, Heart Of The Sunrise
LP: Atlantic 2401 019 (UK) 1 November 1971, Atlantic K 50009 (UK) 1972, Atlantic SD 7211 (US) 4 January 1972, Atlantic SD 19132 (US) 1978, Atlantic ATL 50.009-U (G) Atlantic ATL 50 009 (F) Atlantic HATS 421-88 (S) 1972, Atlantic P-10102A (J) Atlantic P6525A (J), Atlantic P-8206A (J), Atlantic (V) Lyra or Phonogram (Gr), WEA 50009 (Gr)
CD: Atlantic K 250009 (UK) December 1986, Atlantic SD 19132-2 (US) 1986, Atlantic 7567-

The interior imagery used on the gatefold sleeve of Close to the Edge.

82667-2 (US) 18 August 1994 remastered, Atlantic 7567-82524-2 (US) May 1994, Atlantic 250 009 (G), Atlantic 20P2-2052 (J) 10 September 1988, Atlantic AMCY 363 (J) East-West AMCY 2731(J) 25 May 1998 30th Anniversary Limited Edition (Most issues include a free booklet featuring band members' profiles and Roger Dean artwork and photographs)

Close To The Edge (Atlantic)
Close To The Edge: (i) The Solid Time Of Change, (ii) Total Mass Retain, (iii) I Get Up I Get Down, (iv) Seasons Of Man, And You And I: (i) Cord Of Life, (ii) Eclipse, (iii) The Preacher The Teacher, (iv) The Apocalypse, Siberian Khatru
LP: Atlantic K 50012 (UK) 8 September 1972, Atlantic SD 7244 (US) 13 September 1972, Atlantic SD 19133 (US) 1978, Mobile Fidelity Original Master Record MFSL-1-077 (US), Atlantic ATL 50 012-U (G) 13 September 1972, Atlantic 62075 (G) Atlantic HATS 421-95 (S) Atlantic P-10116A (J), Atlantic P 6526A (J), Atlantic P-8274A (J), Atlantic SD-7244 (Au)(NZ) Kong Mei KM-2178 (T) GWEA-5022 (M) First FL-2275 (T), Supraphon E 28 59/1-13-1019 (Cz), Phonogram 2400226 (Gr) WEA 50012 (Gr), Atlantic (Ar)
CD: Atlantic K 250012 (UK) December 1986, Atlantic SD 19133-2 (US) 1986, Atlantic 7567-82666-2 (US) 18 August 1994 remastered

Atlantic 250 012 (G), Atlantic 20P2-2053 (J) 10 September 1988, Atlantic AMCY 364 (J), East-West AMCY 2732 (J) 25/5/98 30th Anniversary Limited Edition

Yessongs (Atlantic)
Opening (excerpt from Firebird Suite), Siberian Khatru, Heart Of The Sunrise, Perpetual Change, And You And I, Mood For A Day, excerpts from The Six Wives Of Henry VIII, Roundabout, Your Move, I've Seen All Good People, Long Distance Runaround, The Fish, Close To The Edge, Yours Is No Disgrace, Starship Trooper
(Includes a free 'Yes live' photo booklet)
3xLP: Atlantic K 60045 (UK) 27 April 1973, Atlantic SD 3-100 (US), Atlantic ATL 60 045-E (G), Atlantic 750-03/04/05 (S), Atlantic P-5503-5A (J), Atlantic P 5087-9A (J)
2xCD: Atlantic 7567-81300-2/SD 100-2 (US) 1987, Atlantic 7567-82682-2 (US) 18 August 1994 remastered, Atlantic 260 045 (UK) February 1987, Atlantic 260 045 (G) February 1987, Atlantic 32P2-2883/4 (J) 19 August 1989, Atlantic AMCY 365/6 (J), East-West AMCY 2733 (J) 25 May 1998 30th Anniversary Limited Edition

Tales From Topographic Oceans (Atlantic)
The Revealing Science Of God, The Remembering, The Ancient, Ritual
2xLP: Atlantic K 80001 (UK) 26 October 1973, Atlantic SD 2-908 (US) 9/1/74, Atlantic ATL 8001/2-A (G) 9 January 1974, Atlantic 500-59 (S), Atlantic P 4612-3A (J), Atlantic P-5508-9A (J), Atlantic 2-SD-908 (NZ), Phonogram 80001 (Gr), WEA (Gr)
2xCD: Atantic 781 325 (UK) September 1989, Atlantic SD 2-908-2 (US) 1989, Atlantic 7567-82683-2 (US) 18 August 1994 remastered, Atlantic 7567-81325-2 (G), Atlantic 32P2-2885/6 (J) 9 August 1989, Atlantic AMCY 367/8 (J), East-West AMCY 2736/7 (J) 25 May 1998 30th Anniversary Limited Edition

Relayer (Atlantic)
The Gates Of Delirium, Sound Chaser, To Be Over
LP: Atlantic K 50096 (UK) 28 November 1974, Atlantic SD 18122 (US) 5 December 1974, Atlantic SD 19135 (US) 1978, Atlantic ATL 50 096-U (G) 5 December 1974, Atlantic HATS 421-148 (S), Atlantic P 10357A (J), Atlantic P-6527A (J) 1974, Atlantic SD 18122 (NZ) CR110PK (Ru), Phonogram 2400215 (Gr), WEA (Gr)
CD: Atlantic SD 19135-2 (US) 1988, Atlantic 7567-82664-2 (US) 18 August 1994 remastered, Atlantic K 250 096 (UK) July 1988
Atlantic 250 096 (G) July 1988, Atlantic

18P2-2887 (J) 10 August 1989, East-West AMCY 2738 (J) 25 May 1998 30th Anniversary Limited Edition

Yesterdays (Atlantic)
America (the full-length version), Looking Around, Time And A Word, Sweet Dreams, Then, Survival, Astral Traveller, Dear Father
LP: Atlantic K 50048 (UK) 14 March 1975, Atlantic

SD 18103 (US) 27 February 1975, Atlantic SD 19134 (US) 1978, Atlantic ATL 50 048-U (G), Atlantic K 50048 B (F)(G)(I), Atlantic HATS 421-161 (S), Atlantic P-6528A (J), Atlantic P-8503A (J), Atlantic P 6528A (J) Atlantic 2313 (V), Atlantic 50067 (V), Phonogram 2400248 (Gr), WEA (Gr), Union TD 1536 (K)
CD: Atlantic 19134-2 (US), Atlantic 7567-82684-2 (US) 18 August 1994 remastered, Atlantic 250 048 (G), Atlantic AMCY 15 (J) 25 February 1990

Going For The One (Atlantic)
Going For The One, Turn Of The Century, Parallels, Wondrous Stories, Awaken

LP: Atlantic K 50379 (UK) 12 July 1977, Atlantic SD 19106 (US) 7 July 1977, Atlantic ATL 50 379-Z (G) 13 July 1977, Atlantic P-10304A (J), Atlantic P-6533A (J), Phonogram 0141 (Gr), WEA (Gr)
CD: Atlantic SD 19106-2 (US), Atlantic 7567-82670-2 (US) 18 August 1994 remastered, Atlantic K 250 379 (UK) July 1988, Atlantic 250 379 (G) July 1988, Atlantic 18P2-2888 (J) 10 August 1989, Atlantic AMCY 370 (J)

Tormato (Atlantic)
Future Times, Rejoice, Don't Kill The Whale, Madrigal, Release Release, Arriving UFO, Circus Of Heaven, Onward, On The Silent Wings Of Freedom

LP: Atlantic K 50518 (UK) 8 September 1978, Atlantic SD 19202 (US) 26 September 1978, Atlantic KSD 19202 (C), Atlantic ATL 50 518 (G), Atlantic P-10572A (J), Atlantic SD 19202 (NZ), SUZY 50518 (Y) 1979, WEA (Gr)
CD: Atlantic 7567-82277-2 (US), Atlantic 7567-82671-2 (US) 18 August 1994 remastered, Atlantic (G), Atlantic 18P2-2889 (J)
08 October 1989

Drama (Atlantic)
Machine Messiah, White Car, Does It Really Happen?, Into The Lens, Run Through The Light, Tempus Fugit
LP: Atlantic K 50736 (UK) 18 August 1980, Atlantic SD 16019 (US) September 1980, Atlantic ATL 50 736 (G) 22 August 1980
Atlantic S 90.272 (S), Atlantic P-10854A (J)
Atlantic SD 16019 (NZ), WEA 50736 (Gr)
CD: Atlantic SD 16019-2 (US), Atlantic 7567-82685-2 (US) 18 August 1994 remastered, Atlantic 7567-81473-2 (G), Atlantic AMCY16 (J) 25 February 1990

Yesshows (Atlantic)
Parallels, Time And A Word, Going For The One, The Gates Of Delirium, Don't Kill The Whale, Ritual (Nous Sommes Du Soleil), Wondrous Stories
2xLP: Atlantic K 60142 (UK) 24 November 1980, Atlantic SD 2-510 (US) December 1980, Atlantic

ATL 60 142 (G) 1 December 1980, Atlantic P-5565-6A (J),
2xCD: Atlantic 7567-81300-2/SD-100-2 (US), Atlantic 7567-82686-2 (US) 18 August 1994 remastered, Atlantic AMCY 372/373 (J) Atlantic 32P2-2890/1 (J) 10 August 1989

Classic Yes (Atlantic)
Heart Of The Sunrise, Wondrous Stories, Yours Is No Disgrace, Starship Trooper: a. Life Seeker, b. Disillusion, c. Wurm, Long Distance Runaround, The Fish (Schindleria Praematurus), And You And I: a. Cord Of Life, b. Eclipse, c. The Preacher The Teacher, d. The Apocalypse, Roundabout, I've Seen All Good People: a. Your Move, b. All Good People
(Includes a free 7" single Roundabout/Your Move, SAM141)
LP: Atlantic K 50842 (UK) 30 November 1981, Atlantic SD 19320 (US), Atlantic ATL 50 842 (G) 4 December 1981, Atlantic P-6842A (J), Amiga 8 56 005 (EG), Atlantic (S), Atlantic (Is)
CD: Atlantic K 250842 –2 (UK) December 1986, Atlantic SD 19320-2 (US), Atlantic 7567-82687-2 (US) 18 August 1994 remastered, Atlantic 250 842 (G), Atlantic AMCY 22 (J) 25 March 1990

90125 (Atco)
Owner Of A Lonely Heart, Hold On, It Can Happen, Changes, Cinema, Leave It, Our Song, City Of Love, Hearts
LP: Atco 790125-1 (G)(UK) 11 November 1983, Atco 7567-90125-1 (US) 7 November 1983, Atco 90125-1 (NZ), Atco P-11356 (J), WEA 790125 (Gr)
CD: Atco 7 90125-2 (UK), Atco 7567 90125-2 (US), Atco 7567-790125-2 (G), Atco 20P2-2054 (J) 10 September 1988 Atco AMCY 374 (J)

9012live – The Solos (Atco)
Hold On, Si, Solly's Beard, Soon, Changes, Amazing Grace, Whitefish
LP: Atco 790474-1 (UK) February 1986, Atco 7567-90474-1-Y (US) 7 November 1985, Atco 790474-1-Y (G) 8 November 1985, Atco VPLP-70464 (J)
CD: Atco 7567-90474-2 (US), Atco AMCY 375 (J)

Big Generator (Atco)
Rhythm Of Love, Big Generator, Shoot High Aim

Low, Almost Like Love, Love Will Find A Way, Final Eyes, I'm Running, Holy Lamb (Song For Harmonic Convergence)
LP: Atco 790522-1 (UK) 29 September 1987, Atco 7567-90522-1 (US) 17 September 1987, Atco WX 70/790 522-1 (G) 25 September 1987, Atco 150649 (G)
CD: Atco 7 90522-2 (UK), Atco 7567-90522-2 (US), Atco 790 522-2 (G), Atco 32XD-559 (J), Atco 18P2-2892 (J) 10 August 1989

Anderson Bruford Wakeman Howe (Arista)
Sound, Second Attention, Soul Warrior, Fist Of Fire, Brother Of Mine, Big Dream, Nothing Can Come Between Us, Birthright, The Meeting, Quartet, I Wanna Learn, She Gives Me Love, Who Was The First, I'm Alive, Teakbois, Order Of The Universe, Order Theme, Rock Gives Courage, It's So Hard To Grow, The Universe, Let's Pretend
LP: Arista AL85-90126 (US), 13 June 1989, Arista 209 970 (G)
CD: Arista ARCD 85-90126 (US) P/D, Arista (US) 1996 20 bit reissue, Arista 259 970 (G)(UK) 13 June 1989, Arista 262 155 (UK) January 1992, Arista A32D-83 (J)

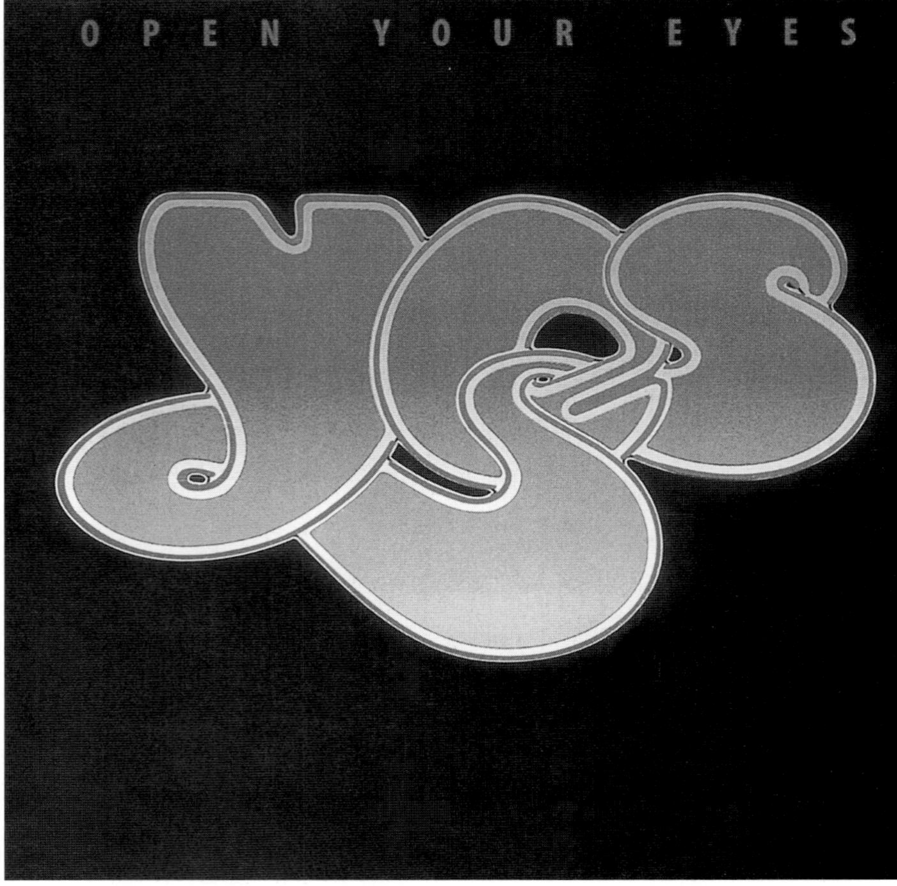

Union (Arista)
I Would Have Waited Forever, Shock To The System, Masquerade, Lift Me Up, Without Hope You Cannot Start The Day, Saving My Heart, Miracle Of Life, Silent Talking, More We Live-Let Go, The Angkor Wat, Dangerous, Holding On, Evensong, Take The Water To The Mountain, Give And Take
LP: Arista 211 558 (UK) April 1991, Arista AL-8643 (US)
CD: Arista 261 558 (UK) April 1991, Arista ARCD-8643 (US) 22 April 91, Arista 261 558 (G) 22 April 1991, Arista BVCA-116 (J)

Yesyears (Atco)
Something's Coming, Survival, Every Little Thing, Then, Everydays, Sweet Dreams, No Opportunity Necessary No Experience Needed, Time And A Word, Starship Trooper: a. Life Seeker, b. Disillusion, c. Wurm, Yours Is No Disgrace, I've Seen All Good People: a. Your Move, b. All Good People, Long Distance Runaround, The Fish (Schindleria Praematurus), Roundabout, Heart Of The Sunrise, America, Close To The Edge: a. The Solid Time Of Change, b. Total Mass Retain, c. I Get Up I Get Down, d. Seasons Of Man, Ritual (Nous Sommes Du Soleil), Sound Chaser, Soon, Amazing Grace, Vevey (Part One), Wondrous Stories, Awaken, Montreux's Theme, Vevey (Part Two), Going For The One, Money, Abilene, Don't Kill The Whale, On The Silent Wings Of Freedom, Does It Really Happen?, Tempus Fugit, Run With The Fox, I'm Down, Make It Easy, It Can Happen, Owner Of A Lonely Heart, Hold On, Shoot High Aim Low, Rhythm Of Love, Love Will Find A Way, Changes, And You And I: a. Cord Of Life, b. Eclipse, c. The Preacher The Teacher, d. Apocalypse, Heart Of The Sunrise, Love Conquers All
(4 CD box set with free booklet showing Yes' history and discography)
4xLP: Atco 7-91644-1 (US) 6 August 1991
4xCD: Atco 7567-91644-2 (UK)(G), Atco 7-91644-2 (US) 6 August 1991, Atco AMCY 280/281/282/283 (J)
4xLP w/Video: Atco 50273-0 (US)

Yesstory (Atco)
Survival, No Opportunity Necessary No Experience Needed, Time And A Word, Starship Trooper, I've Seen All Good People, Roundabout, Heart Of The Sunrise, Close To The Edge, Ritual-Nous Sommes Du Soleil, Soon, Wondrous Stories, Going For The One, Don't Kill The Whale, Does It Really Happen?, Make It Easy, Owner Of A Lonely Heart, Rhythm Of Love, Changes (live version)
(European Version)
2xLP: Atco 7567-91747-1 (UK) (G), 2xCD: Atco 7567-91747-2 (UK)(G) September 1991, Atco AMCY 284/5 (J)
(US Version)
LP: Atco 92202-1 (US), 2xCD: Atco 92202-2 (US) 13 October 1992

Anderson, Bruford, Wakeman & Howe: An Evening Of Yes Music Plus (Fragile Records)
Benjamin Britten's Young Person's Guide To The Orchestra, Time And A Word, Teakbois, Owner Of A Lonely Heart, Clap, Mood For A Day, Gone But Not Forgotten, Catherine Parr, Merlin The

Magician, Long Distance Runaround, Birthright, And You And I, Close To The Edge, Themes 1. Sound, 2. Second, Attention, 3. Soul Warrior, Brother Of Mine, Heart Of The Sunrise, Order Of The Universe, Roundabout
2xCD: Fragile Records CD FRL 002 (CD JMC 005/006) (UK) October 1993, Herald Music CD HER 006 (US) 4 March 1994

Talk (Victory)
The Calling, I Am Waiting, Real Love, State Of Play, Walls, Where Will You Be, Endless Dream a. Silent Spring b. Talk c. Endless Dream
LP: Victory 828 489-1 (US)
CD: Victory 383 480 033-2 (US) 22 March 1994, Victory 828 489-2 (UK)(G) 18/3/94, Victory VICP-5355 (J) 16 March 1994
(Japanese version features The Calling [extended] as a bonus track)

Keys To Ascension Volume 1 (Yes Records)
Siberian Khatru, The Revealing Science Of God, America, Onward, Awaken, Roundabout, Starship Trooper, Be The One, That That Is
2xCD: Castle Music Pictures VACM-1112/3 (J) 23 October 1996, Castle Communication/Alliance 06076 86208-2 (US) 29 October 1996 Eagle Records/Purple Pyramid/Yes Records EDF CD-417/GAS 0000-417 EDF (UK), Castle Communications EDF PR417 (UK)
(Includes a free poster)

Keys To Ascension Volume 2 (Yes Records)
I've Seen All Good People: a. Your Move b. All Good People, Going For The One, Time And A Word, Close To The Edge: a. Solid Time Of Change b. Total Mass Retain c. I Get Up, I Get Down d. Seasons Of Man, Turn Of The Century, And You And I: a. Cord Of Live b. Eclipse c. The Preacher the Teacher d. Apocalypse, Mind Drive, Foot Prints, Bring To The Power, Children Of the Light: a. Children Of The Light b. Lifeline, Sign Language
2xCD: Yes Records EDF CD 457 GAS 0000457EDF (UK), Purple Pyramid/Cleopatra CLP 0159-2 (US) 22 October 1997

Open Your Eyes (Eagle Records)
New State Of Mind, Open Your Eyes, Universal Garden, No Way We Can Lose, Fortune Seller,

Man In The Moon, Wonder Love, From the Balcony, Love Shine, Somehow...Someday, The Solution
CD: Beyond Music/Tommy Boy BYCD3074/6 39857 30742 2 (US) 25 November 1997, Beyond Music/Tommy Boy CDADV (US) 25 November 1997, Eagle Records/Purple Pyramid EDL EAG CD 013-2 (UK), (J) 19 December 1997 plus Bonus Track, Beyond Music/Tommy Boy BYCD3075 39857 30745 2 (US) limited edition special 'Surround Sound' 3D Audio Version, JPCD 980 113 (Ru) 1998

Keys To Ascension Volumes 1 & 2 (Castle Communications)
(Same track listing as Keys 1 & 2)
4XCD BOX: Castle Communications ESF CD 635 (UK) March 1998
(With free Roger Dean album cover cards, the track 'Lightning' missing from CD)

The Ladder (Eagle Records)
Homeworld (The Ladder), It Will Be A Good Day (The River), Lightening Strikes, Can I?, Face To Face, If Only You Knew, To Be Alive (Hep Yadda), Finally, The Messenger, New Language, Nine Voices (Longwalker)
CD: LP: 1 October 1999, (The different variations can be seen detailed under Limited Edition Album Variations)

Yes: House Of Yes: Live From House Of Blues (Eagle Records)
Yours Is No Disgrace, Time And A Word (shortened version), Homeworld, Perpetual Change, Lightning Strikes, The Messenger, Ritual-Nous Sommes Du Soleil (snippet), And You And I, It Will Be A Good Day (The River) Face To Face, Awaken, Your Move - I've Seen All Good People, Cinema, Owner Of A Lonely Heart, Roundabout
2XCD: WB - BEYB780842 (US), Eagle Records EDGCD158, 25 September 2000
(Also available in video and DVD format in the U.S. 2000-1, other regions to follow late in 2001)

Keys to the Studio (Sanctuary Records)
Footprints, Be the One, Mind Drive, Bring Me to the Power, Sign Language, That, That Is, Children of Light.
CMRCD177 (UK)

COMPILATION AND PROMOTIONAL RELEASES

Yes collectors will almost certainly include some promotional and compilation pieces in their collection. These can be the hardest items to find and therefore the most costly. This listing provides the main compilation albums that have featured more than one or two Yes tracks.

Fragile/Close To The Edge - 2 For One
(Atlantic Records)
K 460166 (UK) 1982
80002-4 (US) 1982, Cassette

Yes, By Request (Compilation) (ATCO)
Side 1: Every Little Thing, Time And A Word, America, Yours Is No Disgrace, Roundabout, Wondrous Stories, Owner Of A Lonely Heart
Side 2: Rhythm Of Love, Big Generator, Shoot High, Aim Low, Love Will Find A Way
SAM 395 (G)(UK)
1987, Promotion cassette

Yes, The Story Of Yes (Compilation) (ATCO)
Rhythm Of Love, Owner Of A Lonely Heart, Roundabout, Close To The Edge; (I) The Solid Time Of Change (II) Total Mass Retain (III) I Get Up I Get Down (IV) Seasons Of Man, Going For The One, Don't Kill The Whale, Machine Messiah, Leave It, Love Will Find A Way, Big Generator
PSCD-5 (J)
1987, CD (very limited edition and expensive)

Classic Rock 1966-1988 (Atlantic Records)
I've Seen All Good People: Your Move, All Good People, Heart Of The Sunrise, Owner Of A Lonely Heart
7 81908-1 (US)
1988, 4 X LP

Yesyears Sampler (ATCO)
I've Seen All Good People, Roundabout, Run With The Fox, Money, Make It Easy, Owner Of A Lonely Heart, Love Conquers All
PRCS 4001 (US)
12 July 1991, Cassette

Yesyears Promo (ATCO)
Make It Easy, I've Seen All Good People, Roundabout, America (45 Edit), Money, Run With The Fox, Owner Of A Lonely Heart, Love Conquers All
PRCD 4009-2 (US)
CD BOX (Different cover to released version)

Atlantic Records' Rock & Roll (Atlantic Records)
I've See All Good People ; Your Move, Heart Of The Sunrise, Owner Of A Lonely Heart
82306 (US)
1991, CD

Yes - Special Digest (ATCO)
Owner Of A Lonely Heart, It Can Happen (Cinema), Don't Kill The Whale, Run With The Fox, Love Will Find A Way, Make It Easy (Cinema), Money, Sweet Dreams, Abilene, Roundabout, Changes (Live), Love Conquers All
ASCD-26 (J)
1992, CD (A well presented compilation)

Yes: Highlights - The Very Best Of Yes
(Atlantic Records)
Survival, Time And A Word, Starship Trooper, I've Seen All Good People, Your Move, Roundabout, Long Distance Runaround, Soon (Single Edit), Wondrous Stories, Going For The One, Owner Of A Lonely Heart, Leave It, Rhythm Of Love
7567-82517-2 (US)
21 September 1993, CD

Yes: The Yes Solos Family Album
(Connoisseur Collection)
(Intro) Uncredited - Flash, Catherine Howard - Rick Wakeman, Wind Of Change - Badger, The Nature Of The Sea - Steve Howe, Ram - Steve Howe, Hold Out Your Hand - Chris Squire, Merlin The Magician - Rick Wakeman, Medley; Ocean Song, The Meeting, Sound Out The Galleon - Jon Anderson, Spring (Song Of Innocence) - Alan White, Cachaca - Patrick Moraz, Feels Good To Me - Bill Bruford, I Hear You Now - Jon And Vangelis, All In A Matter Of Time - Jon Anderson, Etoile Noir - Trevor Rabin, Eyes Of Love - Trevor Rabin, Dominating Factor - Peter Banks
VSOP CD 190 (UK)
October 1993, CD

The Symphonic Music Of Yes (RCA)
Roundabout, I've Seen All Good People, Mood For A Day, Roundabout (Radio Edit)
54 PCD (UK)
SYPCD-1 (US) 26 October 1993, CD (Roger Dean cover)

Yes; The Symphonic Music Of Yes (RCA Classic Red Label)
Roundabout, Close To The Edge, Wondrous Stories, I've Seen All Good People, Mood For A Day, Owner Of A Lonely Heart, Survival, Heart Of The Sunrise, Soon, Starship Trooper
09026-61938-2 (US)(G)
26 October 1993, CD (Roger Dean cover)

Soundtrack: Yes: Yessongs (Soundtrack From Video Of The Same Title)
I've Seen All Good People, Clap, And You And I, Close To The Edge, Roundabout, Yours Is No Disgrace, excerpt from Starship Trooper
Qwsd-9608 (J), CD Label Unknown

Tales From Yesterday - A View From The South Side Of The Sky (Magna Carta)
Roundabout - Robert Berry, Siberian Khatru - Stanley Snail, Mood For A Day - Steve Morse, Don't Kill The Whale- Magellan, Turn Of The Century - Steve Howe & Annie Haslam, Release Release - Shadow Gallery, Wondrous Stories – World Trade, South Side Of The Sky - Cairo, Soon - Patrick Moraz, Changes - Enchant, Astral Traveller – Peter Banks, Clap - Steve Morse, Starship Trooper - Jeronimo Road
MA-9003-2 (US)
22 August 1995, CD (Roger Dean cover)

Supernatural Fairy Tales: The Progressive Rock Era (Rhino)
Perpetual Change, Siberian Khatru, And You And I (Edit)
R2 72451 (US)
August 1996
5 X CD BOX (Roger Dean cover)

Yes: ~ Something's Coming The BBC Recordings 1969 - 1970 (UK) / Beyond And Before (US)
Disc 1: Something's Coming (12 January 1969 - Top Gear with John Peel), Everydays (12 January 1969 - Top Gear with John Peel), Every Little Thing (14 June 1969 - Johnnie Walker), Looking Around (04 August 1969 - Dave Symonds), Sweet Dreams (19 January 1970 - Dave Lee Travis), Then (19 January 1970 - Dave Lee Travis), No Opportunity Necessary (German TV)
Disc 2: Astral Traveller (17 March 1970 - Sunday Show), Then (17 March 1970 - Sunday Show), Every Little Thing (17 March 1970 - Sunday Show), Everydays (17 March 1970 - Sunday Show), For Everyone (17 March 1970 - Sunday Show) / Disc 2 - Bonus Tracks: (Intro) Sweetness (14 June 1969), Something's Coming (23 February 1969 - Top Gear with John Peel), Sweet Dreams (23 February 1969 - Top Gear with John Peel), Beyond And Before (French TV)
(New Millennium Communications Pilot) 25/5
018524 145126 (UK) 20 September 1997
(Purple Pyramid/Cleopatra) CLP 0246-2/7-41157-02462-3 (US) 28 April 1998
2 X CD

Yes: Something's Coming The BBC Recordings 1969 – 1970 (New Millennium

Communications)
Disc 1, Side 1: Something's Coming (12 January 1969 - Top Gear with John Peel), Everydays (12 January 1969 - Top Gear with John Peel), Sweetness (12 January 1969 - Top Gear with John Peel), Dear Father (12 January 1969 - Top Gear with John Peel)
Disc 1, Side 2: Every Little Thing (12 January 1969 - Top Gear with John Peel), Sweet Dreams (23 February 1969 - Top Gear with John Peel), Something's Coming (23 February 1969 - Top Gear with John Peel), Beyond And Before - Rare French Broadcast
Disc 2, Side 1: (Intro) Sweetness (14 June 1969 - Johnny Walker), Looking Around (4 August 1969 - Dave Symonds), Sweet Dreams (19 January 1970 - Dave Lee Travis), Then (19 January 1970 - Dave Lee Travis), Astral Traveller (17 March 1970 – Sunday Show)
Disc 2, Side 2: Every Little Thing (17 March 1970 - Sunday Show), Everydays (17 March 1970 - Sunday Show), Then (17 March 1970 - Sunday Show), No Opportunity Necessary - No Experience Needed - Rare German Broadcast
GET BACK RECORDS H89529674 (I) (UK)
28 February 1998, 2 X LP

Yes: Friends And Relatives (Eagle Records/Purple Pyramid)
Disc 1: Owner Of A Lonely Heart (1998 remake) - Jon Anderson, Ice - Rick Wakeman - from Time Machine, Red And White - Steve Howe - from Homebrew 1, The Zone Of O - Esquire - from Coming Home, Up North - Bill Bruford's Earthworks - from Earthworks, The Pyramids Of Egypt - Rick Wakeman - from The Seven Wonders Of The World, Roundabout - Steve Howe - from Not Necessarily Acoustic, Sync Or Swim - Wakeman With Wakeman - from Wakeman With Wakeman, Arthur - Rick Wakeman - from Live At Hammersmith, Close To The Edge - Yes - from Keys To Ascension 2
Disc 2: No Expense Spared - Wakeman With Wakeman - from No Expense Spared, Say - Jon Anderson - from The More You Know, Walk Don't Run - Steve Howe - from Quantum Guitar, Tron Thomi - Esquire - from Coming Home, 10 Million - Jon Anderson - a hidden bonus track on the Japanese release of The More You Know, excerpts From Tales From Topographic Oceans - Steve Howe - from Not Necessarily Acoustic, The More You Know - Jon Anderson - from The More You Know, The Journey- Rick Wakeman - from Live At Hammersmith, America - Yes - from Keys To Ascension
EAG 091-2 (UK) 29 June 1998
0337 (US) 11 August 1998
2 X CD (Roger Dean cover)

Yes: Astral Traveller
(Brilliant Records)
Something's Coming, Everydays, Sweetness, Dear Father, Every Little Thing, Looking Around, Sweet Dreams, Then, No Opportunity Necessary - No Experience Required, For Everyone, Beyond And Before, Astral Traveller
Bt 33019
(UK), 22 November 1999
CD (Reissue of Something's Coming)

Yes: Millennium Collection (Digimode Entertainment Ltd.)
Disc 1: Something's Coming, Everydays, Sweetness, Dear Father, Every Little Thing, Looking Around, Sweet Dreams, Then, No Opportunity Necessary - No Experience Required
Disc 2: Astral Traveller, Then, Every Little Thing (Reprise), Everydays (Reprise), For Everyone, (Intro) Sweetness, Something's Coming (bonus track), Sweet Dreams (bonus track), Beyond And Before (bonus track)
1999 20 4022-1 MI Germany

Yes: Geographic Potions
Yet another budget priced re-release of the *Somethings Coming/Beyond and Before* album of early Yes sessions.
US, 2001

Peter Banks: Can I Play You Something?
Intro: Can I Play You Something?, Intro: Bang Crash, Peter Banks Band – Peter Gun, Peter Banks Band – Hippie Loop, Syn – 14 Hour Technicolour Dream, The Devil's Disciples – You Better Move On, Mabel Greer's Toyshop – Beyond And Before (demo), Mabel Greer's Toyshop – Beyond And Before (What Bass Mix), Peter Banks – Lama Loop, Syn – Grounded, The Devil's Disciples - For Your Love, Syn – Flowerman (demo), Syn – Flowerman, Peter Banks – Yesterdays, Mabel Greer's Toyshop – Electric Funeral (demo), Mabel Greer's Toyshop – Electric Funeral (Radio Fun Mix), Peter Banks – Cinnamon Touch, Mabel Greer's Toyshop – Get Yourself Together (demo), Syn – Created By Clive, Mabel Greer's Toyshop – Images Of You And Me (Radio Fun Mix), Affirmative Duo (Yes) I Saw You (Bang & Crash), Peter Banks – No Time
Blueprint 301CD, 2000, UK

Yes: The Best Of Yes, 1970 – 1987 (Electra)
No Opportunity Necessary - No Experience Needed, America, Heart Of The Sunrise, And You And I, Siberian Khatru, Sound Chaser, On The Silent Wings Of Freedom, Into The Lens, Owner Of A Lonely Heart, Love Will Find A Way
#AMCY-6051 (J)
November 1999

Yes:Friends & Relatives 2 (Eagle Recoeds)
Disc 1: New State of Mind (Yes) – Big Girls (Esquire) – Sad Eyed Lady of the Lowlands (Steve Howe with Jon Anderson) – Merlin the Magician (Rick Wakeman) – Days of Wonder (Chris Squire and Billy Sherwood) – Magic Love (Jon Anderson) – Footloose and Fancy Free (Bill Bruford's Earthworks) – Madman Blues (Rick & Adam Wakeman) – Night Trade (Steve Howe) – New Language (Yes)
Disc 2: Homeworld (Yes) – It's All Over Now Baby Blue (Steve Howe with Annie Haslam) – Catherine Howard (Rick Wakeman) – Faithfully (Jon Anderson) – Coming Home (Esquire) – Red Light Ahead (Chris Squire & Billy Sherwood) – From the Balcony (Yes) – Number 10 (Wakeman with Wakeman) – Dewey Eyed, Then Dancing (Bill Bruford's Earthworks) – Finally (Yes)
EDGCD132 (UK), 2001 (Roger Dean cover)

YES 7"/12", CASSETTE AND CD SINGLES

OFFICIAL & PROMOTIONAL WORLDWIDE

COUNTRIES OF ORIGIN
A = Austria **AR** = Argentina **AU** = Australia
B = Brazil **BE** = Benelux **BEL** = Belgium
C = Canada **CZ** = Czechoslovakia **D** = Denmark
EG = East Germany **F** = France **G** = West Germany **GR** = Greece **H** = Holland **I** = Italy
IS = Israel **J** = Japan **K** = South Korea
M = Mexico **MA** = Maylaysia **N** = Netherlands
NZ = New Zealand **P** = Portugal **PO** = Poland
RO= Romania **RU** = Russia/USSR **S** = Spain
SC = Scotland **SA** = South Africa **SW** = Sweden
SZ = Switzerland **T** = Taiwan **TH** = Thailand
UK = Great Britain **US** = United States
V = Venezuela **Y** = Yugoslavia
Unless stated, the item is a 7" vinyl single.
P/S = Picture Sleeve

Sweetness (Edit)/Something's Coming
(Atlantic Records)
Jon Anderson, Chris Squire, Peter Banks, Bill Bruford, Tony Kaye
584280 (UK),4 July 1969
650171 (F), P/S

Looking Around/Everydays
(Atlantic Records)
Jon Anderson, Chris Squire, Peter Banks, Bill Bruford, Tony Kaye
584298 (UK), October 1969

Sweetness (Edit)/Every Little Thing
(Atlantic Records)
Jon Anderson, Chris Squire, Peter Banks, Bill Bruford, Tony Kaye
45-2709 (US), 27 January 1970

Looking Around/Every Little Thing
(Atlantic Records)
Jon Anderson, Chris Squire, Peter Banks, Bill Bruford, Tony Kaye
ATL 70.425 (G), 1970, P/S

Time And A Word (Edit)/The Prophet
(Atlantic Records)
Jon Anderson, Chris Squire, Peter Banks, Bill Bruford, Tony Kaye
584323 (UK), 27 March 1970

Sweet Dreams/Dear Father
(Atlantic Records)
Jon Anderson, Chris Squire, Peter Banks, Bill Bruford, Tony Kaye
2019 018 (H), 1970, P/S
2091 004 (UK)(H), 19 June 1970

Yours Is No Disgrace (Edit)/Clap
(Atlantic Records)
Jon Anderson, Chris Squire, Steve Howe, Bill Bruford, Tony Kaye
2091 017 (H), 1971

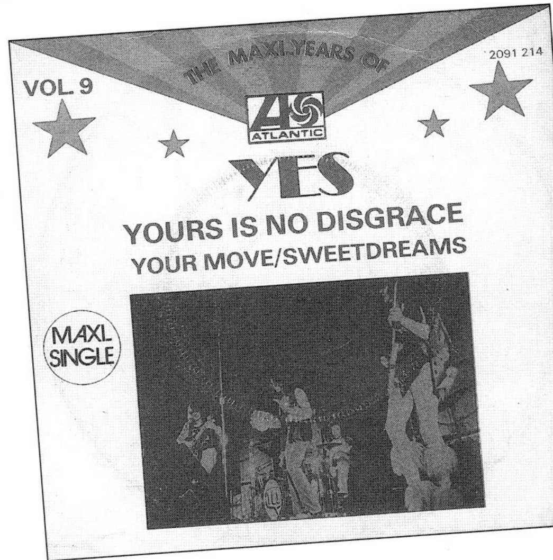

Yours Is No Disgrace Part 1/Yours Is No Disgrace Part 2 (Atlantic Records)
Jon Anderson, Chris Squire, Steve Howe, Bill Bruford, Tony Kaye
K10019 (I), 16 June 1971, P/S

Your Move (Edit)/Your Move (Edit)
(Atlantic Records)
Jon Anderson, Chris Squire, Steve Howe, Bill Bruford, Tony Kaye
45-2819 (US)

Your Move (Edit)/Clap (Atlantic Records)
Jon Anderson, Chris Squire, Steve Howe, Bill Bruford, Tony Kaye
45-2819 (US), 29 July 1971

Your Move (Edit)/Clap (Atlantic Records)
Jon Anderson, Chris Squire, Steve Howe, Bill Bruford, Tony Kaye
AT-2819 (C)
K10037 (F), P/S
N-28-115 (P), P/S
2019 059 (H), P/S
P-1095A (J), P/S
10.046 (G), P/S

Your Move/All Good People
(Atlantic Records)
Jon Anderson, Chris Squire, Steve Howe, Bill Bruford, Tony Kaye
RD-40.028 (AR)
ATL 83 (NZ)

I've Seen All Good People/Your Move/Starship Trooper: Life Seeker
(Atlantic Records)
Jon Anderson, Chris Squire, Steve Howe, Bill Bruford, Tony Kaye
2814-003 (UK), 1971

No Opportunity Necessary, No Experience Needed, A Venture/I've Seen All Good People: (A) Your Move, (B) I've Seen All Good People (Atlantic Records)
Jon Anderson, Chris Squire, Steve Howe, Bill Bruford, Tony Kaye
EPA 225 (AU) P/S
1972, 7" EP

Roundabout (Edit)/Roundabout (Edit)
(Atlantic Records)
Jon Anderson, Chris Squire, Steve Howe, Bill Bruford, Rick Wakeman
45-2854 (US)
Yellow/Gold Vinyl

Roundabout (Edit)/Long Distance Runaround (Atlantic Records)
Jon Anderson, Chris Squire, Steve Howe, Bill Bruford, Rick Wakeman
45-2854 (US), 1 April 1972
OS 13140 (US), 1976
OS 13140 (US), 1985
10133 (F)(I), P/S
ATL 10 133 (G), P/S
MH-31.926 (AR), P/S
ATL 92 (NZ)
2091 178 (GR)(H)
HS 826 (11.615) (S), 1972, P/S
P-1119A (J), P/S
2091 178 (B)
OS 13140 (US), 1976
OS 13140 (US), November 1985

Roundabout
Jon Anderson, Chris Squire, Steve Howe, Bill Bruford, Rick Wakeman
(TH) Includes tracks by three other artists.

Roundabout/I've Seen All Good People
Jon Anderson, Chris Squire, Steve Howe, Bill Bruford, Rick Wakeman
(AR) Promo b/s Led Zeppelin. Mhall no 186

Roundabout - Yes
Jon Anderson, Chris Squire, Steve Howe, Bill Bruford, Rick Wakeman
(J), P/S includes tracks by three other artists.

Something's Coming/Dear Father
(Atlantic Records)
Jon Anderson, Chris Squire, Peter Banks, Bill Bruford, Tony Kaye
2091 199 (H)
1972, P/S

Yours Is No Disgrace/Your Move, Sweet Dreams (Atlantic Records)
Jon Anderson, Chris Squire, Steve Howe, Bill Bruford, Rick Wakeman
2091 214 (H)
1972, P/S

America (Edit)/America (Edit)
(Atlantic Records)
Jon Anderson, Chris Squire, Steve Howe, Bill Bruford, Rick Wakeman
45-2899 (US)

America (Edit)/Total Mass Retain (Edit) (Atlantic Records)
Jon Anderson, Chris Squire, Steve Howe, Bill Bruford, Rick Wakeman
45-2899 (US), 17 July 1972
ATL 10.226 (G), P/S
10226 (H), P/S
P-1161A (J), P/S
HS 871 (S), P/S
M.27.231 (P), 1972
N-28-126 (P), P/S

Interview Record: 14 Minute Interview /Anderson, Offord, Squire, Wakeman, White. Flexidisc :Lyntone
Jon Anderson, Chris Squire, Rick Wakeman, Eddie Offord, Alan White
2535/2536 (US)(UK), 1972

Seasons Of Man - Yes + 3 other artists
Jon Anderson, Chris Squire, Steve Howe, Bill Bruford, Rick Wakeman
(MA), P/S

And You And I (Part I)/And You And I (Part II) (Atlantic Records)
Jon Anderson, Chris Squire, Steve Howe, Bill Bruford, Rick Wakeman
45-2920 (US)
45-2920 (US), 13 October 1972
10259 (G), P/S

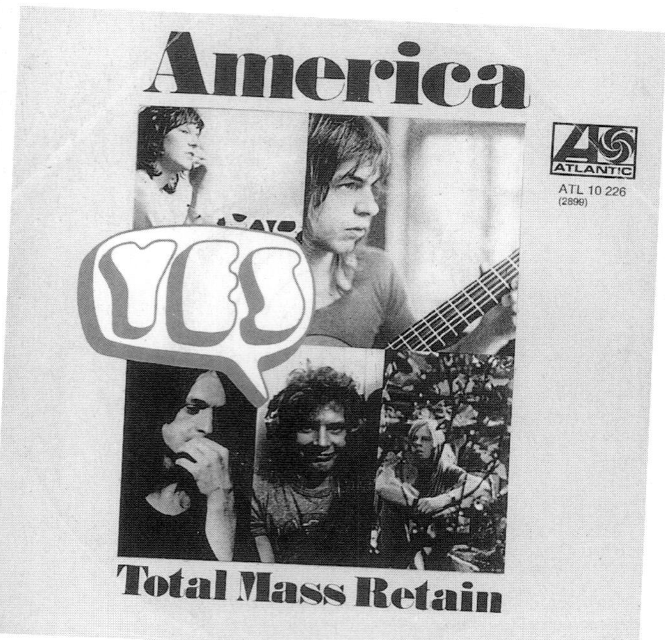

ATL 10 259 (G), P/S
10259 (F), P/S
ATL 10259 (H), P/S
P-1184A (J), P/S
N-28-130 (P), P/S
(AU)
(Y), P/S
(NZ)
ATCS 10.045 (B), 1973

Your Move (Part 1) (Live From Yessongs)/Your Move (Part 2) (Live From Yessongs) (Atlantic Records)
Jon Anderson, Chris Squire, Steve Howe, Bill Bruford, Rick Wakeman
(F), P/S

And You And I/Roundabout (Atlantic Records)
Jon Anderson, Chris Squire, Steve Howe, Bill Bruford, Rick Wakeman
K 10407 EP: Extended Play (UK), January 1974
10.407 (G)
K10407 (Y), P/S

And You And I/Siberian Khatru (Edit)
Jon Anderson, Chris Squire, Steve Howe, Bill Bruford, Rick Wakeman
6-AI/-B1 (UK)
Promo White Label Sampler

And You And I
Jon Anderson, Chris Squire, Steve Howe, Bill Bruford, Rick Wakeman
(G), One Sided Promo White Label Sampler

Soon/Soon (Atlantic Records)
Jon Anderson, Chris Squire, Steve Howe, Alan White, Patrick Moraz
45-3242 (US)

Soon/Sound Chaser (Atlantic Records)
Jon Anderson, Chris Squire, Steve Howe, Alan White, Patrick Moraz
45-3242
(US), 1 August 1975
45-1173 (S), P/S
NS 28-163 (P) 11,644 (P), P/S
181220698 (SW), P/S
3-17-101-021 (B)
CP 254 (S), P/S

Soon/Sound Chaser/Roundabout
(Atlantic Records)
Jon Anderson, Chris Squire, Steve Howe, Alan White, Patrick Moraz
3-17-201-011 (B)

America (Edit)/Your Move (Edit)
(Atlantic Records)
Jon Anderson, Chris Squire, Steve Howe, Bill Bruford, Rick Wakeman
OS 13141 (US)
1976

Going For The One
Jon Anderson, Chris Squire, Steve Howe, Alan White, Rick Wakeman
3 X 12" Promo Boxed Set Issue:

Going For The One/Turn Of The Century
(Atlantic Records)
Jon Anderson, Chris Squire, Steve Howe, Alan White, Rick Wakeman
BY 1/2 (UK)
12" (1 of 3)

Parallels/Wondrous Stories
(Atlantic Records)
Jon Anderson, Chris Squire, Steve Howe, Alan White, Rick Wakeman
BY 3/4 (UK)
12" (2 of 3)

Awaken/ No B-Side (Atlantic Records)
Jon Anderson, Chris Squire, Steve Howe, Alan White, Rick Wakeman
BY 5 (UK)
12" (3 of 3)
3 X 12": (Atlantic Records) DSK 50379 (UK) Box Set

Going For The One/Parallels
(Atlantic Records)
Jon Anderson, Chris Squire, Steve Howe, Alan White, Rick Wakeman
10.985 (G), July 1977, P/S
K 10985 (UK), P/S
K 10985 (UK), P/S

Wondrous Stories/Parallels
(Atlantic Records)
Jon Anderson, Chris Squire, Steve Howe, Alan White, Rick Wakeman
K 10999 (UK)(G)(H), September 1977, P/S 12"
45-1598 (S), P/S
PRO 77 (F), P/S
K 10999 (UK), 12" Issued in both black and blue vinyl

Wondrous Stories/Wondrous Stories
(Atlantic Records)
Jon Anderson, Chris Squire, Steve Howe, Alan White, Rick Wakeman
3416 (US)

Wondrous Stories/Awaken Part 1
(Atlantic Records)
Jon Anderson, Chris Squire, Steve Howe, Alan White, Rick Wakeman
3416 (US)
9 July 1977

Wondrous Stories (WEA)
Jon Anderson, Chris Squire, Steve Howe, Alan White, Rick Wakeman
CP 291 (S)
1977. Includes tracks by three other artists

Turn Of The Century/Wondrous Stories
(Atlantic Records)
Jon Anderson, Chris Squire, Steve Howe, Alan White, Rick Wakeman
ATL 10 036 (B)

Going For The One/Awaken Part 1
(Atlantic Records)
Jon Anderson, Chris Squire, Steve Howe, Alan White, Rick Wakeman
K 11047 (UK), November 1977, P/S
45-1659 (S), P/S
K 11047 (UK), November 1977, P/S 12"

Don't Kill The Whale(Edit)/Abeline
(Atlantic Records)
Jon Anderson, Chris Squire, Steve Howe, Alan

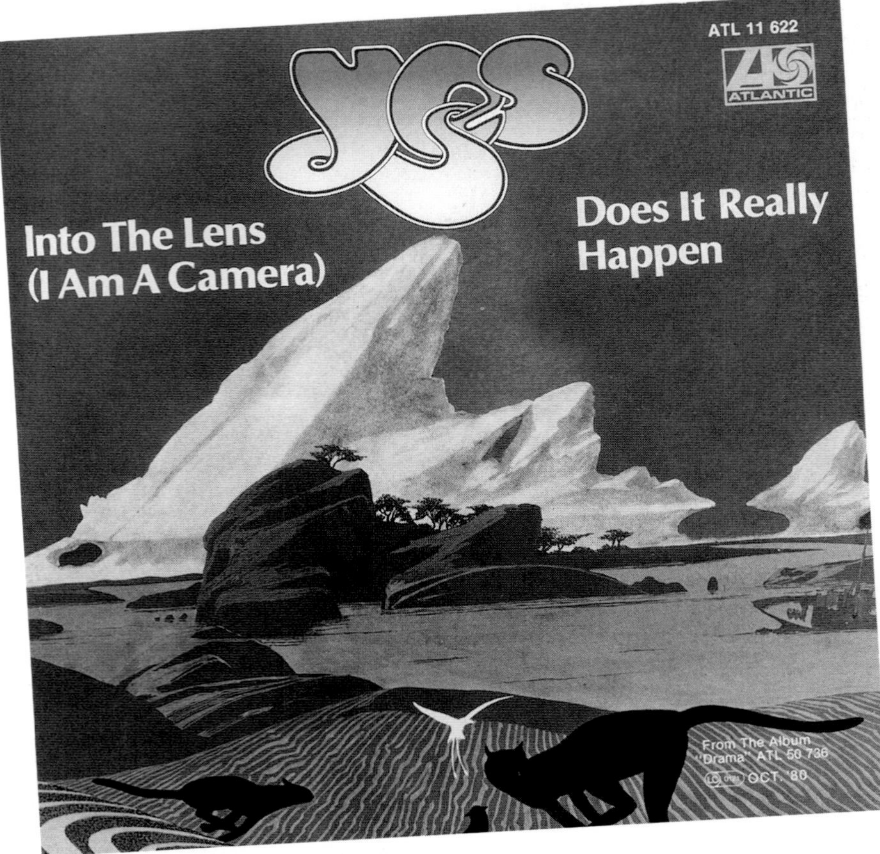

White, Rick Wakeman
K 11184 (UK)(G)(H)(S), August 1978, P/S
45-1786 (S), P/S
P-0334A (J), P/S
(AU)

Release Release/Release Release
(Atlantic Records)
Jon Anderson, Chris Squire, Steve Howe, Alan White, Rick Wakeman
3534 (US)

Release Release/Don't Kill The Whale (Edit) (Atlantic Records)
Jon Anderson, Chris Squire, Steve Howe, Alan White, Rick Wakeman
3534 (US), 11 July 1978
AT 3534 (C)

Into The Lens (I Am A Camera) (Edit)/Into The Lens (I Am A Camera) (Edit) (Atlantic Records)
Chris Squire, Steve Howe, Alan White, Trevor Horn, Geoff Downes
3767 (US)

Into The Lens (I Am A Camera) (Edit)/Does It Really Happen
(Atlantic Records)
Chris Squire, Steve Howe, Alan White, Trevor Horn, Geoff Downes
3767 (US), October 1980
1622 (UK)
September 1980
ATL 11 622 (G), P/S
11622 (BEL)
11.622 (F) (H), P/S
W11622 (I), P/S
202044 (I), P/S
45-2027 (S), P/S

Into The Lens/Test Tone (Atlantic Records)
Chris Squire, Steve Howe, Alan White, Trevor Horn, Geoff Downes
SAM 125 (UK), 12"

Does It Really Happen
Chris Squire, Steve Howe, Alan White, Trevor Horn, Geoff Downes
PROMO 123 (I)

Run Through The Light (Edit)/Run Through The Light (Edit)
(Atlantic Records)
Chris Squire, Steve Howe, Alan White, Trevor Horn, Geoff Downes
3801 (US)

Run Through The Light (Edit)/White Car (Atlantic Records)
Chris Squire, Steve Howe, Alan White, Trevor Horn, Geoff Downes
3801 (US)
January 1981

Roundabout Live/I've Seen All Good People (Atlantic Records)
Jon Anderson, Chris Squire, Steve Howe, Alan White, Rick Wakeman
PR 415 (US), free with Classic Yes LP
SAM 141 (UK), free with Classic Yes LP
ATL 11.694 (G), free with Classic Yes LP
CP 387 (S), free with Classic Yes LP
PZ-6A (J), free with Classic Yes LP

Interview (Atlantic Records)
Chris Squire, Steve Howe, Alan White, Trevor Horn, Geoff Downes
SAM 7 (UK)
1982

Owner Of A Lonely Heart/Owner Of A Lonely Heart (ATCO)
Jon Anderson, Chris Squire, Alan White, Trevor Rabin, Tony Kaye
7-99817 (US), P/S

Owner Of A Lonely Heart/Our Song (ATCO)
Jon Anderson, Chris Squire, Alan White, Trevor Rabin, Tony Kaye
7-99817 (US)
24 October 1983, P/S

Owner Of A Lonely Heart/Our Song (ATCO)
Jon Anderson, Chris Squire, Alan White, Trevor Rabin, Tony Kaye
B 9817 T (UK), P/S
79 9817-7 (G)
799817 (I), P/S
S78 9778-7 (S), P/S
P-1813A (J), P/S
SL 5238 (AR)
10.175 DJ (B), P/S
B9817-P/799817-7 (UK), Shaped P/D issued in both black & blue vinyl

Owner Of A Lonely Heart/Owner Of A Lonely Heart (ATCO)
Jon Anderson, Chris Squire, Alan White, Trevor Rabin, Tony Kaye
PR 529 (US)
P/S 12"

Owner Of A Lonely Heart/Owner Of A Lonely Heart (Red And Blue Re-Mix Dance Version) / Owner Of A Lonely Heart (LP Version) (ATCO)
Jon Anderson, Chris Squire, Alan White, Trevor Rabin, Tony Kaye
DMD 689 (US), P/S 12'

Owner Of A Lonely Heart (Red And Blue Re-Mix Dance Version)/Owner Of A Lonely Heart (ATCO)
Jon Anderson, Chris Squire, Alan White, Trevor Rabin, Tony Kaye
0-96976 (US)
November 1983
P/S 12"

Owner Of A Lonely Heart (Red And Blue Re-Mix Dance Version)/Owner Of A Lonely Heart, Our Song (LP Version) (ATCO)
Jon Anderson, Chris Squire, Alan White, Trevor Rabin, Tony Kaye
796 881-0 (US), November 1983, P/S
79 6976-0 (G), P/S
B 9817T (UK), P/S 12"
SL DA-3032 (AR)

Owner Of A Lonely Heart (WEA)
Jon Anderson, Chris Squire, Alan White, Trevor Rabin, Tony Kaye
787 (S)
One-sided

Owner Of A Lonely Heart (ATCO)
Jon Anderson, Chris Squire, Alan White, Trevor Rabin, Tony Kaye
(AR) Includes a track by another artist.

Changes/Leave It (Atlantic Records)
Jon Anderson, Chris Squire, Alan White, Trevor Rabin, Tony Kaye
(SA), 1983

Leave It/Cinema (ATCO)
Jon Anderson, Chris Squire, Alan White, Trevor Rabin, Tony Kaye
80255 (AR)
1983, P/S

Leave It/Leave It (Acapella Version) (ATCO)
Jon Anderson, Chris Squire, Alan White, Trevor Rabin, Tony Kaye
7-99787 (US), February 1984, P/S
B-9787 T (UK), P/S
79 9787-7 (G)(I)(S), P/S
ATCO P-1845A (J), P/S

Leave It (Hello, Goodbye Mix)/Leave It (Remix), Leave It (Acapella) (ATCO)
Jon Anderson, Chris Squire, Alan White, Trevor Rabin, Tony Kaye
ATCO B 9787T/796964-0 (UK)
14 March 1984 (UK), P/S
0-96964 (US), P/S
796 964-0 (G), P/S

Leave It (Single Version With Edit), City Of Love/Leave It (Hello/Goodbye Mix), Leave It (Acapella) (ATCO)
Jon Anderson, Chris Squire, Alan White, Trevor Rabin, Tony Kaye
PR 587 (US)
May 1984, 12"

12 Inches On Tape: Leave It (Remix)/Owner Of A Lonely Heart (Red & Blue Mix) / Leave It Hello/Goodbye Mix)/Owner Of A Lonely Heart (ATCO)
Jon Anderson, Chris Squire, Alan White, Trevor Rabin, Tony Kaye
B 9787 C (UK) (G), Cassette
90156-4 (US), 14 March 1984, Cassette

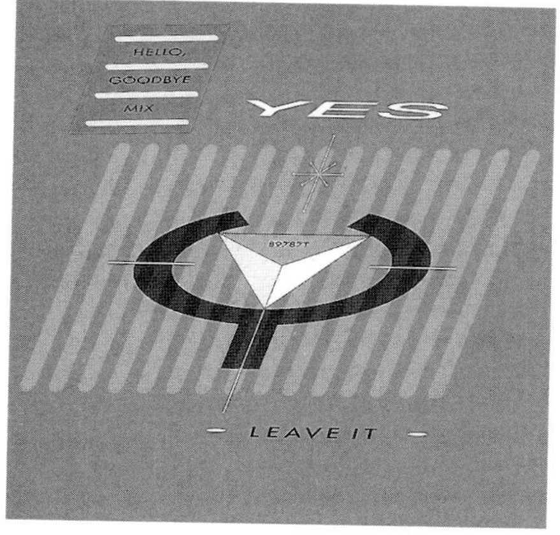

It Can Happen/It Can Happen (Live Version) (ATCO)
Jon Anderson, Chris Squire, Alan White, Trevor Rabin, Tony Kaye
7-99745 (US), 6 April 1984, P/S
B 9745 (UK), P/S
79 9745-7 (G), P/S
799745 (S), P/S
P-1878 (J), P/S
79 9745 (I)
PR 615 (US), 12"

Owner Of A Lonely Heart/Leave It (Atlantic Records)
Jon Anderson, Chris Squire, Alan White, Trevor Rabin, Tony Kaye
7-84999 (US)
November 1985

Hold On/Hold On From 9012-Live (ATCO)
Jon Anderson, Chris Squire, Alan White, Trevor Rabin, Tony Kaye
PR 796 (US)
1986, 12"

Love Will Find A Way (Edit)/Love Will Find A Way (Edit) (ATCO)
Jon Anderson, Chris Squire, Alan White, Trevor Rabin, Tony Kaye
7-99449 (US), P/S

Love Will Find A Way (Edit)/Holy Lamb (Song For Harmonic Convergence) (ATCO)
Jon Anderson, Chris Squire, Alan White, Trevor Rabin, Tony Kaye
A 9449, (UK)
7-99449 (US), 14 September 1987, P/S
799449-7 (G), P/S
799 449-7 (F)
P-2235 (J), P/S
(SA)

Love Will Find A Way (Extended Version), Love Will Find A Way (Rise And Fall Mix)/Holy Lamb (Song For Harmonic Convergence) (ATCO)
Jon Anderson, Chris Squire, Alan White, Trevor Rabin, Tony Kaye
A 9449T (UK), P/S 12"
7-99449 (US), 14 September 1987, P/S 12"
796 743-0/0-96743-A/B (G), 12"
(SA), 12"
(AU), P/S 12"

Love Will Find A Way (Edited Version)/Love Will Find A Way (LP Version) (ATCO)
Jon Anderson, Chris Squire, Alan White, Trevor Rabin, Tony Kaye
PR 2088 (US), 12"
CD: PR 2088-2 (US)
CD: PR 7088-2 (UK)

Love Will Find A Way (ATCO)
Jon Anderson, Chris Squire, Alan White, Trevor Rabin, Tony Kaye
PS-1053 (J), Flexi
878 (S), P/S

Love Will Find A Way (Edit)/Rhythm Of Love (ATCO)
Jon Anderson, Chris Squire, Alan White, Trevor Rabin, Tony Kaye
7-94964 (US), 1987

Rhythm Of Love/Rhythm Of Love (ATCO)
Jon Anderson, Chris Squire, Alan White, Trevor Rabin, Tony Kaye
7-99419 (US)

Rhythm Of Love/Rhythm Of Love (WEA)
Jon Anderson, Chris Squire, Alan White, Trevor Rabin, Tony Kaye
908 (S), P/S

Rhythm Of Love/City Of Love (ATCO)
Jon Anderson, Chris Squire, Alan White, Trevor Rabin, Tony Kaye
7-99419 (US) 7 December 1987 P/S

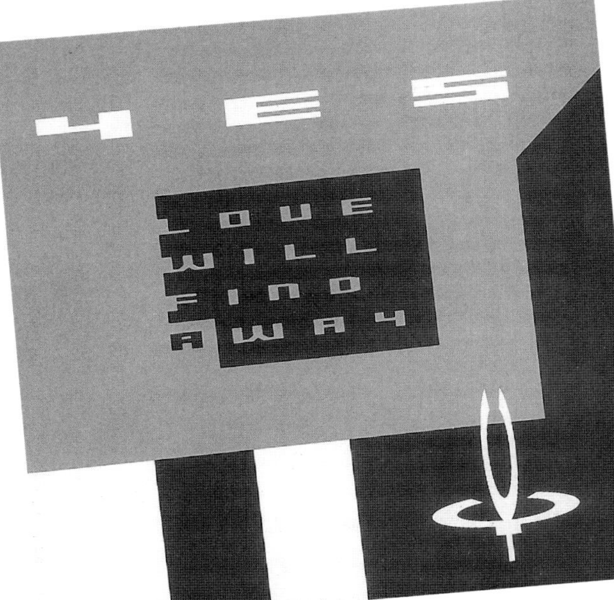

799419-7 (G) P/S
P-2359 (J) P/S
Live From 9012-LIVE Video

Rhythm Of Love (Dance To The Rhythm Mix), Rhythm Of Love (Move To The Rhythm Mix)/Rhythm Of Love (The Rhythm Of Dub), City Of Love (Live Edit) (ATCO)
Jon Anderson, Chris Squire, Alan White, Trevor Rabin, Tony Kaye
0-96722 (US) 21 December 1987 12"
796 722-0 (G) 7
7-96722-4 (US), January 1988, Cassette

Rhythm Of Love (Dance To The Rhythm Mix), Rhythm Of Love (Move To The Rhythm Mix)/Rhythm Of Love (The Rhythm Of Dub) (ATCO)
Jon Anderson, Chris Squire, Alan White, Trevor Rabin, Tony Kaye
DMD 1133 (US)
January 1988, P/S 12"

Rhythm Of Love, Rhythm Of Love (Move To The Rhythm Mix), Rhythm Of Love (Dance To The Rhythm Mix) (ATCO)
Jon Anderson, Chris Squire, Alan White, Trevor Rabin, Tony Kaye
(ATCO), PR 2089-2 (US)
January 1988, CD

Big Generator (Vocal/Remix Version)/Big Generator (LP Version) (ATCO)
Jon Anderson, Chris Squire, Alan White, Trevor Rabin, Tony Kaye
PR 2294 (US)
July 1988, P/S 12"

Lift Me Up (Radio Edit) Lift Me Up (A Cappella Opening), Lift Me Up (Album Version) (ARISTA)
Jon Anderson, Chris Squire, Alan White, Trevor Rabin, Tony Kaye, Rick Wakeman, Steve Howe
ASCD-2218 (US)
June 1991, CD

Lift Me Up (Edit)/Give And Take (ARISTA)
Jon Anderson, Chris Squire, Alan White, Trevor Rabin, Tony Kaye, Rick Wakeman, Steve Howe
AS-2218 (US)
June 1991

Lift Me Up, America (1972)/Lift Me Up, America (1972) (ARISTA)
Jon Anderson, Chris Squire, Alan White, Trevor Rabin, Tony Kaye, Rick Wakeman, Steve Howe
CAS-2218 (US)
June 1991, Cassette

Lift Me Up (Edit Version)/Take The Water To The Mountain (ARISTA)
Jon Anderson, Chris Squire, Alan White, Trevor Rabin, Tony Kaye, Rick Wakeman, Steve Howe
114 256 (G)
June 1991

Lift Me Up, Take The Water To The Mountain (ARISTA)
Jon Anderson, Chris Squire, Alan White, Trevor Rabin, Tony Kaye, Rick Wakeman, Steve Howe
BVDA-19 (J)
June 1991, CDS3

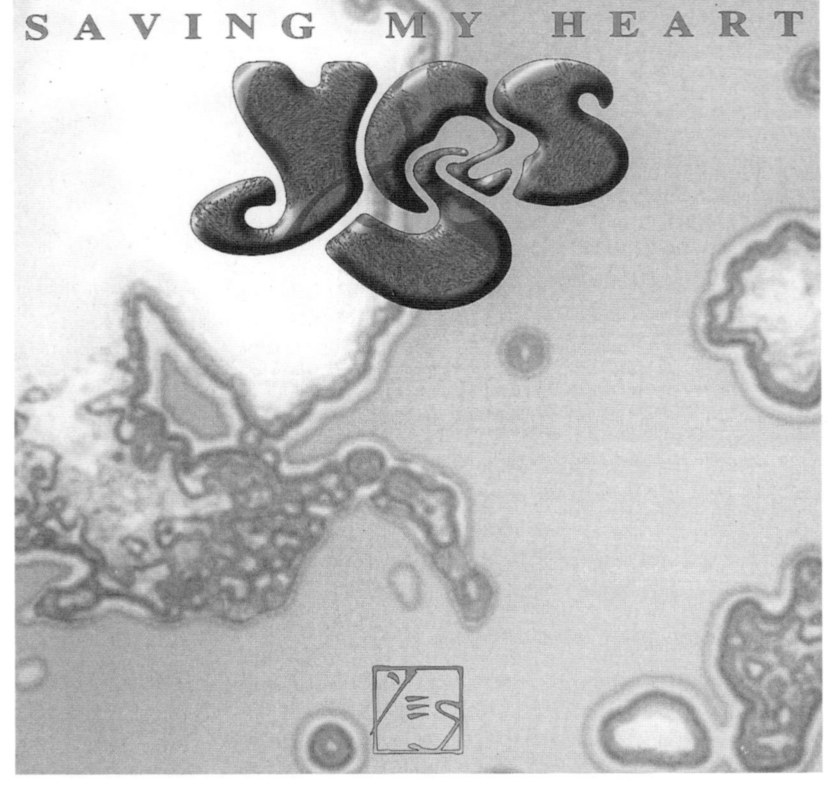

Lift Me Up (Top 40 Edit), Lift Me Up (Rock Radio Edit) (ARISTA)
Jon Anderson, Chris Squire, Alan White, Trevor Rabin, Tony Kaye, Rick Wakeman, Steve Howe
ASCD-2248 (US)
June 1991, CD

Lift Me Up (Album Version), Lift Me Up (Edit Version), Take The Water To The Mountain (ARISTA)
Jon Anderson, Chris Squire, Alan White, Trevor Rabin, Tony Kaye, Rick Wakeman, Steve Howe
614 256 (G)(UK), June 1991, 12" P/S
664 256-(G), June 1991, CD P/S

Lift Me Up (Edit Version) (ARISTA)
Jon Anderson, Chris Squire, Alan White, Trevor Rabin, Tony Kaye, Rick Wakeman, Steve Howe
PROMO132 (AU), CD

Make It Easy, Long Distance Runaround/Make It Easy, Long Distance Runaround (ARISTA)
Jon Anderson, Chris Squire, Alan White, Trevor Rabin, Tony Kaye, Rick Wakeman, Steve Howe
74-98738 (US)
31 July 1991, Cassette

Make It Easy, Make It Easy (ATCO)
Jon Anderson, Chris Squire, Alan White, Trevor Rabin, Tony Kaye, Rick Wakeman, Steve Howe
PRCD 4008-2 (US)
31 July 1991, CD

Saving My Heart (ARISTA)
Jon Anderson, Chris Squire, Alan White, Trevor Rabin, Tony Kaye, Rick Wakeman, Steve Howe
ASCD-2263 (US)
July 1991, CD

Saving My Heart (Album Version)/Lift Me Up (ARISTA)
Jon Anderson, Chris Squire, Alan White, Trevor Rabin, Tony Kaye, Rick Wakeman, Steve Howe
114 553 (UK)
July 1991, P/S

Saving My Heart (Album Version)/America (ARISTA)
Jon Anderson, Chris Squire, Alan White, Trevor Rabin, Tony Kaye, Rick Wakeman, Steve Howe
614 553 (UK)
July 1991, 12" P/S

Saving My Heart (Album Version), Lift Me Up, America (ARISTA)
Jon Anderson, Chris Squire, Alan White, Trevor Rabin, Tony Kaye, Rick Wakeman, Steve Howe
664 553 (UK)
July 1991, CD P/S

I Would Have Waited Forever (Edit Version), I Would Have Waited Forever (Album Version) (ARISTA)
Jon Anderson, Chris Squire, Alan White, Trevor Rabin, Tony Kaye, Rick Wakeman, Steve Howe
ASCD-2344 (US), CD P/S

Owner Of A Lonely Heart/Make It Easy (ATCO)
Jon Anderson, Chris Squire, Alan White, Trevor Rabin, Tony Kaye, Rick Wakeman, Steve Howe
(UK), September 1991, P/S

Owner Of A Lonely Heart (Original Version)/Owner Of A Lonely Heart (Wondrous Mix - Edit) (ATCO)
Jon Anderson, Chris Squire, Alan White, Trevor Rabin, Tony Kaye
B 8713 (UK) September 1991
7567-98713-7 (G)

Owner Of A Lonely Heart (Original Version), Owner Of A Lonely Heart (The Move Yourself Mix) Owner Of A Lonely Heart (2 Close To The Edge Mix), Owner Of A Lonely Heart (Not Fragile Mix) (ATCO)
Jon Anderson, Chris Squire, Alan White, Trevor Rabin, Tony Kaye
7567-96293-0 (B)
8713-T (UK)(G) September 1991, 12"

Owner Of A Lonely Heart (Original Version), Owner Of A Lonely Heart (Wondrous Mix), Owner Of A Lonely Heart (2 Close To The Edge Mix), Owner Of A Lonely Heart (Not Fragile Mix) (ATCO)
Jon Anderson, Chris Squire, Alan White, Trevor Rabin, Tony Kaye
7567-96292-2 (B)
8713 (UK)(G) September 1991, CD

Owner Of A Lonely Heart (Move Yourself Mix), Owner Of A Lonely Heart (Album Mix), Owner Of A Lonely Heart (Wondrous Mix), Owner Of A Lonely Heart (2 Close To The Edge Mix), Owner Of A Lonely Heart (Not Fragile Mix) (ATCO)
Jon Anderson, Chris Squire, Alan White, Trevor Rabin, Tony Kaye
SAM 928 (UK)
September 1991, CD

Owner Of A Lonely Heart, Owner Of A Lonely Heart (2 Close To The Edge Mix) (ATCO)
Jon Anderson, Chris Squire, Alan White, Trevor Rabin, Tony Kaye
7567-98407-2 (G)
September 1991, CD

The Calling, The Calling, The Calling (Victory)
Jon Anderson, Chris Squire, Alan White, Trevor Rabin, Tony Kaye
(US), CD

The Calling (Radio Edit), The Calling (Single Edit), The Calling (Album Edit), The Calling (Original Version)
Jon Anderson, Chris Squire, Alan White, Trevor Rabin, Tony Kaye
(Victory)
VICT CDP 1178 (US)
1 March 1994, CD

The Calling (LP Version), Real Love (LP Version) (Victory)
Jon Anderson, Chris Squire, Alan White, Trevor Rabin, Tony Kaye
CDS3: VICTORY VIDP-57 (J) CDS: VICTORY (J)

The Calling (Victory)
Jon Anderson, Chris Squire, Alan White, Trevor Rabin, Tony Kaye
VICTORY (UK)

The Calling (Radio Edit), I Am Waiting, The Calling (Album Edit) (Victory)
Jon Anderson, Chris Squire, Alan White, Trevor Rabin, Tony Kaye
YESAMP 1 (UK), CD

The Calling (Single Edit), The Calling (Radio Edit) (Victory)
Jon Anderson, Chris Squire, Alan White, Trevor Rabin, Tony Kaye
YESAMP 2 (UK), CD

The Calling, Silent Spring, The Calling (Original Version) (Victory)
Jon Anderson, Chris Squire, Alan White, Trevor Rabin, Tony Kaye
857 589-2 (H), 1994, CD

The Calling (Special Version), I Am Waiting, State Of Play (Victory)
Jon Anderson, Chris Squire, Alan White, Trevor Rabin, Tony Kaye
(J), 1994, CD

The Calling (Special Version), I Am Waiting, State Of Play, Endless Dream (Victory)
Jon Anderson, Chris Squire, Alan White, Trevor Rabin, Tony Kaye
(J), 1994, CD

The Calling - Yes/The Day I Tried - Soundgarden (Polygram)
Jon Anderson, Chris Squire, Alan White, Trevor Rabin, Tony Kaye
280 177-2 (B), 1994, P/S

State Of Play (Album Version) (Victory)
Jon Anderson, Chris Squire, Alan White, Trevor Rabin, Tony Kaye
CDP 1244 (US), 1994, CD

Walls (Victory)
Jon Anderson, Chris Squire, Alan White, Trevor Rabin, Tony Kaye
CDP 1263 (US)
July 1994, CD

Walls (Single Version), Walls (Album Version) (Victory)
Jon Anderson, Chris Squire, Alan White, Trevor Rabin, Tony Kaye
CDP 1282 (US)
July 1994, CD

Walls (Radio Version), Walls (Long Version) (Victory)
Jon Anderson, Chris Squire, Alan White, Trevor Rabin, Tony Kaye
857 637-2 (G)
July 1994, CD

That, That Is/That, That Is/That, That Is (CMC International)
Jon Anderson, Chris Squire, Alan White, Rick Wakeman, Steve Howe
CMC DJ 87207-2 (US)
December 1996, CD

Be The One/That, That Is (CMC International)
Jon Anderson, Chris Squire, Alan White, Rick Wakeman, Steve Howe
ESSP 2054 (UK)
December 1996, CD

America (Single Edit), America (Album Version) (CMC International)
Jon Anderson, Chris Squire, Alan White, Rick Wakeman, Steve Howe
CMC DJ 87203-2 (US)
1997, CD

New State Of Mind (Radio Edit)/New State Of Mind (Dual Solo Edit)/New State Of Mind (Album Version Short Ending)/New State Of Mind (Album Version) (Beyond Music/Tommy Boy)
Jon Anderson, Chris Squire, Alan White, Steve Howe, Igor Khoroshev, Billy Sherwood
BYCD226 (US)
May 1998, CD

For Everyone (17 March 1970 - Sunday Show)
Jon Anderson, Chris Squire, Steve Howe, Bill Bruford, Tony Kaye
1998, Bonus 7" With LP Version Of Something's Coming (I)

Lightning Strikes (Edit) The Messenger/Homeworld (Eagle Records)
Jon Anderson, Chris Squire, Alan White, Steve Howe, Igor Khoroshev, Billy Sherwood
EAGS108 (UK)
1999, CD

Lightening Strikes (Edit 'She Ay...Do Wa Bap') Lightening Strikes (Album Version) (Beyond)
Jon Anderson, Chris Squire, Alan White, Steve Howe, Igor Khoroshev, Billy Sherwood
BYDJ-78060-2 (US)
1999, CD

Homeworld (Edit 4:37) Homeworld (Album Version) (Beyond)
Jon Anderson, Chris Squire, Alan White, Steve Howe, Igor Khoroshev, Billy Sherwood
BYDJ-78105—2 (US)

If Only You Knew (3:39) If Only You Knew (Edit 3:49) If Only You Knew (Album Version) (5:42) (Eagle Records)
Jon Anderson, Chris Squire, Alan White, Steve Howe, Igor Khoroshev, Billy Sherwood
(US) 2000, CD

ANDERSON BRUFORD WAKEMAN HOWE

Brother Of Mine (Album Version), Brother Of Mine (Radio Edit) (ARISTA)
Jon Anderson, Bill Bruford, Rick Wakeman, Steve Howe
ASCD 9842 (US)
May 1989, CD P/S

Brother Of Mine (Edit)/Brother Of Mine (Edit) (ARISTA)
Jon Anderson, Bill Bruford, Rick Wakeman, Steve Howe
AS1-9852 (US), 7" P/S

Brother Of Mine (Single Edit), Brother Of Mine (Rock Edit), Brother Of Mine (Album Version) (ARISTA)
Jon Anderson, Bill Bruford, Rick Wakeman, Steve Howe
ASCD 9852 (US), CD

Brother Of Mine (Edit)/Vultures (ARISTA)
Jon Anderson, Bill Bruford, Rick Wakeman, Steve Howe
AS1-9852/7822-19852-7 (US)(C)
June 1989, P/S

Brother Of Mine (Edit)/Vultures (In The City) (ARISTA)
Jon Anderson, Bill Bruford, Rick Wakeman, Steve Howe
260 018 (UK), 10" P/S

Brother Of Mine (Radio Edit), Brother Of Mine, Vultures (In The City) (ARISTA)
Jon Anderson, Bill Bruford, Rick Wakeman, Steve Howe
ABWH CD1 (UK), CD P/S

Intro Wakeman, Brother Of Mine, Birthright, Order Of The Universe (ARISTA)
Jon Anderson, Bill Bruford, Rick Wakeman, Steve Howe
162 373 (G) (H) (A), CDS3 P/S

Brother Of Mine, Themes: Sound; Attention; Soul Warrior, Vultures (In The City) (ARISTA)
Jon Anderson, Bill Bruford, Rick Wakeman, Steve Howe
612 379 (UK) (G)
June 1989, 12" P/S
662 379 (UK) (G) CD
662 379 (US) CD P/S
162 379 (A) PIC CD/ CDS3

Brother Of Mine (Edit)/Themes (ARISTA)
Jon Anderson, Bill Bruford, Rick Wakeman, Steve Howe
112 379 (G)(UK) P/S P/D
112 444 (UK) P/S

Brother Of Mine, Themes (ARISTA)
Jon Anderson, Bill Bruford, Rick Wakeman, Steve Howe
A10D-129 (J), CDS3

Brother Of Mine (Radio Version)/Brother Of Mine (Single Version) (ARISTA)
Jon Anderson, Bill Bruford, Rick Wakeman, Steve Howe
112 445 (G)

Brother Of Mine (Radio Edit)/Brother Of Mine (ARISTA)
Jon Anderson, Bill Bruford, Rick Wakeman, Steve Howe
ABWH 1(UK), P/S

Order Of The Universe (Short Edit)/Fist Of Fire (ARISTA)
Jon Anderson, Bill Bruford, Rick Wakeman, Steve Howe
112 618 (UK)(G) 1990 P/S
1A 112 618 (S)
662 2693 (UK) 10/89 CDS
A10D-138 (J) CDS3

Order Of The Universe (Long Edit)/Fist Of Fire, Order Of The Universe (Short Edit) (ARISTA)
Jon Anderson, Bill Bruford, Rick Wakeman, Steve Howe,
612 618 (UK)(G) 12" P/S
662 618 (G) CDS

Order Of The Universe (ARISTA)
Jon Anderson, Bill Bruford, Rick Wakeman, Steve Howe
(SA) 7" PRYSPZ

Order Of The Universe (Short Edit), Order Of The Universe (Long Edit), Order Of The Universe (Album Version) (ARISTA)
Jon Anderson, Bill Bruford, Rick Wakeman, Steve Howe
ASCD 9869 (US), CD P/S

I'm Alive, Let's Pretend/Birthright (Live Version) (ARISTA)
Jon Anderson, Bill Bruford, Rick Wakeman, Steve Howe
612 770 (UK)(G) 12" P/S
662 770 (G) CD P/S

Quartet (I'm Alive) (ARISTA)
Jon Anderson, Bill Bruford, Rick Wakeman, Steve Howe
ASCD-9898 (US)
December 1989, CD P/S

Quartet (I'm Alive)/Quartet (I'm Alive) (ARISTA)
Jon Anderson, Bill Bruford, Rick Wakeman, Steve Howe
AS1-9898 (US)
December 1989, P/S

Quartet (I'm Alive)/Let's Pretend (ARISTA)
Jon Anderson, Bill Bruford, Rick Wakeman, Steve Howe
A10D-150 (J) CDS3
AS1-9898/7822-19898-71 (US) December 1989 P/S
ARISTA 112 770 (G)

Quartet (I'm Alive), Let's Pretend/Same (ARISTA)
Jon Anderson, Bill Bruford, Rick Wakeman, Steve Howe
CAS 9898 (US)
1989, Cassette P/S

Live Medley; Time And A Word, Owner Of A Lonely Heart, Roundabout, Starship Trooper (Herald Music)
Jon Anderson, Bill Bruford, Rick Wakeman, Steve Howe
HER PRO 1 (US), CD P/S

Live Medley; Time And A Word, Owner Of A Lonely Heart (Radio Medley), Owner Of A Lonely Heart (Radio Edit), Roundabout, Starship Trooper (Herald Music)
Jon Anderson, Bill Bruford, Rick Wakeman, Steve Howe
HER PRO 2 (US)(UK), CD P/S

Fragile Sampler: Live Medley; Time And A Word, Owner Of A Lonely Heart - Anderson Bruford Wakeman Howe/Roundabout (Live) - Anderson Bruford Wakeman Howe (Fragile Records)
Jon Anderson, Bill Bruford, Rick Wakeman, Steve Howe
CD SAMPLER 001 (UK)
1994, CD

Caroline 1994 Sampler: Roundabout - Anderson Bruford Wakeman Howe (Caroline)
Jon Anderson, Bill Bruford, Rick Wakeman, Steve Howe (US), 1994, CD
(US), 1994, CD

LIMITED EDITION ALBUM VARIATIONS

For the serious collector there have been minor variations in the presentation of some of Yes' albums, which make them more valuable.

Yes

Generally in a gatefold sleeve, but it's speculated that a single sleeve variation was produced, either in Australia, South America or in some Eastern European countries, featuring a photo of the band in the London Architectural Salvage Garden on the cover sleeve. *Yes* was produced in Germany as a joint album with *Time And A Word* which had a totally different cover and came in a gatefold design called *Two Originals Of Yes*. The original release also had a red/plum centre and came with a lyric sheet.

Time And A Word

There are a number of variations to the original, with four different covers known in all, one a US cover (also copied in other countries) which is a fairly well known version due to Steve Howe's inclusion on the cover when he didn't actually play on the album. Another is a German gatefold double album, containing both *Time and a Word* and *The Yes Album* called *Double Dynamite: Two Originals of Yes*. The third is a US version with the cover image of the band in the London Architectural Salvage Garden. The original releases had a red/plum label and came with lyric sheets. There was also a Russian release which featured a slightly different cover and is most probably a bootleg.

The Yes Album

As above, the German gatefold double album of both *Time and a Word* and *The Yes Album* called *Double Dynamite*.
The original release has a red/plum label and is packaged in a gatefold sleeve.

Fragile

There is an american release on a label called Melody Recordings, Inc. Cat. no is SS-6006, which has a thick cover and states on the back – 'This product is manufactured under the highest standards for excellent sound quality and stereophonic reproduction. No expense has been spared in mastering or any stage of production to obtain a startling definition of brilliance and clarity. Our records are moulded on the most modern equipment utilising only the finest quality of pure vinyl to eliminate noise and retain full-bodied tone.' It then carries a guarantee of 10 days from the date of purchase and another statement saying that royalties have been or will be paid – 'pursuant to Title 12, US code as amended by S.646'. Clearly it's an unofficial pressing – a pirate copy – and possibly one of a series on this label.

A Spanish version can be found with an orange and lilac centre label, the cover is a single pocket type not a gatefold, cat No HATS421-88. The cover features a collection of royal jewels photographed on a dark blue velvet sheet. Another version exists from China/Taiwan, different cover, where the painting sits to the bottom centre, it also contains the wording Stereo and a coding number in the border. Original vinyl versions have a red/plum label.

There were a limited amount of re-mastered special edition gold CDs (Atlantic 82542-2) released of *Fragile*, which feature a mini-box (displaying altered cover art), 24 page booklet with extensive notes and additional photos, and a 24 carat gold CD housed in a jewel case. This now commands a high price.

In 1982, Atlantic released an LP in Brazil, with a red, blue and white stars and stripes cover, it is standard LP size but was not actually called *Fragile* since it came as a set of ten with other albums from bands like ELP and Genesis.

Close To The Edge

Although Roger Dean had initially designed the classic Yes logo in eye-catching, sparkling silver, when it went to press it came out grey instead, and it is not confirmed if any silver editions made it into the market place. Another variation of this album is Russian produced with the title in Russian characters in a Dean style. China/Taiwan produced another variation featuring the Yes logo emboldened in yellow. An audiophile vinyl pressing was made by Atlantic P-10116A, with Japanese Yes lyrics.

Yessongs

The US editions of the album were changed from the original UK ones due to the costs involved in flying the necessary copies 3,000 miles across the Atlantic. Roger's UK version had the patented book style folding method which was changed to what is the most common, the four-fold long concertina style. Both issues included the Yes live pictures booklet. The earlier editions would have had the logo printed on the inner sleeves, these disappeared at the reprint stage.

Tales From Topographic Oceans

Two variations to look out for, one a DJ copy which is vinyl banded for airplay, which may have had a stickered cover, the other is a reel to reel 7" tape in a pictured box, (Atlantic 908).

Relayer

The only known change is to the centre of the record label which went from a full circle image to a half circle. The photograph of the band on the inside was taken in Chris Squire's garden at New Pippers, Gorse Hill, West London.

Yesterdays

Some versions were stickered with details that the track America was the full version and not an edited one. For the first pressings, the inner sleeve was cardboard but it gradually became thinner as time went on.

Going For The One

Only two odd changes to be found with this one. Some versions appear to have been made of a different kind of vinyl, when held up to the light they appear to be tinted red.
The other oddball collectible is *The World of Yes* LP. They've used the same *Going For The One* title/logo, but in red and inside, there's a lyric sheet with other releases illustrated on the reverse. The track listing is Roundabout, Wondrous Stories, Mood For a Day, Turn of the Century, Going For The One, Awaken. It purports to be from Japan. Label is Shilla Records - Capuz SCL-1009. It would seem to be an unofficial compilation. This must be in very limited numbers.

Classic Yes

The limited promotional version was made with a cover that had a photograph of the band live on stage in the round 1978-9. The official final release employed a Roger Dean cover, some had stickers relating to the free 7" single inside.

Drama

The only variation of this album is the Japanese audiophile vinyl version which comes with an obi strip.

Big Generator

The only change to this album seems to be that a number of releases sported different colour backgrounds on the cover.

The Ladder

This album is slightly different from any previous Yes album in that it has been released with extra-enhanced material on it. Here is an overview of their contents:
CD Eagle EAGCD088 The European version. This has the demo of the Homeworld PC game, includes a Homeworld screen saver and an interview with the band.
CD Eagle EAGLT088 The European version, limited to 50,000 copies, has a stickered cover, in a cardboard slipcase. It includes a foldout poster of the arty track chart.
CD Beyond 63985-78046-2 The US version, which contains the symbols featured at the live shows and a Homeworld video clip. Other subtle differences are with the sleeve design and it comes with a separate mini foldout poster of the sleeve.
CD – Victor VIZP-6 Japanese version which is a double CD set. As always, it includes an insert of Japanese lyrics and the obi strip of paper. The added disc is 3" in size and features live tracks recorded in Los Angeles, US: I've Seen All Good People and And You And I.
2 x LP (Albums) The UK market was lucky enough to have this limited edition of the album produced in a high quality 12" vinyl as in the old days. Each copy is numbered by a sticker and it's pleasing to see once again Roger's artwork in large scale. The track listing is in the centre of the gatefold.
CD Eagle EAG 254-2 The last version was this special tour edition which has a copy of the standard album plus an extra disc, containing live material from their Los Angeles show:, All Good People, The Messenger and Homeworld.

Promotional Vinyl Albums are the first pressings of an album and are not meant for sale to the general public. They are used for promotional purposes and are sent to radio stations and record company staff. Promos would have been made for each Yes album and were packaged in plain sleeves. Usually they were almost identical to the eventual release. However, what makes them interesting are the variations that can occur occasionally, such as changes to covers, track listings, song title names, and some may be banded for radio play, and one side may be mono while the other is stereo.

SINGLE VARIATIONS

There are many 7" singles in picture sleeves to collect. The bulk of them run from the late 1970s through to the eighties and are relatively easy to find at record fairs or via the internet. They become difficult to find if you are seeking the pre 1977 years. Yes released picture sleeve singles right from the start with their first single Sweetness, released in France. Other European countries were more likely to release picture covers, whereas the UK market often lagged behind in promotional techniques.

About 34 picture covers were released between 1969–76, and the least common are the Japanese items. The rarest Yes single of all, which doesn't have a picture cover, is the 1969 Atlantic 584 298 Looking Around/Everydays promotional copy. From research it appears that the single was intended for official release and was announced to the press, and at the last minute Atlantic had a change of heart and withdrew it from production. They were going to be thrown out but were rescued by an employee who claims that there was no more than a handful made.

The 12" singles began in 1977 with the release of the hit single Wondrous Stories. It was released in standard black vinyl with a blue vinyl limited edition. The covers were black featuring the title Going For The One. A handful of Going For The One/Parallels was pressed but never released and this is a very rare item. The whole of the *Going For The One* album came out as a promotional item pressed as three 12" singles (extremely rare) and was released in box set form in limited numbers. A Japanese version of Wondrous Stories was released in a gatefold cover. The rest of the 12" records are standard and can be obtained easily.

The rarest records connected with Yes are the Hans Christian Anderson singles; the single Autobiography of A Mississippi Hobo is particularly difficult to find and commands a high price. Pre-Yes singles by Syn and the Warriors are also very desirable.

The ten most collectible singles are as follows, all the prices for the items listed below range from £40 – £150 / $60 – $230.

1. Looking Around / Everydays (UK, Atlantic promo 584 298)
2. Going For The One (UK, Atlantic DSK 50379 3 x 12" set)
3. Time And A Word / The Prophet (UK, Atlantic 584323)
4. And You And I (part I & II) (Japan Atlantic P1184A, PS)
5. I've Seen All Good People (UK, Atlantic promo 2814 003)
6. America (Japan Atlantic P1161A, PS)
7. Interview Disc (UK, flexi or vinyl LYN Lyntone 2536 plus songbook)
8. No Opportunity Necessary (Australian EP, PS)
9. Going For The One /Parallels (UK, Atlantic promo K10985/T)
10. And You And I / Siberian Khatru (promo white label sampler 6-ai/-b1 (UK)

CD VARIATIONS

Most of the CDs are current and are not that rare yet, although some are becoming harder to find and will become rarer as time progresses. The set of limited edition mini albums, launched at the end of the 90s, exclusively in Japan but later imported, are now realising high prices. They include *Fragile, Yessongs, Close To The Edge, Relayer* and *Tales From Topographic Oceans*. In the US, Atlantic released a gold edition of the album *Fragile* that was aimed at enthusiasts of superior quality hi-fi. There are a number of CDs that were only released in one country which have become collectible outside that country. Examples include, *Open Your Eyes* Surround Sound, *Beyond and Before* – US only, *The Best Of Yes 1970-87* – Japan only, *Astral Traveller* – UK only and *Millennium Collection* – the German only release, a repackaging of *Somethings Coming*.

Promotional CDs are now a significant collector's area. Many items have been produced since 1983. They are packaged in different cases with varying presentations. From full-colour covers and discs to complete blanks. Promos cover both albums and singles and can include different lengths of tracks, artwork, wording and track order. Made for radio stations, none are meant for resale although they have been traded for years.

LASER DISCS

Popular in the 1980s, this medium is now out of favour since the introduction of DVD. Still interesting items that were quite highly priced from the start and should be available through a specialist dealer or the internet.

Greatest Video Hits (Warner Brothers)
Wondrous Stories, Don't Kill The Whale, Madrigal, Tempus Fugit, Into The Lens, Hold On,

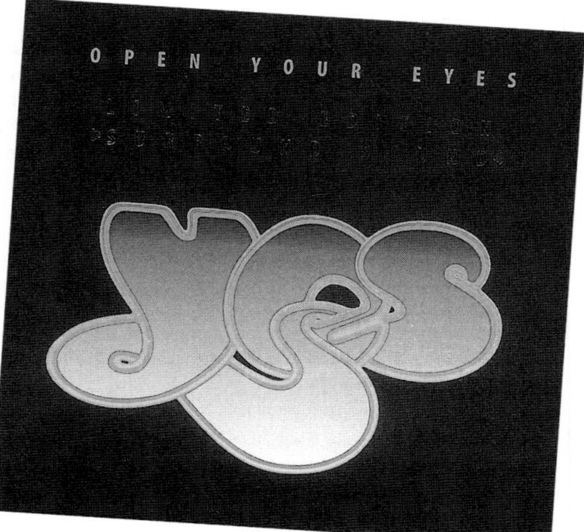

Leave It, It Can Happen, Owner Of A Lonely Heart, Rhythm Of Love, Love Will Find A Way, I've Seen All Good People.
Jon Anderson, Chris Squire, Alan White, Steve Howe, Rick Wakeman, Trevor Rabin, Trevor Horn, Tony Kaye, Geoff Downes.
1991

Live 1975 Queen's Park Rangers
Introduction Firebird Suite, Sound Chaser, Close To The Edge, To Be Over, The Gates Of Delirium, I've Seen All Good People, Long Distance Runaround, Clap, And You And I, Ritual, Roundabout, Sweet Dreams, Yours Is No Disgrace.
Jon Anderson, Chris Squire, Alan White, Steve Howe, Patrick Moraz
VALZ – 2109 / VALZ – 2109/10
Live 1975 vol. 1 Queen's Park Rangers
(Tracks as above)
2 disc set, QPR, VALJ – 3406
Live 1975 vol. 2 Queen's Park Rangers
(Tracks as above)
2 disc set, QPR, VALJ – 3407

Live In Philadelphia 1979 (Warner Brothers)
Siberian Khatru, Circus Of Heaven, Starship Trooper, Alan White's solo, Leaves Of Green, I've Seen All Good People, Roundabout.
Jon Anderson, Chris Squire, Alan White, Steve Howe, Rick Wakeman
VALJ – 3432
JAPAN

9012 Live (Warner Brothers)
Introduction, Cinema, Leave It, Hold On, I've Seen All Good People, Changes, Owner Of A Lonely Heart, It Can Happen, City Of Love, Starship Trooper
Jon Anderson, Chris Squire, Alan White, Tony Kaye, Trevor Rabin
VPLR – 70464
JAPAN

ABWH, An Evening Of Yes Music (Arista)
Benjamin Britten's Young Person's Guide To The Orchestra, Time And A Word, Teakbois, Owner Of A Lonely Heart, Clap, Mood For A Day, Gone But Not Forgotten, Catherine Parr, Merlin The Magician, Long Distance Runaround, Birthright, And You And I, Close To The Edge, Themes 1. Sound 2. Second Attention 3. Soul Warrior, Brother Of Mine, Heart Of The Sunrise, Order Of The Universe, Roundabout.
Jon Anderson, Bill Bruford, Rick Wakeman, Steve Howe
2 disc set, VALJ-3395, VALJ-3396
1989 US Tour
JAPAN

ABWH, An Evening Of Yes Music (Arista)
(Tracks as above)
Jon Anderson, Bill Bruford, Rick Wakeman, Steve Howe
2 disc set VALZ-2111, VALZ-2112.
JAPAN

Yesyears (Warner Brothers)
A retrospective of Yes' history from 1969 to 1991, it includes interviews, behind the scenes footage, studio and live performances. Many Yes classic tracks are aired intertwined with interviews and film.
Jon Anderson, Chris Squire, Alan White, Steve Howe, Rick Wakeman, Patrick Moraz, Bill Bruford, Trevor Rabin, Tony Kaye, Peter Banks, Geoff Downes, Trevor Horn
1991
2 disc set AMLY – 8091

Yessongs (Wienerworld)
Excerpts from Close To The Edge, I've Seen All Good People, Clap, And You And I, Close To The Edge, Excerpts From The Six Wives Of Henry V111, Roundabout, Yours Is No Disgrace, Excerpts From Starship Trooper.
Jon Anderson, Chris Squire, Alan White, Steve Howe, Rick Wakeman
BVLP – 40
JAPAN
Filmed concert in 1972, Rainbow Theatre London.

Yesshows 91 (Warner Brothers)
Firebird Suite, Yours Is No Disgrace, Rhythm Of Love, Heart Of The Sunrise, Clap, Owner Of A Lonely Heart, Changes, I've Seen All Good People, Trevor Rabin solo, Saving My Heart, Chris Squire solo (Amazing Grace), Six Wives, Awaken, Roundabout.
Jon Anderson, Chris Squire, Alan White, Steve Howe, Rick Wakeman, Bill Bruford, Trevor Rabin, Tony Kaye
VPIR –70690
JAPAN

DVDS

Yes launched DVD in 1999, and have a good listing so far. The list can only increase, as DVD becomes the next form of standard music equipment. The majority originate from Japan.

House Of Yes: Live From House Of Blues
(Beyond Music / HOB)
Yours Is No Disgrace, Time And A Word (Snippet), Homeworld, Perpetual Change, Lightning Strikes, The Messenger, Ritual-Nous Sommes Du Soleil (Snippet), And You And I, It Will Be A Good Day (The River) Face To Face, Awaken, Your Move/I've Seen All Good People, Cinema, Owner Of A Lonely Heart, Roundabout.
Jon Anderson, Chris Squire, Alan White, Steve Howe, Igor Khoroshev
USA, September 2000
Region 1 and *Region 2* (Beyond Records) is out in Japan, Nippon Columbia.
The Ladder album and tour live in Los Angeles, the DVD features interactive menus, instant song access, a video press kit of making the album, an exclusive single of Homeworld and a virtual tour book with photographs.
(CMP 1006, region 2)

Yessongs (Warner Brothers)
Excerpts from *Close To The Edge*, I've Seen All Good People, Clap, And You And I, Close To The Edge, Excerpts From *The Six Wives Of Henry V111*, Roundabout, Yours Is No Disgrace, Excerpts From Starship Trooper.
Jon Anderson, Chris Squire, Alan White, Steve Howe, Rick Wakeman
The classic 1972 Rainbow Theatre London.

Keys To Ascension (Castle Music Pictures)
Siberian Khatru, Close To The Edge, I've Seen All Good People, Time And A Word, And You And I, The Revealing Science Of God, Going For The One, Turn Of The Century, America, Onward, Awaken, Roundabout, Starship Trooper.
Jon Anderson, Chris Squire, Alan White, Steve Howe, Rick Wakeman
Castle Music Pictures Europe, Video Arts Japan October 2000, Image US January 2000, Panorama in Hong Kong 2000 and in continental Europe through MAWA.
The great reunion shows of the classic Yes line-up in March 1996 in the small town of San Luis Obispo, California, USA. Includes animated menus and on screen biographies. Recorded in Surround Sound.

Live 1975 Queen's Park Rangers
Introduction Firebird Suite, Sound Chaser, Close To The Edge, To Be Over, The Gates Of Delirium, I've Seen All Good People, Long Distance Runaround, Clap, And You And I, Ritual, Roundabout, Sweet Dreams, Yours Is No Disgrace.
Jon Anderson, Chris Squire, Alan White, Steve Howe, Patrick Moraz
Double pack Volume 1 COBY-90038, Volume 2 COBY 90039. European region under negotiations.
Relayer album tour at the UK football stadium.

Live In Philadelphia 1979 (Warner Brothers)
Siberian Khatru, Circus Of Heaven, Starship Trooper, Alan White's solo, Leaves Of Green, I've Seen All Good People, Roundabout.
Jon Anderson, Chris Squire, Alan White, Steve Howe, Rick Wakeman
Yes playing In The Round, the classic Yes line-up's last big tour together playing the Philadelphia Spectrum 21 June 1979.
COBY-90040 (regions 1 & 2 available)
1997, Europe, US.

Union Tour Live 1991 (VAP Super Rock Series)
Firebird Suite, Yours Is No Disgrace, Rhythm Of Love, Heart Of The Sunrise, Clap, Owner Of A Lonely Heart, Changes, I've Seen All Good People, Trevor Rabin solo, Saving My Heart, Chris Squire solo (Amazing Grace), Six Wives, Awaken, Roundabout.
Jon Anderson, Chris Squire, Alan White, Steve Howe, Rick Wakeman, Trevor Rabin, Tony Kaye, Bill Bruford.
VPBR-11034
The 1991 eight man line-up playing the final show of the US tour at the Shoreline Amphitheatre 8 August 1991.
2000
JAPAN

Musikladen Live (Pioneer)
No Opportunity Necessary, All Good People, Yours Is No Disgrace.
Jon Anderson, Chris Squire, Bill Bruford, Peter Banks, Tony Kaye
Pioneer PA-99-623-D

2000, US
1969 –70 Yes at the Beat Club in Germany, TV programme excerpts. Only three songs but a wonderful piece of Yes history.

ABWH, An Evening Of Yes Music Plus
(Arista)
Benjamin Britten's Young Person's Guide To The Orchestra, Time And A Word, Teakbois, Owner Of A Lonely Heart, Clap, Mood For A Day, Gone But Not Forgotten, Catherine Parr, Merlin The Magician, Long Distance Runaround, Birthright, And You And I, Close To The Edge, Themes 1. Sound 2. Second Attention 3. Soul Warrior, Brother Of Mine, Heart Of The Sunrise, Order Of The Universe, Roundabout.
Jon Anderson, Steve Howe, Rick Wakeman, Bill Bruford
Volumes 1 Coby-90052, Volume 2 Coby-90053.

THE INTERNET MP3

The internet is beginning to reinvent the music business, affecting all areas of the once sacred world of the record company and retailer. With the introduction of the MP3, the 'portable music store in your hand', the music business is getting ready for the biggest shake-up in its history. The US has embraced the new technology to such an extent that its effect has hit the traditional record stores.

Many of the big name retailers have had to close their doors or completely reinvent themselves to keep up with the trend of potential customers acquiring music from the internet. Yes have embraced these technological innovations and have not been slow to act on them, delivering snippets of forthcoming albums and singles and presenting live shows on the Web.

The internet offers Yes fans many benefits, information accessible on all matters Yes related, from their back catalogue to their latest release. What the MP3 does, however, is open up the huge bootleg market, which had previously been going downhill. Within the next five years, it is expected that fifty percent of all music sales will be through MP3. For sheer convenience and choice, the record companies and the bands concerned have to become partners with the MP3 industry or risk losing a great deal.

Yes, seem committed to the use of the internet. It is probably only a matter of time before the whole of the Yes back catalogue will be made available to download, making it ideal for fans to create their ultimate Yes album. We will be able to choose our favourite tracks from an official Yes Website and pay a small amount for it.

OFFICIAL VIDEO RELEASES

Videos are one of the key collecting areas for Yes fans. Since there are so many, this list compiles the official video releases, many of which are now deleted. More than live CDS and records, the videos go a step further towards capturing the atmosphere of a Yesshow and, despite their varied quality, each one documents a stage in the development of Yes on stage. There have been about 200 bootleg videos made over the years showing Yes and the individual solo artists, this is the official list of releases.

Yes, *Yessongs,* recorded in London 1972, first and only released Yes film, soundtrack, 1980, Media Home Entertainment Inc, US.
Yes, *Yessongs*, recorded in London 1972, classic Yesshows, second release of the film soundtrack in a different cover, 1991, Wienerworld, Europe. Also released in a different cover in the US on Betamax and in Brazil in 2000.
Yes, *Queens Park Rangers,* 1975, 1 tape, Relayer tour live in the UK, recorded at the QPR football ground London, JAPAN.
Yes, *QPR,* 1975, 2 tapes, (same show as above) JAPAN. Also available in Asia in VCD format (short lived format available before DVDs) as a set of three.
Yes, *QPR*, 1975, vol. 1, (same show as above) JAPAN.
Yes, *QPR*, 1975, vol. 2, (same show as above) JAPAN.
Yes, *Live in Philadelphia 1979,* released twice, the last tour featuring the classic five man line-up In The Round. 1996. UK, US.
Yes, *9012 Live*, 1985, a wonderfully creative video depicting the 1980s Yes' finest hour, UK, US.
Yes, *Yesyears,* The Yes retrospective looking at 1968-1991, with interviews and rare footage, Two covers available, 1991, UK, US.
Yes, *Greatest Video Hits,* 1991, A compilation of standard video releases, UK, US.
Yes, *Keys to Ascension,* (1 tape released twice) San Luis Obispo shows 1996 in California, the last true Yesshows with Rick Wakeman, UK.
Yes, *Keys to Ascension,* (2 tape set) SLO show as above, 1996, UK.
ABWH, *In The Big Dream,* 1989, making of the album, music and interviews, UK.
ABWH, *An Evening of Yes Music Plus,* 1990, Fragile records, Limited edition box set with CD, ABWH live in concert, UK.
ABWH, *An Evening of Yes Music Plus,* 1989, ABWH live in concert, (Single video) UK.
Jon Anderson, *The Best of South America 1993*, the limited edition of 1,000 copies Video and CD package released privately by Jon. A filmed concert from the fourteen date tour March – May 1993. Comprising a one hour video entitled Indigenous Journey and a forty three minute CD, UK, US.
Jon Anderson, *The Promise Ring Video*, six songs, twenty six minutes. Appearances by Jane Luttenberger Anderson and the Frog'n Peach Orchestra & Dancers. 2000, US.
Steve Howe, *The Turbulent Plan,* making of the album with some personal insights into Steve's philosophies, Starnight Music Masters, UK.
Steve Howe, *Night of the Guitars*, various guitarists play a one-off show in London, UK.
Bill Bruford, *Bruford and the Beat*, 1982, Drum tutorial, UK.
Patrick Moraz, *Patrick Moraz in Princeton*, 1996, Princetown Records, a live show, US.
Asia, *Asia in Asia,* with Greg Lake, Vestron C71009, 1983, US, UK.
Asia, *Live in Moscow,* Geoff Downes, Excellent EXC005, 1991, Europe.
Asia, *Live,* Geoff Downes, MCEG Virgin VVD959, 1991, UK.
Rick Wakeman, *Live,* 1991, Griffin videos, Classic Rick with a backing band, UK.
Rick Wakeman, *The Word and New Gospels,* 1988, Beckmann BMO 003, UK.
Rick Wakeman, *Simply Acoustic,* 1994, Rick live, Hope HRV 001, UK.
Rick Wakeman, *Daley Thompson Body Shop Vol 3*, 1984, Pickwick V9087, Australia, UK.
Rick Wakeman, *The Piano Tour,* 1997, Hope HRV 003, Rick live, UK.
Rick Wakeman, *Listomania,* 1975, Warner Brothers (Film soundtrack)
Rick Wakeman, *Phantom Power,* 1991 (Film soundtrack) UK.

Rick Wakeman, *G'ole*, 1982, Polygram 63236-3 (Film soundtrack) UK.
Rick Wakeman, *Hero*, 1986, Polygram 632378-3 (Film soundtrack) UK.
Rick Wakeman, *Heritage Suite*, 1993, NBC TV Superchannel, (Film soundtrack) US.
Rick Wakeman, *Creepshow*, 1987 (Soundtrack) Vestron 57083, UK.
Rick Wakeman, *Crimes of Passion*, 1986 (Film soundtrack) UK.
Rick Wakeman, *She*, 1983, Royal Films (Film soundtrack) UK.
Rick Wakeman, *White Rock*, 1977, Olympic Games (Soundtrack) UK .
Rick Wakeman, *The Burning*, 1981, Vipco VIP015 (Film soundtrack) UK.
Rick Wakeman, *The Very Best of the Chronicles, Journey* live in 1975 with the Melbourne Philharmonic orchestra, 1981, UK.
Rick Wakeman, *The Making of Circus Surreal*, 1995, TV film, UK.
Rick Wakeman, *Circus Surreal*, 1995, a live show, UK.
Rick Wakeman, *Classical Connection*, 1991, Beckmann O002, UK.
Rick Wakeman, *New Gospels*, 1995, Hope HRV002, UK.
Trevor Rabin, *Starlicks Presents*, 1990, Guitar tutorial, US.
Chris Squire, *Starlicks Presents*, 1990, Bass tutorial, US.
Alan White, *Starlicks Presents*, 1990, Drum tutorial, US.
Various Artists, *Rock Aid Armenia*, 1988, featuring one Yes track + Chris Squire & Geoff Downes on Deep Purple's classic *Smoke On The Water*, UK.
Yesshows 91, Yes Union tour live 1991, the eight man line-up, JAPAN.
Yesfest 1994 (Fan meeting unofficial) US.
Yesfest 1985 (Fan meeting unofficial) US.
Yesfest 1987 (Fan meeting unofficial) US.
Yesfest 1998 (Fan meeting unofficial) US.
Yesfest 1991 (Fan meeting unofficial) US.
GTR, *The Making of GTR*, Steve Howe and Steve Hacket make the GTR album, music and interviews. UK.
Yes: House of Yes: Live From the House of Blues, The Ladder tour live, 2000, US.

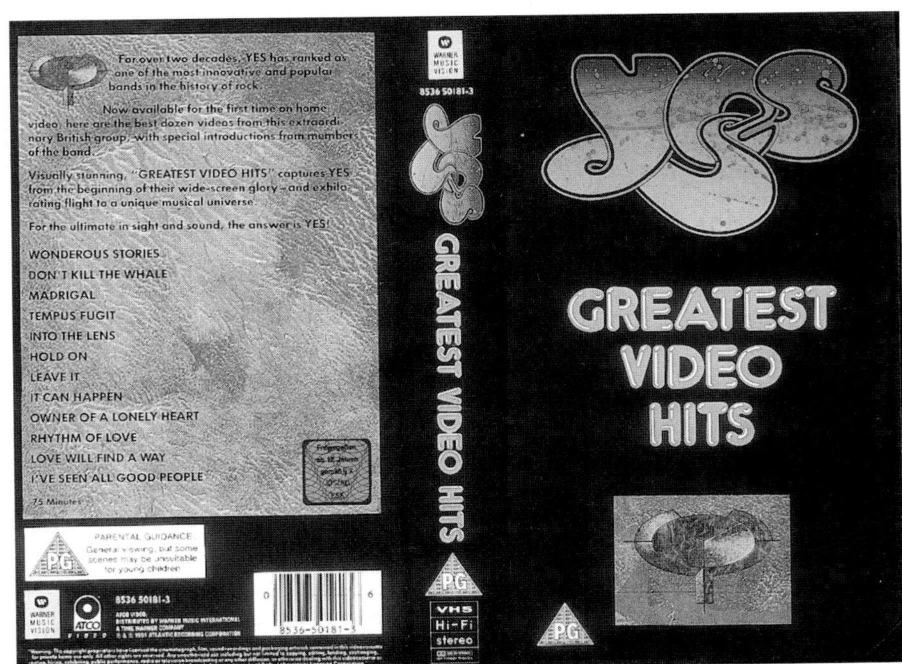

CD-ROMS

Yes Active *(Talk* album*)*: The Calling (CD Version), I Am Waiting (CD Version), I Am waiting (Live), Real Love (CD Version), State Of Play (CD Version), State Of Play (Demo Version), Walls (CD Version), Walls (Live Version), Walls (Instrumental Version), Where Will You Be (CD Version), Where Will You Be (Instrumental), Endless Dream (CD Version), Endless Dream (Demo Version) Compton's New Media 45445 06562 (Deleted)
(US only) November 1994
Containing all the CD music accessed from a visual menu, interviews with the band members, some video clips of the band playing live and video clips of various different-sounding instruments played on one track. Includes interactive drums, guitar and bass guitar for you to play plus much more. Well worth searching out.

Steve Howe Interactive
All-Access Back Stage Pass, Masterclass

Performance, Links & Resources, Acoustic Guitar Composition, Clap, Spanish Guitar, Mood For A Day, All Good People, Slide Show.
Beyond Sound Ltd, 1999
(Available from the official Steve Howe website)

Homeworld
The successful science fiction PC CD-Rom. Yes supplied the soundtrack music, 2000 (Available)

RADIO SHOWS

Radio shows come in both vinyl and CD formats and the odd ones can be found on reel-to-reel tape, but are generally very expensive items to collect. Mainly sourced from the US, the radio shows are extremely well produced documents that often include lengthy interviews and insights into the band. They often come in packages of three or four CDs, which is why they are so costly. However, for the keen and wealthy Yes fan, they are well worth searching out. The list below is the most complete listing to date compiled.

Yes Documentary, 1972, 1 LP, 60mins
Nightbird & Company, 1974, 1 LP, 60mins
WNEW, Biography, June 1977, 1 LP, 55mins
Rock Around the World, 1977, 1 LP, 60mins
Nightbird & Company, 25 September 1977, 1 LP, 60mins
King Biscuit Flower Hour, 25 June 1978, 1 LP, 60mins
Backstage at Madison Square Garden, 9 September 1978, Tape, 20mins
King Biscuit Flower Hour, 16 November 1978, 1 LP, 60mins
Rock Around The World, 3 December 1978, 1 LP, 60mins
Innerview, Series 4, Program 1, 1979, 1 LP, 60mins
Profiles in Rock, 9 March 1980, 1 LP, 60mins
The Source Special, 16 August 1980, 2 LP, 90mins
Retrorock, 19 October 1981, 1 LP, 60mins
Innerview, Series 15, Program 1, 1981, 1 LP, 60mins
Retrorock + ELP, 13 September 1982, 1 LP, 60mins
A Night on the Road, 1982, 1 LP, 60mins
The Source, The Yes Special, 29 January 1984, 3 LPs, 180mins
Captured Live, 19 November 1984, 2 LPs, 120mins
Captured Live, RKO Radio, 1984, 4 LPs, 240mins
Westwood One Off The Record, 7 May 1984, 2 LPs, 90mins
Captured Live, no 'Q' sheet, 17 November 1984, 2 LP, 20mins
Captured Live, 19 November 1984, 2 LPs, 20mins
Legends of Rock, music and interviews, live no 'Q' sheet, 1984, 2 LP, 20mins
King Biscuit Flower Hour, 1985, 1 LP, 60mins
Pioneers in Music, 3 February 1986, 2 LPs, 120mins
Off the Record, music and interviews, 21 December 1987, 2 LPs, 20mins
Legends of Rock parts 1 & 2, March 1987, 4 LPs, 240mins
Legends of Rock, 9 June 1987, 2 LPs, 120mins
Off the Record, 21 December 1987, 2 LPs, 120mins
Up Close, 18 December 1987, 2 LPs, 120mins
Legends of Rock, 31 January 1988, 4 LPs, 240mins
Ticket to Ride: Yes Part 1 & 2, 19 February 1988, 4 LPs, 240mins
Up Close, 25 February 1988, 2 CDs, 70mins
King Biscuit Flower Hour, 6 March 1988, 1 CD, 60mins
Off the Record, 28 March 1988, 2 LPs, 120mins
Westwood One Superstars, 7-8 May 1988, 3 LPs, 180mins
The Yes Album in the Studio, 18 July 1988, 4 CDs, 240mins
Westwood One Superstars, 8 May 1988, 3 LPs, 180mins
The Yes Album in the Studio, 1988, 4 CDs, 240mins
Masters of Rock, 31 December 1989, 1 CD, 60mins
King Biscuit Flower Hour, (chronicles) Pt 1 & 2, 25 June 1989, 2CDs, 120mins
Legends Of Rock, 8 May 1989, 2 LPs, 120mins
Legends of Rock, 21 May 1989, 4 LPs, 240mins
Westwood One In Concert, 29 May 1989, 3 CDs, 180mins
Chronicles Part 1 & 2 King Biscuit Flower Hour, 12 - 19 June 1989, 2 CDs, 120mins
Westwood One Superstars Concert Series, 14 June 1989, 3 LPs, 180mins
90125 In The Studio, 18 September 1989, 1 CD, 48mins
Masters of Rock, 18 December 1989, 1 CD, 60mins
Fragile In The Studio, 1989, 1 CD, 60mins
The Yes Album In The Studio, 10 September 1990, 4 CDs, 240mins
Up Close, music and interviews, 1991, 4 CDs, 240mins
Rockline, 15 April 1991, and one 3 May 1991, 3 CDs, 140mins
King Biscuit Flower Hour, 19 May 1991, 1 CD, 60mins
Close To The Edge, In The Studio, 26 August 1991, 1 CD, 60mins
Global Satellite Close To The Edge, 1991, 3 CDs, 180mins
Close To The Edge, Edge - Labour Day Special, 1 September 1991, 1 CD, 35mins
Westwood One Superstars Concert Series, 3 September 1991, 3 LPs, 180 mins
Westwood One, Off The Record, 9 September 1991, 1 CD, 50mins
Westwood One, Off The Record, 15 September 1991, 1 CD, 50mins
Up Close, May 1991, 4 CDs, 240mins
King Biscuit Flower Hour, (chronicles) Pt 1 & 2, 18 August 1991, 2 CDs, 120min
Westwood One Superstars Concert Series, 9 January 1991, 3 LPs, 180mins
Tower Records, LA, 1991 tour, March 1997, 2 CDs, 120mins
Westwood One Superstars Concert Series, 1 October 1991, 3 LPs, 180mins
Westwood One Superstars Concert Series, 9 July 1992, 2 CDs, 120mins
Close to the Edge, In The Studio, 5 October 1992, 1 CD, 60mins
Superstars, 2 February 1992, 3 LPs, 180mins
King Biscuit Flower Hour, 15 March 1993, 2 CD, 120mins
King Biscuit Flower Hour, 28 March 1993, 1 CD, 60mins
90125, In The Studio, 1 November 1993, 1 CD, 60mins
Up Close, music and interviews, 19 April 1994, 3 CDs, 180mins
Up Close, music and interviews, 4 June 1994, 3 CDs, 180mins
Special music and interviews, (*Yesstory*), 30 May 1994, 3 CDs, 180mins
The Yes Album, In The Studio, 24 January 1994, 1 CD, 60mins
King Biscuit Flower Hour, 28 March 1994, 2 CDs, 120mins
Up Close, March 1994 & April 1994, 2 CDs, 127mins
Talk Listening Party. Album Network, 8 April 1994, 1 LP, 60mins
Westwood One Superstars Concert Series, Yesstory, 27 May 1994, 3 CDs, 180mins
Westwood One Superstars Concert Series, Live in Philly, 2 CDs, 75mins
Musical Biography with Alison Steele, 1 LP, 60mins
Close To The Edge, In The Studio, music and interviews, 1 CD, 60mins
Close to the Edge, In The Studio, 24 July 1995, 1 CD, 60mins
Yes, Superstar Concert, October 1997, 2 CDs, 120mins
Up Close, music and interviews, 1998, 2 CDs, 120mins
YES ALB NET, 18 January 1998, 2 CDs, 20mins
Superstars live, 11 May 1998, 2 CDs, 120mins
In The Studio, 1999, 1 CD, 60mins
Up Close, music and interviews, 2000, 3 CDs, 180mins

King Biscuit Flower Hour, 4 February 2000, 1 CD, 60mins

SHEET MUSIC BOOKS

Yes music songbooks are probably for serious fans who are musicians; the majority of the books are not visually interesting, they just contain music and lyrics. However, those that are visually good are worth getting hold of, even if you are not musically inclined.

For those who want a little bit more of a Yes collectible, then the most interesting sheet music books are the pre 'Best Of' era, the main albums of the 1970s. These songbooks feature the original album covers in colour and contain photographs. The best one is the 1972 *Close To The Edge* songbook published by AMSCO, Code no: 020656, which came with a free interview single stuck on the front. It contains all the music from the Yes LP *Close To The Edge* and in addition, there are 24 pages of photographs – 4 in full-colour – none of which had been published previously. What makes this book so exceptional, however, is the maxi single given free with every copy. This was recorded especially to accompany the book and contains a fascinating 14-minute interview with the group by Karl Dallas. The photographs are by Roger Dean and Doming-Hamilton, the artwork by Roger Dean. The other music book to consider is *Yessongs* which features the same set of photographs. Here is the complete list.

Time And A Word
Amsco Music Publishing, UK, 1970, book No 1163.

The Yes Album
Warner Brothers, UK, 1971, book No 043.

Fragile / The Yes Album
Warner Brothers, 1972, UK.

Fragile
Warner Brothers, 1972, UK, book No T358.

Close To The Edge
Amsco Music Publishing, 1972, UK, book No 020656 plus free 7" interview single and pages of black and white photographs.

Close To The Edge
Amsco Music Publishing, 1972, UK, book No 1163.

Yessongs
Wise Publications, 1973, UK, book No 1163A, includes pages of colour photographs.

Relayer
Warner Brothers, UK, 1974, book No 20753.

Yesterdays
Amsco Music Publishing, UK, 1975, book No 1670F.

Yes / Solo
Warner Brothers, Germany, 1976-7, book.

Yes + Rush
Warner Brothers, US, book No 21861, seventeen songs.

Yes Bass Superstar Series
Warner Brothers, US, book No 21324, eight songs.

Yes The Best Of Yes
Warner Brothers, book No 20104

Yes The Best Of
Warner Brothers, book No 21061

Yes Complete Volume Two
Warner Brothers, 1977, US, UK, book No VF0486.

Yes The Complete Deluxe Edition
Warner Brothers, 1978, US, UK, book No 20752, 58 songs.

Yes The Best Of
Warner Brothers, 1980, UK, book No KY15686.

Yes Drum Superstar Series
Warner Brothers, book No 21315, eight songs.

Yes Guitar Superstar Series
Warner Brothers, US, book No 2155

Yes Big Generator
Warner Brothers, 1988, US, book No 21185

Yes New Best Of
Warner Brothers, US, book No 22333, eight songs.

Yes Selections From Yesyears
Warner Brothers, 1991, UK, book No 22276, Guitar, ten songs.

Yes Union
Warner Brothers, 1991, UK, book No 21850, fourteen songs.

Yes Talk
Warner Brothers, 1994, US, book No 2570a, seven songs.

SINGLE 7" SHEET MUSIC

These were produced by the record companies Although Yes' main success has been through

albums, they did have a number of hits in the singles charts. The short length of the list isn't surprising, but does represent their major hit singles. All of them are A4 in size; the contents generally only show the music and lyrics. All are deleted items now.

Roundabout (Green cover with band photograph) Warner Bothers, 1972, US.
Going For The One (Picture of Yes seated by lake on cover) Warner Bothers, 1977, UK.
Wondrous Stories (Picture of Yes seated by lake on cover) Warner Bothers, 1977, UK.
Don't Kill The Whale (Black and yellow cover with picture of band in forest) Warner Bothers, 1978, UK.
Owner of a Lonely Heart (Cover same as album cover) Warner Bothers, 1984, US.
Leave It (Picture cover of band) Warner Brothers, 1984, US.

PRESS PACKS

These were produced by the record companies and were never intended for the public. They are a great insight into how the company used to market the band at the time. Press packs are not a new phenomenon and they have been available in one form or another since the first album and even before that with the likes of Syn etc. They vary in form from single sheets of paper to glossy folders containing photos, biography, stickers, CD and discography. They are all rare. Here is a short list of known press packs; inevitably there are some missing.

Yes: *Close To The Edge*, biography, photos and stickers.
Yes: *Relayer*, 6 pages 6 photos.
Yes: *Yesterdays*, biography and photos.
Yes: *Going For The One*, 8 pages 6 photos.
Yes: *Tormato*, 12 pages 6 photos.
Yes: *Drama*, 4 pages and 1 photo.
Yes: *90125*
Yes: *Union*, 6 pages 1 photo.
Yes: *Yessongs* video, 2 pages.
Yes: *Big Generator*, 6 pages 1 photo.
Yes: *Symphonic Music Of Yes*, 7 pages 5 photos.
Yes: *Talk*, 10 pages 2 photos.
Yes: *Talk*, 5 pages 1 photo.
Yes: *Talk*, 4 pages.
Yes: *Open Your Eyes*, biography and photos.
Yes: *The Ladder*, two page tour information and dates, a four page biography, one page press release, one page fast facts and a photo.

BOOKS

This has not been a very prolific area over the past thirty years, leaving fans desperate for information. However, the few books that have been published were well received.

The first book on Yes was released in Japan by Ongaku Tomo in 1979 in limited numbers. Not officially approved, it was published in black and white and contained the history of the band plus some memorabilia and photographs.

Out of Print Books

Yes:Yes by Shilow Kuloda, 1979. Ongaku Tomo. Available in Japan only. PB. ISBN: 4-276-23330-5. Black and white, photographs, discography and tour dates.
Yes: Authorised Biography by Dan Hedges, 1981, Sidgewick & Jackson, Hardback ISBN: 0-283-98751-0. PB, 0-283-98761-8. Roger Dean cover, biography, photographs and discography.
Yes:Yes But What Does It Mean by Thomas J. Mosbo, 1994, US, (private publication) Limited numbers, Paperback. Catalogue number: 93-93672. Looks deeply into Yes' songs and lyrics.
Rick Wakeman:Myths & Legends of the Yes Wizard by Jordi Sierra, I Fabfra, 1977, Unilibra, South America.
Rick Wakeman:The Caped Crusader by Dan Wooding, 1978, Hale, Hardback/Paperback. ISBN: 0709164874. Biography and photographs of the keyboard wizard.
The Steve Howe Guitar Book by Steve Howe, 1994, Balafon, Hardback ISBN: 1871547644. Featuring Steve's vast guitar collection in full-colour.
Yes: The System of Rock by T. Vasvary-Toth, 1995, published in Hungary by PCD Multimedia Kft. ISBN: 9630441764. Biography, reviews of albums, discography and videography.

Books in Print

Say Yes by Rick Wakeman, 1995, Hodder & Stoughton, UK, Autobiography,

Paperback. ISBN: 0340621516

Yes Stories: Yes in Their Own Words by Tim Morse, 1996, St. Martins Press US, Paperback ISBN: 0312144539. Snippets of interviews throughout the years. Japanese edition published by Shinko Music in January 1999.

The Music Of Yes:Structure and Vision in Progressive Rock by Bill Martin, 1996, Open Court, US, Paberback ISBN: 0812693337. In-depth look at Yes' music.

Fountains of Gold by Jon Anderson & Wendy Vig, 1997, Heaven Bone Press US, Paperback. ISBN: 096236939X. Poetry by Wendy and art by Jon.

Yes (Group, solos and related works), 1997, Tokyo FM books. Japanese discography with photos.

When In Doubt, Roll! By Bill Bruford, 1988, Hal Leonard Publishing, US, Autobiography, ISBN: 0793535298.

Close To The Edge: The Story Of Yes by Chris Welch, 1999, Omnibus, UK, ISBN Paperback: 0-7119-8041-1, Hardback ISBN: 0711969302. The full Yes history updated including some black and white photographs.

Yes:Uma Raca Musica de Quiriteto by Decio Fsngarnisa, 1999, Paperback. A Brazilian biography. Limited numbers printed, a bootleg or private printing.

Yes Lyrics. US, 2000, limited number printed. Paperback. A private publication/bootleg. Lists all the lyrics from all Yes' studio albums, from *Yes* to *The Ladder*. Also contains pictures of each album cover.

Yes by Jaime Lopez, 2000, private publication, limited amount printed. Paperback. Spain.

FANZINES 1979 – 2000

Before the internet and in particular during the years when the music press turned against Yes, information was very difficult to obtain, but it has now never been easier. Fanzines are some of the best items to acquire, fascinating to look back on and always interesting to read. The difficulty is in finding any of them: most were produced in their hundreds rather than their thousands and a lot of the early ones were probably just thrown away after being read.

Yes fan club magazines started in late 1979 in the UK. With the lack of press coverage at the time and the band in limbo, fans came together to supply the information needed by producing, initially, A4 sized black-and-white fan newsletters. Unbelievably, Yes didn't have an official fan club or organisation until the 1990s when *Yes Magazine* and later the Yesworld internet site, both based in the US (where the Yes fan base is largest) became available. UK fans had to be content with the output from hard-working and dedicated individuals who spent many hours photocopying music paper articles and handwriting material for inclusion. These improved steadily over the years and became glossy, full-colour quality magazines with the official backing of the band. Whatever those early fanzines lacked in quality they certainly made up for in insight, reviews, interviews and information. Yes now have their own official websites and information centres.

(NA) = Not available, now out of print.

Sound Chaser, (UK) 1979 - 80, Editor Barry Smith, seven issues. (NA)

The Revealing, (UK) since 1980 - Editor Ian Hartley, over twenty-six issues. Album, bootleg and live show reviews. Interviews and any releases by Yes and solo artists.

Relayer, (US) 1980s, Editors Tanya Coad & Sue Smith, thirty issues. (NA)

Relayer, (UK) 1980s, Editors Brian and the two Johns, twelve issues. (NA)

Yes Music Magazine, (UK) 1980s, Editor Jon Dee. (NA)

Wondrous Music, (UK) 1980s, Editor T Hay. 5-10 issues. (NA)

Going For The Two, (UK) 1980s, Editor T Hay. (NA)

The Dutch Yes Fan Committee, (BELGIUM) 1985-92, it turned into *Close To Yes* magazine. (NA)

Close To Yes, (BELGIUM) 1985-92, Editors Arno Williems, Carol Pynn, Josephine Jobst, Gert Bakhuizen & Ria Oosting, 15-20 issues. (NA)

Yes Family Fan Club (JAPAN) Since 1990s - forty two issues. Magazine full of all matters relating to the band, Japanese text only.

Yes Music Circle, (UK) 1990s, Editor T Hay. (NA)

Wondrous Stories, (US) 1990s, Editor Susan C, Eleven issues. (NA)

Topographic Sounds, (SPAIN) 1990 – 94, Four issues. (NA)

Awaken Magazine, (US) 1990, advertised but never released.

Yes Magazine,(US) 1990s, Editors Glenn and Doug Gottlieb. The first official Yes magazine, in full-colour and excellent quality. Many issues released before becoming an internet-based magazine. (NA)

Other UK fan publications that have featured Yes over the years are – *Slogans*, *Progressive Forum*, *Yes Talk*, *Progress*, *Wondrous Stories* (Classic Rock Society), *Music News Network* (USA), *Progression* (USA), *South American Khatru* (USA) and *7Cs* (USA), Kozel A Peremhez (Hungarian) 8 issues mainly Yes, 1996-7.

YES FANCLUB/SITES

(these are the main sites)
Yesworld, Yes' official main website www.yesworld.com
Yes information newsletter, Notes From The Edge www.nfte.org
Yes a variety of information and fan sites www.yeshoo.com
Roger Dean, information on all his projects www.rogerdean.com

Jon Anderson – www.jonanderson.com
Steve Howe – www.stevehowe.com
Chris Squire – www.chrissquire.com
Alan White – www.alanwhite.net
Igor Khoroshev – www.khoroshev.com

There is a huge Yes community on the web, with hundreds more websites full of an amazing variety of information. Yes fans seem to be very internet-friendly and from the early days of the web, it has been an important way for the band to communicate with its fan base.

TRIBUTE BANDS

Due to a steady decline in touring activity by many of the world's top rock and pop acts, the market for tribute bands has prospered. There are now tribute bands for Genesis, Rush, ELP and Jethro Tull to name but a few. Yes had to wait some 30 years for their first tribute band, Fragile in the US. Others have arrived on the scene in the last year or two, proving there is a demand from the fans to hear the band's music more often, and they do provide a great night out for Yes fans when the true Yes are not playing.

All have put a great deal of effort into reproducing a Yesshow and, in a scoop for the UK-based Fragile, ex-Yes man Peter Banks played with them at a gig in London in 1999. The tribute bands help to advertise the band, and keep their music alive, promoting the sales of back catalogue.

FRAGILE, (UK) http:/www.yestribute.com
Live At The Half Moon
Roundabout, I've Seen All Good People, Heart Of The Sunrise, Owner Of A Lonely Heart, Yes Medley includes:- Long Distance Runaround, The Fish, The Gates Of Delirium, Soon, Six Wives, Hearts, The Revealing Science Of God, Ritual, Yours Is No Disgrace, Starship Trooper.
Steve Carney (voc), Jon Bastable (bass), Mitch Harwood (drm), Tom Dawe (rtm gtr), Gonzalo Carreras (key), Robert Illes (ld gtr).
FRAGILE-1, *Cybersound* October 2000
Fragile released the live pub gig on CD to the UK market only, recorded in London on 8 June 2000, it is available from their website above.
ASLAN, (JAPAN)
http:/www5a.biglobe.ne.jp/~aslan/aslanhome
Tribute To *Close To The Edge*
Close To The Edge, And You And I, Siberian Khatru, plus bonus tracks Five Per Cent For Nothing and We Have Heaven.
Aslan-1, October 2000
Aslan's studio album produced by Shoji Yamada and ASLAN, contained an enhanced CD movie for the PC featuring the track, The Meeting

originally by ABWH, it is available from their website above.
ENVISION, (US)
http:/ourworld.compuserve.com/homepages/MattRiddle/
A Tribute to Yes
Siberian Khatru, Wondrous Stories, South Side Of The Sky, I've Seen All Good People, Long Distance Runaround, America, Roundabout, Heart of the Sunrise.
Recorded live at Gettysburgh Address Recording Studios in April 1998. The CD available from: MattRiddle@compuserve.com
YESTERDAYS, (US) No longer together
YESSHOWS, (US) No longer together
FRAGILE, (US) No longer together

FANCLUBS & INFORMATION SERVICES

Opio Foundation (JA)
P.O. Box 697
Camp Hill,
PA 17001, USA

Yes Magazine (Gottlieb Brothers)
12 Chelsea Place,
DIX Hills,
New York 11746, USA
(Back issues available. They also trade Yes items.)

Steve Howe Appreciation Society (Pam Bay)
154 Hicks Farm Rise,
High Wycombe,
Bucks, HP13 7SG,
England, UK

The Revealing (Ian Hartley)
35 Field Lane,
Oldswinford,
Stourbridge,
West Midlands, DY8 2JQ
England, UK

Rick Wakeman Communication Centre
Bajonor House,
2 Bridge Street,
Peel, Isle Of Man,
England, UK

Yesterdays Collectibles (Trading in Yes items.)
25 Eden Road,
Gossops Green,
Crawley,
West Sussex, RH11 8LZ, England, UK

Yes Family Fan Club
Mitsuda Corpo 101,
Matsubara 2-32-23,
Setagaya-ku,
Tokyo, 156-0043, Japan

Yes Focus
Verax 39,
6541 LN,
Nijmegen,
Netherlands

TOUR MEMORABILIA AND MERCHANDISE

Yes tour programmes are popular collectors items, the older the programme the rarer it is, and harder to find. Between 1968–70 Yes would only feature as a one-line entry in most programmes since they were generally the support band. After the 1970 Queen Elizabeth Hall gig, Yes had their own programmes. The first colour one to feature the old logo was 1971 Age Of Atlantic, the rest were black and white. The programmes that really made an impression were those from 1973–76, which were full of Roger and Martyn Dean's classic designs and pictures. There may be more undiscovered programmes not on this list but it is as complete as possible up to this point. Should you wish to value your items, then an article doing just that was featured in the May 2000 issue of *Record Collector* magazine number 249 in the UK, and a back copy can be ordered.

The line-up has seen numerous changes over the years: below is a guide to the 59 programmes that accompanied each Yestour and who was in the band at the time.

JA - Jon Anderson, **CS** – Chris Squire, **AW** – Alan White, **SH** – Steve Howe, **TK** – Tony Kaye, **PB** – Peter Banks, **RW** – Rick Wakeman, **TR** – Trevor Rabin, **PM** – Patrick Moraz, **TH** – Trevor Horn, **GD** – Geoff Downes, **BS** – Billy Sherwood, **IK** – Ivor Khoroshev, **BB** – Bill Bruford.

1970 GERMANY - JOINT MEETING
16-18 May (JA, CS, BB, PB, TK)
A rare 32-page item from Dusseldorf in Germany featuring many bands on the bill. Yes get a page with a publicity photograph but no text.

1970 YORKSHIRE FOLK FESTIVAL
14 - 16 August (JA, CS, BB, PB, TK)
7"x5", b&w, 16 page programme. This is an extremely collectible item due to some of the other bands featured (rather than Yes, who were only a minor act). It was reported at the time that the promoter fled with the festival's takings and the weather closed the festival. Whether this means that Yes played or not is unclear, they only received a one-word mention, for Sunday night, and were fourth on the bill. The programme was priced at three shillings!

1970 UK STRAWBS, HARDIN – YORK, RED DIRT
(JA, CS, BB, PB, TK)
A 16"x5" programme, blue in colour, 5" column dedicated to each band and used for both Hull and Newcastle gigs in the UK.

1970 UK 10th NATIONAL JAZZ FESTIVAL
6–9 August (JA, CS, BB, PB, TK)
At this event, Yes moved up the listings from their last outing to be joint bill toppers with Deep Purple and Coliseum. A quarter page write-up covered the top acts.

1970 UK QUEEN ELIZABETH HALL
21 March (JA, CS, TK, BB, PB)
An A5-sized, two-tone yellow and black programme from Atlantic Records, the gig is billed as Yes' first solo concert!

1971 UK UNOFFICIAL YES ALBUM PROMO
(JA, CS, SH, TK, BB)
Extremely rare bootleg programme, it would appear to have been made available to the public in London, in between the releases of *Time and a Word* and the *Yes Album*. A4 with a red cover, 16 pages with 3 pages dedicated to Yes.

1971 QUEEN ELIZABETH HALL (JA, CS, TK, BB, PB)
A simple four-sided, b&w programme, displaying small band photographs inside and containing some information on the evening's show. The back features a logo and promotions for both the first and the new album. There are further copies that are identical in size and detail to the previous programme, but have a light pink colouring on the cover in place of the white. Handbills also exist.

1971 UK ROYAL ALBERT HALL (JA, CS, TK, BB, PB)
13 January
An A5 b&w programme with *Time And a Word* album cover on the front, inside a three-quarter-length photograph of Yes. The back has an Atlantic Records advert for the *Age of Atlantic* album, three different band logos and a plug for the Royal Albert Hall gig on the 13th.

1971 AGE OF ATLANTIC TOUR (JA, CS, TK, BB, PB)
Atlantic Records launched a compilation album of new and existing acts on their label and the groups toured under the "Age of Atlantic" banner. Other acts to use this banner were Led Zeppelin, Iron Butterfly and Delaney & Bonnie (Eric Clapton). A4 with eight pages and a bright yellow cover. Yes were featured over three pages. Handbills/flyers are also available.

1971 UK FRAGILE TOUR (JA, CS, SH, BB, RW)
An unusual size, 8"x4", this full-colour item is one of the smartest early programmes. The main feature of this programme is the free A4 poster. Full-colour pictures of each member with mini biography details.

1971 UK CRYSTAL PALACE GARDEN PARTY II (JA, CS, SH, BB, RW)
An A4 eight-page souvenir featuring the main acts on the bill, Elton John, Fairport Convention and Rory Gallagher. Yes appear on the bottom of the bill, and only get a single page.

1972 US LONG BEACH ARENA (JA, CS, SH, BB, RW)
Sized 5" x 8". This is the nearest thing to a *Close To The Edge* tour programme that exists, with eight pages in b&w and two pages dedicated to Yes, one page to Edgar Winter, and the Eagles receive a mention.

1972 UK RAINBOW THEATRE (JA, CS, SH, BB, RW)
One of many free souvenir programmes given out by the Rainbow, London's main rock venue. A5 with three pages on Yes, this consisted of a cover photo of Steve Howe in full flight with his trusty Gibson, a *Fragile* album promotional page and a write-up of the band with an excellent picture of Bill Bruford.

1972 UK CRYSTAL PALACE GARDEN PARTY V (JA, CS, SH, AW, RW)
This was the premiere of Yes' classic *Close To The Edge* album and was Alan White's first live appearance with Yes in the UK. The programme gives plenty of space to all bands on the bill: Lindisfarne, Mahavishnu Orchestra, Wright's Wonderwheel and Capability Brown. Yes have a small section in this die-cut covered item, the back cover showing for the first time the classic Roger Dean logo.

1973 AUSTRALIA / NEW ZEALAND (JA, CS, SH, AW, RW)
A very short tour produced this very rare collectible programme. Unfortunately, the classic Yes logo did not appear on the front cover, which is surprising. This is not a great looking item but a real rarity now; probably the hardest Yes programme to find. The centre spread has a good group shot. A handbill for the tour would be very collectible, as would a tour poster, but neither item has come onto the market as yet.

1973 JAPAN (JA, CS, SH, AW, RW)
Anything Japanese is very collectible and this is no exception. This giant-sized programme is certainly one of the hardest to find. It features unusual artwork (not Roger Dean), live pictures and text. It is an excellent quality programme. The tour only lasted nine days in March 1973. It won't be cheap if you find one but this is a must.

1973 UK UNOFFICIAL TALES TOUR (JA, CS, SH, AW, RW)
An A4-sized eight-page show souvenir that is very scarce these days. It has a bright yellow cover featuring a picture of Jon Anderson. The first two pages provide a Yes biography; the centre spread shows photographs of the band.

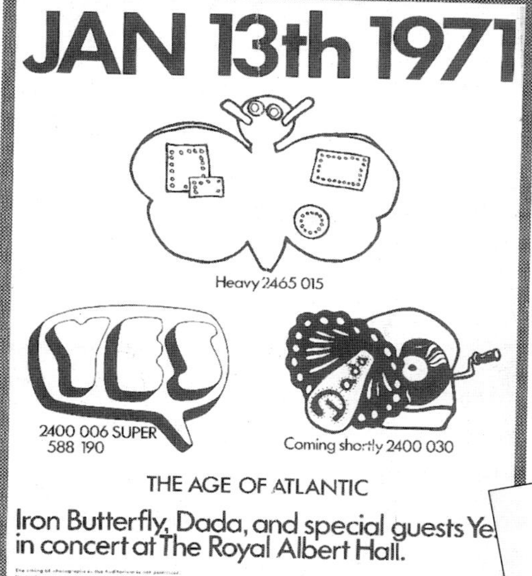

The following pages are filled with the *Fragile* album cover and insert designs plus some tour dates for the UK.

1973 UK TALES TOUR (JA, CS, SH, AW, RW)
This programme has a die-cut cover sized A4-ish and Roger Dean provides the cover logo. Inside are twelve pages covering album sleeve notes, band member details, Rick's Festival Hall gig advert and a great centre-spread live photo. This is a fantastic looking item from a great period for the band.

1974 USA TALES TOUR (JA, CS, SH, AW, RW)
This has a classic Yes logo cover with great tour photos inside. With tour dates, band member features and a thought-provoking piece of earthy cosmic prose by Donald Lehinkuhl, this is a must for any fan. There are twenty-two pages in all, with Chris Welch contributing a biography.

1974–5 USA UNOFFICIAL RELAYER TOUR (JA, CS, SH, AW, PM)
One that has recently come to light, six pages of mostly well-known pictures of the band, with one page of text. It has a yellow cover with a Dean logo. A good quality bootleg.

1974 USA WINTER RELAYER TOUR (Yellow Cover) (JA, CS, SH, AW, PM)
Designed by Martin Dean, this is quite a hard programme to find nowadays. It has fourteen pages that cover tour dates, art work and band member pages. Very similar in content to the following three programmes produced, these are a real treat and capture Yes at their seventies peak.

1975 UK SPRING TOUR RELAYER **(JA, CS, SH, AW, PM)**
Featuring Roger Dean's design, green cover with a yellow bird and the Yes logo, contains information on the instruments played. Two pages promote Yes' previous and current releases as well as a page devoted to each of the new solo albums from SH & CS.

1975 US (Red Cover) **(JA, CS, SH, AW, PM)**
With red cover this is one of the rarer mid seventies programmes. A4 in size with live shots and band member features, it covers solo works, new releases and the Yes back catalogue. It also has a section on Ace, the support act on the tour, and features lots of Roger and Martyn Dean's artwork and photographs.

1975 UK READING FESTIVAL **(JA, CS, SH, AW, PM)**
Yes shared the bill with the likes of Wishbone Ash and others at Reading and, consequently, featured on only a few pages in the programme. In newspaper format, similar to *Melody Maker* at the time, Yes shared the cover with Wishbone Ash.

1976 USA RELAYER (Promo) **(JA, CS, SH, AW, PM)**
A limited-edition, promotional item, used to encase the green coloured 1976 *Relayer* programme, album-sized with a Roger Dean Yes logo on the front.

1976 USA RELAYER TOUR **(JA, CS, SH, AW, PM)**
This item ends the first era of the massive Dean involvement with the band. This 12" x 12" full-colour item has Yes in the centre pages in a Queen (bo-rap) style pose. Very arty, features (solo album material) photos for each member.

1977 UK GOING FOR THE ONE TOUR **(JA, CS, SH, RW, AW)**
A4 in size, it has many colour pictures, little text.

1977 USA GOING FOR THE ONE TOUR **(JA, CS, SH, RW, AW)**
It is quite easy to get hold of this due to the number produced and the length of the tour and, as with the UK version, it has good pictures of each member of the band.

1977 UK UNOFFICIAL TOUR SOUVENIR **(JA, CS, SH, RW, AW)**
A5 in size, it has a colour cover with pictures taken from the sleeve of *Going For The One*. Inside the eight pages there are lyrics to Wondrous Stories, a biography, discography and a centre album cover spread. Hard to come by and is one of the better bootlegs.

1977 USA UNOFFICIAL SOUVENIR **(JA, CS, SH, RW, AW)**
This appears to be the last bootleg programme produced. It is A5 in size with a mauve and white cover, featuring the sun setting behind a tree. It was specifically produced for the Detroit, Michigan show in the Cobo Hall Arena, 22-23 August.

1978 UK UNOFFICIAL TORMATO **(JA, CS, SH, RW, AW)**
Featuring a die-cut Yes logo on the red cover, this bootleg programme is one of the best. 11" x 7", it has 13 pages which include a biography, photographs taken from press articles and the official Yes programmes, a page of album covers and a small discography.

1978 UK TORMATO TOUR **(JA, CS, SH, RW, AW)**
A sixteen page programme with album cover artwork done by Hypgnosis. There is a page devoted to each band member and a map of Yestor in Devon where, from the top, we are kindly informed, 'You can see forever'.

1978 US TORMATO **(JA, CS, SH, AW, RW)**
This programme is almost the same as the UK one and is probably only of interest to the completist.

1979 USA NORTH AMERICAN **(JA, CS, SH, AW, RW)**
This programme features live pictures and text written by Dan Hedges (author of *Yes: The Authorised Biography* published 1981). Last look at this great era makes this programme a must, but it's not easy to find since it was printed in limited numbers.

1980 UK DRAMA TOUR **(CS, SH, AW, TH, GD)**
The artwork is a combination of Roger Dean and Hypgnosis style photography. Twenty-four pages include studio shots, lyrics, album art and a group photograph of Yes. Slightly larger in size than A4, it includes individual double-page spreads on each member.

1980 USA DRAMA TOUR **(CS, SH, AW, TH, GD)**
This is the US version featuring a superior Steve Howe photograph displaying his massive collection of guitars.

OFFICIAL PROGRAMME
No. 3064 SATURDAY, AUGUST 16, 1975
READING ROCK '75
15p
Wishbone Ash
PLUS
Hawkwind
Robin Trower
CARAVAN
Soft Machine
—and many more
YES
It's a great Festival
Six albums to be won

1984 EUROPEAN (JA, CS, AW, TR, TK)
Features computer-generated album artwork and tour pictures. A4 in size, it's probably the most easily available programme due to the huge success of the tour and the huge number of dates played all over the world.

1984 US (JA, CS, TR, AW, TK)
This programme is slightly more difficult to find, it's larger in format to the European programme.

1984 US NORTH AMERICAN (JA, CS, TR, AW, TK)
The third tour programme is the hardest one to find from 1984, featuring a pink cover.

1988 ATLANTIC RECORDS 40th ANNIVERSARY (JA, CS. TR, AW, TK)
Along with other top acts such as Led Zeppelin, Yes helped to celebrate Atlantic Records' 40th anniversary with this big bash in New York. An album-sized programme was available on the night, in which Yes featured over two pages, including a short biography.

1988 JAPAN (JA, CS, TR, AW, TK)
20 pages. Has some good live pictures and a text by a long-term Yes admirer, Lee Abrams.

1989 UK/US ABWH (JA, BB, RW, SH)
These two programmes differ slightly, text variations and different Jon Anderson pictures.

1989 US ABWH (JA, BB, RW, SH)
Features plenty of photos alongside a biography and Roger Dean designs, stage sets and album artwork. A smart, glossy, large format, good quality item.

1990 JAPAN ABWH (JA, BB, RW, SH)
As with all Japanese items, this is highly collectible but will be difficult to find.

1991 UK UNION TOUR (JA, CS, TR, AW, TK, RW, BB, SH)
A full-colour programme with a good band history, full of Roger Dean's influences and packed with photos.

1991 US UNION TOUR (JA, CS, TR, AW, TK, RW, BB, SH)
A great programme marking both a fantastic tour and a strange album. The *Yes* magazine editors in the US wrote the text, which contains a history up to that date. Only slight differences alter this programme from the Japanese.

1991 JAPAN UNION TOUR (JA, CS, TR, AW, TK, RW, BB, SH)
Similar to the US programme, except for added Japanese inserts, totalling eight sides of added Yes material along with a slightly different text.

1994-5 US / JAPAN TALK TOUR (JA, CS, TR, AW, TK)
As usual for a Japanese item, it's excellent quality, a 12" x12" glossy programme, full of live photos, visuals and some text. Peter Max's interesting Yes logo adorns the cover which was also used for the front of the CD. Although it's hard to find, it is worth the effort as it is high quality and represents the end of the 1980s Yes.

1996 US SLO MASTERWORKS (JA, CS, SH, AW, RW)
This A5-sized programme opens to reveal photos of this classic line-up, a cheaply produced item that was only made available for the three nights. Difficult to find because of the importance of the concerts and the fact that no fan would want to part with it!

1997 US OPEN YOUR EYES TOUR (JA, CS, SH, AW, IK, BS)
A glossy 12" x 12" featuring the classic Yes logo cover artwork by Roger Dean. Inside are live photographs from the US tour along with two pages devoted to each member of the band. For the first part of the tour, the programme was not available, which now makes it a desirable item.

1998 UK/EUROPE OPEN YOUR EYES TOUR
(JA, CS, SH, AW, IK, BS)
This is similar to the US programme but has slight text differences and is probably for the complete collector only.

1998 US 30th ANNIVERSARY TOUR
(JA, CS, SH, AW, IK, BS)
A special edition for the big 30th anniversary. Using the same format as the two previous programmes, it has additional pages (on the Surround Sound details), and an excellent new cover design with a Roger Dean logo.

1998 JAPAN OPEN YOUR EYES TOUR 30th ANNIVERSARY **(JA, CS, SH, AW, IK, BS)**
Similar to the US programme but contains a free flyer for the few dates played there.

1999 AMERICAN LADDER TOUR
(JA, CS, SH, AW, IK, BS)
With a familiar format and presentation, the first programme produced for the South American tour was altered slightly for all the different countries on the world tour. Judging by the last tour programme for the 1998 tour, the alterations included listing the road crew and featuring some changed photographs of the band. 12" x 12" in size, it features a Roger Dean cover. It has eight more pages of photographs (all taken on the 1998 US tours) and includes short up-to-date interviews with all band members. Yes' new-ish (1991) square Roger Dean logo had gradually been introduced into all official work, making a visual change for the new millennium.

1999 SOUTH AMERICAN LADDER TOUR
(JA, CS, SH, AW, IK, BS)
Colourful 3-4 page programme featuring (unusually) the classic Dean logo, but is very hard to find.

2000 US LADDER WORLD TOUR
(JA, CS, SH, AW, IK, BS)
One of the best ever programmes with lots of new information on the band. Produced in a large square format, similar to the old album covers, it features *The Ladder* (Roger Dean) sleeve on the cover and also contains an updated mini-history of the band, complemented by some Yes memorabilia from days gone by. Excellent photographs and artwork accompany the text (including interviews with the band) along with an amusing cartoon portrait of the band and internet addresses for the official sites.

2000 UK/EUROPE LADDER WORLD TOUR
(JA, CS, SH, AW, IK, BS)
Very similar to the US version with minimal text variations, this is only for the completist really. The cover border is different, as is some of the layout and text in the history section.

2000 US MASTERWORKS TOUR (JA, CS, SH, AW, IK)
Comprising thirty-two pages and the same size as the last tour programme. Full-colour with standard Yes logo in red, the bands' history presented in the form of a timeline, featuring key dates such as album release dates and notable concerts. Heavily illustrated with memorabilia fitting around the timeline, mostly 45s, posters and magazines, each page features a quote from a song of that particular year. The programme ends with 2 pages of live photos, the back cover features the dragonfly image. This programme won an award for quality of design in the US.

Promotional programmes were also produced: a 30-page magazine in the style of a programme was created in the US in 1977 for the release of *Going For The One*. It was published by Cash Box, the music industry paper at the time. It features interviews and information on the band around the time of release. A 1991 German promotional item, released by Atco, has about 70 pages of information including a discography, reviews, history and facts on the releases of *Yesstory, Yesyears* and the *Greatest Hits* video compilation.

If you want to know which are the most valuable programmes to collect, the following list details those which are extremely hard to find.

1. 1972 Australia (A5-sized unremarkable to look at, but very rare)
2. 1973 Japan (Large size, small number produced)
3. 1970 UK Yorkshire Folk and Jazz Festival (small black and white)
4. 1968–70 Any item
5. 1971 UK *Fragile* (Colour, odd shape with a centre page poster)
6. 1996 San Luis Obispo (Simple small flyer/programme, approximately 2,000 printed)
7. 1975 US North American (Red cover, Dean logo)
8. 1974 US Winter Tour (Yellow cover, Dean logo)
9. 1999 South America (Full-colour, limited number printed)
10. 1979 US North America (A4 size, In The Round cover shot)

TOUR MERCHANDISE AND MEMORABILIA

Yes posters fall into two different categories; the high street retailer's standard release and the record companies' promotional release.

Promotional posters started early on with the release of the first album, although very few must survive now. They range in size from the counter-top to massive 100 feet long billboard posters for the release of *Going For The One* in 1977. The earliest known Yes tour posters come from the Age Of Atlantic tour in 1971. There are a number of variations, changes to the line-up lists, the design sometimes included pictures of the album cover alongside the tour plus the support act's album cover. Any poster from the 1970s commands a very high price. Posters from the Yes tour of Japan and Australia in 1973 must be at the top of the list for collectors, as they are very rare indeed! Tour posters are rare because they are only displayed for a relatively short period, and then torn down. The arrival of Roger Dean's artwork saw the demand for Yes posters boom: in the 1970s many

students wanted Yes/Roger Dean's album covers on their walls. The company responsible for providing most of the reproductions of Roger's work was called Big 'O', who produced the full-colour, large-sized posters for the first 1973 tour. Two were made available, one of the Yes logo and one of the Topographic collage by Roger and Martyn Dean which combined photos with original artwork.

Two posters were released for *Yessongs* the movie, showing Yes playing live in 1972, one from the UK and the other from the US. Both are very rare as they were only displayed for the film run, a matter of weeks, and then removed. There are press ads and flyers, which promote the film, but little else has been found. A single, which has remained elusive to me as well as most other serious Yes collectors, is 'Yessongs – Radio Spots' which was reportedly a promotional one-sided single made to plug the movie. The movie has been available for some years now on video and has had four different covers.

Yes tour T-shirts are also a popular collector's item. The earliest ones are very hard to find and are inevitably in poor condition due to the sub-standard materials used back in the early 1970s. The first T-shirts produced had ironed-on, flimsy, paper-thin images. The first attempt at marketing Yes memorabilia was on the *Close To The Edge* tour, with Roger Dean's marvellous logo transforming the way the band was marketed. Instantly recognisable, the logo was applied to T-shirts and stickers. T-shirts were produced for every tour after this, so collectors have 30 years' worth to seek out.

It is important to point out that prior to the *Tales From Topographic Oceans* Tour all Yes merchandise came from pirate/illegal sources and was not official. What often happened was that local entrepreneurs would steal the logo and apply it to T-shirts and even the odd programme, they would approach Yes' management and would knock out some agreement allowing them to sell the goods at the gig. Every one was happy, they all made some money.

What soon happened was the management's realisation that selling merchandise could be so much more successful if it was brought under the Yes team umbrella. The main person responsible for the explosion of Yes merchandise was Roger Dean who organised for all the merchandise to be produced by one supplier and delivered directly to each of Yes' scheduled venues. He co-ordinated the whole process which would become a landmark event in rock merchandising, something that has blossomed into a multi-million dollar business for many. No-one before this tour had ever designed, produced, shipped and sold specific official merchandise at a rock show, it was a huge logistical operation that worked very well.

Sweatshirts and jackets first appeared about 1975–6. These can be difficult to source, but tend to be in better condition than the T-shirts. Notable collector's pieces are the San Luis Obispo T-shirts; not surprisingly, because any fan that made it to the event isn't too keen to give it up. The *90125* sweatshirt, in black with details on the arms, was highly priced for the time at £30. Undeterred by the cost, Yes fans loved them and consequently they sold out in the first day. Tour jackets are rare too; known examples were made for the *Relayer* and *Drama* tours.

There are many different Yes badges to collect and they come from both official and bootlegged sources. It seems that the first badges appeared during the *Close To The Edge* tour. The official ones can usually be told apart from the bootleg by the quality of images used and many in the mid 1970s had the manufacturing company name on the side.

Concert memorabilia is an increasingly popular area for collectors, specifically the none too glamorous concert ticket. These are split into two categories; firstly the completely unused items and secondly, the stub or portion left when torn away on entry to the gig. Before the days of concert halls Yes would play in pubs and clubs and these venues wouldn't always have issued tickets. The earlier tickets 1969–74 were quite plain and it wasn't until 1974–80 that they

featured the classic Yes logo. The earliest known ticket is from 18 January 1969; and there may well be one lurking in someone's old treasures from an even earlier date.

The earliest known pieces of Yes tour memorabilia are the flyers from the Marquee club in London. These double-sided information sheets, with coloured logo, give the live appearance details of all the bands over a one-month period. There is one which shows Yes' first London gig with a support act. This came directly after their East Mersea Youth Camp gig in Essex. Pre-Yes bands like the Syn and Mabel Greer's Toyshop are also featured on early Marquee handbills too, if you can find them. Flyers were then produced sporadically throughout the band's history, mainly in colour and A5 in size, both single and double-sided. The main source of flyers now seems to be Japan, although others have been issued around Europe and a small number in North America.

Tour passes were an area of little or no interest some years ago, but have now become popular collectors items. The internet has aided the searching capacity for such items, they are easy to post due to their size. They look good when framed, generally they come in two forms; plastic coated (laminated) or sticky-backed fabric. There are different types of passes used while the band are on tour, such as road crew, special event, working crew, restricted areas, press, access all areas and guest passes. All come in a variety of sizes, shapes and colours and there are 30 years' worth to collect.

On a number of occasions, key items have come up for auction at one or two of the main auction houses. Steve Howe and Chris Squire have both sold guitars through them. A Jon Anderson harp came up from the *Olias* days, about five gold discs came from the old 1970's Yes offices in Hill Gate Street in London, as have framed and glazed paintings and awards. A Roger Dean stage piece from the ABWH tour and video once went up for sale, as did the original painting for the *Fragile* album cover. Not many appear, but they are interesting items that any fan would treasure. Other items to come up for sale have been a huge back lot of unreleased work by Jon Anderson, including Yes' live material and the whole of the ABWH tour. Rick Wakeman also had an auction, which included his old Moog and Hammond organ keyboards.

Many years earlier he auctioned some of his famous capes. Sales of this type are obviously very rare but it is amazing how collectible items like these can turn up in the most surprising of places. The serious collector should always have his/her eyes open for the opportunities that might be there for just a fleeting moment...

BOOTLEGOGRAPHY

Bootlegography is a debatable area, probably the most potentially damaging to any band but one which all music acts have to deal with. Out of the whole collecting area, this is the top one for Yes fans.

Bootlegging will be apparent for as long as the band has a fan base. The record company can't release an official recording of every gig performed so, in order to provide souvenirs, the bootleggers keep supplying their recordings.

The bootlegs listed here are historical documents in themselves, sometimes providing an indication of how well Yes were performing and what they were performing in any particular year. The first bootleg recordings go back a long way, to around 1969, when live recordings were released of Bob Dylan named *Great White Wonder*. Until the rise of the CD, most bootlegs started out in tape and vinyl format. Yes recordings came thick and fast in the 1970s, disappearing in the 1980s making way for the CD.

The early Yes bootlegs were a mixed bunch, the quality of recording and the sleeve presentation varied greatly. The first bootleg vinyl Yes album was called *The White Yes Album*. It had a red cover, which informed you that Mr William Bruford was playing drums! The albums were very expensive when first released in the seventies, and came down in price many years later and the CD format was introduced in around 1989 with ABWH. Yes have never been a top league bootleg band like, say, the Beatles, Led Zeppelin, Pink Floyd, Queen or the Stones, but the floodgates opened up for fans in 1996 when a Japanese company called Highland started producing Yes bootlegs. Apparently, the head of the company is a Yes fan!

The first one they produced was called *Lost Yesyears*; during their first three years, they produced about 200 different Yes titles! In the late nineties the UK bootleg trade was hit badly when local authorities clamped down and most dealers went underground. Now, with the internet making detection harder and providing an easily accessible on-line market bootlegs are now making a comeback.

BOOTLEG VINYL ALBUMS

The White Yes Album
I've Seen All Good People, Heart Of The Sunrise, Keyboard solo, Long Distance Runaround, Yours Is No Disgrace
Offshore Records
OF 722
Amsterdam, Holland January 1972
Deluxe red and white cover

On Tour
I've Seen All Good People, Heart Of The Sunrise, Keyboard solo, Long Distance Runaround, Yours Is No Disgrace
TMOQ 71066
Amsterdam January 1972

On Tour
I've Seen All Good People, Heart Of The Sunrise, Keyboard solo, Long Distance Runaround, Yours Is No Disgrace
TMOQ 71066
Amsterdam January 1972
Deluxe pressing in stamped cover plus insert coloured vinyl

On Tour
I've Seen All Good People, Heart Of The Sunrise, Keyboard solo, Long Distance Runaround, Yours Is No Disgrace
TMOQ Y116
Amsterdam January 1972
(As above) Reissue from master plates

Live In Amsterdam
I've Seen All Good People, Heart Of The Sunrise, Keyboard solo, Long Distance Runaround, Yours Is No Disgrace
TAKRL 1375RS
Amsterdam, Holland January 1972
Kornyphone reissue from TMOQ plates

Live At The Rainbow Theatre
And You And I, Clap, Six Wives, Jingle Bells, Roundabout, Yours Is No Disgrace
TAKRL 915
UK December 1972
Deluxe B/W cover

At The Rainbow Theatre
And You And I, Clap, Six Wives, Jingle Bells, Roundabout, Yours Is No Disgrace
Flat Records 8235
UK December 1972

Chord Of Life
Siberian Khatru, Your Move, I've Seen All Good People, Mood For A Day, Clap, Close To The Edge, Heart Of The Sunrise, And You And I, Yours Is No Disgrace, Rick's solo, Roundabout

RSR, International Records 07995 (RSR 231)
Canada 30 October 1972
Waterloo University, Ontario, Canada, a double album - deluxe colour cover

Live in Europe
January 1972
Hard to find - minimal number of pressings made

Guess Who's Coming To Dinner
I've Seen All Good People, One Day Old (Clap), Live or Die (And You And I), Close To The Edge, Roundabout
CWRPK-YS-3241 Various sources
UK 1972/3
Cuts are from the soundtrack of the film Yessongs

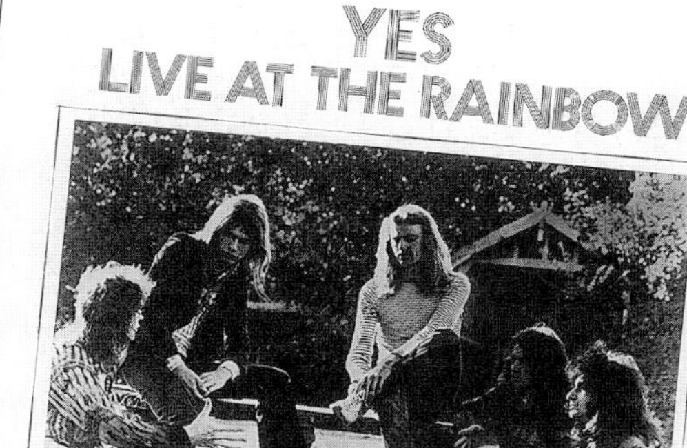

Yes...Indeed
Roundabout, Starship Trooper, Close To The Edge, Wakeman solo
Contraband Music CBM3815
Tampa Bay, Florida, USA 21 April 1973
Some copies have strip cartoon printed on back cover

Live in Japan
Tokyo, Japan March 1973
Possibly the most rare Yes vinyl bootleg.

The Affirmatives
The Revealing Science Of God, The Remembering, The Ancient, Ritual
Chance Records Inc YEP21874
Madison Square Garden, New York, USA
18 February 1974
Double album - Deluxe colour cover

Live At The Long Beach Arena, California
Close To The Edge, The Revealing, The Ancient, Roundabout, Starship Trooper
Pig's Eye PE-YES 1
Long Beach Arena, California, USA
19 March 1974
Double album

The Affirmery
Sound Chaser, Roundabout, The Gates Of Delirium
TAKRL-1981
Boston Gardens, Massachusetts, USA
12 November 1974
Original pressings have tri-colour insert

The Affirmery
Beacon Island Records 2S-710
Rainbow Theatre, London, UK
1972 and
Boston Gardens, Massachusetts, USA
12 November 1974
Double album - Sides 1 & 2 are a reissue of The Affirmery (TAKRL 1981) Sides 3 & 4 are a reissue of At The Rainbow (FLAT 8235) All from the master plates Deluxe colour cover

Stellar Attraction
Sound Chaser, Close To The Edge, Gates Of Delirium, And You And I, Roundabout
Singer's Original Double Disk SODD 006
Boston Gardens, Massachusetts, USA
12 November 1974
Double album

Stellar Attraction
Sound Chaser, Close To The Edge, Gates Of Delirium, And You And I, Roundabout
Beacon Island Records 2S-719
Boston Gardens, Massachusetts, USA
12 November 1974
Reissue of the SODD double album with deluxe colour cover

Re-Evolution
Sound Chaser, To Be Over, Close To The Edge
Flashback 08 90 0124-33
Boston Gardens, Massachusetts, USA
12 November 1974 and
Wembley Arena, London, UK
28 October 1978
Deluxe colour cover

Sorceror's Apprentice
The Gates Of Delirium, Your Move, Mood For A Day, Long Distance Runaround, Patrick Moraz solo, Clap, And You And I
Idle Mind Productions IMP 1100
Hollywood Bowl, California 1975
Original pressings were on multicoloured vinyl. Later versions have coloured insert, different text and IMP logo (lady holding apple) is missing

Mark's LP
Siberian Khatru, Sound Chaser, The Gates Of Delirium, Ritual, Heart Of The Sunrise, I'm Down, I've Seen All Good People
Dancin' Discs DD1002
Roosevelt Stadium, New Jersey, USA
17 June 1976
Very limited pressing - one of the rarest Yes bootlegs. Double album

Live In London
Firebird suite, Parallels, I've Seen All Good People, Close To The Edge, Wondrous Stories, Colours Of The Rainbow, Turn Of The Century, Tour Song, And You And I, Going For The One
K & S Records 035
Empire Pool, Wembley, London
28 October 1977
Double album. Deluxe B/W cover

Yesshows - World Tour 1977
Parallels, Wondrous Stories, Medley: Colours Of

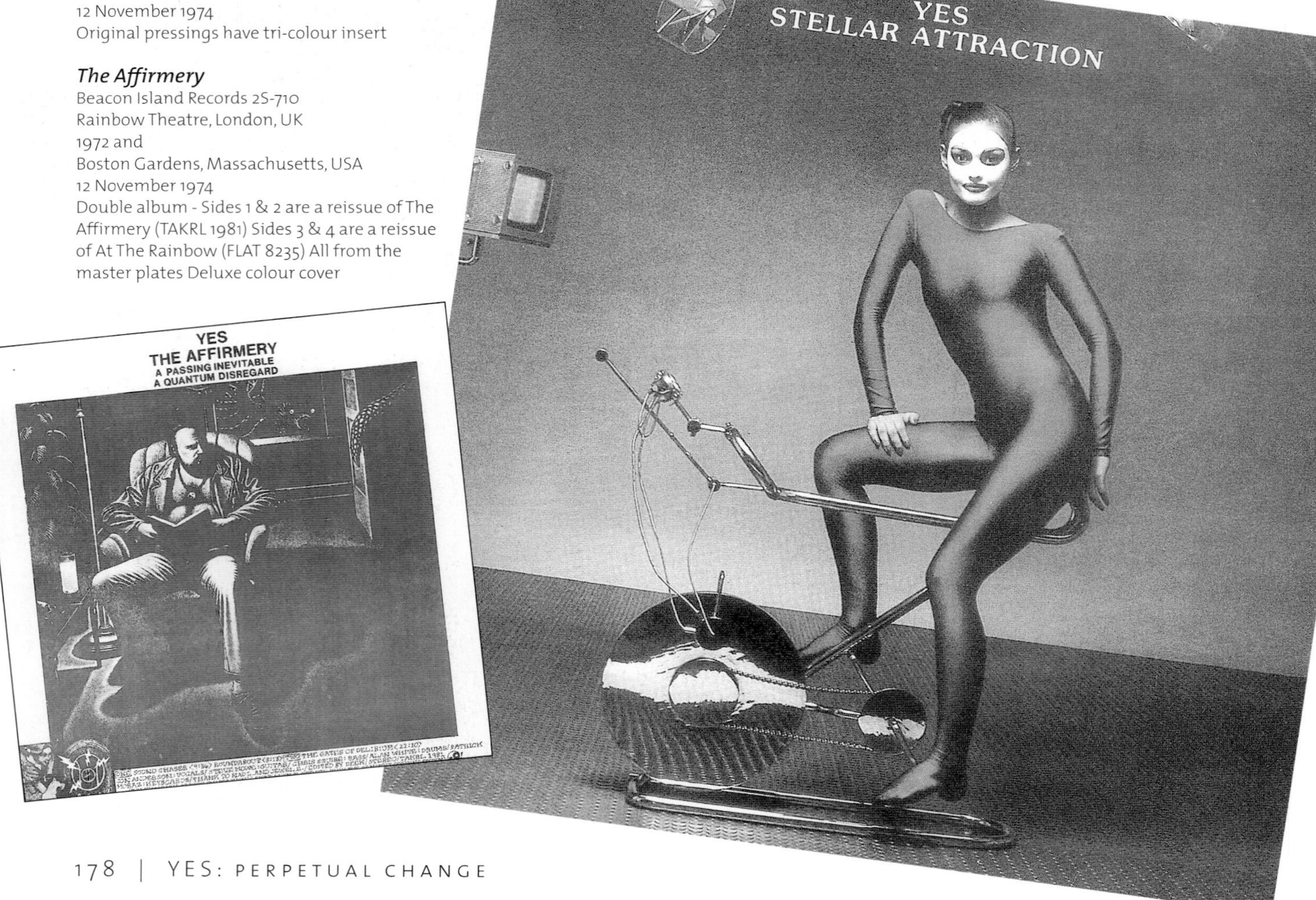

LIVE IN LONDON

The Rainbow-Turn Of The Century, Here in Long Beach, Going For The One, Roundabout
Ruthless Rhymes YES LB
Long Beach Arena, California, USA
26 September 1977

File Under: YES
I've Seen All Good People, Roundabout
I've Seen All Good People-74, R AB-74
Wembley Arena, London, UK
28 October 1978
12" white vinyl EP with B/W picture labels

The Twelve Towers At Dawn
Time And A Word, Long Distance Runaround, Fish, Perpetual Change, Don't Kill The Whale, Circus Of Heaven, Awaken, I've Seen All Good People, Roundabout
T K Records AFF3
Wembley Arena, London, UK
28 October 1978
Full-colour gatefold card sleeve

Periphet
Siberian Khatru, Starship Trooper, Heart Of The Sunrise, Circus Of Heaven, Don't Kill The Whale, Clap, Madrigal, On The Silent Wings Of Freedom, I've Seen All Good People, Roundabout
Impossible Recordworks IMP 2-17
Wembley Arena, London, UK
28 October 1978
Double album. Deluxe B/W cover

In The Round
Siberian Khatru, Heart Of The Sunrise, Circus Of Heaven, Don't Kill The Whale, Clap, Starship Trooper, Madrigal, On The Silent Wings Of Freedom, I've Seen All Good People, Roundabout
YS-1600
Wembley Arena, London, UK
28 October 1978
Double album. Deluxe cover. First run copies have grey/white covers, others green

In The Round
YS1600
Wembley Arena, London, UK
28 October 1978
Reissue of sides 1 & 2 of above with paper insert sleeve

In The Round
LXXXIV Series #57
Wembley Arena, London, UK
28 October 1978
Reissue of sides 1 & 2 of YS1600. Red vinyl. Only

100 numbered copies made

The Affirmative – Tales From Mabel Greer's Toyshop
Everybody Loves You, Flower Girl, Awaken (live, Wembley, London 28 October 1978), Dancing Through Light (Run Through The Light), Golden Age, Tango, In The Tower, Friend Of A Friend
AVD2383: Studio demos
Paris, France 1979
Deluxe colour cover

Our Song
Opening, Cinema, Leave It, Yours Is No Disgrace, Hold On, Hearts, Changes, And You And I, Soon (not listed on cover) , Owner Of A Lonely Heart, It Can Happen, Cinema (again - cover states Long Distance Runaround) I've Seen All Good People (cover states Roundabout)
Anto Records 94330-1
San Francisco Cow Palace, California, USA
30 March 1984
Double album with full-colour deluxe cover. Production credits and the back cover are a pastiche of the 90125 album

World Tour 1984
Cinema, Leave It, Hold On, Hearts, I've Seen All Good People, Changes, And You And I, Reason To Be Here (Soon), Owner Of A Lonely Heart, It Can Happen, City Of Love, Long Distance Runaround, Starship Trooper, Roundabout
XL1587-1588
Meadowlands Stadium, New Jersey, USA
7 May 1984
Double album. Japanese with deluxe colour cover

Domino
Owner Of A Lonely Heart, Hold On, It Can Happen, Changes, City Of Love, Starship Trooper
Laughing Clown Records LC58055
Westfalenhall, Dortmund, Germany
24 June 1984
Deluxe colour cover

Domino
Owner Of A Lonely Heart, Hold On, It Can Happen, Changes, City Of Love, Starship Trooper
Laughing Clown Records LC58055
Westfalenhall, Dortmund, Germany
24 June 1984
Picture Disc using same colour cover design on the vinyl

File Under YES, The Beat Goes On, Part 1
Cinema, Leave It, Yours Is No Disgrace, Alan White solo, Hold On, Tony Kaye solo, Trevor Rabin solo, Owner Of A Lonely Heart, It Can Happen
Anon (matrix no 311843)
Dortmund, Germany 24 June 1984
Double album in stamped sleeve

The Evolution Continues
Leave It (intro), Cinema, Leave It, Yours Is No Disgrace, Hold On, Hearts, I've Seen All Good People, solo, Changes, Owner Of A Lonely Heart, And You And I, Soon, Starship Trooper, Long Distance Runaround, City Of Love, It Can Happen, Roundabout, I'm Down
Trap Records Embeeigh 90126-1
Dortmund, Germany 24 June 1984
Triple album in deluxe colour cover. Jimmy Page guests on final song, A rare bootleg - many copies were seized

Five Masters Live In Germany
Owner Of A Lonely Heart, Hold On, It Can Happen, Changes, City Of Love, Starship Trooper
Lounging Records NO A/B
Dortmund, Germany
24 June 1984
Pirated bootleg allegedly limited to 150 copies

Lonely Hearts
It Can Happen, Yours Is No Disgrace, Long Distance Runaround, Drum solo, Hold On, Changes, Owner Of A Lonely Heart
Arc Records ARC0085
Dortmund, Germany 24 June 1984 and Milan, Italy 18 July 1984
Limited edition of 300 numbered copies with blue, black printed cover insert

Say Yes
Cinema, Leave It, Yours Is No Disgrace, Drum solo, Hold On, Hearts, I've Seen All Good People, Solly's Beard, Changes, And You And I, Soon, Owner Of A Lonely Heart, It Can Happen, Long Distance Runaround, Whitefish 1, Whitefish 2, The Fish, Amazing Grace, City Of Love, Starship Trooper 1,Starship Trooper 2, Roundabout
Metropol Records Y 84001/2/3
Festhalle, Frankfurt, Germany
26 June 1984
Triple album in deluxe colour cover

Say Yes
Cinema, Leave It, Yours Is No Disgrace, Drum solo, Hold On, Hearts, I've Seen All Good People, Solly's Beard, Changes, And You And I, Soon, Owner Of A Lonely Heart, It Can Happen, Long Distance Runaround, Whitefish 1, Whitefish 2, The Fish, Amazing Grace, City Of Love, Starship Trooper 1, Starship Trooper 2, Roundabout
Metropol Records Y 84001/2/3
Festhalle, Frankfurt, Germany
26 June 1984
Multicoloured vinyl discs. Sticker on cover. Very limited reissue

Rock In Rio
Yours Is No Disgrace, Hold On, Hearts, Roundabout, Leave It, I've Seen All Good People, Intro, Keyboard solo, Guitar solo, Changes, And You And I, Light (Soon), Owner Of A Lonely Heart
Anon YRR-01
Rio Festival, Rio De Janeiro, Brazil
January 1985
Double album in deluxe (if plain) colour cover

Live At The Hollywood Sportatorium On The 1988 World Tour
Rhythm Of Love, Hold On, Heart Of The Sunrise, Big Generator, Changes, Shoot High - Aim Low, Holy Lamb, Trevor Rabin Guitar solo, Owner Of A Lonely Heart, Yours Is No Disgrace, Duet (Soon), And You And I, Wurm
Hollywood Sportatorium, Miami, Florida, USA
24 January 1988
Double album. Stickered sleeve - limited to 300 copies only. Cover erroneously lists Wondrous Stories on side four

Yesshows '88
Rhythm Of Love, Hold On, Heart Of The Sunrise, Big Generator, Changes, Shoot High - Aim Low, Owner Of A Lonely Heart
Main Event ME-004
Houston, Texas, USA 19 February 1988
Deluxe colour cover

Big Tour - Volume 1
Dancing Through The Light, The Golden Age, Tango, Rhythm Of Love, Hold On, Heart Of The Sunrise, Big Generator, Changes, Shoot High - Aim Low, Holy Lamb, Solly's Beard, Owner Of A Lonely Heart
Toasted Records TRW 1903
Pacific Amphitheatre, Costa Mesa, USA 5 March 1988 and Paris, France demos 1979
Double album with deluxe colour cover

Big Tour - Volume 2
Yours Is No Disgrace, Nous Sommes Du Soleil, Amazing Bass, And You And I, Wurm, Love Will Find A Way, Your Move, I've Seen All Good People, Roundabout, In The Tower, Friend Of A Friend, Everybody Loves You, The Flower Girl
Toasted Records TRW 1904
Pacific Amphitheatre, Costa Mesa, USA 5 March 1988 and Paris, France demos 1979
Another double album with full-colour deluxe cover

Roundabout '88
Rhythm Of Love Theme, Rhythm Of Love, Hold On, Heart Of The Sunrise, Big Generator, Changes, Shoot High - Aim Low, Holy Lamb, Tony Kaye solo, Trevor Rabin solo, Soon, Owner Of A Lonely Heart, Yours Is No Disgrace, And You And I, Starship Trooper, Love Will Find A Way, I've Seen All Good People, Roundabout
Y 8471/2
Olympic Pool, Tokyo, Japan 4-7 April 1988
Double Album. Japanese bootleg with deluxe colour cover

ABWH - Long Distance Roundabout
Time And A Word, Owner Of A Lonely Heart, Teakbois, Howe solo, Wakeman solo, Long Distance Runaround, Birthright, And You And I, I've Seen All Good People, Close To The Edge, Close To The Edge (cont'd), Brother Of Mine, Brother Of Mine (cont'd), The Meeting, Heart Of The Sunrise, The Order Of The Universe, Roundabout
Chance Records YES-01
Shoreline Amphitheatre, Mountain View, USA 9 September 1989
Double album with deluxe colour cover

BOOTLEG CDs
What follows is a list of all the known Yes bootlegs that were professionally produced, i.e. in a proper factory/pressing plant. The CDs are all silver disc originals made from glass masters in a CD pressing plant. We have not listed CD-Rs (recordable CDs), as these are far too numerous to mention and, in any event, have little or no value as an artefact. CD-Rs are always worth checking out for the recorded material on them but, for collectors, the original silver disc is the essential item to look for. To distinguish between original CDs and CD-R copies, a check of the playing side is all that is usually necessary, as CD-Rs have a colour tint whereas professionally produced CDs are clear, bright silver. Another give-away is the inner clear plastic circle - CD-Rs will nearly always have the model number (RX74 for example) printed on them.

The Goddess Of Mercy
Crawdaddy Simone (Syndicats), You Came Along, Don't Make Me Blue (Warriors), Never My Love, All Of The Time, Autobiography Of A Mississippi Hobo, Sonata Of Love (Hans Christian), Out Of My Mind, Someone In Heaven Knows (Hans Christian unreleased demos), Marlena, What I'd Say (Federals), The Only Ones, Pageing Sullivan (Wild Ones w/ Rick, J. Page and Jon Hiseman), Shy Boy, Angel Fallen Night Vom Himmel (Keith West & Steve Howe), My Sly Sadie, Please Stop The Wedding, Freedom, I Don't Need No Doctor (Paul Williams set w/Alan White), I'm The Noise In My Head, Don't You Know (Griffin w/Alan White), Satisfied Street, Do Right Woman Do Right Man, Who Belongs To You, Beautiful Land (Happy Magazine), Mary Man (Alice Cooper w/Rick Wakeman), No More Mr Nice Guy (Alice Cooper w/Chris Squire), Fight For My Country #1, Hound Dog Down, Janie Slow Down, Fight For My Country #2, Fight For My Country #3 (Balls With Alan White & Denny Laine demos), Marshwood (instr), West country, Wherever My Love Goes, Sad Song, Leit Molit, The Visit, I Hope You Feel Better, Company Going Home Song, Wherever My Love Goes #2 (Keith West & Steve Howe)
Highland HL405/406
Pre-Yes recordings 1964-71
Japanese Double CD – Studio recordings (Taken from somewhat scratchy vinyl)

Moments
Revealing Science Of God, Beyond & Before, Images Of You & Me, Jeanetta, Dear Father, Beyond & Before, For Everyone, Dear Father, Eleanor Rigby, I See You, Witchi-Tai-Po
The Third Eye Liquid Sky KT003
Mabel Greer's Toyshop sessions 1968 and Sheffield, UK 1969 and BBC sessions (+) Digipak sleeve

Sons Of Olias
Flowerman, 14 Hour Technicolour Dream, Created By Clive, Grounded(The Syn), Beyond & Before, Images Of You & Me, Jeanetta (Mabel Greer's Toyshop), Do You Remember?, I Want You, Mr Jones, 1,000 years (Bodast), Blow Up, Strawberry Fields, Now Your Time Has Come, Journey Of Timothy Chase, Shy Boy, My White Bicycle, Real Life Permanent Dream, Colonel Brown (Tomorrow Live BBC), I Lied To Auntie May (Peter Banks's first band), Things She Says, Stop Wait A Minute, You're On Your Own, Why Must They Criticise? (In Crowd), Eleanor Rigby, I See You (Yes live 69)
Tendolar TDR 063
Pre-Yes recordings plus Yes live UK 1969
Japanese CD

Yessessions
Created By Clive, Grounded, Flowerman, Fourteen Hour Technicolour Dream (The Syn), Beyond & Before, Images Of You And Me, Jeanetta (Mabel Greer's Toyshop), Looking Around (session 4 June 1969), For Everyone (session 7 April 1970), America (session 20 October 1970), I've Seen All Good People, Astral Traveller, Everydays , Bye Bye Goodbye Baby (w/Iron Butterfly, Sweden 25 January 1971), Yours Is No Disgrace, I've Seen All Good People (Beat Club, Bremen 28 January 1971), Starship Trooper (Top Of The Pops 1 April 1971), Clap, Perpetual Change, America (Sportpalast, Berlin 5 June 1971), Roundabout (Demo September 1971), I've Seen All Good People (Crystal Palace 31 July 1971), The Fish, Heart Of The Sunrise, Steve solo (Fragile tour rehearsals October 1971), I've Seen All Good People – Perpetual Change – Long Distance Runaround – Heart Of The Sunrise – Mood For A Day – Yours Is No Disgrace (BBC Hempstead 3 October 1971), The Revealing Science Of God (Bob Harris Top Gear 1 November 1973), Don't Kill The Whale, Madrigal, On The Silent Wings Of Freedom (promo versions)
Highland HL 296/297/298
Various sessions, recordings, out takes and appearances 1967-1978
Japanese Triple CD

In The Beginning
Introduction, No Opportunity Necessary- No Experience Needed, Dear Father, Every Little Thing, Something's Coming, Eleanor Rigby, Dear Father, I See You (Peter solo)
Highland HL055 #Y12
Essen, Germany 9 October 1969 and Hamburg, Germany October 1969 and Penthouse, Sheffield, UK 1969
Japanese CD

BBC Sessions 1969-70
Dear Father, Everydays, Sweetness, Something's Coming, Sweetness, Every Little Thing, Looking Around, Astral Traveller, Then, Everydays, For Everyone
8 Ball 024
Top Gear w/John Peel, Johnny Walker Show + Sunday Show w/John Peel
Japanese CD

First Steps
Sweetness, Something's Coming, Looking Around, Everydays, Sweet Dreams, Then, Time And A Word, Starship Trooper, Roundabout, No Opportunity Necessary - No Experience Needed, Yours Is No Disgrace
Abraxas Aulica A 114
BBC sessions 1970/71

Live in London 1970-71
Roundabout, Sweet Dreams, Everydays, Yours Is No Disgrace, Looking Around, Sweetness, Then, Looking Around
Armando Curio DIR 60
Wembley 1978, DLT show 25 January 1970, Symonds on Sunday show 10 August 1969, Beat Club 28 January 1971, Top Gear 12 January 1969

Looking Around
Everydays, Sweetness, Something's Coming, Sweet Dreams, Then, Looking Around, America, Starship Trooper, No Opportunity Necessary - No Experience Needed, Something's Coming
The Early Years 02-CD-3340
BBC Sessions, live cuts 1969/70 + Something's Coming (mono)

Looking Around
I've Seen All Good People, Astral Traveller, Everydays, Sweetness, Something's Coming, Sweet Dreams, Then, Looking Around, No Opportunity Necessary - No Experience Needed
Lost Rose LR07
BBC 1969/70 and Gothenburg, Germany 24 January 1971 and Belgium TV 1970

Cracks Appeared In The Air
Opening (excerpt from 'Also Sprach Zarathusra'), Yours Is No Disgrace, I've Seen All Good People, Clap, Classical Gas, Perpetual Change (incl. drum solo)
Highland HL486
Berlin Arts Festival, Germany 27 March 1971
Japanese CD

Every Little Thing
No Opportunity Necessary - No Experience Needed, Then, Every Little Thing, Astral Traveller, Everydays
Highland HL419
Cologne Pop Festival, Germany 4 April 1970
Japanese CD

Roundhouse '71
Yours Is No Disgrace, I've Seen All Good People, Clap, Perpetual Change, Everydays, America
Highland HL392
The Roundhouse, London 27 February 1971 (date unconfirmed)
Japanese CD

2001
Opening (2001), Yours Is No Disgrace, I've Seen All Good People, Clap-Classical Gas, Perpetual Change (incl. drum solo), Everydays (incl. keyboard solo), America
Highland HL068 #Y13
Rome, Italy May 1971
Japanese CD

Milano Stage '71
Yours Is No Disgrace, I've Seen All Good People, Clap, Perpetual Change, Everydays, America
Highland HL392
Teatro, Milan, Italy 10 May 1971

Lost Yesyears
Dear Father, Eleanor Rigby, I See You, Clap, Perpetual Change, America, For Everyone, I've Seen All Good People, Astral Traveller, Everydays, Sweetness, Something's Coming, Dear Father, Beyond And Before, Looking Around, Sweet Dreams, America, Starship Trooper
Highland HL001/2 #Y1
Sheffield, UK 1969 and Gothenburg, Sweden 1971 and Berlin, Germany 1971 + sessions
Japanese double CD

It's Love
Introduction, Yours Is No Disgrace, I've Seen All Good People, Clap, Perpetual Change (incl. drum solo), It's Love (incl. bass solo)
Highland HL308
Gaelic Park, New York, USA 23 July 1971
Japanese CD

In The Beginning Is A Future
Yours Is No Disgrace, Your Move, All Good People, Clap, Perpetual Change, Roundabout (demo)
Rocket Sound RS 1002
Yale Bowl, Newhaven, USA 24 July 1971
Japanese CD

Perpetual Change
Yours Is No Disgrace, Your Move, All Good People, Clap, Classical Gas, Perpetual Change, America
Hiwatt YS001
Yale Bowl, Newhaven, USA 24 July 1971 and Berlin 5 June 1971
Japanese CD

The Model For Success
Yours Is No Disgrace, I've Seen All Good People, America, Clap, Perpetual Change (23 August 1971), Astral Traveller, I've Seen All Good People, Clap, America (9 August 1970)
Highland HL409
Crystal Palace Garden Party IV 23 August 1971 and Plumpton Jazz Festival 9 August 1970, UK
Japanese CD

Out The Valley
Opening, Roundabout, I've Seen All Good People, Mood For A Day, Clap, Heart Of The Sunrise, Rick solo, Long Distance Runaround, The Fish, Perpetual Change , Yours Is No Disgrace, I've Seen All Good People, Astral Traveller, Everydays, America, I've Seen All Good People
Highland HL169/170
Civic Centre, Wolverhampton, UK 10 November 1971 and Gothenberg, Germany 24 January 1971 and Berlin, Germany 5 June 1971 and Plumpton, UK 14 August 1970

A Venture Seeker
Opening, Roundabout, I've Seen All Good People, Mood For A Day, Clap, Heart Of The Sunrise, Rick solo, Long Distance Runaround, The Fish, Perpetual Change , Yours Is No Disgrace, I've Seen All Good People, Astral Traveller, Everydays, America, I've Seen All Good People, plus bonus cuts
Highland HL341/342
Civic Hall, Wolverhampton, UK
10 November 1971 (cover states 9 November 1971)
Japanese Double CD (Different source tape – same show)

Down At The Edge
Opening, Siberian Khatru, I've Seen All Good People, Close To The Edge, Mood For A Day, Clap, Heart Of The Sunrise, And You And I, Six Wives, Roundabout, Yours Is No Disgrace, Clap-Classical Gas, Perpetual Change (incl. drum solo), Everydays (incl. keyboard solo)
Highland HL110/111 #Y20
Hartford, Connecticut, USA 14 August 1972 and Stuttgart, Germany 16 April 1971
Japanese double CD

The White Album
I've Seen All Good People, Heart Of The Sunrise, Rick solo, Long Distance Runaround, Yours Is No Disgrace, The Gates Of Delirium
TKCD 1015
Amsterdam, Holland 1972 and Hollywood Bowl, California, USA 1975

The White Album
Live Storm LSCD 51015: (as above)
Pirate of TKCD 1015

Not Fragile
Introduction (Firebird Suite), Roundabout, I've Seen All Good People, Mood For A Day, Clap, Heart Of The Sunrise, Six Wives, Long Distance Runaround-The Fish, Perpetual Change (incl. drum solo), Yours Is No Disgrace (incl. guitar solo)
Highland HL076/77 #Y14
San Francisco, California, USA
10 March 1972
Japanese double CD

Guessing Problems Only
Firebird Suite, Siberian Khatru, I've Seen All Good People, Mood for A Day, Clap, And You And I, Heart Of The Sunrise, Close To The Edge, excerpts from Six Wives, Roundabout, Yours Is No Disgrace
Highland HL414/5
Glasgow, UK 4 October 1972
Japanese Double CD

Suite Distance
Opening (Firebird Suite), Siberian Khatru, I've Seen All Good People, Mood For A Day, Clap, Heart Of The Sunrise, And You And I, Six Wives Of Henry VIII, Roundabout, Yours Is No Disgrace
Music Nation MN001
Columbia Post Pavilion, Maryland, USA
13 August 1972
Japanese CD - Soundboard recording

Crystal Palace Garden V
Opening, Siberian Khatru, I've Seen All Good People, Mood For A Day, And You And I, Heart Of The Sunrise, Close To The Edge, Roundabout, Yours Is No Disgrace
Highland HL420/421
Crystal Palace Garden Party V, London, UK
2 September 1972
Japanese Double CD

Alternate Yessongs
Opening, Siberian Khatru, I've Seen All Good People, Heart Of The Sunrise, Clap, And You And I, Close To The Edge, Rick's Symphony (Six Wives), Roundabout, Yours Is No Disgrace, I've Seen All Good People, Clap, Perpetual Change
Highland HL003/4 #Y2
Duke University, North Carolina 11 November 1972 and Yale Bowl, Connecticut 24 July 1971
Japanese double CD

Heart Of The Sunrise
Roundabout, Heart Of The Sunrise, And You And I, Close To The Edge, Starship Trooper
Easy Rider Years 9409279
Live 1972 (all cuts from Yessongs album)

Yessongs
I've Seen All Good People, Clap, Close To The Edge, Roundabout, And You And I, Yours Is No Disgrace, excerpts from Starship Trooper
Pigeon GIG-10
Rainbow Theatre, London, UK
1972 (Part of Yessongs film soundtrack)
Japanese CD

Yessongs
I've Seen All Good People, Clap, Close To The Edge, Roundabout, And You And I, Yours Is No Disgrace, excerpts from Starship Trooper
QWSC-9608: (As above)
Copy of Pigeon GIG-10

Gold Stainless Nail
Siberian Khatru, I've Seen All Good People, Mood For A Day, Heart Of The Sunrise, And You & I, excerpts from Six Wives, Roundabout, Yours Is No Disgrace
Highland HL418
Gaelic Park, New York, USA 16 August 1972
Japanese CD

The Wizard Of Yes
Siberian Khatru, I've seen All Good People, Clap (incl. Mood for a Day), Heart Of The Sunrise, And You And I, Close To The Edge, excerpts From Six Wives, Roundabout, Yours Is No Disgrace
Highland HL507/8
US Tour 8/72 + 4/73
Japanese 2CD set (superb audience recordings)

An Eve Of "Autobiography"
Opening, Siberian khatru, I've Seen All Good People, Heart Of The Sunrise, Mood For A Day, Clap, And You And I, Close To The Edge, excerpts From Six Wives, Roundabout, Yours Is No Disgrace, Starship Trooper
Highland HL425/426
Koseinenken Hall, Tokyo, Japan 8 March 1973
Japanese Double CD – Box Set with miniature tour book and ticket stub. Picture discs

Hallelujah
Opening theme, Siberian Khatru, I've Seen All Good People, Heart Of The Sunrise, Mood For A Day, Clap, And You And I, Close To The Japanese Edge, Close To The Edge (cont'd), keyboard solo, Hallelujah, keyboard solo, Roundabout, Yours Is No Disgrace, Starship Trooper
Dirty 13 Volume 1 D13-01 A/B
Tokyo, Japan 9 March 1973
Double CD

And You And I
Siberian Khatru, Heart Of The Sunrise, Sakura - Sakura, Mood For A Day, And You And I, Close To The Edge, The Six Wives Of Henry VIII, Roundabout, Yours Is No Disgrace, Starship Trooper
Rag Doll Music RDM-942007 A/B
Live, Tokyo, Japan 12 March 1973
Japanese double CD

Absolutely Necessary
Yours Is No Disgrace, I've Seen All Good People, Clap-Classical Gas, Perpetual Change-drum solo, Siberian Khatru, I've Seen All Good People, Heart Of The Sunrise, And You And I, Close To The Edge, Roundabout, Starship Trooper
Red Hot RH024/025
Adelaide, Australia 21 March 1973 and Yale Bowl, Connecticut 24 July 1971
Japanese double CD in card sleeve

Cans And Brahms
Opening, Siberian Khatru, I've Seen All Good

People, Heart Of The Sunrise, And You And I, Six Wives (incl. Cans and Brahms), Roundabout, Starship Trooper
Highland HL084 #Y16
Adelaide, Australia
21 March 1973 (Same source tape as above)
Japanese CD

Du Soleil
Opening, Siberian Khatru, Heart Of The Sunrise, Close To The Edge, The Revealing Science Of God, The Remembering, The Ancient, Ritual
Highland HL090/91 #Y18
Sheffield City Hall, UK 27 November 1973
Japanese Double CD

Topographic Ocean View
Firebird Suite, Siberian Khatru, And You And I, Close To The Edge, The Revealing Science Of God (this track actually from Detroit 28 February 1974), The Remembering, The Ancient, Ritual, Roundabout
Highland HL384/385
Miami Stadium, Florida, USA
8 February 1974
Japanese Double CD in digipak sleeve

Songs From Topographic Ocean
The Revealing Science Of God, The Remembering, The Ancient, Ritual
ZA 75/76
Madison Square Garden, New York, USA
18 February 1974
Japanese double CD

Science Of God Story
Firebird Suite, Siberian Khatru, And You And I, Close To The Edge, The Revealing Science Of God, The Remembering, The Ancient, Ritual – a prelude, Ritual, Roundabout
Highland HL416/417
Cobo Hall, Detroit, Michigan, USA
28 February 1974
Japanese Double CD

Topographic
The Revealing Science Of God, The Remembering, The Ancient, Ritual, The Revealing Science Of God
Highland HL044/45 #Y11
Detroit, Michigan, USA 28 February 1974 and BBC Top Gear 1 November 1973
Japanese Double CD

Long Beach Arena
Close To The Edge, The Revealing Science Of God, The Ancient, Roundabout, Starship Trooper
Pig's Eye BS6
Long Beach Arena, California, USA
19 March 1974
Japanese CD - cover design matches original vinyl bootleg

Tales From The Edge
Opening, Siberian Khatru, And You And I, Close To The Edge, The Revealing Science Of God, The Ancient, Ritual, Roundabout, Starship Trooper
Highland HL141/142 #Y30
Ludwigshapen, Germany 14 April 1974
Japanese Double CD

Paris '74
Opening, Siberian Khatru, And You And I, Close To The Edge, The Revealing Science Of God, The Ancient, Ritual, Roundabout, Starship Trooper
Highland HL132/33 #Y26
Paris, France 19 April 1974
Japanese Double CD

South Side Of The Tulsa
Firebird Suite, Sound Chaser, Close To The Edge, To Be Over, Ritual (incl. Dance Of The Dawn), Roundabout, South Side Of The Sky
Highland HL482/3
Civic Centre, Tulsa, Oklahoma, USA
5 December 1974
Japanese Double CD

Experience The Future
Sound Chaser, To Be Over, The Revealing Science Of God, The Ancient
Diamonds In Your Ear DIYE 25
Boston Gardens, Massachusetts, USA
12 November 1974 and Long Beach Arena, Miami, Florida, USA 19 March 1974

Re-Evolution
Sound Chaser, To Be Over, Close To The Edge, And You And I, Roundabout, I've Seen All Good People
Flashback 08 90 1024
Boston Gardens, Massachusetts, USA
12 November 1974 and Wembley Arena, London UK 28 October 1978

Roundabout
Sound Chaser, To Be Over, Close To The Edge, And You And I, Roundabout, I've Seen All Good People
Oil Well RDC CD 060
Boston Gardens, Massachusetts, USA
12 November 1974 and Wembley Arena, London UK 28 October 1978

Close To The Edge
Sound Chaser, To Be Over, Close To The Edge, And You And I, Roundabout, I've Seen All Good People
Allegra CD 9018
Boston Gardens, Massachusetts, USA
12 November 1974 and Wembley Arena, London UK 28 October 1978

Sound Chaser
Sound Chaser, Roundabout, The Gates Of Delirium
Chapter One CO 25140
Boston Gardens, Massachusetts, USA
12 November 1974

Something Wonderful
To Be Over, And You And I, Gates Of Delirium, Roundabout
Prime Of Rarities PRCD 1009
Boston Gardens, Massachusetts, USA
12 November 1974 (cover states Dallas, Texas, USA 1975)

The Gates Of Boston Garden
Opening, Sound Chaser, Close To The Edge, To Be Over, The Gates Of Delirium, And You And I, Roundabout (12 November 1974), I've Seen All Good People, Mood For A Day, Long Distance Runaround, Moraz solo, Clap, Ritual, Sweet Dreams, Yours Is No Disgrace (10 May 1975)
Highland HL339/340
Boston Gardens, Massachusetts, USA
12 November 1974 (from master reel) and QPR Stadium, London, UK 10 May 1975
Japanese Double CD - Soundboard

Full Of Nightmarish
Opening, Soundchaser, Close To The Edge, To Be Over, Gates Of Delirium, And You And I, Ritual (incl. Dance Of The Dawn), Roundabout, Siberian Khatru
Highland HL478/9
Hollywood Sportatorium, Florida 28 November 74
Japanese 2CD

Siberian Khatru
Your Move, I've Seen All Good People, And You And I, Siberian Khatru, Starship Trooper, Close To The Edge, Roundabout
Lobster Records CD 021
Wembley, London, UK 28 October 1978 and Boston Gardens, Massachusetts, USA
12 November 1974

Roundabout
Your Move, I've Seen All Good People, And You And I, Siberian Khatru, Starship Trooper, Close To The Edge, Roundabout
Wembley, London, UK 28 October 1978 and Boston Gardens, Massachusetts, USA
12 November 1974
Living Legend LLRCD 082
Cover misnames track 1 as 'All Your Love'

Roundabout
Your Move, I've Seen All Good People, And You And I, Siberian Khatru, Starship Trooper, Close To The Edge, Roundabout
Wembley, London, UK 28 October 1978 and Boston Gardens, Massachusetts, USA
12 November 1974
MRL 045

Live in L.A. Forum 1974 & 1987
Best Of Live Series BOLS 004
Boston Gardens, Massachusetts, USA
12 November 1974 and Houston, Texas, USA
5 March 1988

Live At L.A. Forum, L.A. USA 1974 & 1987
International Pop - INP 041
Boston Gardens, Massachusetts, USA
12 November 1974 and Houston, Texas, USA
5 March 1988

Siberian Khatru
Boston Gardens, Massachusetts, USA
12 November 1974 and Houston, Texas, USA
5 March 1988
Live Line LL 15486

The Remembering
Close To The Edge, To Be Over, Gates Of Delirium, And You And I, Ritual (incl. The Remembering), Roundabout
Highland HL145/146
Fort Worth, Texas, USA 4 December 1974
Japanese Double CD

Electric Freedom
The Firebird Suite, Sound Chaser, Close To The Edge, To Be Over, The Gates Of Delirium, Your Move, Mood For A Day, Long Distance Runaround, keyboard solo, Clap, And You And I, Ritual, Roundabout, Sweet Dreams, Yours Is No Disgrace
The Gold Standard EF-122
Queens Park Rangers Football Stadium, London, UK 10 May 1975
Double CD - Soundboard recording

Yes
Introduction, Sound Chaser, Close To The Edge, To Be Over, The Gates Of Delirium, I've Seen All Good People, Long Distance Runaround, Clap, And You And I, Ritual, Roundabout, Sweet Dreams, Yours Is No Disgrace
HQ 08/2
Queens Park Rangers Football Stadium, London, UK 10 May 1975
Double CD in deluxe digipak cover. Soundboard recording

Soon The Light
Opening, Sound Chaser, Close To The Edge, To Be Over, The Gates Of Delirium, I've Seen All Good People (acoustic), Mood For A Day, Long Distance Runaround (acoustic), keyboards solo, Clap, And You And I, Ritual, Roundabout, Sweet Dreams
Highland HL099/100 #Y19
Long Beach, California, USA 23 June 1975
Japanese Double CD

The Swiss Poodle
Firebird Suite, Sound Chaser, Close To The Edge, And You And I, Gates Of Delirium, Ritual, Roundabout
Highland HL480/1
Ryhearson Stadium, Ypsilanti, Michigan, USA
20 July 1975
Japanese Double CD

Reading 23/8/75
Opening, Sound chaser, Close To The Edge, And You And I, Awaken (improvising), The Gates Of Delirium , I've Seen All Good People (acoustic), Ancient (acoustic), Ritual, Roundabout
Highland HL048/49 #Y10
Reading Festival, UK 23 August 1975
Japanese Double CD

Solo Rehearsals
Heart Of The Sunrise (vocal by Chris Squire), Heart Of The Sunrise (vocal by Jon), excerpts From 'I', Flight Of The Moorglade, Sound Chaser, The Remembering
Highland HL089 #Y17
Millersville, Pennsylvania, USA May 1976
Japanese CD

Excerpts From "Solo Album"
Opening – And You And I (Eclipse), Siberian Khatru, I've Seen All Good People, Ram, Hold Out Your Hand, You By My Side, Roundabout, Break Away From It All, Beginnings (incl. Australia), One Way Rag, Ritual (drum solo),excerpts From Story Of I, Heart Of The Sunrise, Sweet Dreams
Highland HL408
Roanoke, Virginia, USA 28 May 1976
Japanese CD

Quasi-Mystical Vision
Siberian Khatru, Sound Chaser, I've Seen All Good People, Gates Of Delirium, Long Distance Runaround, Clap, Sunhillow, Heart Of The Sunrise
Turtle Records TR-235
Roosevelt Stadium, New Jersey, USA
17 June 1976
Four way foldout card sleeve

Live Vol 1
Siberian Khatru, Sound Chaser, I've Seen All Good People, Gates Of Delirium, Long Distance Runaround, Clap, Sunhillow, Heart Of The Sunrise
Joker Records JOK-026-A
Roosevelt Stadium, New Jersey, USA
17 June 1976
Australian CD - FM Broadcast

The Story Of Relayer
Opening - And You And I (Eclipse), Siberian Khatru, Sound Chaser, I've Seen All Good People, Long Distance Runaround-keyboard solo, Clap, Tour instrumental jamming, Heart Of The Sunrise, The Gates Of Delirium, Ritual, I'm Down, Roundabout
Highland HL034/35 #Y8
Roosevelt Stadium, New Jersey, USA
17 June 1976
Japanese double CD - FM broadcast

Song Of Relayer
Opening - And You And I (Eclipse), Siberian Khatru, Sound Chaser, I've Seen All Good People, Long Distance Runaround-keyboard solo, Clap, Tour instrumental jamming, Heart Of The Sunrise, The Gates Of Delirium, Ritual, I'm Down, Roundabout
Highland HL348/349
Roosevelt Stadium, New Jersey, USA
17 June 1976
Japanese Double CD – FM Broadcast. Reissue in slipcase with gold discs and better sound quality

Solo Tour '76
And You And I (Eclipse), Siberian Khatru, Sound Chaser, I've Seen All Good People, Clap, Gates Of Delirium, Long Distance Runaround, Patrick solo, Dance Of Ranyart, Heart Of The Sunrise, Ritual, Roundabout
Highland HL371/372
Vancouver Coliseum, Canada
22 July 1976
Japanese Double CD

Alternate Yesshow
Opening (And You And I), Siberian Khatru, Sound Chaser, I've Seen All Good People, Gates Of Delirium, Long Distance Runaround, Patrick solo (incl. Story Of I), Clap, Jon harp solo (incl. Olias), Heart Of The Sunrise, Ritual, Roundabout
Highland HL492/3 – Cobo Hall, Detroit, Michigan
7 August 76
Japanese 2CD

Making For The One
Parallels #1, Parallels #2, Steve's acoustic covers solo, Going For The One #1, Awaken #1, Steve's electric solo #1, Parallels #3, Rick's solo (incl. Turn Of The Century), Parallels #4, Parallels #5-10, Parallels #11, Jam #1, Awaken #2, Turn Of The Century #1, Turn Of The Century #2, Jam #2, Awaken #3, Awaken #4, Turn Of The Century #3, Awaken #5, Turn Of The Century #4, Parallels #12, Steve's acoustic covers solo #2, Going For The One #2, Jam #3, Steve's electric solo #2, Jam #4, Wondrous Stories, Going For The One #3, Awaken #6
Highland HL121/122 #Y22
Studio sessions, Mountain Studios, Montreux, Switzerland 1976/77
Japanese Double CD

Going For The One Tour Rehearsals
Awaken, Parallels #1, And You And I #1, And You And I #2, Solos, Parallels #2, Turn Of The Century
Highland HL024 #Y6
Lititz, Pennsylvania, USA July 1977
Japanese CD

Listen In Time
Opening, Parallels, I've Seen All Good People, Close To The Edge, Wondrous Stories, And You And I, The Colours Of The Rainbow, Turn Of The Century, Ram, Awaken - a prelude, Awaken, Starship Trooper, Going For The One, Roundabout
Highland HL114/15 #Y21
Wheeling, West Virginia, USA
31 July 1977
Japanese Double CD

Light Of Images
Opening, Parallels, I've Seen All Good People, Close To The Edge, Wondrous Stories, Colours Of The Rainbow, Turn Of The Century, And You And I, Going For The One, Awaken - a prelude, Awaken, Starship Trooper, Roundabout
Highland HL143/44
Philadelphia Spectrum, Pennsylvania, USA
3 August 1977
Japanese Double CD

Wondrous Mystery Tour
Firebird Suite, Parallels, I've Seen All Good People, Close To The Edge, Wondrous Stories, Colours Of The Rainbow, Turn Of The Century, And You And I, Awaken – a prelude, Awaken, Starship Trooper, Parallels, Close To The Edge, Wondrous Stories, Colours Of The Rainbow, And You And I
Highland HL248/249
Springfield, Massachusetts, USA 10 August 1977 and Madison Square Garden, New York, USA
6 August 1977
Japanese Double CD

Prelude To Awaken
Opening, Parallels, I've Seen All Good People, Close To The Edge, Wondrous Stories, Colours Of The Rainbow, Turn Of The Century, And You And I, Prelude to Awaken, Awaken, Starship Trooper, Roundabout, Yours Is No Disgrace
Highland HL212/213
Boston Gardens, Massachusetts, USA
12 August 1977
Japanese Double CD

High Vibration Ship
Firebird Suite, Parallels, I've Seen All Good People,

Close To The Edge, Wondrous Stories, Colours Of The Rainbow, Turn Of The Century, And You And I, Awaken – a prelude, Awaken, Starship Trooper, Yours Is No Disgrace
Highland HL412/413
Cobo Hall, Detroit, Michigan, USA
22 August 1977
Japanese Double CD

A Wondrous Evening With Yes
Firebird Suite, Parallels, I've Seen All Good People, Close To The Edge, Wondrous Stories, Beautiful Land (Colours Of The Rainbow), Turn Of The Century, Tour Song, And You And I, Going For The One, Flight Jam, Awaken, Roundabout
Anon
Midsouth Coliseum, Memphis, Tennessee, USA
7 November 1977
Japanese double CD

Going For The Germany
Firebird, Parallels, I've Seen All Good People, Close To The Edge, Wondrous Stories, Colours Of The Rainbow, Turn Of The Century, Tour Song (thank you Germany), And You And I, Going For The One, Awaken – a prelude, Awaken, Roundabout, Sound check (before the show)
Highland HL390/391
Nurenberg, Germany 19 November 1977
Japanese Double CD

Soleil Our Sights
Firebird, Parallels, I've Seen All Good People, Close To The Edge, Wondrous Stories, Turn Of The Century, Tour Song, And You And I, Going For The One, Awaken – a prelude, Awaken, Roundabout, Nous Sommes Du Soleil, Starship Trooper
Highland HL410/411
Rhein Necke Halle, Heidelberg, Germany
21 November 1977
Japanese Double CD

Swan Lake Stories
Opening, Parallels, I've Seen All Good People, Close To The Edge, Wondrous Stories, Colours Of The Rainbow, Turn Of The Century, And You And I, Rick intro, Going For The One, Awaken – a prelude, Awaken, Roundabout, Yours Is No Disgrace (12 November), Tour Song, And You And I, Swan Song jam, Going For The One (28 November)
Highland HL354/355
Gothenberg, Sweden 12 November 1977 and Berlin, Germany 28 November 1977
Japanese Double CD

Moment's Delight
Firebird Suite, Parallels, I've Seen All Good People, Close To The Edge, Wondrous Stories, Colours Of The Rainbow, Turn Of The Century, The Tour Song (Paris), And You And I, Cosmic Mind Jam - Going For The One, Prelude to Awaken, Awaken, Roundabout, Nous Sommes Du Soleil, Starship Trooper (5 December), Nous Sommes Du Soleil, Yours Is No Disgrace, Roundabout (6 December)
Highland HL272/273
Paris, France 5 & 6 December 1977
Japanese Double CD

On Digital Reels
Picasso #4, Picasso #5, Amazing Grace #1, Amazing Grace #2, Money #5, Money #6, Celestial Seasons, Richard #1, Richard #2, Jon's Song #1 (Days), Jon's Song #2 (Days), Some Are Born, Rail Fourteen, Tempus Fugit, Untitled 1, Does It Really Happen, Untitled 2, Untitled 3
Diamonds In Your Ear DIYE 29
Studio Demos 1978 & 1980
1,000 numbered copies

Digital Reels & Master Reels
Picasso #1, Picasso #2, Amazing Grace #1 #2, Money #5, Money #6, Celestial Seasons, Richard #1, Richard #2, Days #1, Days #2, Some Are Born, Rail Fourteen (incl. Arriving UFO), Dance Thru The Light, The Golden Age, In The Tower, Friend Of A Fiend, To Let You Know, Everybody Loves You, Flower Girl
Highland HL123 #Y24
Studio Demos 1978 & 1979
Japanese CD

Releasing The Parallels
Opening, Siberian Khatru, Heart Of The Sunrise, Time And A Word, Long Distance Runaround, The Fish, Perpetual Change, Soon, Circus Of Heaven, Parallels, Release - Release, Awaken - A Prelude, Awaken, I've Seen All Good People
Highland HL433/434
Boston, Massachusetts, USA
31 August 1978
Japanese Double CD

Circus Of New Heaven
Opening, Siberian Khatru, Heart Of The Sunrise, Future Times – Rejoice, Circus Of Heaven, Time And A Word, Long Distance Runaround, The Fish, Perpetual Change, Soon, Don't Kill The Whale, Clap, Parallels, Madrigal (vocal version), On The Silent Wings Of Freedom, Excerpt from Six Wives, Awaken
Highland HL214/215
The Coliseum, New Haven, Connecticut, USA
4 September 1978
Japanese Double CD

Madrigal Mystery Tour
Opening - Siberian Khatru, Heart Of The Sunrise, (A) Future Times (B) Rejoice, Circus Of Heaven, Medley: Time And A Word, Long Distance Runaround, The Fish (incl. Survival, Ritual), Perpetual Change, The Gates Of Delirium (Soon), Don't Kill The Whale, Madrigal - Clap, Starship Trooper, Rick solo Incl. Catherine Of Aragon & Catherine Howard, The Battle, Awaken, I've Seen All Good People, Roundabout, Madrigal, On The Silent Wings Of Freedom, And You And I
Highland HL046/47 #Y9
Richfield Coliseum, Cleveland, Ohio, USA
19 September 1978 and Inglewood Forum, California, USA 6 October 1978
Japanese Double CD. All tracks FM stereo

Wembley Arena 1978
Siberian Khatru, Heart Of The Sunrise, The Circus Of Heaven, Time And A Word, Long Distance Runaround, Perpetual Change, The Sun Will Lead Us (Soon), Don't Kill The Whale, Clap, Starship Trooper, Bass solo, I've Seen All Good People, Roundabout
Electric Monkey EM-05/06
Wembley Arena, London, UK 28 October 1978
Double CD

Live In London 1975
Siberian Khatru, Heart Of The Sunrise, I've Seen All Good People, Starship Trooper, Roundabout
Super Golden Radio Shows SGRS 021
Wembley Arena, London, UK
28 October 1978

Outside The Window
Siberian Khatru, Heart Of The Sunrise, Circus Of Heaven, Don't Kill The Whale, Clap, Starship Trooper, On The Silent Wings Of Freedom, I've Seen All Good People, Roundabout
Sugarcane SC52003
Wembley Arena, London, UK
28 October 1978

Survivors Of The Future
Siberian Khatru, Heart Of The Sunrise, I've Seen All Good People, Starship Trooper, Roundabout, Heart Of The Sunrise, Starship Trooper, Time And A Word, Perpetual Change, Siberian Khatru, Don't Kill The Whale
Off The Record OTR 65509/10
Wembley Arena, London, UK 28 October 1978 and Quebec City, Canada 18 April 1979
Double CD

Rocking The Orchestra
Siberian Khatru, Heart Of The Sunrise, Circus Of Heaven, Don't Kill The Whale, Clap, Starship Trooper, Madrigal, On The Silent Wings Of Freedom, I've Seen All Good People, Roundabout, Leave It, Hold On, I've Seen All Good People, Changes, Owner Of A Lonely Heart, It Can Happen, City Of Love, Yours Is No Disgrace, Starship Trooper
Sound Carrier System SCS847011/12
Wembley, London, UK 28 October 1978 and Edmonton, Canada September 1984 and Dortmund, Germany 24 June 1984
Double CD

Anniversary Of Decade
Opening, Siberian Khatru, Heart Of The Sunrise, Circus Of Heaven, Time And A Word, Long Distance Runaround, The Fish, Perpetual Change, Soon, Don't Kill The Whale, Clap, Starship Trooper, On The Silent Wings Of Freedom, Awaken, I've Seen All Good People, Roundabout, Opening, Siberian Khatru, Future Times-Rejoice, Circus Of Heaven, Birthday Song, Time And A Word, Long Distance Runaround
Highland HL210/211
Wembley Arena, London, UK
28 October 1978 and
University of Illinois, Champaign, Illinois, USA
23 April 1979
Japanese Double CD – FM/Soundboard

Dreams Supreme
Opening, Siberian Khatru, Heart Of The Sunrise, Future Times – Rejoice, Circus Of Heaven, Time And A Word, Long Distance Runaround, The Fish, Perpetual Change, Soon, Don't Kill The Whale, Madrigal, Clap, Starship Trooper, Madrigal, On The Silent Wings Of Freedom, excerpts From Six

Wives – The Forest, Awaken, I've Seen All Good People, Roundabout
Highland HL378/379
Wembley Arena, London, UK
28 October 1978 (Matinee Show)
Japanese Double CD

Circus Of Heaven
Opening, Siberian Khatru, Heart Of The Sunrise, Future Times - Rejoice, Circus Of Heaven, Medley: Time And A Word-Long Distance Runaround-The Fish-Survival-Ritual-Perpetual Change-Soon, Don't kill the whale, Clap, Starship Trooper, Rick solo, Awaken, Tour Song, I've Seen All Good People, Roundabout-Ending
Dynamite Studio DS 94F059/60
Quebec City, Canada 18 April 1979
Double CD. Soundboard

Live In Quebec 1979
The Gates Of Delirium (Heart Of The Sunrise - first part), Heart Of The Sunrise (Cont'd), Starship Trooper, Time And A Word, Perpetual Change, Siberian Khatru, Don't Kill The Whale
Super Golden Radio Show SGRS 046
Quebec City, Canada 18 April 1979

Starship To The Gates Of Eternity
Heart Of The Sunrise, Starship Trooper, Time And A Word, Perpetual Change, Siberian Khatru, Don't Kill The Whale
American Concert Series ACS 011
Quebec City, Canada 18 April 1979

Live In Quebec City, Canada
Heart Of The Sunrise, Starship Trooper, Time And A Word, Perpetual Change, Siberian Khatru, Don't Kill The Whale
International Pop INP042
Quebec City, Canada 18 April 1979

Live In Quebec
Heart Of The Sunrise, Starship Trooper, Time And A Word, Perpetual Change, Siberian Khatru, Don't Kill The Whale, Yours Is No Disgrace
Trade Service Rare Recording Collection RRC 003
Quebec City, Canada 18 April 1979 and Dortmund, Germany 24 June 1984

Rehearsal Tales
Siberian Khatru, Gates Of Delirium (Heart Of The Sunrise, Pt. One), Heart Of The Sunrise (Pt. Two), Time And A Word, Perpetual Change, Don't Kill The Whale, Starship Trooper
No Pig NP 8842
Quebec City, Canada
18 April 1979

Tourmato (Part One + Two)
Introduction, Siberian Khatru, Heart Of The Sunrise, Future Times - Rejoice, Circus Of Heaven, Time And A Word, Long Distance Runaround, The Fish - Survival, Perpetual Change, Soon, Clap, And You And I, Starship Trooper, Rick solo, Awaken, Vancouver Song, I've Seen All Good People, Roundabout
Silver Rarities Sira 25/26 Vancouver Coliseum, Canada
5 May 1979
Double CD. FM Stereo

Seventh Age Imagination
Opening, Siberian Khatru, Heart Of The Sunrise, Future Times – Rejoice, Circus Of Heaven, Time And A Word, Long Distance Runaround, The Fish, Perpetual Change, Soon, Clap (incl. Beginnings), And You And I, Starship Trooper, excerpts From Six Wives – The Forest, Awaken, Tour Song (Vancouver), I've Seen All Good People, Roundabout
Highland HL229/230
Vancouver Coliseum, Canada
5 May 1979
Japanese Double CD. FM Stereo

Chicago Of Heaven '79
Siberian Khatru, Heart Of The Sunrise, Future Times, Rejoice, Time And A Word, Long Distance Runaround, The Fish, Perpetual Change, Soon, Clap, And You And I, Rick solo, Awaken, Circus Of Heaven, Starship Trooper, Tour Song, I've Seen All Good People, Roundabout
Cat Food 002
Chicago Amphitheatre, Chicago, Illinois, USA
4 June 1979
Double CD. FM broadcast

The Gates Of Heaven
Opening, Siberian Khatru, Heart Of The Sunrise, Future Times – Rejoice, Circus Of Heaven, Time And A Word, Long Distance Runaround, The Fish, Perpetual Change, Soon, Clap, And You And I, Excerpts From Six Wives – The Forest, Awaken, Starship Trooper, Tour Song (Chicago), I've Seen All Good People, Roundabout
Highland HL240/241
International Amphitheatre, Chicago, Illinois, USA 9 June 1979
Japanese Double CD – FM Stereo

Arriving UFO
Opening, Siberian Khatru, Heart Of The Sunrise, Future Times – Rejoice, Circus Of Heaven, Time And A Word, Long Distance Runaround, The Fish, Perpetual Change, Soon, Clap, Arriving UFO, Alan solo, And You And I, Starship Trooper, Rick solo, Awaken, Tour Song, I've Seen All Good People, Roundabout
Highland HL356/357
Miami, Florida, USA 30 June 1979
Japanese double CD

Solo works
Various solo recordings & performances 1973 - 1996, incl. Montreux Jazz Festival 19 July 1979 Anne Of Cleves, Catherine Howard, Catherine Parr (BBC Session 1 February 1973), Heartsong (Wakeman, Howe, Brian May w/Gordon Giltrap 1994), Database, Lytton's Diary (TV Themes), Catherine Howard (Korg Demo 1992), Turn Of The Century, Midnight Sun, Mood For A Day, Beginnings, Gates Of Delirium, Clap, Close To The Edge, Heat Of The Moment (Steve Howe live Danbury Connecticut 13 October 1993), Yes Medley: Intro-To Be Over-Perpetual Change-Long Distance Runaround-Wondrous Stories-Rejoice-I've Seen All Good People-The Revealing Science Of God-The Remembering-Ritual (Jon Anderson live, Albert Hall, London, UK 1 December 1980), Harp & piano intro, Leaves Of Green, Flight Of The Moorglade, Festival Jam (Montreux Jazz Festival 19 July 1979), Time And A Word (incl. Soon), Owner Of A Lonely Heart, And You And I (Jon Anderson live, Paso Nobles, California, USA 12 May 1996)
Highland HL323/324
Japanese Triple CD

SUPER GOLDEN RADIO SHOWS N° 046 — LIVE IN QUEBEC 1979

Golden Age
Dance Thru Lights, Golden Age, Tango, In The Tower, Friends Of A Friend, Everybody Loves You, Flower Girl, Awaken
Mongoose Records Mong CD004
Paris, France demos 1979 plus Awaken - Wembley Arena, London, UK 28 October 1978

The Golden Age
Chapter One CO 25182
Solo Material 1976 (TV) plus Paris, France demos 1979

The Age Of Buggles
Into The Lens, And You And I, Go Through This, keyboard solo, We Can Fly From Here, Tempus Fugit, Machine Messiah, Starship Trooper, Roundabout
Microphone Records MPH 012
Madison Square Garden, New York, USA

6 September 1980
FM Broadcast (Poor Tape)

Complete Dramatized Tour
Intro: Britten, Does It Really Happen?, Yours Is No Disgrace, Into The Lens, Clap, And You And I, Go Through This, keyboard solo, Parallels, We Can Fly From Here, Tempus Fugit, Amazing Grace - Whitefish, Machine Messiah, Starship Trooper, Roundabout
Highland HL025/26 #Y7
Japanese Double CD

Dramashow
Clap, And You And I, Go Through This, keyboard solo, We Can Fly From Here, Tempus Fugit, Into The Lens, Machine Messiah, Starship Trooper, Roundabout
Highland HL014 #Y4
Madison Square Garden, New York, USA
6 September 1980
Japanese CD. FM

Into The Drama
Opening (Britten), Does It Really Happen?, Yours Is No Disgrace, Into The Lens, Clap, And You And I, Go Through This (w/drum intro), Geoff solo, We Can Fly From Here, Tempus Fugit, Amazing Grace, The Fish, Amazing Grace (reprised), Machine Messiah, Starship Trooper, Roundabout (24 November), Go Through This (bass intro), White Car (acappella) (6 December)
Highland HL363/364
De Montford Hall, Leicester, UK 24 November 1980 and Apollo, Manchester, UK 6 December 1980
Japanese Double CD

After The Crash
Instrumental 1, Instrumental 2, Untitled 1, Untitled 2, Easily Lead, Pink And Black, Trouble Your Money, Hip To Hoo, Sixes And Sevens, Hip To Hoo-Doo Doo A Do Do, Rude World (rough mix 1), Rude World (isolated tracks), Rude World (rough mix 2)
Midas Touch Md72911
XYZ Sessions 1991 plus Robert Plant out-takes 1985 / Page & Plant remixes
Japanese Double CD

XYZ-Cinema-90XYZ
Believe It, Telephone Secrets, Instrumental, Fortune Hunter, Telephone Secrets (instr.), Make It Easy (instr.), I'm With You, Moving In, Moving With The Times, Changes, Girl It Ain't Easy, Hold On, Fools, Who Were You With Last Night, Mussorgsky excerpt – Promenade, Marmony, Tonight's Our Night, Owner Of A Lonely Heart, Would You Feel, Baby I'm Easy, It's Enough, Turn It On, Heart Beat, Slow Dancer, Don't You Know, Make It Easy, I'm Down
Highland HL294/295
Sessions / demos 1980-1982 plus live Dortmund, Germany 24 June 1984
Japanese Double CD

Cinema Sessions
Run Through The Light, Tempus Fugit, Untitled #1, Does It Really Happen? , Untitled #2, Run Through The Light, Jamming #1, Don't You Know Everyone, Make It Easy, Jamming #2, Open Your Door, Run With The Fox (demo version)
Highland HL023 #Y5
Studio demos 1980, Studio sessions 1982
Squire/White demo
Japanese CD

They!
Intro, Cinema, Leave It, Yours Is No Disgrace, Keyboards - guitar solo, Owner Of A Lonely Heart, It Can Happen, Hold On, Changes, Soon, City Of Love, Chris solo, Starship Trooper, Owner Of A Lonely Heart (2)
Beech Marten BM020/2
Montreal, Canada 27 August 1984
Double CD

G.O. 1984
Leave It, Hold On, I've Seen All Good People, Changes, Owner Of A Lonely Heart, It Can Happen, City Of Love, Yours Is No Disgrace, Starship Trooper
American Concert Series ACS 074
Edmonton, Canada September 1984
Soundtrack to the official 9012-Live Video

Live In Argentina
Introduction, Cinema, drum solo, Hold On, keyboard solo, guitar solo, Changes, Improvisation, Owner Of A Lonely Heart, It Can Happen, Amazing Grace, The Fish, Whitefish, Roundabout, Gimme Some Lovin'
Meteorite MR-06
Buenos Aires, Argentina 9 February 1985

The Alternate Generator
Love Will Find A Way, Big Generator, Rhythm Of Love, Final Eyes, I'm Running, Shoot High - Aim Low, Shoot High -Aim Low (2nd Take), Big Generator (2nd Take), Holy Lamb - backing track (not listed on cover), Let's Pretend, All Through The Night, Say What You Will, The Arms Of Love, Distant Thunder (listed but not included!)
Dancing Discs 1002
Studio demos 1987 plus Jon/Vangelis demos 1986
Limited to 300 copies

Domino
Rhythm Of Love, Hold On, Heart Of The Sunrise, Big Generator, Changes, Shoot High - Aim Low, Owner Of A Lonely Heart, And You And I, Yours Is No Disgrace, Roundabout
Three Cool Cats Tcc009/010
Houston, Texas, USA 5 March 88 and Roundabout - Boston Gardens, Massachusetts, USA 12 November 1974
Double CD

Resurrecting Dragons
Rhythm Of Love, Hold On, Heart Of The Sunrise, Big Generator, Changes, Shoot High - Aim Low, Owner Of A Lonely Heart, And You And I, Yours Is No Disgrace, I've Seen All Good People, Roundabout, Long Distance Runaround, Friends Of Mr Cairo, Lancelot And The Black Knight, When The Heart Rules The Mind, Roundabout, Three Of A Perfect Pair
Papillon CD 007/2
Houston, Texas, USA 5 March 1988 plus various solo & Yes-related tracks
Double CD

Live USA
Rhythm Of Love, Hold On, Heart Of The Sunrise, Big Generator, Changes, Shoot High, Aim Low, Owner Of A Lonely Heart, Roundabout, And You And I, Yours Is No Disgrace, Sound Chaser, The Gates Of Delirium
Imtrat Imt 2 CD 920.038
Houston, Texas, USA 5 March 1988 and Boston Gardens, Massachusetts, USA 12 November 1974
Double CD

Yesshows '88
Rhythm Of Love, Hold On, Heart Of The Sunrise, Big Generator, Changes, Shoot High - Aim Low, Owner Of A Lonely Heart, And You And I
Main Event Me CD-004
Houston, Texas, USA 5 March 1988
Vinyl version also released

Big Generator Show & Rare Tracks
Rhythm Of Love, Hold On, Heart Of The Sunrise, Big Generator, Changes, Shoot High - Aim Low, Owner Of A Lonely Heart, And You And I, Yours Is No Disgrace, Love Will Find A Way, Big Generator, Rhythm Of Love, Final Eyes, I'm Running, Shoot High - Aim Low #1, Shoot High - Aim Low #2, Rhythm Of Love (Dance To The Rhythm mix), Love Will Find A Way (extended version), Owner Of A Lonely Heart (Special Red & Blue Remix Dance Version), Leave It (Hello, Goodbye mix)
Highland HL005/6 Y3
Houston, Texas, USA 5 March 1988 plus studio demos 1987 & 12" remixes
Japanese Double CD

We Make Believe
Intro, Hold You In My Arms, Watching The Flags That Fly, Make Believe, Is It Love, Instrumental 2, Untitled, Take The Water To The Mountain, To The Stars, Richard, Richard (cut), Santa Barbara, Touch Me Heaven, Axis Of Love, Instrumental 1, After The Storm, Tall Buildings, God With A Southern Accent, Without A Doubt, Big Love, Picasso, Railway 14 (cut)
Diamonds In Your Ear Diye 26/27
Studio demos 1989 & 1978
Double CD

Dialogue
Intro, Hold You In My Arms, Watching The Flags That Fly, Make Believe, Is It Love, Instrumental 2, Untitled, Take The Water To The Mountain, To The Stars, Richard, Richard (cut), Santa Barbara, Touch Me Heaven, Axis Of Love, Instrumental 1, After The Storm, Tall Buildings, God With A Southern Accent, Without A Doubt, Big Love, Picasso, Railway 14 (cut)
Y.E.S.001/2
Studio demos 1989 & 1978
Japanese Double CD

Hunting Like The Dinosaurs
Intro Theme, Second Attention, Third Theme, Fist Of Fire, Brother Of Mine, Birthright, Distant Thunder, Quartet, Themes, Teakbois, Rock Gives Courage, The Order Of The Universe, Let's Pretend
Diamonds In Your Ear Diye 33
Studio demos 1989
Limited edition of 1,000 copies made

Songs Of The Earth
Time And A Word, Owner Of A Lonely Heart, Teakbois, Time And A Word, Clap, Mood For A Day, keyboard solo incl. Madrigal, Long Distance Runaround, drum solo incl. Heart Of The Sunrise, Birthright, And You And I, I've Seen All Good People, Close To The Edge, Themes, bass-drum duet, Brother Of Mine, The Meeting, Heart Of The Sunrise, Order Of The Universe, Roundabout, Starship Trooper
The Gold Standard CBT-839/STE-345
Jones Beach, California, USA 10 August 1989
Double CD - Soundboard recording

Incas Valley
Time And A Word, Owner Of A Lonely Heart, Brother Of Mine, And You And I, Heart Of The Sunrise, Long Distance Runaround, Roundabout, Close To The Edge, Order Of The Universe
Beech Marten Records BM016
Shoreline Amphitheatre, Mountain View, California, USA 10 September 1989
FM broadcast

Yes
Medley, Brother Of Mine, And You And I, Heart Of The Sunrise, Close To The Edge, Order Of The Universe, Roundabout
Rock Dreams Rocks 92056
Shoreline Amphitheatre, Mountain View, California, USA 10 September 1989
FM broadcast

1989 European Tour
Birthright, And You And I, I've Seen All Good People, Themes, drums-bass duet, Brother Of Mine, Heart Of The Sunrise, The Order Of The Universe, Roundabout
Microphone Records MPH 11
Europe 1989

A Young Person's Guide To Yes
Young Person's Guide To The Orchestra, Time And A Word – Owner Of A Lonely Heart - Teakbois, Clap – Areda, Mood For A Day, Madrigal (Gone But Not Forgotten – Catherine Parr – Merlin The Magician), Long Distance Runaround, Bill's solo (incl. Heart Of The Sunrise), Birthright, And You And I, I've Seen All Good People, Close To The Edge, Themes, Bill Bruford & Tony Levin duet, Brother Of Mine, The Meeting, Heart Of The Sunrise, Order Of The Universe, Roundabout, Starship Trooper (incl. Soon), I've Seen All Good People (Part Missing), Close To The Edge, Roundabout, Starship Trooper (incl. Soon), Sweet Dreams
Highland HL235/236/237
Edinburgh Playhouse, Edinburgh, UK 21 October 1989 and Stockholm, Sweden 8 November 1989
Japanese Triple CD – Soundboard

An Evening Of Yes Music Plus
Time And A Word-Owner Of A Lonely Heart-Teakbois, Clap, Mood For A Day, Madrigal-Journey To The Centre Of The Earth, Long Distance Runaround, Birthright, And You And I, I've Seen All Good People, Soon, Close To The Edge, Themes, Brother Of Mine, The Meeting, Heart Of The Sunrise, Order Of The Universe, Roundabout, Starship Trooper
Anon. - ABWH 10291/10292
Wembley Arena, London, UK 29 October 1989
Japanese Double CD

The Perfect Union
I Would Have Waited Forever, Shock To The System, Without Hope You Cannot Start The Day, Lift Me Up, Dangerous (club version 1), Angkor Wat, Silent Talking, The More We Live - Let Go, Holding On, Take The Water To The Mountain, Mountain Exit, Dangerous (club version 2), Dangerous, Give & Take, She Walks Away (Instrumental), She Walks Away, It Must Be Love, Shot In The Dark (demo), Shot In The Dark, She Walks Away (instrumental), Without Hope You Cannot Start The Day, Dangerous, Lift Me Up, The More We Live - Let Go, Say Goodbye, Distant Thunder, Some Are Born, Yesterday Boulevard, On A Still Night
Blue Moon Records BMCD 16/17
Studio demos 1990/1
Double CD

Master Of Dream
I Would Have Waited Forever, Shock, Masquerade, Must Be Love, Lift Me Up, Dangerous, Angkor Wat, Silent Talking, Let Go, Holding On, Bill-Tony intro, Take The Water, She Walks Away # 1, She Walks Away # 2, She Walks Away # 3, She Walks Away # 4, Dangerous #1, Dangerous #2, Must Be Love, Shot In The Dark, Give & Take # 1, Give & Take # 2, Say Goodbye, Lift Me Up, The More We Live – Let Go, Saving My Heart, Be The One (promo only version), That - That Is (promo only version), The One (demo take), That, That Is – That Is, All In All (demo take), Owner Of A Lonely Heart ('98 remake)
Highland HL343/344
Studio demos 1991
Japanese Double CD

The Ancient Yes
Opening, Yours Is No Disgrace, Rhythm Of Love, City Of Love, Heart Of The Sunrise, The Ancient (Leaves Of Green), Clap, Owner Of A Lonely Heart, And You And I, Hold On, Shock To The System, Trevor solo, Changes, Take The Water To The Mountain, Soon, Long Distance Runaround, The Fish-Tempus Fujit-Amazing Grace, Lift Me Up, Six Wives, Awaken, Roundabout, Starship Trooper, Clap-Mood For A Day-Clap, I've Seen All Good People, Shock To The System
Anon.CDY001/002/003
Pensacola, Florida, USA 9 April 1991 and Philadelphia 16 April 1991 and Uniondale, N.Y. 20 April 1991
Japanese 3CD set

Union Of Dreams
Yours Is No Disgrace, Rhythm Of Love, Shock To The System, Heart Of The Sunrise, Make It Easy – Owner Of A Lonely Heart, And You And I, Lift Me Up, Changes, I've Seen All Good People, Roundabout, Awaken, Holding On demo (take1), (take 2), (take3), (take 4), (take 5), (take 6), (take 7), Holding On part two (take 1), (take 2), (take 3)
Highland HL238/239
Montreal, Canada 24 April 1991 and Wembley Arena, London, UK 22 June 1991 plus studio out takes
Japanese Double CD – Soundboard

To The Union
Yours Is No Disgrace, The Rhythm Of Love, Shock To The System, Steve solo, Heart Of The Sunrise, Owner Of A Lonely Heart, And You And I, Hold On, Changes, Trevor solo, Long Distance Runaround, Chris solo, Amazing Grace, Lift Me Up, Rick solo, Awaken, Roundabout
Silver Dollar G.N. 5/6 - S.D. 01188

Frankfurt, Germany 1991
Double CD in digipak sleeve

Round The World In Eighty Dates
Rhythm Of Love, Cinema (Make It Easy), Owner Of A Lonely Heart, Changes, Lift Me Up, Shock To The System, Awaken, Heart Of The Sunrise, Keyboard solo-Rick-Six Wives, Guitar solo-Trevor
FM 800
Stuttgart, Germany 31 May 1991 and ABWH 9 September 1989
FM broadcast

They Are Back
Yours Is No Disgrace, Rhythm Of Love, Shock To The System, Heart Of The Sunrise, acoustic set by Steve , Owner Of A Lonely Heart, And You And I, Hold On, I've Seen All Good People, Changes, acoustic set by Trevor, Long Distance Runaround, electric set by Chris
Great Live Recordings GLR 9115/16
Cologne, Germany 2 June 1991
Double CD

Say Yes
Yours Is No Disgrace, Rhythm Of Love, Shock To The System, Heart Of The Sunrise, Clap, Mood For A Day, Owner Of A Lonely Heart, And You And I, Changes, I've Seen All Good People, Solly's Beard, Long Distance Runaround, The Fish, Lift Me Up, Six Wives, Awaken, Roundabout
Red Phantom RPCD 2055/56
Wembley Arena, London, UK 29 June 1991
Double CD

Live USA
Shock To The System, Clap, Mood For A Day, I've Seen All Good People, Solly's Beard, Long Distance Runaround, The Fish, Lift Me Up, Six Wives, Awaken
Immtrat Imm 40.90120
Source is Wembley Arena, London, UK
29 June 1991
From same audio tape as Say Yes

The Return To Fantasy
Rhythm Of Love, Shock To The System, Owner Of A Lonely Heart, And You And I, Changes, I've Seen All Good People, Lift Me Up, Awaken (part two), Roundabout
Beech Marten BM055
Wembley Arena, London, UK 29 June 1991
FM broadcast

U.S.A. 1991
Rhythm Of Love, Shock To The System, Owner Of A Lonely Heart, And You And I, Changes, I've Seen All Good People, Lift Me Up, Awaken (part two), Roundabout
Post Script PSCD 1243
Wembley Arena, London, UK
29 June 1991

U.S.A. 1991
Rhythm Of Love, Shock To The System, Owner Of A Lonely Heart, And You And I, Changes, I've Seen All Good People, Lift Me Up, Awaken (part two), Roundabout
Live Storm LSCD 51243

Live In Montreal
Rhythm Of Love, Shock To The System, Heart Of The Sunrise, Owner Of A Lonely Heart, And You And I, Lift Me Up, Changes, I've Seen All Good People, Roundabout
Flashback 09.92.0187
Source is Wembley Arena, London, UK
29 June 1991
From the FM broadcast

Union Review '91
Yours Is No Disgrace, Shock To The System, Changes, Heart Of The Sunrise, Owner Of A Lonely Heart, And You And I, I've Seen All Good People, Roundabout
Dr. Gig DGCD004
Denver, Colorado, USA 1991
From TV broadcast - FM stereo

Ultimate Reunion
Firebird, Yours Is No Disgrace, Rhythm Of Love, Shock To The System, Heart Of The Sunrise, Clap, Make It Easy - Owner Of A Lonely Heart, And You And I, I've Seen All Good People, Solly's Beard, Saving My Heart, The Fish, Lift Me Up, Keyboard solo, Awaken, Roundabout
Highland HL217/218
Jones Beach, New York, USA 21 July 1991
Japanese double CD - soundboard

Yesshows
1991, 'Round The World In A Last Day
Firebird, Yours Is No Disgrace, Rhythm Of Love, Shock To The System, Heart Of The Sunrise, Clap, Owner Of A Lonely Heart, And You And I, Changes, I've Seen All Good People, Trevor solo, Saving My Heart, Chris solo (Amazing Grace), Lift Me Up, Six Wives, Awaken, Roundabout
Whatever Wer-03/04
Shoreline Amphitheatre, Mountain View, California, USA 8 August 1991
Japanese double CD - soundboard recording

Close To VIII Progressers
Firebird, Yours Is No Disgrace, Rhythm Of Love, Shock To The System, Heart Of The Sunrise, Clap (incl. Georgia's Theme), Make It Easy – Owner Of A Lonely Heart, And You And I, I've Seen All Good People, Solly's Beard, Saving My Heart, The Fish,

Amazing Grace (Jon & Chris), Lift Me Up, excerpts from Six Wives, Awaken, Roundabout, Keyboard & drum jam (Rick & Alan), guitar & drum jam (Trevor & Alan), keyboard, guitar & drum jam (Rick, Trevor & Alan) (sound check, Chicago, Illinois, USA 5 May 1991), Close To The Edge (I Get Up, I Get Down), Saving My Heart (instr.), Saving My Heart, Close To The Edge (The Solid Time Of Change), Seasons Of Man (sound check, Birmingham NEC, Birmingham, UK 26 June 1991)
Highland HL345/6/7
Shoreline Amphitheatre, Mountain View, California, USA 8 August 1991
Japanese Triple CD – part soundboard

Reunion 1992
Firebird Suite, Yours Is No Disgrace, Rhythm Of Love, Shock To The System, Heart Of The Sunrise, Winter (Diary Of A Man Who Vanished), Mood For A Day, Make It Easy, Owner Of A Lonely Heart, Bill Bruford & Alan White drum battle, Changes, I've Seen All Good People, Solly's Beard, Saving My Heart, White Fish, Amazing Grace, Roundabout
TNT Studio TNT-930128/9
Yoyogi Olympic Pool, Tokyo, Japan
29 February 1992
Double CD

Masters Of Time
Firebird Suite, Yours Is No Disgrace, Rhythm Of Love, Shock To The System, Heart Of The Sunrise, All's A Chord, Mood For A Day, Make It Easy, Owner Of A Lonely Heart, And You And I, drum duet, Changes, I've Seen All Good People, guitar solo, Saving My Heart, The Fish-Tempus Fugit-Amazing Grace, Lift Me Up, keyboard solo, Awaken, Roundabout
Silver Rarities SIRA 98/99/100
Century Hall, Nagoya, Japan 3 March 1992
3CD Set

Look Through The Dragonfly
Firebird, Yours Is No Disgrace, Rhythm Of Love, Shock To The System, Heart Of The Sunrise, Clap, Make It Easy - Owner Of A Lonely Heart, And You And I, twin drum battle, Changes, I've Seen All Good People, Solly's Beard, Fish, Lift Me Up, Tombo No Megan (Look Through The Dragonfly), keyboard solo, Awaken, Roundabout
Highland HL221/222: Budokan, Tokyo, Japan
5 March 1992
Japanese Double CD

Gimme More
Perpetual Change - The Calling, I Am Waiting, Rhythm Of Love, Hearts, Real Love, Changes, Heart Of The Sunrise, Cinema, City Of Love, Owner Of A Lonely Heart, And You And I, Where Will You Be?, I've Seen All Good People, Walls, Endless Dream, Roundabout
Insect IST75/76
Broome County Arena, Binghampton, New York, USA 18 June 1994
Double CD

Endless Dream
I'm Waiting, The Calling, Rhythm Of Love, Hearts, Real Love, Changes, Heart Of The Sunrise, Roundabout, Cinema, City Of Love, Make It Easy, Owner Of A Lonely Heart, And You And I, Where Will You Be?, I've Seen All Good People, Walls, Endless Dream
Octopus OCTO 031/032
Canidegua, New York, USA 19 June 1994
Double CD

Can't Stop Lovin'
I'm Waiting, The Calling, Changes, Heart Of The Sunrise, Roundabout, Owner Of A Lonely Heart, Walls, Endless Dream
Planet-X PLAN 053 Canidegua, New York, USA 19 June 1994

Time For A Planet
Perpetual Change, The Calling, I Am Waiting, Rhythm Of Love, Hearts, Real Love, Changes, Heart Of The Sunrise, And You And I
RHP 678
World Theatre, Chicago, Illinois, USA
2 July 1994

Endless Road
Opening (Perpetual Change), The Calling, I Am Waiting, Rhythm Of Love, Hearts, Real Love, Changes, Heart Of The Sunrise, Make It Easy, Owner Of a lonely Heart, And You And I, Where Will You Be, I've Seen All Good People, Walls, Endless Dream, Roundabout, Cinema, City Of Love, The Calling #1, The Calling #2, I Am Waiting, State Of Play, Real Love, Walls (single version), Walls (promo only radio version), The Calling (promo only edit), The Calling (radio edit)
Highland HL488-490
Orlando, Florida 11 August 1994 and Maryland, 29 June 1994 and Talk demos 1994 and edit versions
Japanese 3CD (Soundboard tapes)

Yes Live Meeting 1996
Opening (Firebird Suite), Siberian Khatru, Close To The Edge, I've Seen All Good People, Time And A Word, And You And I, The Revealing Science Of God, Going For The One, Turn Of The Century, America, Onward, Awaken, Roundabout, Starship Trooper, Outlawed, Night Trade (take 1), Night Trade (take 2), Travellin' Man, Welcome To Steve's Place (take 1), Welcome To Steve's Place (take 2), Lowlife Baby, The Moment Of Release (take 1), The Moment Of Release (take 2), Spanish Heritage (take 1) (listed but not included), Spanish Heritage (take 2) (listed but not included)
Dancin' Disc Records 1003/5
San Louis Obispo, California, USA
6 March 1993
plus Steve Howe - 'Guitar Player'
3CD set. Howe songs are credited to Peter Banks on the sleeve!

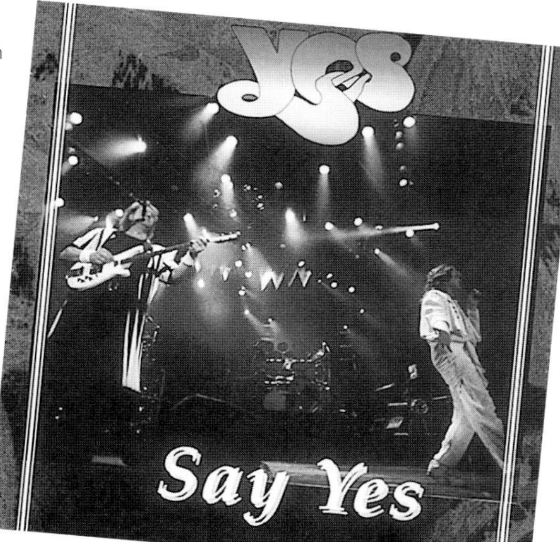

Keys To Chris' Birthday
Opening, Siberian Khatru, Close To The Edge, I've Seen All Good People, Time And A Word, Happy Birthday Song, And You And I, The Revealing Science Of God, Going For The One, Turn Of The Century, America, Onward, Awaken, Roundabout, Starship Trooper
Highland HL124/25/26 #Y25
Fremont Theatre, San Louis Obispo, California, USA 4 March 1996
Japanese 3CD Set

New Yes Announcement
America, I've Seen All Good People, Roundabout, Starship Trooper
Highland HL08 #Y15
Tower Records, Los Angeles, California, USA
27 November 1996
Japanese CD FM stereo

Yestower
America, I've Seen All Good People, Roundabout, Starship Trooper, Rhythm Of Love, Owner Of A Lonely Heart, Heart Of The Sunrise, And You And I
Anon YT 1196
Tower Records, Los Angeles, California, USA
27 November 1996 and Wembley Arena London, UK 29 June 1991
Both sources FM stereo

The Demos And The Tower
Siberian Khatru, Long Distance Runaround, South Side Of The Sky, I've Seen All Good People, Wondrous Stories, Roundabout, America, I've Seen All Good People, Roundabout, Starship Trooper
Anon HW098
Tribute Band (possibly 'Envision') plus Tower Records, Los Angeles, California, USA
27 November 1996
Cover mischievously suggests the first six cuts are 1997 Yes demos

Open Your Ears
Siberian Khatru, Rhythm Of Love, America, Open Your Eyes, And You And I, Heart Of The Sunrise, From The Balcony, Children Of Light, Owner Of A Lonely Heart, I've Seen All Good People, Roundabout, Shoot High - Aim Low, Yours Is No Disgrace
Anon YT1297
Universal Amphitheatre, Los Angeles, California, USA 1 December 1997 and Houston, Texas, USA 5 March 1988
Double CD

Yes Magic

Opening-Siberian Khatru, Rhythm Of Love, America, Open Your Eyes, And You And I, Heart Of The Sunrise, From The Balcony, Children Of Light, Owner Of A Lonely Heart, I've Seen All Good People, Roundabout
Highland HL134/35 #Y23
Universal Amphitheatre, Los Angeles, California, USA 1 December 1997
Japanese Double CD

Yessounds
Firebird Suite, Siberian Khatru, Rhythm Of Love, America, Open Your Eyes, And You And I, Heart Of The Sunrise, Mood For A Day, Indian Woman, Clap, From The Balcony, Wondrous Stories, piano solo, Long Distance Runaround, Tempus Fugit-Ritual-The Fish, Sound Chaser, Owner Of A Lonely Heart, The Revealing Science Of God, Roadcrew Blues, I've Seen All Good People, Roundabout, Starship Trooper, Soon, Second Initial, Masquerade, Clap, Leaves Of Green, Children Of Light, Heart Of The Sunrise, Shock To The System
Sisyphus Records THWS 002-3
Rosengarten, Mannheim, Germany
18 March 1998 and Beacon Theatre, New York, USA 30 November 1997 and Mountain View, California, USA 8 August 1991
3CD set - limited edition of 500 numbered copies

Revealing Science Of San Diego
Rhythm Of Love, Open Your Eyes, Heart Of The Sunrise, From The Balcony, Children Of Light, Long Distance Runaround, Owner Of A Lonely Heart, Revealing Science Of God, I've Seen All Good People
Highland HL223
San Diego, California, USA
7 December 1997
Japanese CD soundboard

Open The Show
Opening, Siberian Khatru, Rhythm Of Love, America, Open Your Eyes, And You And I, Heart Of The Sunrise, Mood For A Day, Ram, Clap, State Of Mind (From The Balcony), Wondrous Stories, piano solo, Long Distance Runaround-The Fish (incl. Tempus Fugit, Ritual and Sound Chaser), Owner Of A Lonely Heart, The Revealing Science Of God, Jam, I've Seen All Good People, Roundabout, Starship Trooper
Highland HL165/166/167 #Y29
Liederhalle, Stuttgart, Germany
20 March 1998
Japanese 3CD set

Yes Stage '98
Opening, Siberian Khatru ('sound trouble effect and try once more'), Rhythm Of Love, America, Open Your Eyes, And You And I, Heart Of The Sunrise, Mood For A Day, Ram, Clap, From The Balcony, Wondrous Stories, Change The World - piano solo, Long Distance Runaround-The Fish (incl. Tempus Fugit And Sound Chaser), Owner Of A Lonely Heart, I've Seen All Good People, The Revealing Science Of God
Highland HL190/91
Warsaw, Poland 26 March 1998
Japanese Double CD

Tour De France
Firebird, Siberian Khatru, Rhythm Of Love, America, Open Your Eyes, And You And I, Heart Of The Sunrise, Mood For A Day, Django Reinhardt homage, Masquerade, Clap, Nous Sommes Du Soleil, From The Balcony, Wondrous Stories, Igor solo, Long Distance Runaround, The Fish, Owner Of A Lonely Heart, The Revealing Science Of God, I've Seen All Good People, Roundabout, Starship Trooper
Highland HL232/233/234
Palais De Congres, Paris, France 6 March 1998
Japanese triple CD

Unplugged Show
Band introduction, Yes jam, Owner Of A Lonely Heart, Children Of Light, excerpt from Turn Of The Century & Awaken, Alan discusses with fans #1, Open Your Eyes, Jon discusses with fans #2, I've Seen All Good People, Corkscrew, Masquerade, Clap, Leaves Of Green, Children Of Light, Soon, happy birthday song to Jon
Highland HL 231
FNAC Record Store, Paris, France
7 March 1998 and Tower Theatre, Philadelphia, Pennsylvania, USA 25 October 1997
Japanese CD – Not soundboard!

Lonely Runaround
Firebird, Siberian Khatru, Rhythm Of Love, Yours Is No Disgrace, And You And I, Open Your Eyes, Heart Of The Sunrise, Wondrous Stories, Close To The Edge, Long Distance Runaround, America, I've Seen All Good People, Owner Of A Lonely Heart, Roundabout (24 June 1998), Ram, Clap (6 July 1998)
Highland HL369/370
Pittsburgh, Pennsylvania, USA 24 June 1998 and Cincinnati, Ohio, USA 6 July 1998
Japanese double CD

Evening Sunburst 1998
Firebird, Siberian Khatru, Rhythm Of Love, Yours Is No Disgrace, Open Your Eyes, And You And I, Heart Of The Sunrise, Steve solo – Arada, Mood For A Day, Sketches In The Sun, Clap, Aka- Tombo, Wondrous Stories, keyboard solo, Long Distance Runaround, The Fish, Owner Of A Lonely Heart, Close To The Edge, I've Seen All Good People, Roundabout, Firebird Suite, Siberian Khatru, Rhythm Of Love, Yours Is No Disgrace, Open Your Eyes, And You And I, Heart Of The Sunrise, Steve solo – Surface Tension, Mood For A Day, Second Initial, Clap, Aka –Tombo, Wondrous Stories, keyboard solo, Long Distance Runaround, The Fish, Owner Of A Lonely Heart, Close To The Edge, I've Seen All Good People, Roundabout
Highland HL257-260
Shibuya Kohkaido, Tokyo, Japan
8 & 9 October 1998
Japanese Four CD Set

Luna Park 1999
Firebird, Yours Is No Disgrace, America, Lightning Strikes, excerpt from Time And A Word, New Language, excerpt from Survival, Perpetual Change, Interviews 1, excerpts from Nous Sommes Du Soleil, Homeworld, It Will Be A Good Day, Nine Voices, Owner Of A Lonely Heart, Roundabout, I've Seen All Good People, Interviews 2
Highland HL458/459
Luna Park Stadium, Buenos Aires, Argentina
12 September 1999
Japanese double CD – taken from TV broadcast

Ladders On The Strip
Firebird, Yours Is No Disgrace, Time And A Word, Homeworld, Perpetual Change, Lightning Strikes, The Messenger, Nous Sommes Du Soleil, And You And I, Close To The Edge, It Will Be A Good Day, Face To Face, Hearts, Awaken, I've Seen All Good People, Cinema, Owner Of A Lonely Heart, Roundabout, Las Vegas Jam
Highland Hl454/5/6
House Of Blues, Las Vegas, Nevada, USA
31 October 1999
Japanese triple CD – soundboard

The Masterworks Songs – Fireworks & Masterworks
Opening (Young Person's Guide to The Orchestra), Close To The Edge, Starship Trooper, The Gates Of Delirium, Leaves Of Green (The Ancient), Heart Of The Sunrise, Ritual, Roundabout, Outroduction, (bonus track) I've Seen All Good People(Hartford, Connecticut, USA 22 July 2000)
Highland HL494/5
Reno Amphitheatre, Reno, Nevada, USA
20 June 2000
Japanese Double CD

Real Masterworks
Intro (Young Person's Guide To The Orchestra), Close To The Edge, Starship Trooper, Gates Of Delirium, Leaves Of Green, Heart Of The Sunrise, Ritual, I've Seen All Good People, Roundabout, Radio Tour Promo, The Messenger, Lightning Strikes, Face To Face, I've Seen All Good People
Highland HL517/8 – Holmdel, NJ 19 July 2000 + Masterworks Tour Radio Promo + KLOS Radio, L. A. 1 November 1999
Japanese 2CD set (Soundboard tapes)